A MOHAWK MEMOIR FROM THE WAR OF 1812

D1452572

A Mohawk Memoir from the War of 1812 presents the story of John Norton, or Teyoninhokarawen, an important war chief and political figure among the Grand River Haudenosaunee (or Iroquois) in Upper Canada. Norton saw more action during the conflict than almost anyone else, being present at the fall of Detroit; the capture of Fort Niagara; the battles of Queenston Heights, Fort George, Stoney Creek, Chippawa, and Lundy's Lane; the blockades of Fort George and Fort Erie; and a large number of skirmishes and front-line patrols. His memoir describes the fighting, the stresses suffered by indigenous peoples, and the complex relationships between the Haudenosaunee and both their British allies and other First Nations communities.

Norton's account, written in 1815 and 1816, provides nearly one-third of the book's content, with the remainder consisting of Carl Benn's introductions and annotations, which enable readers to understand Norton's fascinating autobiography within its historical contexts. With the assistance of modern scholarship, *A Mohawk Memoir* presents an exceptional opportunity to explore the War of 1812 and native-newcomer issues not only through Teyoninhokarawen's Mohawk perspective but in his own words.

CARL BENN is a history professor at Ryerson University. His other books include *The Iroquois in the War of 1812*, also published by University of Toronto Press.

A Mohawk Memoir from the War of 1812

JOHN NORTON – TEYONINHOKARAWEN

Introduced, Annotated, and Edited by Carl Benn

UNIVERSITY OF TORONTO PRESS
Toronto Buffalo London

© University of Toronto Press 2019
Toronto Buffalo London
utorontopress.com
Printed in Canada

ISBN 978-1-4875-0432-8 (cloth)
ISBN 978-1-4875-2326-8 (paper)

Printed on acid-free paper.

Library and Archives Canada Cataloguing in Publication

Title: A Mohawk memoir from the War of 1812 / John Norton –
Teyoninhokarawen ; introduced, annotated, and edited by Carl Benn.
Names: Norton, John, 1770–1827, author. | Benn, Carl, 1953– editor.
Description: Includes bibliographical references and index.
Identifiers: Canadiana 20190048743 | ISBN 9781487523268 (paper) |
ISBN 9781487504328 (cloth)
Subjects: LCSH: Norton, John, 1770–1827. | CSH: Canada – History –
War of 1812 – Personal narratives.
Classification: LCC FC443.N67 A3 2019 | DDC 971.03/4–dc23

This book has been published with the help of a grant from the Federation
for the Humanities and Social Sciences, through the Awards to Scholarly
Publications Program, using funds provided by the Social Sciences
and Humanities Research Council of Canada.

University of Toronto Press acknowledges the financial assistance to its
publishing program of the Canada Council for the Arts and the Ontario
Arts Council, an agency of the Government of Ontario.

Canada Council Conseil des Arts
for the Arts du Canada

ONTARIO ARTS COUNCIL
CONSEIL DES ARTS DE L'ONTARIO
an Ontario government agency
un organisme du gouvernement de l'Ontario

Funded by the Financé par le
Government gouvernement
of Canada du Canada

Canadä

MIX
Paper from
responsible sources
FSC
www.fsc.org FSC® C016245

For my family

Contents

Abbreviations   ix

Map: The Iroquois/Haudenosaunee Lower Great Lakes, 1812–15   xi

Map: Six Nations Iroquois/Haudenosaunee Grand River Lands, 1812–15   xii

Introduction

John Norton's Memoir   3
Editorial Decisions, Terminology, and Numbers   9
The Haudenosaunee to the 1790s   13
John Norton's Early Life and Transformation into Mohawk
  Leader Teyoninhokarawen   24
Teyoninhokarawen's Service to the Six Nations of the Grand
  River and Views on Haudenosaunee Society and Independence   39

A Mohawk Memoir from the War of 1812
BY JOHN NORTON – TEYONINHOKARAWEN

1 Uncertainties, Diplomacy, and the Outbreak of War, 1811–12   75

2 Opening Moves, Disunion, and the Capture Of Detroit, 1812   97

3 Niagara and Victory at Queenston Heights, 1812   115

4 Ambiguity and Frustration on the Detroit Front, 1813   141

5 The Fall of Fort George, Desperate Moments, and the
  Battle of Stoney Creek, 1813   165

6 The Blockade of Fort George, Intrigue, and the Capture
of Fort Niagara, 1813   181

7 Quebec, Burlington, and the Battle of Chippawa, 1814   222

8 Discredit, Battles at Lundy's Lane and Fort Erie, Murders,
and the Defence of Grand River, 1814   240

Epilogue

John Norton in Upper Canada and Great Britain   275
Final Years   292

*Appendix A: The Six Nations Population on the Grand River,
1811 and 1814*   299

*Appendix B: John Norton's Spelling of Native Names Where It
Differed from Current Practice*   302

Acknowledgments   305

Image Credits   309

Bibliography   313

Index   329

Colour plates follow page 180

Abbreviations

AFC407	John Norton (Teyoninhokarawen) Collection (WU)
AO	Archives of Ontario
BFBSA	British and Foreign Bible Society Archives, Cambridge University
BL	British Library
CO42	Colonial Office Fonds (LAC)
D1/5/2	Correspondence Books, vol. 2 (BFBSA)
F3/Shore	Lord Teignmouth's Letters (BFBSA)
F440	John Norton Fonds (AO)
F1015	Alexander Fraser Fonds (AO)
JMJN	John Norton, *The Journal of Major John Norton, 1816,* edited by Carl F. Klinck and James J. Talman, 1816/1970, with a new introduction by Carl Benn (Toronto: Champlain Society, 2011)
JN	John Norton – Teyoninhokarawen
LAC	Library and Archives Canada
MG19–F1	Manuscript Group 19–F1, Daniel Claus and Family Fonds (LAC)
MG19–F35	Manuscript Group 19–F35, Superintendent of Indian Affairs in the Northern District of North America Fonds (LAC)

MG21–Add.MSS–8075	Joseph-Geneviève de Puisaye Fonds (LAC)
MS234	Russell Copy Book (AO)
MS654	John Norton Letter Book (NL)
MS3204	Edward E. Ayer Manuscript Collection (NL)
NA	National Archives (U.K.)
NL	Newberry Library
NYPL	New York Public Library
NYSL	New York State Library
RG7	Record Group 7, Governor-General's Papers (LAC)
RG8	Record Group 8, C Series, British Military and Naval Records (LAC)
RG10	Record Group 10, Indian Affairs Records (LAC)
RG31	Statistics Canada Fonds; Upper Canada/Canada West Census Returns (LAC)
SC10440	Phelps and Gorham Papers, 1772–1895 (NYSL)
TPL	Toronto Public Library – Toronto Reference Library
WO	War Office Papers (NA)
WU	Western University

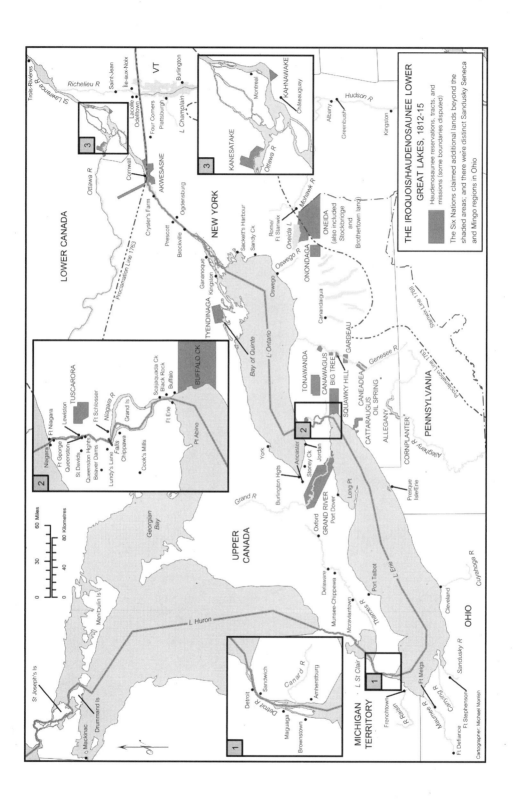

THE IROQUOIS/HAUDENOSAUNEE LOWER GREAT LAKES, 1812–15 (some boundaries disputed)

Haudenosaunee reservations, tracts, and missions

The Six Nations claimed additional lands beyond the shaded areas; and there were distinct Sandusky Seneca and Mingo regions in Ohio

3 KANESATAKE KAHNAWAKE Montreal Châteauguay Ottawa R

LOWER CANADA St Lawrence R Trois-Rivières Saint-Jean Richelieu R Île-aux-Noix Lacolle Odelltown Four Corners Plattsburgh Burlington L Champlain VT

Hudson R Albany Greenbush Kingston

Proclamation Line 1763 Cornwall AKWESASNE Crysler's Farm Ogdensburg Prescott Brockville Gananoque Kingston NEW YORK Sackett's Harbour Sandy Ck Oswego Rome/ Ft Stanwix Oneida L Mohawk R ONEIDA (also included Stockbridge and Brothertown land) ONONDAGA

TYENDINAGA Bay of Quinte L Ontario York Canandaigua Genesee R GARDEAU BIG TREE TONAWANDA CANAWAGUS SQUAWKY HILL CANEADEA OIL SPRING CATTARAUGUS ALLEGANY CORNPLANTER PENNSYLVANIA Allegheny R Sydenham Line 1788 Pennsylvania Line 1789

2 TUSCARORA Ft Niagara Niagara Lewiston Ft Schlosser Niagara R Grand Is Scajaquada Ck Black Rock Buffalo BUFFALO Ck Ft George Queenston St David's Queenston Hghts Beaver Dams Lundy's Lane Falls Chippawa Ft Erie Cook's Mills Pt Abino

60 Miles 30 0 80 Kilometres 40 0

Georgian Bay Manitoulin Is St Joseph's Is Mackinac Drummond Is L Huron UPPER CANADA Grand R Burlington Hgts Ancaster Stoney Ck Jordan Oxford Delaware GRAND RIVER Port Dover Long Pt L Erie Port Talbot Munsee-Chippewa Moraviantown Thames R Presque Isle/Erie Cleveland Cuyahoga R

MICHIGAN TERRITORY Detroit Sandwich Maguaga Brownstown Amherstburg Canard R Detroit R L St Clair Frenchtown R Raisin Maumee R Ft Meigs Ft Stephenson Ft Defiance Sandusky R OHIO

1

Cartographer: Michael Morrish

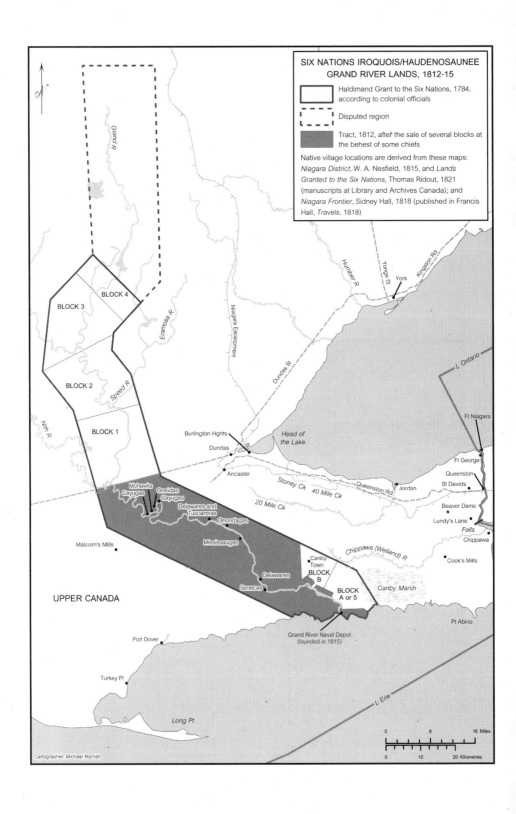

SIX NATIONS IROQUOIS/HAUDENOSAUNEE
GRAND RIVER LANDS, 1812-15

Haldimand Grant to the Six Nations, 1784, according to colonial officials

Disputed region

Tract, 1812, after the sale of several blocks at the behest of some chiefs

Native village locations are derived from these maps: *Niagara District*, W. A. Nesfield, 1815, and *Lands Granted to the Six Nations*, Thomas Ridout, 1821 (manuscripts at Library and Archives Canada); and *Niagara Frontier*, Sidney Hall, 1818 (published in Francis Hall, *Travels*, 1818)

Grand R.

Eramosa R.

Niagara Escarpment

Humber R.

Yonge St.

York

Kingston Rd.

L. Ontario

BLOCK 4

BLOCK 3

BLOCK 2

Speed R.

BLOCK 1

Nith R.

Dundas St.

Ft Niagara

Burlington Hghts

Head of the Lake

Dundas

Ft George

Ancaster

Queenston

Mohawks
Cayugas
Oneidas
Cayugas

Stoney Ck 40 Mile Ck

Queenston Rd

Jordan

St Davids

Delawares and Tuscaroras

20 Mile Ck

Beaver Dams

Onondagas

Lundy's Lane

Falls

Malcolm's Mills

Mississaugas

Chippawa (Welland) R.

Chippawa

Delawares

Canby Town

BLOCK B

Cook's Mills

Senecas

BLOCK A or 5

Canby Marsh

UPPER CANADA

Pt Abino

Grand River Naval Depot (founded in 1815)

Port Dover

Turkey Pt

L. Erie

Long Pt

0   8   16 Miles

0   10   20 Kilometres

Cartographer: Michael Morrish

A MOHAWK MEMOIR FROM THE WAR OF 1812

Introduction

John Norton's Memoir

At the time of the War of 1812, the Six Nations Haudenosaunee (or Iroquois) comprised the Mohawks, Oneidas, Onondagas, Cayugas, Senecas, and Tuscaroras, along with others who lived with them, such as the Tutelo and Nanticoke peoples, as well as individuals of diverse indigenous, white, black, and mixed origins. Most of their homes sat on reservations, tracts, and missions in the American states of New York, Pennsylvania, and Ohio, or in the British colonies of Upper and Lower Canada (now parts of Ontario and Quebec). A particularly fascinating and influential individual among them was John Norton, or Teyoninhokarawen.[1] Born to a Cherokee man and a Scottish woman in 1770, and adopted by the Mohawks in the 1790s, Norton rose to important leadership positions among the Six Nations of the Grand River north of Lake Erie. Like many figures in native society, he enjoyed connections to aboriginal communities beyond his own and, like some, exercised meaningful roles among them as well. As a diplomatic and political figure, Teyoninhokarawen encouraged indigenous people across the

---

1 The most detailed secondary accounts of JN's life at the time of writing this book are the Klinck and Talman introductions to his journal (*JMJN*), supported by my research on him recorded in the bibliography (which sometimes corrected those authors as well as enlarged our understanding of JN). I wrote "Missed Opportunities" to examine JN's Cherokee ethnicity in more detail than was possible in this book. *JMJN* itself provides additional biographical data. Another useful source is Willig, *Restoring the Chain of Friendship*, chapter 5. Timothy Willig's forthcoming study of JN will be the first book-length biography of this important individual.

lower Great Lakes to ally with Great Britain against the United States in 1812. As a war chief, he took men into battle, and saw more combat than most, being present at the capture of Detroit and Fort Niagara; the battles of Queenston Heights, Fort George, Stoney Creek, Chippawa, and Lundy's Lane; the multi-week blockades of Forts George and Erie; and a remarkable number of skirmishes and front-line patrols. Not only did he hope to thwart American expansionary desires directed at both the First Nations and the British North American provinces, he expected the government of King George III to recognize indigenous contributions to Canadian defence by affirming and respecting native aspirations for independence and secure lands of their own. In fact, his desires to protect aboriginal freedoms and territories through an alliance with the Crown are fundamental to understanding his willingness to fight between 1812 and 1814. Beyond his efforts in the war, he sought to modernize native economies as the environment around them changed, not only for people's comfort and security but also to prevent Euro-Americans from exploiting the imperatives generated by poverty to oppress and manipulate indigenous communities. Like his mentor, the famous Mohawk Joseph Brant (Thayendanegea), he promoted Christianity, although he respected and participated in aboriginal expressions of spirituality, as was common among church-going natives during that time. Furthermore, John Norton wrote one of the most extensive, absorbing, and historically useful autobiographies from the War of 1812 by any of its participants, regardless of ethnicity or status. That alone makes his memoir worthy of critical attention. More importantly, it possesses deep utility as a detailed insider description of indigenous involvement in the traumatic events of 1812 to 1814. It is that text that forms the heart of this book.

His description of the hostilities that engulfed the Great Lakes region and the world beyond, presented below, comprises one-quarter of a thousand-page manuscript he wrote over a number of years before completing the surviving version during a visit to the United Kingdom after the war. One of its other components describes a journey he made in 1809–10 from Upper Canada to the Cherokees, then living in Tennessee, Georgia, and today's Alabama. Another section explores the war between the First Nations and the United States in the Ohio country south and west of Lake Erie in the 1780s and 1790s. His text also preserves an extensive and important history of the Haudenosaunee, based on indigenous traditions, first-hand memories, and Euro-American sources. Adding to the significance of that part of the manuscript is the likelihood that it incorporates material assembled or prepared by Joseph Brant, who had wanted to write such a work of his own. Furthermore, Norton's document preserves the first written mention of a number of critical moments and details in Haudenosaunee history, extending back to the foundation of the confederacy itself, along with material of additional interest, such as some of the variations in Iroquois oral traditions that existed in his day. The manuscript includes a word list of native terms and a suggested set of chapter divisions (the latter produced by someone other than Norton).[2] Teyoninhokarawen dedicated the text to the second Duke of Northumberland (Hugh Percy), who had befriended Brant and Norton, and titled his effort "Journal of a Voyage, of a Thousand Miles, Down the Ohio; From the Grand River, Upper Canada; – Visit to the Country of the Cherokees: – Through the States of Kentucky and Tenessee [sic]: and an Account of the Five Nations, Etc. from an Early Period, to the Conclusion of the Late War between Great

---

2 JN thought of publishing a book as early as 1804 (Murray, "John Norton," 11) and had produced a document he called a "journal" by 1808, which he thought was almost finished (Robert Barclay to JN, 31 October 1808, AO, F440). Despite his early optimism about it being suitable for release, JN continued to work on the manuscript, which by 1810 resembled part of the existing *JMJN*. At that time, he had written 220 pages addressing the "manners and customs, traditions, and languages of the different nations I am acquainted with," which he hoped to finish by the spring of 1811 (JN to John Owen, 15 November 1810, NL, MS654, 133). One person he met in 1814 said that JN had written a "history of the Five Nations and a journal of his own travels" that "now" was "in London ready for publication" (Thomas Scott to Walter Scott, March 1814, quoted in Klinck, "Biographical Introduction," in *JMJN*, xxix). That manuscript was not published, but JN completed the surviving journal before mid-1816 (second Duke of Northumberland to JN, 23 June 1816, AO, F440). For links to Joseph Brant's aspirations to write a history of the Six Nations, see Kelsay, *Brant*, 3, 387–8, 533–4; Klinck, "Biographical Introduction," in *JMJN*, xxiv; Fenton, *Great Law and the Longhouse*, 59–64, 72, 98–101. JN's history of the Six Nations comprises *JMJN*, 84–108, 126–7, 190–277, with additional historical and cultural information spread elsewhere across its pages. He also responded to a questionnaire on Haudenosaunee history and society in 1801 (Boyce, "Iroquois Cultural History," 292–4). JN wrote about historical themes in some of his correspondence, with a good example being his description of the "Covenant Chain" that bound the Six Nations to Great Britain (JN to the second Duke of Northumberland, 4 February 1807, BL, Northumberland MSS, 64:24–5). Additional reports on indigenous society that originated with him exist elsewhere, most notably in Headley, "Account," 12 March 1805, NYSL. A modern study that used *JMJN* to explore indigenous history as understood in JN's day is Anderson, "The Storied Landscape of Iroquoia."

Britain and America." The title page also says "By Major John Norton (Teyoninhokarawen)" and "1816."[3] Upon its completion, an "A.W." wrote out a fair copy for him. It is that document that has been preserved, although there is a small part of an earlier draft of the Cherokee journey in Norton's handwriting at Western University. A.W. may have been either Andrew Wilson, the printer for the British and Foreign Bible Society, who was connected to people Norton associated with when he visited Great Britain, or Adam Wilson, the deputy clerk of the Court of Sessions in Edinburgh, married to Susan Wilson (née Barclay), who was related to Norton's mother.[4]

John Norton expected to publish his efforts in 1816 or shortly afterwards. A note even appeared in the Scottish press anticipating the event, proclaiming "we have heard that a most interesting work, viz., *The History of the Late War in Canada*, may be shortly expected from the pen of *Teyoninhokarawen*."[5] (That statement suggests that Norton may have intended to separate his memoir of the period from 1811 to 1814 from the rest of the journal.) A friend of his in London, the Reverend John Owen of the British and Foreign Bible Society, intended to edit and abridge the work (or works), but several challenges prevented the manuscript from progressing beyond A.W.'s fair copy. The extent of the revisions that Owen and others thought it needed, the other demands the Anglican priest faced on his time, a shortage of funds, and the death of John Norton's ducal patron all were factors.[6] At some point, the fair copy arrived at Alnwick Castle in Northumberland, where it remains today. The Historical Manuscripts Commission catalogued it in the 1870s; then, the American Council of Learned Societies microfilmed it in the 1940s as part of a project to copy archival materials rendered vulnerable by the Second World War and to make them broadly available to researchers.[7] Nevertheless, it sat ignored until 1970, when the

---

3 JN, "Journal," Alnwick Castle, Duke of Northumberland Collection.

4 JN, Diary, n.d., WU, AFC407–F1; Klinck, "Biographical Introduction," in *JMJN*; Klinck, "New Light," 170; Communication from Paul Barnaby to Timothy Willig, 23 July 2012, courtesy of Dr Willig.

5 *Edinburgh Annual Register for 1816* 9 (1820): xxiv.

6 Robert Barclay to JN, 7 April 1817, AO, F440. For an extensive discussion of the manuscript's history, see Klinck, "Biographical Introduction," in *JMJN*, xxiii–xxxii, lviii–lix, lxxiv–lxxv.

7 Great Britain, *Third Report of the Royal Commission on Historical Manuscripts*, 125; Born, *British Manuscripts Project*, ix, 85. There are microfilms of the fair copy of JN's text at the British Library, Library of Congress, and Western University.

Champlain Society issued a scholarly edition as *The Journal of Major John Norton, 1816*, edited by Carl F. Klinck and James J. Talman (reissued in 2011 with a new introduction that I wrote). The Alnwick manuscript, however, might not be Norton's final version. There is a hint that he recognized the need to revise and abridge his text, because one person in the 1820s wrote that Teyoninhokarawen had retired, with "his literary acquirements affording him the principal source of amusement."[8] Whatever he may have been doing during those years, a text like the journal, apart from A.W.'s fair copy, does not seem to have survived. (Norton worked on a translation into Mohawk of the Gospel of Saint Matthew after returning to Canada in 1816, but that does not seem to have represented enough of a challenge to have been a "principal source of amusement," assuming that the author of that statement was accurate.)[9]

While we might lament the loss to generations of historical inquiry brought on by the long delay in putting Norton's manuscript into print, we now can be thankful that nobody revised it in his day, altered the problematic parts, or cut down the text. Consequently, Teyoninhokarawen's vision for it as of 1816 remains whole, and the document tells us more about its author and his world than it would have had he revised and shortened it at the suggestion of his acquaintances, or had it gone through the hands of a Georgian-era editor to smooth its rougher components. One of the gratifying revelations in the unpolished journal, as I discovered across several research projects (as did Klinck and Talman), was that he rarely misinterpreted his first-hand experiences (although his estimates of battle casualties and other such figures often were wrong). If he did not like something in his personal history, he usually chose not to speak about it or only mentioned it obliquely instead of misleading his intended audience. The words he did pen about the events he witnessed possess an unusual degree of reliability in comparison to many primary sources. We can verify this partly through comparing his words to other contemporary observers. In those instances, his accounts align well with the consensus generated by surviving documents, while texts by people associated with incidents where he said little provide at least partial access to other

---

8 Morgan, *Emigrant's Note Book*, 190.
9 For the Gospel translation, see Robert Addison, Report and Journal, various dates between 1817 and 1824, quoted in Young, "Addison," 184–9.

segments of his story. The War of 1812 section of his manuscript is not as polished as the earlier portions, and there are indications that he had not revised it to his satisfaction. We can see examples of this in Norton's comments on his difficult relationship with the British government's Indian Department, in which his text presents unclear and incomplete allusions to his frustrations and embarrassments with that bureaucracy and its agents. The most logical interpretation of these vague and partial statements is that Norton had written more on the subject and then deleted some of it, but had not edited his wartime memoir as thoroughly as the other parts before A.W. wrote out the fair copy. Fortunately, we have other primary documents – many written by Norton – that allow us to explore his story comprehensively, as we shall see below.

My objectives in this book are to present this wartime narrative with sufficient historiographical support to maximize access to it, enrich its utility as an important text from the native world of the early 1800s, and explore its content in relation to other primary sources written by Norton and his colleagues, friends, enemies, and others. At the same time, I recognize that the documentary record, strong as it is, is incomplete. For instance, the memoir mentions letters that sometimes no longer can be found, and other documents that must have existed have disappeared (such as some of the correspondence that led the governor-in-chief of British North America, Sir George Prevost, to think highly of Norton). In addition, only a fraction of Teyoninhokarawen's personal papers survive. Beyond annotating his wartime story, I wrote a comprehensive introduction to enable readers to understand Norton and his world with sufficient depth to appreciate his commitment to native independence, within the story of First Nations participation in the conflict. I also added an epilogue to cover relevant themes in Teyoninhokarawen's story up to his death in 1827.

Aside from presenting only John Norton's wartime autobiography rather than his entire multi-sectioned work, my efforts differ from those of the Champlain Society in that I researched and annotated his account of the 1812–14 conflict in much more detail than my predecessors did in their broadly focused edition. (I hope that other scholars will examine the rest of the manuscript with the depth that it deserves, given that it is one of the most significant indigenous-authored works of the early nineteenth century.) I sincerely hope that John Norton's autobiography, accompanied by my editorial and other contributions, will serve readers well as an interesting and scholarly exploration of Teyoninhokarawen's life, the events in which he figured prominently, the War of 1812 on the Canadian front, and the First Nations during a formative period in the history of North America.

Editorial Decisions, Terminology, and Numbers

In transcribing Norton's words, I used the Champlain Society's *Journal of Major John Norton, 1816* as the base text, and then confirmed its accuracy against a microfilmed copy of the original handwritten document. There were very few discrepancies between the two, and I noted those of any meaning but corrected insignificant errors without drawing attention to them. Page references cited as *JMJN* in the notes are to the society's 2011 edition. The material from Norton's journal below encompasses pages 276–357 of that version (or 286–370 of the 1970 volume and 741–967 in the manuscript).

While I did not present John Norton's entire manuscript, because of my focus on his War of 1812 autobiography, the text covering the conflict is complete, with nothing cut from the contiguous manuscript (except for some marginalia consisting of dates indicating when events occurred but which are redundant, which Klinck and Talman also excluded, and the articles "a" and "the" on two occasions each where they were incorrectly included and made the prose confusing). I did add some words to enhance intelligibility, but have presented them in square brackets. I corrected some minor pronoun, verb, and similar errors silently where it seemed appropriate to do so and where leaving them alone would distract readers from Teyoninhokarawen's meaning, but refrained from doing so where it seemed unnecessary. In a handful of instances I changed obviously incorrect words (e.g., "our/one"), which in some cases may have been mistakes made when A.W. transcribed Norton's draft in 1816. I did this silently where the words were insignificant but documented more important corrections (e.g., "Grand Island/Grand River"). In order to facilitate understanding of the autobiography and the other historical documents quoted below, I wrote out abbreviations and regularized spelling, numbering, capitalization, and punctuation. For the sake of clarity and in recognition of modern word-search practices, I changed proper names when they were misspelled or when Norton's approach did not align with today's common usage, but in the case of indigenous nations, villages, and individuals I noted his use in Appendix B where it differed. In my own prose, I recorded aboriginal people's names in native and newcomer forms when I could determine both, but did not add the extra information to Norton's text.

I modified sentence and paragraph breaks to enhance intelligibility, but left grammatically incorrect sentences alone when I could not mend them through adjusting the punctuation or by adding a word in square brackets, or where fixing a problem seemed to be unnecessarily intrusive. A few of my changes might appear to have altered the meaning of some sentences, but I believe the modifications capture Norton's intentions better than the unedited version of the text did (and, of course, anyone may compare my transcription easily with Norton's unaltered work in the Champlain editions). The example below provides a sense of my copyediting.

A. Norton's text from the 1816 manuscript (excluding the long "s" used in the period's writing)

Those, who with more distant assault annoyed the Enemy, – attracted his attention, – until the Fusil's Flash & near report, discovered the Friends, – then the Foe raged like a Hive of Bees disturbed, – Volleys of Bullets flew towards them, but all passed harmless over; – viewing each other with a smile, they acknowledged it rather too hot, & retired towards the more numerous body,

B. As copyedited for this book

Those, who with more distant assault annoyed the enemy, attracted his attention until the fusil's flash and near report discovered the friends. Then the foe raged like a hive of bees disturbed. Volleys of bullets flew towards them [i.e., the warriors], but all passed harmless over. Viewing each other with a smile, they acknowledged it rather too hot, and retired towards the more numerous body.

I also divided John Norton's unitary memoir into sections to accommodate contextual introductions to its discrete chronological elements. In addition, I presented a further level of detail in the notes, typically elucidating his points and providing information on the people, places, and events he described. Given the biographical nature of this book and the extensive length of the annotations, I generally did not encumber the notes by providing citations to points beyond Norton's immediate experiences where my descriptions and factual statements align with the current scholarly consensus. There is, however, a full bibliography at the end of the book to guide readers to additional materials.

Opinions differ on approaches to terminology in describing native peoples and communities, while terms seem to fall in or out of favour with some rapidity. Thus, an explanation of my practices seems appropriate for those parts of the text that present my words rather than those of John Norton and the other historical figures I quoted. My intentions were to affirm the equality of First Nations polities with their Euro-American equivalents, be as clear as possible to the greatest number of readers, and provide appropriate nuance. Therefore, I employed speech patterns for First Nations that align with those I would use for Europeans, such as using the common English word for a people (e.g., "Onondagas") rather than the nation's own term, as I also would for Europeans (e.g., "Germans"). I used "First Nations" as a structural equivalent to "European." I did this because "Indian" has fallen out of use, and because it often evokes distressing images due to the legacy of how "Indians" have been misrepresented in history, literature, and popular culture. I did not use "Native-American," despite the term's widespread acceptance in the United States, because it does not resonate in Canadian ears, and because its structure implies that aboriginal peoples do not have a distinct place in North America from, say, Chinese-Canadians or Swedish-Americans. I used collective confederacy names equally, (e.g., "Iroquois" and "British"), as I did national names (e.g., "Senecas" and "Americans"). As English is an evolving language and some aboriginal words have become common in recent decades, they have entered my prose, such as "Kahnawake," which has replaced "Caughnawaga," just as "Beijing" has succeeded "Peking" in my lifetime. As the language changes, and as other indigenous words appear commonly in print but have not become standard in Canadian prose, I sometimes employed them to indicate their growing use and to add variety to the text where clarity can be preserved (e.g., "Haudenosaunee" appears along with the older but widely recognized term "Iroquois"). I did not do so, however, where native words would be unfamiliar to most readers (e.g., "Gayogohono" instead of "Cayuga"). There is a wide range of spellings for native names (e.g., Haudenosaunee, Hodinöhsö:ni', Rotinonshonni). In those instances, the imperative to be clear meant that I used the most common form of the word, as determined by the *Canadian Oxford Dictionary*. One deviation is my use of "Chippewa" instead of "Ojibwa" or "Anishinabe" in deference to Norton's use of the former (while that word also tends to be used in reference to the specific descendant communities he generally associated with when working with the Anishinabek, such as the Chippewas of the Thames). I frequently used John Norton's Mohawk name, Teyoninhokarawen. (He usually signed his letters with both his white and native names.) Despite their utility, the terms "native," "indigenous," and "aboriginal" seem limiting within the world that

Teyoninhokarawen inhabited, because of intermarriage, cross-cultural migration, the characteristics of borderland communities, and other factors, and so I did not capitalize them, as I did not capitalize the similarly limited but functional words, "white" and "black." Using lower case also helps emphasize how race is not a valid categorization of people. Some individuals today object to the word "aboriginal," but in its etymology from the Latin, *ab* simply means "from," while *origine* conveys the idea of "beginning" or "origin," so "aboriginal" seems appropriate because it means "from the beginning" in understanding a group's history in a region. I used "tribe" interchangeably with "nation," as was common in early-nineteenth-century speech among both natives and newcomers, and which respects the freer political structures of indigenous societies in a non-judgmental way, just as "republic" and "constitutional monarchy" should be read as descriptive rather than value-laden terms for other forms of nationhood. Some people object to the word "chief," but I use it because native people in Norton's day used it normally when communicating in English.

Statistical information, such as the number of combatants in battles, is regularly difficult to determine with precision. Therefore, I generally rounded figures from what I believed were the most credible sources available and restricted use of such words as "about" and "approximately" to some degree. It seemed necessary to review battle figures carefully, because Teyoninhokarawen cited such statistics and thus I needed to check them for accuracy. Some numbers below differ from those in my closely related book, *The Iroquois in the War of 1812*, because this text has benefited from newer scholarship since the other's release in 1998, especially in terms of detailed battle studies that have appeared over the last two decades. I also reviewed primary data on numbers carefully in relation to these more recent publications. Consequently, I believe that my notations on the strength of the opposing forces and casualty figures are reliable, even when they differ from other histories of the conflict, which often accepted data produced by previous scholars. To align with Norton's text, my part of the book does not use metric measurements, but in his rough calculations we can assume a yard and a metre are about the same (although the former is 0.9 metres), and a mile is equivalent to 1.6 kilometres (although his figures tend only to be estimates). His "paces" mimicked human steps, but with the added precision that he knew the British army's marching pace of thirty inches (0.8 m) from the time he served in the military in the 1780s.

The Haudenosaunee to the 1790s

When John Norton was born in 1770, the majority of Iroquois, or Haudenosaunee, belonged to the Six Nations Confederacy (or League).[1] Unlike the situation in 1812, when most of their independent territories had been lost, they maintained extensive homelands in "Iroquoia," located westwards of Albany in New York and northern Pennsylvania. Others lived separately from the confederacy along the Ottawa and St Lawrence rivers to the north or in the Ohio country south of Lake Erie. While the Haudenosaunee owned much of the territory they occupied, Great Britain claimed sovereignty over these regions, as it had for over a century in some areas, and elsewhere since 1763, when France relinquished its claims to most of its North American possessions at the end of the Seven Years' War. The league comprised six of the many tribes of the large Iroquoian language group, with each inhabiting a particular part of Iroquoia: the Mohawks towards the east, the Tuscaroras and Oneidas next, then the Onondagas (near today's Syracuse), the Cayugas in the area around the eponymous lake, followed by the Senecas farther west. In forming their confederacy over a period of time between the mid-1400s and early 1600s, the member nations agreed to abide by a Great Peace, which had expanded and modified existing spiritual and political structures to a supranational level in order to address collective needs. Its primary function was to end inter-tribal violence and other evils that had afflicted their lives. To a lesser degree, it enabled them to face the rest of the world with some degree of unanimity. Achieving widespread harmony in relations with foreigners, however, was harder than preserving internal peace. Decisions arose through a process of consensus politics, from lower to higher levels of association (such as from the village to the nation and then to the league). They incorporated

---

1 Literature on Haudenosaunee history is vast. Recommended studies include: Aquila, *Iroquois Restoration*; Bradley, *Onondaga Iroquois*; Committee of Chiefs, "Tradition of the Origin of the Five Nations' League"; Engelbrecht, *Iroquoia*; Fenton, *Great Law and the Longhouse*; Graymont, *Iroquois in the American Revolution*; Hill, *Clay We are Made of*; Jennings, *Ambiguous Iroquois Empire* and *Empire of Fortune*; Jennings et al., *Iroquois Diplomacy*; Johnston, *Six Nations* (which includes primary documents associated with JN); Jordan, *Seneca Restoration*; Kelsay, *Brant*; Parmenter, *Edge of the Woods*; Rice, *Rotinonshonni*; Richter, *Ordeal of the Longhouse*; Snow, *Iroquois*; Stone, *Brant*; Tanner, *Atlas of Great Lakes Indian History*; Taylor, *Divided Ground*; and Wallace, *Death and Rebirth of the Seneca*.

the opinions of most adults, but with male leaders and clan matrons exercising greater influence than others within each community. One result of this inclusiveness was that it often was not possible to achieve agreement at levels above village polities, where regional relationships with outsiders dominated people's views. Even within villages, families and clans, or less-formally structured parties or groups, might respond differently to the challenges they faced.

The creation of the confederacy is a striking example of indigenous dynamism, because it emerged through people's willingness to contemplate new solutions in solving their problems. At the same time, it reflected conservative thought, because its formation protected traditional values, including respect for personal, family, clan, and community freedoms, which had to be balanced with the obligations owed by the diverse components that formed Iroquoian society to care for each other. Another example of dynamism and people's ability to respond to challenges and opportunities dates to the mid-1600s, when part of the population moved north to establish villages at Roman Catholic missions within New France. By the middle of the eighteenth century there were four such communities: Akwesasne, where today's Ontario, Quebec, and New York meet; Kahnawake, near Montreal; Kanesatake, on the Ottawa River (which also included a sizable number of Algonquian speakers until the 1860s); and Oswegatchie, at modern Ogdensburg, New York, which no longer survives. Along with several non-Iroquois missions on the St Lawrence River, these settlements formed the Seven Nations of Canada. Although Haudenosaunee members of that alliance maintained close connections with their relatives to the south, they lived outside of the confederacy's structures for the most part. In contrast to those who went north, other individuals moved from Iroquoia to the Ohio country in the 1700s. Known as the Mingos, they too generally pursued lives beyond the league's influence.

Alongside migration away from Iroquoia, many foreign natives settled amid or near the confederates in New York and Pennsylvania. Many of them were captives, such as thousands of Iroquoian-speaking Hurons (or Wendat) from today's southern Ontario, seized by war parties during the terrible conflicts of the 1600s. Despite the violence of their entry into the Haudenosaunee world, prisoners regularly went through an adoption process that saw them become full members of the league's communities, although their captors treated some as inferiors and put others to death. Other people voluntarily left their homes to reside among the Iroquois, and they too normally found acceptance within the families and clans that made up the confederacy's different nations. Adoptions occurred without reference to ethnicity. Thus, not only Iroquoians but also indigenous people from other language groups (such as Algonquian Shawnees and Odawas) entered Haudenosaunee society, as did non-natives from European and African backgrounds, along with individuals of mixed ancestries. In addition, large portions of distinct communities chose to relocate in Iroquoia. One such group comprised a significant percentage of the Iroquoian-speaking Tuscaroras, who left North Carolina in the early eighteenth century to flee war, enslavement, the theft of their lands, and other cruelties inflicted on them by settlers. They then formed the sixth nation of the league in the 1720s. Other aboriginal people, such as non-Iroquoian Delawares (or Lenni Lenapes) and Tutelos from the Atlantic seaboard and Mesquakies (or Foxes) from the west, relocated in Iroquoia in the eighteenth century, primarily to escape newcomer persecution. Unlike the Tuscaroras, however, they did not become formal members of the confederacy at the tribal level, but generally accepted Six Nations suzerainty over them, with some exceptions (such as most of the Delawares, who took up land farther west than those who settled under Haudenosaunee protection). So many outsiders joined the confederacy – native, white, black, and people of varied ancestries – that, combined with intermarriage, their societies exhibited a considerable degree of diversity within a larger Iroquois political and cultural milieu several decades before John Norton's birth.

In 1770, the Six Nations in Iroquoia had a population of eight thousand (including adoptees), while eight hundred other native people lived among them. The Haudenosaunee members of the Seven Nations of Canada numbered two thousand, while the Mingos in the Ohio country counted six hundred souls within their villages. (The total Great Lakes native population at the time was eighty thousand, spread across thirty or so tribes.) Due to disease, war, and the other disasters that marked intertribal conflict and the profound troubles associated with native-newcomer relations, these numbers were less than half of what they had been when Europeans first travelled to Iroquoia in the early 1600s. In contrast, before the 1630s and the first outbreaks of devastating epidemics from Europe in the lower Great Lakes, indigenous societies had been growing steadily through the decades, primarily through natural increase.

The Mohawks, Oneidas, Onondagas, Cayugas, and Senecas who originally founded the confederacy pursued lives shaped by their own development across the centuries and changes arising from interactions with other peoples. Iroquoians primarily were farmers, as they had been for hundreds of years before Norton's birth. The "three sisters" of corn, beans, and squash met the bulk of their dietary needs in comparison to other crops and foods derived from gathering, hunting, fishing, and trading. Corn (or maize), for instance, had been grown in the lower Great Lakes since at least the sixth century. As time passed, farming increased in importance, which in turn led people to choose lives that were relatively sedentary so they could cultivate their fields efficiently. Horticulture accelerated population growth, and that rise naturally led to increased interpersonal and other complexities, along with a corresponding expansion of social structures to address evolving needs, as was common across human societies throughout the millennia. By the 1300s, for instance, the clusters of longhouse-dominated farming villages that dominate our images of pre-contact Haudenosaunee society had become fully established after several centuries of evolution (and would remain so until architectural and landscape transformations due to the adoption of Euro-American forms occurred in the eighteenth century). From some point in the 1500s, the arrival of European goods, carried inland from coastal regions by aboriginal traders, began to affect the native world of the lower Great Lakes. Direct contact with white people for the Haudenosaunee in New York occurred early in the 1600s. For the Tuscaroras and others who moved to Iroquoia later, similar patterns had marked their history, with some variations, such as earlier encounters with Europeans for those whose homelands had lain closer to the Atlantic coast. In the 1600s, exchanges with newcomers from the other side of the ocean led the Iroquois to begin cultivating European foods; by the 1700s, some raised pigs, cattle, and horses, expanding the range of produce they consumed beyond traditional foods and adding animal labour to their endeavours. Outside of diversifying their diets and easing their work, these changes enhanced their food security. In addition to farming, the Haudenosaunee of the 1700s supported themselves through gathering, fishing, hunting, trading, craft production, waged work, receiving gifts and supplies from allies, and, to a small degree, taking spoils in war. None of these activities was simple. For example, we know the people of the Six Nations gathered over four hundred different plants for medicinal purposes alone (to say nothing of collecting them for food and other uses).[2] Using so many plants

---

2 Herrick, *Iroquois Medical Botany*.

speaks to the development of knowledge through observation, experimentation, and awareness of the environment, and it demonstrates that native societies were vibrant, not static, as one generation passed its accumulated knowledge to the next, which then built upon that wisdom with intelligence and creativity to make its contributions to the well-being of those who came after.

While the Iroquois accepted outside influences, especially when it suited their needs, tastes, and desires, they likewise possessed – and continue to possess – a proud history of preserving their identity and independence against external intrusions. Despite the advent of Christianity among some, and the widespread consumption of foreign goods, foods, ideas, practices, and technologies, the Six Nations at the time of John Norton's birth vigorously guarded their culture and sought to control their development as distinct societies, despite the immense pressures posed by the rapidly growing colonial presence. Often they welcomed new things that made life easier but rejected influences that undermined cherished values, with different people making individual choices and expressing varied opinions on what should be accepted or rejected. Beyond protecting their separate cultures, the Haudenosaunee defended their sovereignty and their lands as proficiently as they could against outsiders, in a world where the changing weight of population numbers worked relentlessly against them while favouring ever-expanding Euro-American interests. To achieve their goals, they took advantage of divisions between whites and among foreign indigenous nations skilfully, and they engaged in diplomacy, war, and trade adroitly. They did this while facing enormous challenges from enemies and competitors in both the white and native worlds, and while confronting internal divisions and social tensions, brought on in part through the severity of the conflicts of the 1600s and 1700s, white greed for Haudenosaunee territory, and other threats to their well-being. The Six Nations had lost some of their lands in the easterly regions and along the southern borders of Iroquoia by 1770, yet remained remarkably strong politically and culturally on the eve of the great transformations that would come a few years later due to the American Revolution of 1775–83. Their success contrasted conspicuously with the fate of other Iroquoians during the upheavals of the seventeenth and eighteenth centuries, who had disappeared as distinct societies (such as the Wenros) or become shadows of their former glory (such as the Hurons), and in both these instances had been defeated by Haudenosaunee warriors. Furthermore, the Six Nations enjoyed an enviable standard of material comfort compared to neighbouring Euro-Americans and other natives. Many of them also found cautious hope for their future welfare through the relationships they had developed with the British Crown since the latter 1600s.

At the end of the Seven Years' War, King George III affirmed Iroquois ownership of most of their territories through provisions made in the Royal Proclamation of 1763. In part, it divided the Crown's possessions in North America along a line that separated areas of white-dominated settlement from indigenous lands, with most of Iroquoia falling within the realms designated as "Indian Territory." At the same time, white officials proved willing to collude with the Six Nations to advance combined imperial and Haudenosaunee desires against those of other native peoples. The most arresting example of that bond occurred at a treaty negotiated in Oneida country in 1768 at Fort Stanwix (in modern Rome, New York). The Iroquois asserted an old but no longer justifiable claim to the lands occupied by other tribes to the south and west of them, and then sold those territories to the British (who knew the title was weak). In the process, the Haudenosaunee collected almost all of the money from the transaction for themselves. In part, this sale attempted to reduce pressure to alienate parts of Iroquoia by opening other regions for white settlement. The treaty also recovered some confederacy territory endangered by the Proclamation Line. While Six Nations actions towards the Shawnees and others whose lands they traded away were egregious, the threats to their independence from Euro-American expansion were tremendous; and conflict with diverse aboriginal peoples had created models of how the Iroquois could align with, or compete against, others regardless of the colour of their skin. Six Nations deeds contrasted with ideas of trans-tribal solidarity against the common Euro-American danger, and the corresponding demands for native unity that some began to advocate in the mid-1700s in the lower Great Lakes, which grew in strength as the decades passed (and which John Norton would embrace as he came to maturity). The people of the Six Nations in the 1760s, however, believed they had little choice but to protect their interests forcefully if they hoped to preserve their well-being in an environment marked by settler prejudice and greed, while long-standing inter-tribal tensions and conflicting objectives undermined aspirations to find strength through broadly based indigenous alliances.

The relief from settlement pressures that came with the 1768 treaty was short-lived. The American Revolution generated a period of dreadful violence, hardship, and dislocation for the Haudenosaunee, and then forced stunning land losses on them in its aftermath, causing many to leave their homeland once the rebellious colonists won independence from Great Britain. Most Iroquois people chose not to participate in the early stages of this civil war between Euro-American loyalists and revolutionaries. Nevertheless, they found themselves drawn into the conflict. Internal divisions prevented the Six Nations Confederacy from maintaining unity. Individuals felt the need to align with their friends and partners in the white world to protect their communities and families as they thought best, and men wished to prove themselves in combat in conformity with cultural values that honoured the warrior spirit. While none of the tribes entirely adopted a particular position, and while support for belligerency or neutrality varied from year to year, there were certain trends in Iroquois behaviour during the conflict. Sizeable numbers of Oneidas and Tuscaroras sided with the rebellious colonists. Their decision seemed to lack logic, given that the revolutionaries represented the graver threat to Iroquois security, because of their agenda of agrarian expansion and their rejection of the protections offered by the Royal Proclamation and other efforts and promises made by the government in London. These tribes, especially the Oneidas, however, had enjoyed good relations with missionaries and other whites who supported the rebel side and advocated support for its cause. They also had experienced problems with Sir William Johnson, the Crown's superintendent-general of the Indian Department and patriarch of the region's most eminent loyalist family. (Created in 1755, the department oversaw Anglo–First Nations relations.) Moreover, they were surrounded by white communities dominated by revolutionaries who could threaten them should they support the King's cause, while they hoped these same people might offer protection if they befriended them, which seemed promising due to efforts by rebel leaders to assuage Oneida and Tuscarora fears and to strengthen the bonds between them. Not all agreed. Some members of these two nations aligned with the Crown, as the Mohawks, Cayugas, and Senecas generally did. Neutrality enjoyed greater support among the Onondagas than among other league members, at least until 1779, when many of them took up arms beside loyalist forces after rebels arbitrarily and ignorantly burned their villages.

The conflict proved to be devastating from an early date. In 1777, for instance, in an event that horrified the Six Nations when they contemplated what they had done, pro- and anti-loyalist Iroquois fought and killed each other at the battle of Oriskany near Fort Stanwix. As the war progressed, the Haudenosaunee who allied with the Crown proved to be valuable combatants, especially in raids against agricultural settlements in New York and Pennsylvania that provided much of the food consumed by rebel forces on the eastern seaboard. In 1779, George Washington, commander-in-chief of the revolutionary army, ordered his troops to invade Iroquoia to force the King's Six Nations allies out of the war. Soldiers burned several dozen Haudenosaunee villages and destroyed the extensive fields and orchards that surrounded them, but most of the indigenous people themselves escaped. Thousands fled to the loyalist stronghold of Fort Niagara in the western part of Iroquoia. In contrast, many members of the now-divided league who had aligned against George III left their exposed villages to seek shelter at the eastern end of Iroquoia among their rebel allies. Like their relatives to the west, they suffered greatly from the starvation, disease, degradation, and uncertainty common to the experience of wartime refugees throughout the centuries. Despite General Washington's hopes, Six Nations warriors continued to fight into 1782. In addition, the Mingos to the west of Iroquoia aided the Crown, but without experiencing the depth of suffering that their easterly relatives endured. The Iroquois of the Seven Nations of Canada negotiated neutrality with the revolutionaries in 1775 when the rebels occupied Montreal for a time, but afterwards more of them provided assistance to the loyalist side than to its opponents. Like the Mingos, they too escaped most of the horrors that afflicted the people of Iroquoia.

As the war moved towards its conclusion, Crown forces and their allies from Iroquoian- and Algonquian-speaking nations controlled most of the lands north of the 1768 Fort Stanwix line, which ran south of Iroquoia and then along the Ohio River. Hence, indigenous people reasonably expected to retain these territories within a truncated British Empire upon the return of peace, despite the success of the rebels in other theatres of the conflict. To their horror, in the 1783 Treaty of Paris, in which Great Britain recognized the independence of the United States, diplomats created a boundary through the middle of the Great Lakes waterways between the new republic and the remnants of the King's North American possessions. A new government had formed in London to bring the costly and unpopular struggle to a hurried close while obtaining as many advantages for the empire as possible. This meant signing a generous peace with the revolutionaries, including giving away sovereignty over First Nations territory south of the lakes that otherwise might have been retained through more resolute bargaining. Outraged, Joseph Brant (Thayendanegea), who had fought so hard against the rebels largely in response to British promises to protect the Six Nations, captured native shock when he declared, "England has sold the Indians to Congress."[3]

In the treaty's aftermath, mortified British officials who disagreed with their government's decisions told their stunned aboriginal allies that their government only had transferred sovereignty over, not ownership of, the land. Bad as that was, it reflected the pre-war situation where the Crown had claimed dominion over, but not possession of, indigenous territories. For a time, however, representatives of the new republic acted as if the revolutionaries had conquered the tribes, arguing that natives had to move away when settlers – now freed from royal restraint – wanted their land. The thirst for expansion was immense. The value of these territories promised to help the federal and state governments retire their wartime debts, allow land speculators to grow rich, and enable ordinary people to pursue their dreams. Within a few years, however, American officials changed their views on conquest and acknowledged native ownership of their holdings within the boundaries of the United States. Nevertheless, they continued to engage in relentless efforts to coerce the tribes to sell their territories by forcing land surrenders on them through treaties that did not respect indigenous concerns. Shamefully, the Oneidas and Tuscaroras, who had supported the rebels, were among the first to be compelled to give up most of their land. Between 1784 and 1797, the Haudenosaunee in Iroquoia lost most of their holdings and removed to reservations consisting of small fractions of their former territories. Almost immediately, Americans then worked to shrink and even eliminate those remnant lands. By the outbreak of the War of 1812, only fourteen Iroquois reservations or tracts remained in New York and Pennsylvania. Many were very small, and most were separated from the others by regions occupied by Euro-Americans, whose surrounding settler population grossly outnumbered that of the Six Nations in the tribes' former territories.

Not all of the people of Iroquoia in the 1780s stayed within the boundaries of the United States. One-third of those who survived the American Revolution moved to British territory to start their lives anew

---

3 Joseph Brant cited by Allan Maclean to Frederick Haldimand, 13 May 1783, quoted in Kelsay, *Brant*, 372.

alongside the war's United Empire Loyalist refugees. They received grants of land from the government to resettle within the King's dominions as partial compensation for their wartime losses (and the Crown provided payments and other forms of support to them). One hundred Mohawks took up residence north of Lake Ontario at Tyendinaga (near today's Belleville, Ontario). Eighteen hundred others, from all of the confederacy's nations and the other peoples who lived among them, moved to the Grand River north of Lake Erie. Joseph Brant was one of the central figures in founding that community. Other Haudenosaunee moved to the Ohio country within the United States and contributed to the formation of a new and distinct Iroquois cluster near the shores of Lake Erie, known as the Sandusky Senecas. (Despite the name, a large percentage of them were Cayugas.)

To the west of Iroquoia, the peace of 1783 between the First Nations and the United States lasted only a short while. White settlers, on the one side, and on the other, Shawnees, Miamis, Odawas, Potawatomis, Wyandots, Mingos, Chippewas, and others, renewed hostilities by 1786 for control of the Ohio country. Low-level violence escalated into war, with the aboriginal side winning decisive battles in 1790 and 1791. Although at peace with the new republic, the British, who had developed second thoughts about the 1783 treaty, provided supplies, advice, and other aid to the tribes, which naturally offended the government of President George Washington. By the winter of 1793–4, an American invasion of Canada seemed possible as relations between the two white powers deteriorated. Therefore, the King's soldiers reoccupied Fort Miamis, fifty-five miles south of Detroit (in today's Maumee, Ohio), in order to guard the approach to the border and encourage the First Nations to carry their struggle to a successful conclusion. The British also had not transferred Detroit and other "Western Posts" within the United States to the Americans, despite requirements to do so in the Treaty of Paris. They garrisoned them ostensibly to force their former enemies to meet treaty obligations to compensate loyalists for property losses in the recent conflict, and to give Canadian-based individuals time to liquidate their interests south of the Great Lakes.

Yet the main fear of the government in London centred on protecting the refugee settlements on the north side of the border. Its ministers not only worried about American threats, but also feared that native peoples, enraged that the terms of the peace had disregarded their concerns, might retaliate against their old ally. In the turmoil of the early 1790s, the Crown's servants hoped that the tribes would force the Americans into making concessions in favour of indigenous desires, and wanted to help engineer treaties between the First Nations and the United States to relieve tensions that threatened to spill into British territory. Through their services to the tribes, these officials also sought to keep the indigenous populations aligned with King George in case an Anglo-American war should erupt in the future. Some even wanted to reopen discussions on the boundary between the white powers, to improve Canadian security and create an independent – but British-allied – First Nations territory in part of the broad region historians refer to as the "Old Northwest" (south of Canada, north of the Ohio River, west of Pennsylvania, and east of the Mississippi River). Such an outcome would undo part of the injustice of having ignored aboriginal desires in 1783. Nevertheless, it was not in Britain's interests to go to war to achieve such a goal if it could not be attained through diplomacy or indigenous military efforts undertaken without overt British participation in combat. Thus, seeking to avoid a confrontation, Crown officials did not provide sufficient help to the natives, who lost the critical battle of Fallen Timbers in 1794 near Fort Miamis. In the Treaty of Greenville that followed in 1795, the Americans forced the defeated tribes to surrender much of the Ohio country that they had hoped to preserve for themselves and their descendants, and created new boundaries, although these did not last for any substantial length of time. That agreement occurred after Anglo-American diplomats resolved tensions between their two countries in Jay's Treaty of 1794, which, in part, required the British to leave the Western Posts by 1796 in return for some American concessions. Indigenous peoples – whether or not they had participated in the Ohio war – interpreted both the events of the 1790s and the previous formation of the border between the white powers in 1783 as betrayals of their liberties and rights by the King's servants.[4] That belief naturally undermined Anglo–First Nations relations across the Great Lakes. Yet ongoing economic links with British subjects and efforts by Crown officials to repair their standing with aboriginal communities, combined with aggressive American expansion at the expense of native security, tempered indigenous anger. Consequently, Great Britain and the majority of the First Nations of the Old Northwest would ally with each other – albeit warily – against their common enemy in 1812.

---

4 For JN's thoughts on these betrayals, see *JMJN*, 180, 184, 270.

John Norton's Early Life and Transformation
into Mohawk Leader Teyoninhokarawen

A teenaged John Norton arrived in the Great Lakes region in the 1780s, when indigenous peoples were dealing with the painful challenges brought on by the post-revolutionary political order, the violence of the Ohio war, the loss of vast quantities of land, the influx of antagonistic settlers, and the social and economic stresses generated by their deteriorating circumstances. During this time he first encountered Haudenosaunee society, subsequently became an adopted Mohawk, and began to take on a leadership role under Joseph Brant's patronage among the Iroquois of the Grand River north of Lake Erie. Like many people before him, Norton entered Six Nations society through adoption rather than by birth; and like others in the aboriginal world, he was a person of mixed white and native ancestry. Most such people had a white father and an aboriginal mother, or parents of mixed origins. A much smaller number had a white mother and a native father. Rarer still were babies born in Europe with an aboriginal parent. In terms of his ethnicity, John Norton's birth was thus unusual: his father was a Cherokee, his mother was a Scot, and he was born in Great Britain. He came into the world on 16 December 1770, in or near the fishing village of Crail on Scotland's east coast. The next day, a Presbyterian minister baptized him in the town's medieval church.[1] Norton's origins have generated confusion over his identity, both in his day and since. His enemies' efforts have aggravated the problem, because they worked to discredit his legitimacy within the Haudenosaunee world by asserting that he was a Scot, telling a small truth about his place of birth while hiding the larger truth that his father was a Cherokee. One such person was William Claus, the deputy superintendent-general in the Indian Department in Upper Canada. Claus made his claims knowing that Norton was a legitimate adoptee by the Mohawk standards of his day, and had every right to rise to a prominent role among the Iroquois. Indeed, Norton noted that when he was appointed a chief, "according to custom," representatives from the council presented Claus "with a belt of wampum on the occasion for his information," also confirmed in a letter from Joseph

---

1 *Scotland's People* Website, Church of Scotland, Parish Church of Crail, Baptismal Record for JN, 17 December 1770.

Brant to Claus.[2] By denying these realities, the deputy superintendent-general not only lied about one individual; he effectively rejected the right of indigenous communities to determine their own membership, although controlling membership was a vital factor in self-determination and sovereignty. Even if Norton's father had not been a Cherokee, Claus knew enough about native societies to realize that Norton did not need aboriginal ancestry in order to be adopted (with issues of blood quotient largely being imposed on First Nations by white authorities in later decades). By the Haudenosaunee standards of the period, John Norton was a Mohawk.

Norton's father had been born among the Iroquoian-speaking Cherokees, most likely in or near the northwestern regions of South Carolina where many of their villages stood in the mid-1700s. Given that people knowledgeable about aboriginal identities later described his son as a "half-breed," Norton's father had to be at least partially, if not entirely, indigenous ethnically, with the latter being more likely.[3] As the senior Norton grew up, relations with white society deteriorated at the time of the Seven Years' War, leading to the outbreak of the Anglo-Cherokee War of 1759–61.[4] During the conflict, British forces raided aboriginal villages. On one occasion – most likely in June 1760 – Norton's father, then an older child or a younger teenager, suffered burns when soldiers torched the house where he was hiding from the violence. His son later recorded that his father's older sister, a now-unnamed woman (and widow of a chief by the name of Kennitea) recalled seeing an "officer rescue him after he had been scorched, on which account he was taken away in a wagon, and they were separated."[5] The senior officers on the expedition were dismayed that non-combatants had suffered injuries due to the actions of their men, which might account at least in part for the care Norton's father received. He did not return to his people with other women and children captured at the time, however, perhaps because of the severity of his wounds. Nonetheless, he recovered, and

---

2 JN to the second Duke of Northumberland, 4 February 1807, BL, Northumberland MSS, 64:25 (quote); Six Nations Chiefs to William Claus, 3 September 1806, NL, MS654, 62–3.
3 As noted earlier, I examined JN's Cherokee identity in more detail in Benn, "Missed Opportunities."
4 For JN's description of the Cherokee War, see *JMJN*, 131–3.
5 Ibid., 114. See also Benn, "Missed Opportunities," 266.

then lived with the soldiers of the 1st Regiment of Foot (the Royal Scots), where it seems that one or more men by the name of Anderson became his friends and protectors. Possibly during that time, he received the name John Norton, as later would his son, the man who would become an adopted Mohawk. John Sr sailed with the regiment to Britain in 1764, and appeared on its muster rolls in 1769 as a drummer when the Royal Scots garrisoned Berwick in northern England (and his son's baptismal record a year later indicated that his father was a soldier). John Sr left the regiment in 1770, although we do not know whether he received a discharge or deserted. He moved to Scotland and married or otherwise entered a relationship with Christian Anderson, who was likely a relative of the Andersons in the 1st Foot. It was from this union that John Jr was born, shortly before Christmas 1770.[6]

John Sr seems to have valued his Cherokee heritage. For instance, he apparently taught some of the language to his son, as John Jr recorded that when he met his aunt in 1809–10 on his journey to visit the tribe she "derived much pleasure when she perceived that I could understand her language."[7] (His skills in Cherokee, however, were limited.)[8] His son's Scottish family seems to have been equally important to his formation, as John Jr embraced both his First Nations and European identities, benefited from the education derived from each culture, and maintained contact with relatives in Scotland through letters and visits to that country after moving to North America. John Jr went to school in Scotland and apparently worked for, or apprenticed with, a printer in Edinburgh.[9] John Sr seems to have planned to return to the native

---

6 Benn, "Missed Opportunities," 268. No documents confirm that John Sr and Christian were married, although she was called John's "spouse" (*Scotland's People* Website, Church of Scotland, Parish Church of Crail, Baptismal Record for JN, 17 December 1770). Scottish law assumed that marriage was based on consent rather than ceremony; thus, a couple did not need to take part in a church wedding if they declared that they were married in front of witnesses.

7 *JMJN*, 114.

8 Ibid., 140; John Gambold to Charles Gotthold Reichel, 2 October 1809, published in Crews and Starbuck, *Records of the Moravians*, 3:1323.

9 Years later, for instance, someone recorded that JN was "acquainted with printing" (Robert Addison, Report and Journal, 15 July 1818, quoted in Young, "Addison," 185). JN brought a (presumably small) printing press to Canada from England in 1805, ostensibly to serve the needs of the Bible Society (JN to William Wilberforce, 29 August 1805, NL, MS654, 6; see also Klinck, "Biographical Introduction," in *JMJN*, xxxvii).

world, and stirred desires in his son's mind to visit the land where his father had been born. In 1784, the older man began the process of fulfilling his dream when he enlisted in the 65th Regiment of Foot. Like others who wanted to travel to North America but had no means of doing so, he found a regiment destined to be sent across the ocean and joined it. John Sr likely took Christian and their son into barracks with him, as was common in the eighteenth century. Then in 1786, in his sixteenth year, John Jr entered the army as a drummer. Detachments of the 65th Foot sailed to Quebec in 1785 and 1786. In Canada, Christian became a domestic servant to John Coffin, one of several Coffins in government service in Montreal and Quebec. We do not know, however, if she accompanied her husband and son in 1787 when they went to Fort Niagara (one of the Western Posts Britain retained on American soil until 1796), or what happened to her later on. One possibility is that she died at Grand River in 1804 or 1805, because John Jr wrote that his child's grandmother had passed away then, but of course this could have been the mother of his wife or partner instead. As with so much of Norton's story, limited documentation makes it difficult to answer all the questions we might want to pose, necessitating some presumption based on fragmentary information, or requiring that some subjects remain unexplored.[10]

As was not uncommon among individuals who joined the army in hopes of gaining passage across the ocean, both Norton men deserted. John Jr ran away from Fort Niagara on two occasions, in March and June 1787, most likely seeking shelter with the Cayugas in western New York (because he gained some proficiency in their language about that time, and had made friends with native people who visited the fort). Desertion, while widespread, regularly carried severe consequences for those who were caught. Yet instead he received a discharge in February 1788, apparently at least partly due to the intervention of

---

10 "Z," Article, *Missouri Gazette*, 15 June 1816; Janson, *Stranger*, 287n; Robert Addison, Report and Journal, 15 July 1818, quoted in Young, "Addison," 185; JN to Robert Barclay, 15 January 1806, NL, MS654, 23; Benn, "Missed Opportunities." Corroborating evidence across several sources is important for exploring JN's early life because many documents contain mistakes. "Z," for instance, preserved both useful information and errors while conflating John Sr and Jr as one person. Attempts to identify "Z," who seems to have worked in the fur trade, were unsuccessful, but we can be confident that JN did not write the article because of the numerous errors.

someone in the Coffin family. No record seems to survive to tell us why the authorities treated him so leniently, although perhaps one of the Coffins arranged to buy Norton out of the army, as was allowed in that period, or there may have been some other reason lost to history.[11] In any case, his desertion, which normally would be have been regarded as disreputable, did not seem to affect the readiness of army officers to work with or respect him during the War of 1812, suggesting that there were mitigating circumstances surrounding the events of the 1780s. John Sr (who had been promoted to corporal) deserted in 1789, when stationed on the Richelieu River south of Montreal. He then disappeared, and may have lived in the Ohio country for a time, but almost certainly made it back to his Cherokee relatives, who had moved west from South Carolina by that point. Evidence for his successful return comes from the memory of a missionary who recalled that John Jr visited the tribe in 1809–10 partly to "cover the grave of his father with wampum."[12]

During the latter 1780s, John Norton Jr probably lived in western New York. He also may have visited the Ohio country, where the Cayugas and other Haudenosaunee had a presence, and where some Cherokees had their homes after moving there from the south. In late 1790 or early 1791, he crossed the border between American and British territory to work as a teacher among the Mohawks of Tyendinaga on the Bay of Quinte for the Society for the Propagation of the Gospel, an Anglican missionary body. Norton, however, did not like teaching and stayed for only a short time. His supervisor, the Reverend John Stuart, noted that he "was tired of the confinement and could not subsist on the salary, and the Indians expect that a schoolmaster should be more under their direction than most men are willing to submit to."[13] Another, now anonymous, source echoed Stuart's comment, reporting that Norton found "teaching school to be tedious, and confinement was more than he could bear" and instead "he associated with the young Indians in all their diversions and became at once as perfect an Indian

---

11 65th Foot, 1783–97, various documents from the 1780s, NA, WO 12/7378; Benn, "Missed Opportunities," 271–2, 288n47.
12 [Loskiel], *Moravian Mission*, 305 (quote); Anna Rosina Gambold, Memorandum, September 1809, published in McClinton, *Mission to the Cherokees*, 1:329–30.
13 John Stuart to the Society for the Propagation of the Gospel, 5 July 1791, quoted in Klinck, "Biographical Introduction," in *JMJN*, xli.

as ran in the woods."[14] John Norton then travelled to the Six Nations on the Grand River for a short while. According to a speech he gave in 1807, this was his first visit to the Iroquois settlements north of Lake Erie. He did not stay long, because he wanted to support the indigenous peoples of the Ohio country in the war to protect their lands against American expansion. He noted that "the relation I bear to some" had animated his heart.[15] We do not know what that statement meant, but there are several possibilities. First, some Cherokees had travelled north to fight in the war for the Ohio country. Second, his father might have been there, not yet having gone home. Third, he may have been referring to the Cayugas, with whom John Jr had established connections, and who formed the majority of the Sandusky Senecas. Fourth, a source in 1793 noted that he had "great interest among the Mohawks" on the Scioto River in Ohio, which, geographically, suggests a link to the Mingos or other Haudenosaunee living there, but this "interest" may have been established after his arrival in 1791, and may have alluded to a woman whom he had married or otherwise lived with.[16] Naturally, there is no reason to suppose that his associations south of Lake Erie were restricted to one community or did not evolve through the years. Not knowing the details of his family or other personal relationships is frustrating, because kinship ties through marriage and blood were crucial in creating opportunities and obligations for individuals in the indigenous world.[17]

---

14 "Z," Article, *Missouri Gazette*, 15 June 1816. Some of JN's thoughts on indigenous schooling survive in Headley, "Account," 12 March 1805, NYSL.

15 JN, Speech, 19 February 1807, NL, MS654, 119.

16 Thomas Smith to John Askin, 3 March 1793, published in Quaife, *Askin Papers*, 1:467.

17 In addition to records associated with JN, searches through online and printed genealogical sources, local histories, other databases, and consultations with various individuals did not clarify JN's relationships, and often generated conflicting, inaccurate, and undocumented information. We know that in an Anglican ceremony in 1813, he wed Catherine (Karighwaycagh or Kitty), a young Delaware woman, who had been born on the Grand River in the 1790s and who had a white father and native mother. Karighwaycagh's surname is unclear, with sources suggesting Mons, Moss, Maus, Huff, and Docherty. At least one previous partner still was alive when JN married her. That woman was a Mohawk and the mother of his son, John, born in 1799, and, apparently, another child about whom we know nothing, just as we do not know the identity of the woman. JN also had a relationship with an unidentified Onondaga at Six Nations (between his Mohawk and Delaware partners), and they had children (one of whom was named Tehonakaraa, born in 1805). Both children

John Jr reached the Ohio country sometime in the latter part of 1791 and worked as a trader over the next few years while supporting the native cause. He obtained merchandise from the prominent Detroit River family of John Askin, such as blankets, clothing, hunting gear, hardware, rum, tobacco, and luxury items. In return he collected furs, mainly raccoon, muskrat, and mink. He also seems to have worked directly as an employee of the Askins from time to time. He fell into debt with them, creating a burden that weighed on him and his creditors for years afterwards. An anonymous source recorded that Norton "frequently had a few goods on credit, but always, like an Indian, he never traded for profit. All he wished for was to collect ... enough ... furs to pay his merchant, and the remainder of his goods was given to his Indian friends and relations."[18] Aside from supporting the idea that Norton had family connections in the Ohio country, this observation suggests that he regarded possessions in the same way that others in the native world did, tending to think of them as a means not of accumulating wealth but of addressing everyday needs and satisfying obligations to share with others.

John Norton Jr's trading activities placed him at the heart of aboriginal resistance in the war for the Ohio country. There were a number of villages in the Miami River area founded by people who had abandoned their homes farther south and east because of the influx of settlers, and diplomatic councils among the tribes and between natives and whites took place there. The details of his participation in the struggle are vague. He apparently went on small-scale raids against aboriginal

---

from that relationship died during the War of 1812, but we do not know how their lives ended (and childhood mortality was high in the early 1800s independent of wartime traumas). Carl Klinck made the mistake of conflating Tehonakaraa and JN's son John as one person (e.g., *JMJN*, 373). The relationship with at least the Mohawk woman probably had not been solemnized in a Christian ceremony because of the Church's restrictions on remarriage at the time JN wed Catherine. See Klinck, "Biographical Introduction," in *JMJN*, lxxix, xciv; Benn, *Iroquois in the War of 1812*, 236n83; Claus, Account, 4 December 1813, published in Cruikshank, "Campaigns," 33–4; JN to Robert Barclay, 15 January 1806, NL, MS654, 25; JN to J.F. Addison, 13 June 1818, LAC, RG10, 489:29364; Robert Thomson to JN, 8 August 1823, AO, F440; Lukenbach and Haman, "Extract from the Diary of the Indian Congregation at Fairfield," 16 January 1827, 146–7; Canada West Personal Census, Kent County, 1861, LAC, RG31, 5317. For JN's description of indigenous marriage, see Headley, "Account," 12 March 1805, NYSL.

18 "Z," Article, *Missouri Gazette*, 15 June 1816. For debts, see Quaife, *Askin Papers*, 2:179.

enemies. More significantly, he fought at the great native victory on 4 November 1791, where indigenous warriors destroyed an American force at the battle of the Wabash (in modern Fort Recovery, Ohio), killing, wounding, and capturing a thousand of their enemies while suffering only sixty losses of their own.[19] He was twenty years old at the time. His later participation in the War of 1812 – in which he obviously was a competent warrior and leader – implies that he had developed some degree of combat proficiency in the Ohio country. In addition, he had trained in the British army, and undoubtedly had studied tactics and strategy through his subsequent association with Joseph Brant and other men of the generation who had fought in the American Revolution. Norton's participation in action in the 1790s gave him more military experience than most of his contemporaries along the Grand River had acquired before 1812, because the Six Nations generally had not taken part in the Ohio war.

He also was present at diplomatic events in the region, and witnessed tensions between the Haudenosaunee, who preferred moderation, and the indigenous peoples of the Old Northwest, who advocated belligerency. Despite American unwillingness to compromise, most Iroquois thought that only negotiations could resolve the crisis, and feared that ongoing hostilities to the west of their lands might spread to their own vulnerable communities in Canada, New York, and Pennsylvania. They failed, however, to convince the other tribes to accept their views. At a council in 1792, for instance, Norton witnessed the acrimony between representatives of the two groups. He recalled that Haudenosaunee representatives "offered to become mediators for a peace" but that, "their

---

19 Headley, "Account," 12 March 1805, NYSL noted JN's participation at the Wabash, as did James Currie, who met JN in 1804 and said he saw combat in other actions too (Currie, *Memoir*, 1:373). *JMJN*, 171–3 describes the fighting at the Wabash in the third person but in ways that align with his accounts of battles in which he participated (such as Queenston Heights) rather than those he described secondhand (such as York). His narrative of the 1791 battle presents details that accord with those we would expect a combatant to remember, while a close reading indicates that he served with a native column that consisted of Iroquoians from the Cherokee, Wyandot, and Mingo nations rather than with one of the Algonquian-dominated columns, which makes sense in terms of his Cherokee origins. For an analysis of the battle of the Wabash that compares well to *JMJN*, see Heath, *William Wells*, 141–51. JN described some of the characteristics of native warfare in this period (*JMJN*, 122–6, with briefer notations elsewhere).

proposals not being well-received, they rather upbraided the Shawnees with continuing the war from an avidity for plunder." In response, the people they addressed "retaliated by hinting that" the Iroquois "had so far degenerated as to become the tools of the Americans, to sacrifice their independence and honour for paltry presents."[20] These mutual accusations sadly discounted the intricacies of each party's position in favour of simple invective. Harsh words marked tensions that undermined relations between the Six Nations and other tribes, which had marred their interactions across many decades and which recalled memories of the wars they had fought against each other in earlier times. These denunciations also symbolized how indigenous peoples had incompatible concerns and agendas, which made it difficult to unite against common threats posed by Euro-Americans.

Although John Norton fought at the battle of the Wabash in 1791, he came under suspicion in 1794 of having warned the Americans of an impending attack near Fort Recovery, a post the republic's army had established in 1793 on the site of their great defeat two years earlier. We know this to be false: only one person, a Chickasaw scouting for the American army by the name of Jimmy Underwood, provided intelligence to them at that moment. Norton, who had been missing from the native force at the time, reappeared saying he had been lost in the woods, although the now-unknown author of this story seemed to doubt him.[21] The manner in which Crown officials treated Norton after the Ohio war ended, offering him land and preferment in Upper Canada, indicates that the idea that he had betrayed the aboriginal cause was untrue, although his enemies within the colony – such as William Claus – affirmed a variety of falsehoods to undermine his credibility and promote their interests. Nevertheless, the details of his participation in the 1794 campaign are unclear due to a lack of documentation. His journal does not help, because he presented the events of that year as a historical narrative rather than as an autobiographical text. We do know, however, that Norton did not participate in that year's major battle, at Fallen Timbers (in today's Maumee, Ohio). Most of the native army was absent, because the chiefs had miscalculated the timing of the

---

20 *JMJN*, 173.
21 Anonymous Diary associated with the Claus Family, 29 June and 2 July 1794, published in Cruikshank, *Correspondence of … Simcoe*, 5:93–4; Benn, *Iroquois in the War of 1812*, 208n18; Atkinson, *Splendid Land*, 168.

American advance. He may have been with other warriors away from the site of the battle, or he may have taken up arms alongside British troops inside Fort Miamis with other traders and militiamen. In either case, his description of events surrounding Fallen Timbers suggests that he was not far from the fighting.[22]

While Norton was a minor figure in the Ohio country of the 1790s, he was not without promise. Since leaving the 65th Regiment, he had established connections in various aboriginal and white communities across the lower Great Lakes, had developed a range of useful skills and expertise that could benefit both natives and newcomers as they dealt with each other, and had become proficient in several languages. In fact, he seems to have possessed remarkable linguistic gifts, becoming fluent in spoken and written Mohawk and developing some facility in other First Nations and European tongues, which enabled him to serve as a translator and intermediary. (He even amused himself by translating Walter Scott's celebrated 1810 poem, *The Lady of the Lake*, into Mohawk.)[23] A now-unknown person who knew him in the 1790s remembered Norton as "a very intelligent, modest, and unassuming young man" who "could discourse on any subject, but in all his conversations about Indians he complains of the injustice they receive from the intrigues of white people."[24]

Around this time, Joseph Brant (Thayendanegea) considered drawing Norton into his circle to employ his talents for the benefit of the Six Nations of the Grand River. Earlier, Brant had failed to have his volatile son Isaac (Karaguantier) assume a prominent political role; and then, in 1795, Isaac, who had aligned with people on the Grand opposed to his father, assaulted Joseph. In the ensuing struggle, Isaac received a wound that led to his death two days later. Joseph had other children; however, his boys were too young to participate in the public capacities associated with men in the 1790s. Only one daughter, Christina (Aoghyatonghsera), was an adult then, but women's political roles were different from those of men. Furthermore, Thayendanegea thought that few

---

22 *JMJN*, 178–82, 184. See also, White, *Selkirk's Diary*, 26 February 1804, 244.
23 Peter Russell to Alexander McKee, 10 June 1797, AO, MS234; Farmer's Brother (Honayawas), Speech, 19 June 1797, ibid.; White, *Selkirk's Diary*, 26 February 1804, 244; Janson, *Stranger*, 287n; Fenton, "Cherokee and Iroquois Connections," 242–5; Fogelson, "Norton as Ethno-Ethnologist," 252–3, 255n18; Thomas Scott to Walter Scott, March 1814, quoted in Klinck, "Biographical Introduction," in *JMJN*, xxix.
24 "Z," Article, *Missouri Gazette*, 15 June 1816.

people in the community had the literary skills, knowledge of Euro-American society, and other abilities needed to assist him in fulfilling his responsibilities to the Haudenosaunee.[25]

At the same time that Joseph Brant was considering John Norton's potential, the war for the Ohio country concluded with the defeat of the tribes, as we saw earlier, while Anglo-American diplomacy prevented a confrontation between the two white powers. The changes brought on by those events led Norton to move to Canada, despite his reluctance to leave the Old Northwest.[26] Writing from Detroit in 1796, he petitioned colonial authorities for land by the shores of Lake Erie where he might "settle in assurance of having his home under the British government."[27] Crown officials offered him a generous grant of twelve hundred acres, which presumably reflected his utility as a translator and prospects for further service. For reasons unknown, he never acquired the property. (Details of his land holdings and attempts to obtain grants before and after the War of 1812 are elusive in the historical record).[28] Instead, efforts that had begun earlier to employ Norton as an Indian Department interpreter came to fruition through discussions between Thayendanegea and Upper Canada's senior official, Lieutenant-Governor John Graves Simcoe. The appointment gave Joseph Brant an ally and observer within the department.[29] Norton began his new job in November 1796. It came with a recommendation that he be given six hundred acres of land, as well as a one-acre town lot on the Canadian side of the mouth of the Niagara River so he could settle close to Fort George, where the department's officials addressed

---

25 Joseph Brant's biographer, Isabel Kelsay, suggested that JN became his "secretary and confidant" towards the end of the Ohio war in the mid-1790s, writing that the Mohawk chief "had finally found an educated friend whom he could trust, who would not tell everything he knew about Indian affairs to the first British official he met" (*Brant*, 516).

26 JN, Speech, 19 February 1807, NL, MS654, 120.

27 JN, Petition, 30 August 1796, with notation, 21 July 1797, AO, F440.

28 Minutes of the Upper Canadian Executive Council, 8 October 1796, published in Cruikshank and Hunter, *Correspondence of ... Russell*, 1:65; Communication from Timothy Willig, 15 July 2013, on his research on JN's properties at the AO and LAC.

29 J.G. Simcoe to Lord Dorchester, 22 December 1795, published in Cruikshank, *Correspondence of ... Simcoe*, 4:165; JN, Speech, 19 February 1807, NL, MS654, 119–20; JN to the second Duke of Northumberland, 4 February 1807, BL, Northumberland MSS, 64:25.

Anglo-Haudenosaunee affairs.[30] The Six Nations, according to Norton, also gave him "an equal right with themselves to occupy and possess any unassigned part of the lands on the Grand River" to farm. (He later gave the site he had chosen to relatives of his Onondaga wife or partner, with whom he had lived for a time before the War of 1812.)[31] While thus employed by the department he volunteered to work for the Six Nations of the Grand, after obtaining permission from the commandant at Fort George at Niagara to do so.[32]

By about 1797, John Norton's relationship to Joseph Brant had progressed far enough for him to serve as a deputy to the famous Mohawk leader.[33] A year later, the twenty-six-year-old Norton participated as part of the Six Nations delegation at a council at the Haudenosaunee community of Buffalo Creek on the American side of the Niagara River, near Lake Erie. On another occasion, he headed a delegation to meet Mohawks from Kahnawake and officials from New York in Albany, to deal with concerns arising from the alienation of native land in the northern part of the state.[34] It was around this time that Brant adopted Norton as his "nephew." This gave Norton status as a Mohawk, along with a new name, Dowwisdowwis (the Snipe), although another reference says that the Mohawks at Tyendinaga had adopted him in 1791 when he taught school there. This might imply that he went through two adoptions or that the processes fulfilled different purposes.[35]

---

30 Joseph Chew to Alexander McKee, 26 September 1796, published in Cruikshank and Hunter, *Correspondence of ... Russell*, 1:43; Minutes of the Upper Canadian Executive Council, 8 October 1796, ibid., 1:65; Peter Russell to Robert Prescott, 30 June 1797, ibid., 1:201–2; JN, Petition, 30 August 1796, with notation, 21 July 1797, AO, F440; Farmer's Brother, Speech, 19 June 1797, AO, MS234; Russell to William Claus, 31 December 1797, ibid.; JN, Petitions, 21 July 1797 and 11 April 1798, published in Cruikshank, "Petitions," 262–3; Joseph Brant, Speech, 24 November 1796, LAC, MG19–F35, series 2, lot 713:1–4; Joseph Chew to James Green, 10 April 1797, LAC, RG8, 250:478.

31 JN to J.F. Addison, 13 June 1818, LAC, RG10, 489:29364.

32 John McDonell to James Green, 22 August 1797, published in Cruikshank and Hunter, *Correspondence of ... Russell*, 1:261; Proposed Establishment of the Indian Department, n.d. (1797), published in ibid., 2:53; JN, Speech, 19 February 1807, NL, MS654, 119–20.

33 JN, Speech, 19 February 1807, NL, MS654, 107.

34 E.g., Joseph Brant to James Givins, 24 July 1798, published in Cruikshank and Hunter, *Correspondence of ... Russell*, 3:233; Brant to Thomas Morris, 4 April 1799, quoted in Stone, *Brant*, 2:412–13; JN to J.F. Addison, 16 June 1818, LAC, RG8, 262:90.

35 Stone, *Brant*, 2:411–12; Young, *Parish Register*, 15. The 1791 reference to JN's adoption is in Owen, *Bible Society*, 1:126n.

In 1800 John Norton wrote that he resigned from the Indian Department, intending "to go to the westward because it is a better country for Indians and easier to live in, there being plenty of game and the like, but Captain Brant ... prevailed on me to remain a while here yet."[36] At first he resisted Thayendanegea's request, thinking he might have to abandon his "western friends," but yielded when the Six Nations "represented to me that the good of the community required I should become a chief to be enabled to act in a public capacity without incurring blame when I defended their cause, but as it might respect my other concerns I should be at liberty."[37] Thus, it seems that Norton had not intended to stay permanently among the Six Nations, and that he regarded his place in the aboriginal world – then and later – as extending beyond the Grand River. Nevertheless, he agreed to continue serving the Haudenosaunee in a prominent role, which the Six Nations council had asked him to assume in 1799.[38] With increased responsibilities, he received the name Teyoninhokarawen, which translates as "it keeps the door open." Norton said it signified "frankness and an open heart," and that it recalled the life of an earlier Mohawk chief, Hendrick (Tejoninhokarawa), who Norton and the people around him believed had been a Mahican adoptee, and thus, like him, had foreign origins. Hendrick had risen to prominence a century earlier, and was part of a famous delegation that visited Queen Anne in London in 1710.[39] As we saw above, the absorption of outsiders into Iroquois society was

---

36 JN to Oliver Phelps, 26 December 1800, NYSL, SC10440, Box 22. See also Headley, "Account," 12 March 1805, NYSL; Review of *The History of the British and Foreign Bible Society*, 11n; Robert Nichol to John Askin, 18 August 1800, published in Cruikshank, "Some Letters of Robert Nichol," 52. Joseph Brant held the rank of captain in the Indian Department, but he had led his warriors (along with white and black followers) during the American Revolution as a traditional war chief.

37 JN, Speech, 19 February 1807, NL, MS654, 119–20.

38 Headley, "Account," 12 March 1805, NYSL.

39 Ibid. provides JN's translation of the name, while JN to the second Duke of Northumberland, 4 February 1807, BL, Northumberland MSS, 64:24 notes the link to Hendrick. There were two Hendricks, who scholars often have conflated as one. The person associated with JN's name lived c.1660–c.1735; the other lived c.1691–1755 (Hinderaker, *Two Hendricks*, 2). Eric Hinderaker differentiated the older figure as Tejoninhokarawa and the later as Theyanoguin. He believed that it is not certain whether the first Hendrick was a Mahican (27, 305n15), but Mohawks of JN's generation thought he was.

a normal occurrence, and in becoming an adopted Mohawk, Norton participated in that long-standing practice. While the Six Nations integrated people from diverse backgrounds into their communities, including some with no native heritage, Brant may have selected Norton partly because of his indigenous ancestry, in addition to his skills and strengths. The Haudenosaunee and Cherokees realized that they shared cultural similarities as Iroquoians, even though their societies had developed separately over many centuries. There was already a Cherokee presence on the Grand River, as recorded in a 1785 census, which enumerated fifty-three Cherokees and Creeks (another southern native people). In seeking someone to groom as an assistant and possible successor, Brant may have thought that Norton had a better chance of assimilating into, and being accepted by, the Six Nations because of his aboriginal identity.[40]

Lord Headley (Charles Allanson-Winn) heard Teyoninhokarawen speak on Iroquois governance in 1805. He recorded that there were two main kinds of chiefs: civil leaders, who usually gained office through hereditary succession, and war chiefs, whose offices were "wholly elective," with a successful candidate being "any amiable man remarkable for his bravery and courage, who has lived quietly and conducted himself with propriety."[41] The realities of Six Nations political structures were more complex, and Headley's notes display instances where he misunderstood or simplified Norton's thoughts. Traditionally, the clan matrons selected the hereditary civil or peace chiefs – who had spiritually important obligations as part of their offices – from a group of eligible candidates. If these men did not execute their duties adequately, the women might chasten them and convince them to change their behaviour, or they might "dehorn" them and raise up others in their place. Once installed, each held one of the fifty titles of the original chiefs of the Iroquois Confederacy. (Unfortunately, one scholar – Carl

---

40 Grand River Census, 1785, published in Johnston, *Six Nations*, 52. JN recorded examples of Cherokee-Haudenosaunee historical, linguistic, and family connections (e.g., *JMJN*, 36, 44, 48, 53, 60, 62, 67, 79, 83, 253–5, 259–60). There were Cherokees living at the Grand during and after the War of 1812, although census records from the time overlook them by incorporating them into other tribes (JN to J.F. Addison, 16 August 1817, LAC, RG8, 261:281; see also Appendix A of this book).
41 Headley, "Account," 12 March 1805, NYSL.

Klinck – generated confusion in recent decades by erroneously assuming that John Norton's name – Teyoninhokarawen – was that of one of the hereditary positions.)[42] In contrast, most war chiefs achieved their positions through a combination of merit and the ability to attract a following, but women exerted influence over them as well by ensuring that everyone heard the women's views on questions of peace or war clearly. There also were "pine tree chiefs" who helped civil leaders, and who gained their status through such abilities as their speaking or negotiating skills. Naturally, some people were prominent in more than one role. Tehaosemsghte, a Seneca at Six Nations in 1806, explained that "according to our customs" someone became a chief either through the "hereditary line on the female side," or from having become "distinguished through meritorious conduct so as to be accepted as such."[43] Judging from their work at Grand River, Brant and Norton (who respectively had been or would become war chiefs) were pine tree chiefs in the manner Tehaosemsghte described, which did not put them within the hereditary succession but gave them status, as people recognized their ability to serve community interests. Other individuals exercised influence because their particular gifts and insights – spiritual or temporal – might contribute to a significant decision. As time passed through the eighteenth and early nineteenth centuries, the hereditary chiefs retained their spiritual functions, based on the religious nature of the confederacy's origins and purposes, but other people often overshadowed them in civil and external affairs. In the years surrounding the American Revolution, for example, Thayendanegea rose to positions of authority as a war and alliance chief, partly through his skills as a military leader and his abilities to represent the Haudenosaunee when dealing with outsiders, but then exercised tremendous influence over the internal management of Six Nations society afterwards. Other factors that enhanced Brant's authority included his marriages to prominent women in Iroquois society and his links to powerful whites, especially

---

42 Klinck, "Biographical Introduction," in *JMJN*, xliv–xlv, especially note 2 on xlv, was in error when he suggested the name was associated with the roll call of the Haudenosaunee Confederacy's fifty hereditary titles, being that of the Seneca chief, Deyonihnhogawen, which means "doorkeeper" (Fenton, Review of *JMJN*, 1259; see also Fenton, *Great Law and the Longhouse*, 193–4).

43 Tehaosemsghte, Speech, 28 July 1806, NL, MS654, 51.

the family of Sir William Johnson, who played critical roles in Great Lakes region native-newcomer relations from the mid-1700s through to the early 1800s.

Whatever someone's source of authority or influence, no one had a right to command. The Six Nations valued personal freedoms, and so influential individuals only could use their powers of consultation, example, and persuasion to try to fashion a consensus that would enable people to face a challenge with some degree of unity. Consensus-building in Norton's time might prove difficult, because communities often divided into rival parties, and because almost everyone enjoyed the liberty to oppose collective decisions or limit his or her commitments to them. This combination of parties, personal autonomy, and a large number of different kinds of chiefs in relation to the comparatively small population allowed groups of people to ignore or oppose one cluster of leaders with some ease if public opinion shifted because of changing circumstances or new information. For his part, Teyoninhokarawen found Iroquois politics to be difficult and frustrating, and he experienced periodic setbacks during his years on the Grand River, as did most prominent Haudenosaunee figures during that period. At the time he assumed a leadership role within Joseph Brant's circle, for example, relations with Upper Canadian authorities were tense. This was largely because of Thayendanegea's efforts to protect indigenous rights and pursue objectives he felt would benefit his people, in opposition to alternative views held both by others within the Six Nations world and in colonial society. Those stresses contributed to the formation of groups of native and newcomer friends and enemies of Joseph Brant, John Norton, their supporters, and the vision they promoted.

Teyoninhokarawen's Service to the Six Nations of the Grand River and Views on Haudenosaunee Society and Independence

Two important issues for the people of the Grand River Tract in the years surrounding John Norton's adoption were the nature and extent of Six Nations tenure of their territory, and the degree to which they could control their affairs. As part of the compensation they had received for their losses in the American Revolution, the governor-in-chief of Quebec, Frederick Haldimand, had bought land in 1784

from the Mississaugas for Mohawks and other Iroquois who wanted
to leave the United States. Located in today's southern Ontario (which
was part of Quebec before the creation of Upper Canada in 1791), the
tract was twelve miles wide, centred on the Grand, and ran, according to Haldimand, from its mouth on Lake Erie to its then-uncertain
source, which the Haudenosaunee "and their posterity" were to
"enjoy forever."[1] Joseph Brant assumed that the governor had provided the hundreds of thousands of acres along the river in perpetuity within the legalities of fee simple ownership, as had been the
case with Mohawk land in New York before the revolution, which had
stood outside of the realms farther west covered by the restrictions of
the Royal Proclamation of 1763. (The grant's specific reference to the

---

1 Frederick Haldimand, Proclamation, 25 October 1784, quoted in Johnston, *Six
Nations*, 50–1. Some modern commentators affirm that the Six Nations owned the
territory before 1784 through ancient conquest, use, occupation, or treaty. Neither
Joseph Brant and his followers nor colonial authorities in the late 1700s and
early 1800s, however, argued the legalities of Haudenosaunee ownership except
through the conditions of the 1784 grant, which made sense in acknowledging
Mississauga ownership of the lands prior to the Haldimand Purchase. (The
Mississaugas had moved into the region in the late 1600s from today's central
Ontario at about the same time that the Iroquois abandoned a number of villages
they had established a few decades earlier after the wars of the mid-1600s in
which they dispersed the pre-existing Iroquoian populations.) For instance, JN
stated that "the claim of the Five Nations is not insisted on from the ancient
right of possession, but from the grant of Sir Frederick Haldimand" (JN to
William Windham, 27 May 1807, BL, Northumberland MSS, 64:81). His phrasing,
especially "insisted," however, suggests that there may have been other views
current at the time that might be used to advance Iroquois claims if necessary. He
made this statement knowing at least some of the history of southern Ontario,
including the Haudenosaunee conquest of the region in the mid-1600s (JN to
Henry Goulburn, 1 December 1815, published in American and British Claims
Arbitration Tribunal, *Cayuga Indians*, 3:967). He also affirmed that the Haldimand
Tract formed "part of the territory over which their ancestors roamed from time
immemorial, and [which] they occasionally occupied as a hunting country" and
that it was "part of their ancient territory" (JN to Lord Camden, 18 September
1804, published in ibid., 3:1036–7). Grand River land issues are complex, and
there is a large body of literature on the subject, including some listed in the
bibliography. The relevant sections of Kelsay, *Brant*, Johnston, *Six Nations*, and
Good, "Crown-Directed Colonization" offer extensive assessments for the early
decades of the tract. For concise histories, see Paxton, *Brant*, 47–76; Talman,
"Historical Introduction," in *JMJN*, xcix–cxii.

Mohawks rather than to all of the Haudenosaunee suggests that Thay-endanegea's interpretation was reasonable.) Thus, Brant believed that the Iroquois owned the tract outright and could manage it to suit their needs and desires, which included selling or leasing surplus parts to whomever they wanted in order to generate revenue and other ben-efits for his people. In contrast, the proclamation only allowed natives to alienate land to the Crown, a decision designed to protect indig-enous peoples from exploitation, but which government officials in Upper Canada often used to the advantage of settler society and at the expense of aboriginal interests.

Subsequently, when doubts about the extent of Six Nations author-ity arose, Brant gave a speech on behalf of the Grand River council, saying that the problem was nothing more than a simple bureau-cratic oversight caused when authorities had not registered the grant properly in 1784, because the governor had made it in haste while preparing to leave Canada.[2] In contrast, colonial authorities usually thought the Crown held the land in trust for the Six Nations, which gave the King's officials authority, obligations, and opportunities to manage the tract. Some of these people worried that speculators and others might exploit its residents if the Haudenosaunee admin-istered their lands on their own, and others responded attentively to Six Nations people who disagreed with Brant's desire to gener-ate revenue by disposing of parts of the grant. In general, however, most individuals in the colonial government expected to direct indig-enous affairs primarily to benefit Euro-American agendas, and often themselves; and sometimes they were perfectly comfortable doing so through corrupt practices. Their attitudes and behaviour created tremendous distress over the security of the grant, and undermined the hopes of Iroquois people who thought many of their friends and relatives in New York would move to the Grand and strengthen the Six Nations presence in Upper Canada. As John Norton wrote, American-resident Haudenosaunee did not come in substantial numbers after the great exodus of the early 1780s, mainly because of "the constant rumour of the uncertain tenure on which these lands were held," which even caused some of those already settled on the

2 Joseph Brant, Speech, 28 July 1806, NL, MS654, 38–47. See also associated texts, 18–24 July 1806, LAC, RG10, 1:390–413.

Grand to leave.[3] Consequently, Brant and his supporters thought they needed to have Iroquois ownership of the tract confirmed in accordance with their understanding of Haldimand's intentions. If this could be achieved, then they could be confident in their tenure, their right to manage the tract, and their ability to enjoy its benefits free from outside interference, and in the process they could assert Haudenosaunee sovereignty over their internal affairs. At an intrinsic level, Brant, Norton, and most Six Nations leaders during this period generally accepted some degree of Euro-American suzerainty, along with other limitations on indigenous sovereignty, as represented by the characteristics of a large portion of their negotiations and agreements with British and American officials. They also recognized, if resented, the inequalities in power between natives and newcomers; thus, they often sought protection from white governments and acknowledged some degree of dependency on them. As well, they frequently – but not always – worked within the legal contexts of settler society in cross-cultural interactions, but nevertheless tried to preserve as many of their freedoms as possible.

Beyond the characteristics of Haudenosaunee tenure, another contentious issue concerned the size of the grant, a problem that arose because the source of the Grand River was farther north than colonial officials had thought it was in 1784. Thus, the Crown's purchase of Mississauga land did not include the upper reaches of the waterway. For that reason, its servants argued that the tract had to be accepted as smaller than the area promised by Governor Haldimand.

Brant's attempts to secure control of the Haldimand Tract for the Six Nations prior to Norton's adoption proved to be intensely frustrating, because colonial officials would not provide a fee simple deed equivalent to the grants they had given to United Empire Loyalist refugees as partial compensation for their losses in the former colonies. The Crown's servants already were nervous about Joseph Brant because he frequently negotiated with American authorities through the 1780s and 1790s, mostly to represent Iroquois interests in postwar affairs in New York, but also to affirm Six Nations independence from Britain by playing the white powers off each other. Tensions reached a point in

---

3 *JMJN*, 273.

the 1790s where Upper Canadian authorities worried that Thayendanegea even might lead the Grand River's warriors – alone or in concert
with their Mississauga neighbours, disloyal settlers, American filibusters, or foreign forces – against the colony's government. This fear was
especially grave because there were few soldiers in the province, while
Britain's war with France (which broke out in 1793) precluded sending sufficient reinforcements across the Atlantic Ocean. The Ohio war
had ended in 1795; nevertheless, ongoing military threats plagued the
Great Lakes region almost continuously until about 1802. In the latter
1790s, for example, while colonial officials feared both a native rising
by the Mississaugas and a foreign invasion, Brant intimidated them by
taking a large number of warriors to the capital of York (now Toronto).
His objective was to force them to accede – at least in part – to some of
his demands (although historians generally do not think he actually
was willing to resort to violence). During that crisis, Crown authorities
managed to satisfy Thayendanegea by allowing the transfer of several
blocks of territory that he wanted to alienate, but they did so within a
framework that they believed affirmed the restrictions and legalities of
the Royal Proclamation.[4]

With deep distrust afflicting Anglo-Haudenosaunee relations when
John Norton left the Indian Department to become an adopted Mohawk
at the heart of Brant's circle, it is not surprising that the colonial establishment regarded him with suspicion. Consequently, they tried to
undermine Norton's attempts to serve as a leader, as part of their strategy to weaken Thayendanegea and his supporters. In 1800, Teyoninhokarawen articulated his sense of how outlandish official apprehensions
could be when he wrote about the reaction his resignation caused when
he planned to move to the Old Northwest for personal reasons, before
being convinced to stay and serve the Iroquois. He wrote, "It is rather
odd the strange ideas my resignation has given the gentlemen here [at
Niagara]. They directly seemed to think my going to the westward was
on some project detrimental to government. Such as are particularly
acquainted with me and the country cannot but highly ridicule these
suspicions. As for my part, I can see no grounds they can have even

---

4 JN's views on how the government managed to oblige Brant and some of the
problems that arose are in JN, Memorials, n.d. (1804), published in American and
British Claims Arbitration Tribunal, Cayuga Indians, 3:1029–31, 1033.

of supposing me capable of doing them mischief – unless they think I can by magic … turn trees and stumps into armed warriors."[5] Deputy Superintendent-General William Claus of the Indian Department was the most virulent among those who held hostile views of Norton and his efforts to serve the Haudenosaunee. Claus was in a good position to challenge Teyoninhokarawen, as he was the primary individual responsible for the Crown's relations with the Six Nations and a well-connected member of Canadian society, being the grandson of Sir William Johnson and the nephew of Sir John Johnson, the department's superintendent-general (who lived in Montreal and played only a small role in Upper Canadian affairs). Norton was an easy target for Claus, who claimed that he was a mere common soldier of obscure origins, a deserter from both the British army in the 1780s and the native force in the Ohio country in the 1790s, and a man who lived under a cloud for his connections to Joseph Brant in his conflicts with colonial authorities.

Thayendanegea and Teyoninhokarawen aggravated their troubled relationships with the provincial government when they patronized land speculators its officials did not like. Their poor standing fell further when the King's servants suspected that they might have participated in discussions on overthrowing the government of Upper Canada. In 1802, about the same time that Brant was speaking out against the Crown for its treatment of the First Nations, he asked Norton to represent him in Albany on some business. Around the same moment, a group of aspiring filibusters, seeking profits through speculating in land, gathered in the New York capital to consider an attempt to annex the colony to the United States. While there is a chronological link between Norton's visit and the filibusters' scheming, surviving letters by Brant and Norton indicate that Teyoninhokarawen travelled to New York or otherwise corresponded with Americans only to address questions related to Haudenosaunee land and other prosaic matters in the state.[6] The scheme to annex the province attracted the support of

---

5 JN to Oliver Phelps, 26 December 1800, NYSL, SC10440, Box 22.
6 E.g., Joseph Brant to Oliver Phelps, 22 January 1800, NYSL, SC10440, F2; Brant to Phelps, 20 February 1804, ibid.; JN to Phelps, 5 February 1799, ibid., Box 20; JN to Phelps, 19 September 1802, ibid.; Box 25; JN to Phelps, 20 August 1803, ibid.; JN to Phelps, 24 July 1804, ibid.; Brant to James Caldwell, 17 February 1802, NYPL, Thomas Addis Emmet Collection. We might interpret the last letter to suggest that its first section addressed a confidential matter independent of the rest of its contents, which

influential individuals, such as Upper Canadian road builder Asa Danforth and American Vice-President Aaron Burr. Even if Brant followed the deliberations surrounding the conspiracy, he only may have wanted to force colonial authorities to respect Haudenosaunee interests and independence, which would conform to his general behaviour when dealing with the Crown after the American Revolution. Nevertheless, the historical record is vague, and a change in sovereignty might have seen the Grand River lands confirmed to the Six Nations in fee simple.

In the same period, Brant sought land in the Sandusky region of Ohio, possibly in a semi-autonomous association with the United States. As we have seen, the Iroquois already had a presence south of Lake Erie, and Thayendanegea said that natives who wanted to pursue a Christian and agricultural life could settle there among their relatives. On the one hand, having property in the United States offered a retreat should Brant participate in a failed uprising in British territory. On the other hand, his desire to procure this land (or have existing rights to it affirmed) may have had nothing to do with any plotting. Rather, he may have thought of acquiring it as either an investment or an alternative place for the Six Nations to settle, especially given his concern over the legal vulnerabilities of the Grand River territory. Furthermore, he only pursued the idea of acquiring land in Ohio when the Chippewas in the Georgian Bay area within Upper Canada rebuffed his requests to provide a home within their territories to the Six Nations. We know that the idea of moving appealed to people, and in 1809 and 1810, for instance, a sizeable number of individuals left the Haldimand Tract for Ohio (while others moved to New York). For his part, John Norton advocated a general relocation of indigenous people at various

---

dealt with a land issue, but it represents very thin evidence for participation in a plot. The document reads: "I have hardly time to acknowledge receipt of your letters, and take the liberty to introduce you to Mr Norton, to whom I also refer you for the particulars of the subject of our letters. I have understood that the deceased Captain Dockstader had a farm at Cherry Valley, which had never been confiscated, and [is] in the possession of a Captain Whitaker. I wrote to Philip Fry Esquire to inquire into the particulars and leave it with you. I hope you may make it convenient to attend to it." (John Dockstader was a United Empire Loyalist who had several indigenous children and lived at Grand River before passing away in 1801.) Only a portion of Brant's papers survive or were recorded by historians before they disappeared, but of them, the letter quoted above is the closest we have to suggesting JN had any connection to the plot, unless further documentation can be found.

times, including to the Ohio country. More often, he promoted the idea of relocating to the Lake Huron and Georgian Bay area, within British territory. He dreamt of forming a strong, pan-tribal, agricultural community, with secure patents to the land, where aboriginal peoples could free themselves from unwanted external influences (but within an alliance to the Crown).

Whatever Joseph Brant's thoughts were, nothing came of the filibusters' dreams. They had depended, in part, on gaining President Thomas Jefferson's support, which he would not provide. Their plans did not fit American interests at that moment, and Jefferson wanted to see Aaron Burr's power and status diminished. The scheme also required an uprising within Canada, which did not occur because few people were willing to support a *coup d'état*, if they even had heard about the plot at all.[7]

Years later, John Norton wrote a letter defending his loyalty, saying he had not been in Albany during this period. We do not know if he failed to mention some of his visits to New York deliberately, or simply forgot about his travels after the passage of time.[8] His activities as an adopted Mohawk and chief in these years, nevertheless, raise questions about his allegiances as a British subject, a status he neither gave up, nor could give up by the laws of the period. Even if he had met the filibusters in Albany, this does not necessarily mean he supported the conspiracy; and, as Brant's deputy, he may not have had much choice but to go if his mentor sent him. While he shared Brant's deep frustrations with the treatment the Six Nations received from Canadian officials, and while we cannot fathom his views in 1802 with the records available to us, we know that he habitually expressed anger at Americans for their treatment of native peoples. He had seen combat against

---

7 The two leading historians who have examined Brant's connection to the idea of overthrowing the Upper Canadian government disagree on his enthusiasm for it, with Alan Taylor giving some credence to the story that Brant took an interest in bringing it to fruition while Isabel Kelsay did not (Taylor, *Divided Ground*, 352–7; Kelsay, *Brant*, 620–3, 626–7). For a fuller discussion on the conspiracy, see Taylor, "Northern Revolution," which noted JN's presence in Albany (394, 407n29), and Gates, "Roads, Rivals, and Rebellion." For the 1809–10 move to Ohio, see *JMJN*, 190. Records of JN advocating settlement in the Georgian Bay and Lake Huron area include White, *Selkirk's Diary*, 26 February 1804, 245; JN to Unknown, 10 August 1808, LAC, CO42, 140:175–7; JN to John Harvey, 30 September 1816, LAC, RG8, 260:21–3.
8 JN to J.F. Addison, 16 June 1818, LAC, RG8, 262:90–1.

them in 1791, and would fight with distinction against the republic in 1812–14. Yet he criticized British behaviour towards the First Nations, especially in relation to the Crown's actions in 1783 and 1794, when he felt that it had abandoned its indigenous allies in its treaties with the United States.[9] As well, his anti-American opinions did not prevent him from thinking of settling in the republic on occasion, and we know that his hostility was not absolute. A now-unknown person, for instance, remembered that Norton had expressed support for American desires to help convert native economies to resemble those of agrarian settler society; Teyoninhokarawen thought the indigenous future lay in this kind of modernization, even though he realized that settler society encouraged such changes to facilitate the appropriation of indigenous land, which he opposed.[10] Essentially, he thought that older ways of life could not provide the wealth and security aboriginal people needed as newcomers transformed the landscape around them, but they could find prosperity – and hence, freedom – by changing their economy with white help. In reflecting on these ambiguities, he recorded that "as it often occurs in the affairs of the world, the Merciful Father of all may cause the event to be different from which is intended. A little industry introduced among our people without any diminution of the hunting exertions of the warriors, and unattended by any pernicious influence … might tend to increase our independence."[11]

Despite the Indian Department's conduct and its opposition to the aspirations of many Iroquois people, it was not without influence in combating Norton, Brant, or its other opponents. Government presents, which were important in meeting needs and honoured the Anglo-Haudenosaunee alliance, came through its agents, who distributed them to promote Crown – and sometimes personal – objectives. These officials generally spoke at least one indigenous language and understood tribal politics, which helped them challenge anyone who resisted them with some skill. They also patronized people friendly to their goals, aligned with chiefs who opposed Brant and Norton, and gathered information from within native communities to

---

9 *JMJN*, 270, 180, 184.
10 "Z," Article, *Missouri Gazette*, 15 June 1816.
11 JN to the second Duke of Northumberland, 9 September 1809, BL, Northumberland MSS, 63:161. For more on his views of modernization, see NL, MS654, with JN to John Owen, 12 August 1806, 26–37 being a good example.

help them plan their strategies. Moreover, some of the department's employees were married to First Nations women or otherwise had relatives in aboriginal society – or were natives themselves – and thus had familial connections that they could use to promote their views. Conversely, indigenous people might use the Indian Department's agents to advance aboriginal interests in the relationship with the Crown, and therefore found it advantageous to cultivate ties with agents, sometimes requiring them to align against people like Thayendanegea and Teyoninhokarawen to achieve some objective unrelated to the two men. Moreover, Joseph Brant's willingness to alienate parts of the tract was controversial, principally because Euro-American investors who acquired sections of it found it difficult to meet their financial obligations to the Six Nations, as the King's servants had warned would happen. Such troubles naturally undermined Brant's position along the Grand, while a significant number of Haudenosaunee simply opposed alienating land in the first place. Therefore, Indian Department agents often held positions of strength when confronting those they did not like, especially when their actions helped address concerns shared by people within indigenous communities.

During the American Revolution, the people of Iroquoia had "covered" their collective council fire, and their post-1784 separation into American- and Canadian-resident communities had divided the Haudenosaunee further. One of Brant's responses to the Indian Department's actions was to reunite the Six Nations Confederacy at a rekindled, cross-border council fire at Buffalo Creek in New York in 1801. Thayendanegea thought that a joint council in the United States would weaken the Crown's control over Grand River affairs. He also believed that restoring the confederacy to its earlier status (and encouraging other natives to ally with it) would enhance the ability of aboriginal peoples to face the threats to their well-being and freedoms posed by both the British and Americans. In the end, however, the relit fire subverted his plans, as we shall see below.

Resisting the pressures imposed by settler society proved to be a constant and unequal battle. At one point in 1803, as Norton recalled, he, Joseph Brant, and leading Mohawk hereditary chief Henry Tekarihogen, acting on the authority of the "full council of the longhouse," travelled seventy miles through the winter snows from their homes to York to see the lieutenant-governor, Peter Hunter. They wanted "to have the Grand River confirmed in perpetuity according to the sense of the original grant," or to hear Hunter's reason why that was not possible (as well as address related issues). This was to be a "last request," before making an appeal to the authorities at the imperial centre in London if a satisfactory answer could not be obtained in the province. Hunter recently had issued a proclamation, which, among other provisions, invalidated leases that native people had arranged with Euro-Americans along the Grand. This not only affected the Iroquois financially, because some of the white settlers abandoned the tract soon afterwards, but also represented yet another assault on their independence. Despite their efforts in the colonial capital, Teyoninhokarawen recorded, "His Excellency did not see us, and said he would only hear from the Five Nations through the medium of the Indian Department. This we had frequently attempted without better success, so we were in a manner debarred communication with His Excellency, except through a certain gate, and that gate to be kept shut."[12] (Norton usually used the anachronistic "Five" rather than "Six" Nations in his prose.)[13] Although the governor insultingly would not meet the Mohawk delegates, they did see the province's chief justice, Henry Allcock, who said he would look into their affairs, but his subsequent report only dealt with problems related to parts of the tract that had been alienated already rather than the fundamental issue of confirming the intent of the Haldimand Grant.[14]

Later that year, in the summer of 1803, John Norton learned that the war between France and Britain that had begun in 1793 had resumed after a brief lull in 1802–3. He decided to leave the Grand River and sail to England to seek an officer's commission in the military.[15] Aside

12 JN, Speech, 19 February 1807, NL, MS654, 107–8.
13 Even though he referred to the Iroquois as the "Five Nations," JN wrote that, since the adoption of the Tuscaroras early in the 1700s, the Haudenosaunee Confederacy "has generally been called the Six Nations" (*JMJN*, 253). We do not know why he preferred "Five Nations" but sometimes people excluded the late-joining Tuscaroras as not being full members of the confederacy (e.g., Enclosure with Robert Kerr and John Brant to Lord Bathurst, 6 September 1821, published in American and British Claims Arbitration Tribunal, *Cayuga Indians*, 3:1046). JN also tended not to mention others who lived within Haudenosaunee communities, such as the Tutelos. Joseph Brant's biographer, Isabel Kelsay, noted that Brant used the term "Five Nations" after the American Revolution to exclude the Oneidas, who had taken up arms against the Crown and the majority of the Iroquois, but there is no evidence that JN followed that practice (*Brant*, 463, 489).
14 JN, Speech, 19 February 1807, NL, MS654, 108–9.
15 Ibid., 108, 112. JN wanted to do more than enlist as a private soldier, because he did not join the army, even though no recruiting party would have turned away a robust

from a possible desire for adventure and a sense of British patriotism – despite problems with colonial authorities and the conflicting pull of his aboriginal identity – he presumably felt discouraged by the lack of success that Thayendanegea, Tekarihogen, and he had experienced. There also may have been reasons for his departure that have been lost to history. Norton was married to or living with someone at the time, who would give birth to a son while he was away, and thus a move across the Atlantic Ocean promised a long if not permanent separation from his family.[16] Perhaps domestic troubles influenced his thinking, although he seems to have been anxious to see his family when he returned home a year later. (Nevertheless, the relationship with his wife or partner subsequently ended.) This was not the first time he had thought of leaving the Haudenosaunee in pursuit of adventure. Earlier, conversing with prominent people in New York while travelling on Six Nations business, he had heard that the United States intended to send an overland expedition to the Pacific Ocean, and in 1801 he expressed enthusiasm for the idea. He even wanted his American connections to advise him on how he might participate in the journey, providing that "any discovery which may be made will never be turned to the detriment of our western brethren, but rather to their advantage."[17]

Despite his desires to join Great Britain's struggle against Napoleon Bonaparte's France, Norton did not intend to abandon efforts to confirm the promise of the Haldimand Grant while in London. Thayendanegea thought about joining him but lacked the funds to do so, and perhaps believed that he ought to remain in Canada to attend to Six Nations and personal affairs. In the tradition of a well-connected gentleman who could harness social networks to advance a cause, however, Brant wrote letters of introduction for Norton to important people he had known from fighting during the American Revolution and from his journeys across the Atlantic in the 1770s and 1780s. These included the Earl of Moira (Francis Rawdon-Hastings), the Duke of

---

male at a time when maintaining the military's strength was difficult. Therefore, logic tells us he tried to obtain an officer's commission. (Contrary to common opinion, the majority of officers at the time of the Napoleonic Wars did not purchase their commissions, so a lack of funds would not have excluded JN.)

16 JN to Robert Barclay, 15 January 1806, NL, MS654, 25 stated that his son was a year-and-a-half old, which meant that he was born while JN was away. The baby was conceived late in 1803, so it is unclear if JN knew that his partner was pregnant.

17 JN to Oliver Phelps, 14 October 1801, NYSL, SC10440, Box 23.

Northumberland (Hugh Percy), and Sir Evan Nepean. The mission was meant to be secret, in order to prevent the Indian Department from undermining it, so only a limited number of people participated in the deliberations surrounding the journey. In subsequent months, Joseph Brant even felt he had to deny his role in planning the enterprise, although he expressed his words carefully to absolve Norton of any blame and to ensure that Teyoninhokarawen could discuss Six Nations issues in London, while other letters he wrote made it clear that the chiefs had authorized the appeal to the imperial government.[18] This secrecy gave the Indian Department's William Claus an opportunity to undermine Brant and Norton once he learned about Teyoninhokarawen's plans, as he invariably would, even though Norton travelled with authorization signed by representatives of the three Mohawk clans – Turtle, Wolf, and Bear – and with directions from the broader Six Nations council to attend to its interests. Unfortunately, we do not know how representative this particular council was, and the confidentiality of its deliberations seems to have weakened its legitimacy on the politically divided Grand River.[19]

In February 1804, at age thirty-three, John Norton left the Grand for Great Britain, charged with the task, as he wrote, of giving "such representation of our affairs as might cause the great and good men in England to order them to be rectified to our satisfaction."[20] He made his way on foot and by sleigh to New York City to find a ship sailing

---

18 Kelsay, *Brant*, 632–5; William Claus, Memorandum, 7 January 1805, LAC, RG10, 1:445; Joseph Brant to Alexander Grant, 12 February 1806, ibid., 1:323; JN to W. Walton, 3 September 1806, ibid., 1:443–4. An example of a letter of recommendation is Brant to the second Duke of Northumberland, 20 February 1804, BL, Northumberland MSS, 62:29. Northumberland had become a friend of Brant's during the American Revolution while serving in the British army, and later became one of the richest men in England upon succeeding his father to the dukedom. The Earl of Moira and Sir Evan Nepean also knew Brant and were prominent in various official and social realms within British society.

19 JN, Speech, 19 February 1807, NL, MS654, 107–11; Headley, "Account," 12 March 1805, NYSL. Lord Headley recorded that he saw the three-clan document.

20 JN, Speech, 19 February 1807, NL, MS654, 98–124 (quote on 111). This document describes his visit to the United Kingdom. Klinck, "Biographical Introduction," in *JMJN*, xlvii–lxv provides additional detail about the journey. See also Talman, "Historical Introduction," in *JMJN*, cvi–cvii; Headley, "Account," 12 March 1805, NYSL; Morgan, *Travellers through Empire*, 19–39.

to England, as the Canadian route across the ocean from Quebec could not be used during the winter. In Albany, he met the Earl of Selkirk (Thomas Douglas), with whom Norton shared his thoughts on the condition of native peoples and recounted details about the war for the Ohio country. Selkirk described him as "Brant's secretary, councillor, and probable successor," while noting that he had been told that Teyoninhokarawen's objective was "to complain about General Hunter's behaviour" towards aboriginal peoples.[21] In New York City, Norton met a now-anonymous Quaker. Impressed with Teyoninhokarawen, this person gave him letters of introduction to influential co-religionists in the Society of Friends.[22] That spring, Norton docked in Liverpool and proceeded on to London, where, on 2 June 1804, he called upon the well-connected Lord Moira to present documents listing Six Nations grievances and start the process of obtaining a deed granting secure tenure for their Grand River lands. Moira afterwards gave Norton a letter of introduction to Earl Camden (John Pratt), the secretary of state for war and the colonies, who provided money for Teyoninhokarawen to defray his expenses, while his undersecretary, Edward Cooke, tried to find a copy of the Haldimand Grant to help resolve the issue, but could not discover one in the government's files. At the same time, officials sent a letter to Peter Hunter in Canada, directing him to attend to Six Nations matters equitably. Norton also tried to obtain a copy of the deed by writing to at least one person in England he thought might have it, but without success. As well, he contacted other people he hoped could address Iroquois concerns, such as the former governor of Quebec, Lord Dorchester (Guy Carleton), who offered to testify in favour of the Six Nations. Teyoninhokarawen received help from other influential people. Some he met through his letters of introduction, and he then encountered others through their circles of friends and associates. A number of them welcomed him into their homes. They provided advice, assisted with his correspondence, facilitated access to high-ranking officials, and intervened directly on behalf of the Six Nations. These supporters included Joseph Brant's friend, the Duke of Northumberland, along

---

21 White, *Selkirk's Diary*, 26 February 1804, 243–6, quote on 243.
22 Headley, "Account," 12 March 1805, NYSL; JN, Speech, 19 February 1807, NL, MS654, 111–12.

with members of the reformist and evangelical Clapham Sect, such as the abolitionist William Wilberforce and Lord Teignmouth (John Shore), former governor-general of Bengal and president of the British and Foreign Bible Society.[23]

Honour was important in John Norton's mission. Writing to Northumberland, he said that "my heart is earnestly engaged to have this affair accomplished to the credit of Great Britain and the satisfaction of the Six Nations." He added that he would be "ashamed" if he failed to succeed, "considering the strong terms in which I set forth to the discontented [people of the Grand] the justice of His Majesty's government and the confidence I had of their wishes being obtained at the fountainhead," in contrast to the behaviour of officials in Canada.[24] He also explained to His Grace how Frederick Haldimand had given the tract to the Iroquois as partial compensation for the territories lost or threatened in New York, as well as to satisfy some of the promises made to the King's Six Nations allies during the American Revolution. In addition, he noted that the Grand River tract was a hundred miles long, a greater distance than colonial officials acknowledged, but which reflected native opinion that the grant extended beyond the parts that had been purchased from the Mississaugas (and which created a demand that the Crown acquire the rest of the land for the Haudenosaunee). Norton further stated that the Iroquois had not received clear title, despite their belief that such had been Haldimand's intention – an intention aligned to the promises made by London in the 1770s. Thus Teyoninhokarawen, articulating the thoughts of the party that had formed around Brant, asked that George III have the tract "fully confirmed to" the Iroquois, "that hereafter the Six Nations may enjoy the

---

23 Headley, "Account," 12 March 1805, NYSL; JN, Speech, 19 February 1807, NL, MS654, 112–15; JN to J.G. Simcoe, 24 December 1804, quoted in Scadding, *Leaves*, 19; JN to D.W. Smith, 7 May 1805, TPL, Smith Papers, S126, A11–4:203–5; Shore, *Reminiscences*, 1:6–7; Shore, *Memoir*, 2:80–5; William Wilberforce to Viscount Melville, 6 September 1804, NL, MS3204. Talman, "Historical Introduction," in *JMJN*, cvii, suggests government officials only claimed they could not find a copy of the Haldimand Grant, perhaps to gain time until they heard from the Upper Canadian authorities, but period documents do not support his interpretation. The archival record also indicates that the government in London intended to resolve Six Nations concerns fairly. This is worth noting, given the not unreasonable tendency of historians to regard the behaviour of imperial authorities critically.

24 JN to the second Duke of Northumberland, 21 July 1804, BL, Northumberland MSS, 62:19.

said lands and river, immediately from the King himself, this beloved father, and thus insure to themselves and their children the perpetual enjoyments of their agricultural improvements without the possibility of any vexations in future from those who may be appointed governors of Canada."[25] Fundamentally, Teyoninhokarawen, Thayendanegea, Tekarihogen, and their supporters wanted His Majesty to affirm their interpretation of the Haldimand Grant as being offered as compensation for their New York lands through an act of unchallengeable royal authority, and thus prevent corrupt and incompetent colonial officials from intervening in Six Nations affairs.[26]

Beyond these issues, John Norton promoted ideas that he shared with Brant, but which were divisive in the eyes of a good portion of the residents of the Grand River. He thought the land regime should change, in part, from one based on collective to individual ownership. This view arose from two concerns. First, he stressed that whites used common ownership against the welfare of indigenous people by finding "two or three chiefs" to sell land that the majority of inhabitants wanted to keep. This practice, while not serious on the Grand at that time, had caused tremendous anguish, poverty, and tragedy across the lower Great Lakes for decades, particularly south of the Canadian-American border, and Norton thought his community could become vulnerable to similar exploitation. He also wanted land divided among "every tribe and family" because he thought that confederacy ownership acted as a disincentive to "the more industrious" to improve their holdings and enjoy the benefits from doing so, which fitted with his advocacy of Euro-American farming practices as a way of ensuring prosperity. He believed that such a modification also would benefit the security of Upper Canada. Norton claimed, "There is not the smallest doubt that the major part of the Six Nations (more than one-half of whom yet remain within the American line) would soon remove to their brethren within British territory," but attracting more Haudenosaunee people to the Grand "cannot be expected from the present unsettled and undecided nature of

25 JN, Memorial, n.d., (1804), BL, Northumberland MSS, 62:27. Similar documents by JN from 1804–5 may be read in American and British Claims Arbitration Tribunal, *Cayuga Indians*, 3:1028–46. He affirmed the longer Grand River Tract ("to its source") in *JMJN*, 271.
26 Examples of his comments on Indian Department corruption and incompetence include JN to John Owen, 12 August 1806, NL, MS654, 26–37; JN to (Robert?) Barclay, 20 October 1806, ibid., 77; JN to Barclay, 16 June 1810, ibid., 130.

their grant and possession."[27] He assumed that the adoption of European-style farming did not have to come at the expense of older hunting and other means of sustaining people. Nevertheless, he recognized that growing newcomer settlement diminished the game population and degraded the environment's capacity to supply traditional foods and materials that had been so important in earlier times.[28] In contrast, the Duke of Northumberland thought that it would be a mistake to convert to a European-style agricultural economy, because it would weaken the ability of Six Nations "hunters and warriors" to defend their communities. He believed that "nine hundred or a thousand warriors, inured to hardship by hunting, are a most respectable and independent body; but what would the same number of men become who were merely husbandmen?" Obviously, His Grace had heard Norton's views on the subject and disagreed with them. Nevertheless, he affirmed that Teyoninhokarawen's efforts to secure title to the Haldimand Tract for the Haudenosaunee had been made with "constant attention and the most unremitting zeal," and that "no person could possibly execute the missions on which he was sent with more ability."[29]

Back in Canada, Peter Hunter and William Claus learned about John Norton's work. They decided to prevent the authorities in England from scrutinizing their management of Grand River affairs, and to stop the Haudenosaunee from gaining control over their lands or otherwise asserting more independence than colonial officials thought was appropriate. Claus gave Hunter information to send to London, stating that Norton had seditious tendencies and denouncing him as merely a white man masquerading as a Mohawk. He also claimed that the Six Nations were "perfectly ignorant of the memorial," except for Brant, Norton, and a few others, "not exceeding a dozen." As we have seen, the people in Thayendanegea's circle had felt they needed to conduct the mission with discretion in order for it to have a chance of success, because they knew that Claus and his associates would try to sabotage it. The deputy

---

27 JN, Memorial, July? 1804, BL, Northumberland MSS, 62:22–4. See also JN to John Owen, 12 August 1806, NL, MS654, 26–37.

28 JN, Petition, n.d. (1804–5), published in American and British Claims Arbitration Tribunal, *Cayuga Indians*, 3:1033; JN to the second Duke of Northumberland, 9 September 1806, BL, Northumberland MSS, 63:161–2; JN, Speech, 19 February 1807, NL, MS654, 107; JN to Unknown, 10 August 1808, LAC, CO42, 140:175–7.

29 Second Duke of Northumberland to Joseph Brant, 5 May 1806, BL, Northumberland MSS, 69A:342, 339–40. See also Northumberland to JN, 6 May 1806, ibid., 344–7.

superintendent-general assaulted the integrity of the people behind the
plan by proclaiming that Brant's followers only aligned to him "by
reason of constant drunkenness," and claimed that the "whole" had
"originated" with Teyoninhokarawen and Thayendanegea, to whom
"the warriors as well as the Indians in general are decidedly opposed."
His view on native discontent was partially correct, because there were
people antagonistic to Brant's agenda, but of course, Claus exaggerated
by saying this was "general," and made callous and false claims about
the motivations of Brant's supporters and Norton's identity.[30] As Thayendanegea recorded, Claus also worked against Teyoninhokarawen
by calling together a coalition of his supporters within the Haudenosaunee community, including younger males without chiefly status (in
contrast to the older men and matrons who supported the mission).
According to a document that Brant wrote, Claus told these people that
"Norton was about effecting in England something much to their detriment if they did not immediately prevent it." Claus organized councils at Buffalo Creek and Niagara between some Grand River people
and American-resident Iroquois who were hostile to Brant so that, as
Thayendanegea continued, "the mission and proceedings of Teyoninhokarawen should be disallowed of and disavowed," and to arrange
for Brant to be "displaced from being chief."[31] In fact, both Joseph Brant
and John Norton claimed that William Claus had dictated the terms
of the disavowal to the assembled representatives.[32] Thus, the Indian
Department used the newly united confederacy council at Buffalo
Creek, along with people without legitimate claims to decision-making
roles, against its founder, Joseph Brant, who had rekindled its flames
partly to diminish the department's influence. (American officers at
Fort Niagara corroborated Thayendanegea's story, noting that someone
representing forty Iroquois from their side of the border had said that
"they were going into Upper Canada for the express purpose of breaking Captain Brant.")[33] Among the Claus-allied natives were people who

---

30 William Claus to Peter Hunter, 19 January 1805, quoted in Good, "Crown-Directed
Colonization," 189.
31 Joseph Brant to the second Duke of Northumberland, n.d. (1805), quoted in Stone,
Brant, 2:417.
32 JN to the second Duke of Northumberland, 13 January 1806, BL, Northumberland
MSS, 63:3; Joseph Brant to Northumberland, 24 January 1806, ibid., 63:5.
33 Certificate of Nathaniel Leonard et al., 20 October 1805, quoted in Stone, *Brant*,
2:xxxiv (appendix).

would support the Americans in the War of 1812, such as the Seneca chief Red Jacket (Sagoyewatha), one of Thayendanegea's long-standing political adversaries. Joseph Brant later gave a speech, supported by the "principal chiefs of that part of the Five Nations" inhabiting "the Grand River who obtained the grant from General Haldimand in consequence of our services and losses" in the American Revolution. In it, he insisted that the chiefs from Buffalo Creek had exceeded the limits of normal Haudenosaunee politics, because they had interfered in the internal governance of the Grand River rather than addressing issues of common concern to both communities. Some of Brant's opponents beyond the Grand maintained an interest in the tract, however, while there also was some movement across the Anglo-American border by Six Nations people, which generated confusion over the issue of council legitimacy. Brant and the leaders aligned to him were absent from the meetings that Claus had organized, which undermined the authority of these assemblies because of their lack of inclusiveness (but then, the council that had sent Norton to England also had been limited in its membership).[34]

While efforts to thwart the mission were occurring in Canada but before word of their success reached England, Teyoninhokarawen's labours, with the help of his supporters, began to suggest the possibility of a positive resolution to the question of the Grand River lands when the cabinet took up the matter. First, the authorities decided to interview Lord Dorchester to determine what the original intent of the 1784 grant had been because they could not find a copy of the document and Frederick Haldimand had passed away. Second, the cabinet wanted the Upper Canadian lieutenant-governor to report on how Haudenosaunee concerns might be redressed satisfactorily. John Norton captured a sense of the progress in a letter to a retired colonial official. He quoted Dorchester, who wrote "that if it was necessary for the satisfaction of the Five Nations that the terms of General Haldimand's Grant should be enlarged, he would acquiesce thereon, but by no means to have it in any wise curtailed." Dorchester also thought that the Six Nations should enjoy the right to lease land if they wished to do so.[35]

---

34 Joseph Brant, Speech, 28 July 1806, NL, MS654, 38–47, quote on 43. See also Red Jacket, Speech, 8 April 1805, published in Ganter, *Collected Speeches of Sagoyewatha, or Red Jacket*, 135–7. (That document referred to JN as "Plover," a variant of "Snipe," in reference to his other name, Dowwisdowwis.)

35 JN to D.W. Smith, 7 May 1805, TPL, Smith Papers, S126, A11–4:203–5.

Dorchester believed – optimistically – that Iroquois worries over the nature of the grant might have been misplaced, writing that Norton had "many unnecessary fears concerning the land allotted by General Haldimand for the Five Nations" because the government "can never mean to deprive them of the benefit thereof." Nevertheless, the behaviour of the Crown's servants in Canada was a problem, which created "doubts concerning the proper arrangements," and thus, "the sooner these matters are settled with the entire approbation of the Indians, the better I shall think it for that province."[36] One issue in the minds of the authorities in London lay in the possibility that the Iroquois might alienate land to Americans and thereby weaken colonial security. Therefore, they thought the Six Nations should be required to obtain government permission when they wanted to sell or otherwise provide land to people who were neither British subjects nor members of the Haudenosaunee Confederacy, with such a view indicating that officials in England inclined in favour of Teyoninhokarawen's position.[37] Drawing on his memory of the events of the 1780s, Sir Evan Nepean held a somewhat different perspective of the Haldimand Grant, but thought about it in terms meant to protect rather than control the natives. He assumed that the Six Nations did not have to perform the normal settlement duties that other refugees from the American Revolution in the province needed to fulfil in order to retain ownership of their lands, because of their different ways of supporting themselves. Yet, relieved of those duties, he believed the Iroquois would be restricted in disposing of land without government control because of worries that unscrupulous whites might exploit them, which reflected some of the ideals behind the Royal Proclamation of 1763. He also supposed that, with the passing of time and the settled conditions of the Haudenosaunee in Canada, it had become reasonable to allow them to alienate land if they no longer needed it, with the proceeds being invested for the long-term benefit of the Six Nations or used to support agricultural modernization.[38] One notable point about these discussions related to

---

36 Lord Dorchester to the second Duke of Northumberland, 21 June 1805, BL, Northumberland MSS, 62:194.
37 Second Duke of Northumberland to Joseph Brant, 5 May 1806, ibid., No. 6 Letter Book, 69A:340–1.
38 Sir Evan Nepean, "Sketch of Captain Norton's Claim," 1805?, Bodleian Library, Wilberforce Papers, C.4, Fol. 109.

Joseph Brant's loyalty to the British alliance. The government in London as well as York had wanted to limit his influence among aboriginal peoples because of the threats he had posed to the safety and development of the province in the 1790s. In 1804–5, however, the issue of the land regime established in 1784 was a different matter, and it seems that the decision-makers in England intended to accept Norton's arguments and implement measures to meet Six Nations demands.

Before the land question could be resolved, however, word reached the United Kingdom that the Iroquois – through the councils that William Claus had managed – had repudiated John Norton's mission. Edward Cooke wrote to Teyoninhokarawen on 13 July 1805 with the bad news: "According to the intimation given you" in a letter of 2 July, "the memorial, which you had transmitted to Lord Camden, has been forwarded to the privy council. By dispatches since received from Canada, it appears that at two councils of the Six Nations, the chiefs assembled unanimously declared that you have not been authorized by them to undertake any mission to this country in their behalf; and they have disavowed the whole of your proceedings, which they state to have been conducted in a clandestine and underhanded manner." Thus, the undersecretary continued, "these communications will be also transmitted to the privy council in order that their lordships may be aware of the real merits of the case that you have laid before them." When Norton read Cooke's devastating letter, as he later told an assembly of the Six Nations, he "suspected it to be some misrepresentation from Fort George" because, he said (perhaps with some restraint), "I could not imagine that any of you on this river would have acted a part so inconsistent with your honour and your interests." Nonetheless, Brant's party had been foiled, because the communication from Canada, as Norton wrote, "came in such a manner that the government could do no otherwise than credit it," and thus he "could not with any propriety persist any further in praying [for] the confirmation of the title to the lands we occupy."[39]

Not only did his primary task in England end in failure, but Norton also could not find a place in the army. He had sought Lord Moira's assistance in both the matter of the Grand River lands and his military ambitions, but Teyoninhokarawen found himself abandoned by

---

39 JN, Speech, 19 February 1807, NL, MS654 (which quotes Edward Cooke to JN, 13 July 1805), 115–17.

officials once they received the hostile news from Canada, which, combined with the accusation that he had misrepresented himself in London, must have made his application for an officer's commission seem particularly impertinent.[40]

Despite these depressing failures, John Norton's travels were not without some satisfaction. At a personal level, he spent time in Scotland, presumably pleasantly with his mother's relatives and friends. He enjoyed the company of influential people at places as diverse as the University of Cambridge, the assembly rooms at Bath, and the residences of leading Anglican and Quaker figures. During these visits, he spoke about the conditions of native peoples to curious audiences, corrected misconceptions about the aboriginal world, described indigenous beliefs and customs, and promoted liberal policies towards the tribes. He also gathered information on agricultural practices, craft production, and other matters that he thought might benefit the Six Nations. Often he wore Mohawk clothing, and sat for his portrait in these garments.[41] Sometimes, to the delight of his audiences, he demonstrated

---

40 JN to John Owen, n.d. (1805), ibid., 1; JN, Speech, 19 February 1807, ibid., 108, 112; Robert Barclay to JN, 31 October 1808, AO, F440; Headley, "Account," 12 March 1805, NYSL.

41 Mary Ann Knight painted a miniature of JN (owned by the Reverend John Owen, as proven by his handwriting on the back, now at LAC), which she copied at least once. Knight exhibited her original at the Royal Academy in 1805. JN hoped to have her paint another portrait during his second visit to the United Kingdom in 1815–16, but it does not seem to have been done due to a combination of Knight's poor health and JN's travel schedule (LAC, Catalogue data for the miniature; Communication from Andrew Potter, Royal Academy, 20 July 2017; Mary Ansted to JN, 17 December 1815, AO, F440; Klinck, "Biographical Introduction," in *JMJN*, liv). During JN's time in Britain in 1804–5, Solomon Williams painted a portrait (now at the Canadian War Museum), as did another artist, with that work now located in the collection of Yale University. Attributed to Mather Brown, it may have been created by John Francis Rigaud instead (Benn, "Norton Portraits"). Thomas Pole created a silhouette (offered for sale by Samuel Gedge Limited, *Catalogue 23* [2016] and subsequently by the William Reese Company [2017], online catalogue "A Collection of Profiles by Thomas Pole, MD"). During JN's visit to Great Britain, in 1815–16, Thomas Phillips painted him (on display at Syon House, the London home of the Duke of Northumberland). Philips exhibited it at the Royal Academy (*London Morning Post*, 29 April 1816). JN's wife Catherine also sat for her portrait during JN's second visit. One version remained in the Northumberland Collection until the 1920s but efforts by several scholars to locate it have been unsuccessful. Another image – now lost – was sent to her in Canada in 1818 (John Ferguson to JN, 15 February 1818, AO, F440).

Iroquois cultural practices, such as the war dance, and in the process perhaps flaunted his taste for the romantic, the dramatic, and the grand gesture.[42] (Years later, the strength of Teyoninhokarawen's personality inspired John Richardson to model Wacousta after him in part in his 1832 novel of the same name.)[43] Generally, Norton impressed the people he met. For instance, Charles William Janson, whose views were typical, recalled that he possessed "numerous traits of an amiable disposition and a vigorous intellect" which "produced the most pleasing impressions on all who were introduced to him."[44] A now-unknown individual wrote that his "observations were acute, and the language in which they were conveyed is strong and elegant. In history, both ancient and modern, he is well versed ... On every subject connected with his country, his knowledge is minute ... His thirst after every species of knowledge is extreme; but his particular attention is directed to obtain every information that may improve the condition of his country."[45] Lord Teignmouth recorded that Teyoninhokarawen exhibited "strong sense, sound judgement, and upright principles," which "distinguish his character and give him a superiority over those who think slightly of him."[46] Unfortunately, Teignmouth did not identify these detractors or their views. Yet, when he heard that his friend's mission had been repudiated, he maintained that he could not "bring my mind to believe John Norton to be an imposter." Instead, he wrote, "I think I could resolve the whole into the manoeuvres of the Canadians, who, from what I hear, act systematically upon the principles of defaming the Indians in hopes of driving them westward."[47] Sir Edward Nepean expressed similar views. He believed that Teyoninhokarawen's mission, while not authorized according to conventional practices among the Six Nations, nevertheless was legitimate, and that William Claus's efforts to undermine

42 For a sense of what JN said and did, as well as the impressions he made, see Headley, "Account," 12 March 1805, NYSL; *Bath Chronicle and Weekly Gazette*, 20 December 1804. Klinck, "Biographical Introduction," in *JMJN*, xlvii–lviii covers JN's British travels, with quotes from various primary documents.

43 Finlayson, "Major John Richardson," 32–55.

44 Janson, *Stranger*, 287n.

45 D. "C__L" to the Editor, 21 July 1805, *Monthly Magazine; or British Register* 20, no. 133 (1805): 101–2.

46 Lord Teignmouth to William Wilberforce, 22 September 1804, quoted in Shore, *Memoir*, 2:85.

47 Lord Teignmouth to William Wilberforce, 26 July 1805, ibid., 92.

him were duplicitous, as was the provincial government's management of Grand River affairs. Sir Evan also wrote that he did not think "a more honest and able negotiator" than Norton "could be found among the Indian nations, or a man more deserving the confidence and protection of government."[48]

Through Lord Teignmouth, the Reverend John Owen, and others, Teyoninhokarawen established links to Christian mission work. As we saw earlier, a Presbyterian minister had baptized him, and he had worked as a schoolteacher at Tyendinaga for the Anglican Society for the Propagation of the Gospel. Like Thayendanegea, he supported the state-connected and comparatively broad-minded Church of England along the Grand over other denominations (and he interpreted for the Reverend Robert Addison when the rector of Niagara visited the Six Nations).[49] One lasting outcome of Teyoninhokarawen's visit to the United Kingdom was a decision by the British and Foreign Bible Society to employ his skills to translate the Gospel of Saint John into Mohawk (which may have been based on an earlier effort by Joseph Brant).[50] This was the first non-English text that the recently founded society undertook in its subsequently long history of distributing Scripture in the world's languages. Norton also wrote an introduction to accompany his edition, but the society would not bind it with the Gospel because it did not permit attachments to its editions of the Bible, although people associated with the project thought Norton's words were fine. Of the initial printing of two thousand copies of Saint John, Norton brought five hundred back to the Grand River, a quantity he thought was appropriate for the number of literate Haudenosaunee people on the tract at the time. The society sent an equal number to the Seven Nations on the St Lawrence (whose Christianity was Roman Catholic), and it forwarded copies to the Ohio country and to the Oneidas in New York. Other people printed his translation, such as American Quakers, who

---

48 Sir Evan Nepean, "Sketch of Captain Norton's Claim," 1805?, Bodleian Library, Wilberforce Papers, C.4, Fol. 109.

49 Robert Addison, Report and Journal, 14 January 1809, quoted in Young, "Addison," 181.

50 JN, trans., *Nene Karighwiyoston Tsinihorighhoten ne Saint John*. A rumour of uncertain value stated that Brant felt that he had not received enough credit in the translation (Samuel Kirkland, Journal, 27 December 1806, published in Pilkington, *Kirkland*, 417–18). Kirkland heard this second- or third-hand, so it is difficult to know if he was right, and he had a habit of saying things to make the British and people associated with them look bad. For JN's translation efforts, see Shore, *Memoir*, 2:80–1.

published an edition in 1806 with his introduction incorporated into their volume.[51]

Despite his Protestantism, Norton apparently had married once or twice through native custom rather than through the rites of the Church, and he participated in spiritually charged indigenous rituals such as the war dance, while his desire to cover his father's grave with wampum, as we have seen, reflected aboriginal religious practice.[52] (In a related context, John Norton noted that "a man who had lost either his friend or his cousin in war or by natural death, was required, by the law of honour, to replace him with a prisoner or scalp or to cover him with wampum.")[53] He also spoke with esteem of the nativist spiritual reform associated with the Seneca prophet Handsome Lake (Ganeodiyo). Norton showed him respect when they met in 1809, telling the Seneca "I am thankful that it has pleased the Almighty to make you the means of bringing many to walk in the paths he has marked out for us."[54] As well, he used both native and newcomer religious language in more or less the same breath, and equated the Great Spirit with the Christian God.[55] It seems that, like many aboriginal people, he was comfortable practising both native and white spirituality, although he regarded himself primarily as a Christian. A Moravian missionary, George Loskiel, for instance, noted that part of John Norton's motivation for his Cherokee journey of 1809–10 was to "declare to his own countrymen the love of God in Christ Jesus," before sighing "but to the great regret of the missionaries, he was unable to accomplish … his design."[56]

---

51 JN to John Owen, 28 January 1807, BFBSA, D1/5/2 (literate people); Owen, *Bible Society*, 1:126–34, 169 (which includes JN's introduction to Saint John in English, published as *Ne Raowenna Teyoninhokarawen Shakonadonire ne Rondaddegenshon ne Rondadhawakshon Rodinonghtsyoni Tsiniyoderighwagennoni ne Raorighwadogenghte ne ne Sanctus John*). See also Horne, *Critical Study*, 2:296; Browne, *Bible Society*, 1:291.

52 Headley, "Account," 12 March 1805, NYSL; Shore, *Reminiscences*, 1:6–7; [Loskiel], *Moravian Mission*, 305.

53 *JMJN*, 108.

54 Ibid., 9. JN spelled Handsome Lake's Seneca name Skanyadarigo. Lord Selkirk wrote positively of Handsome Lake, based on information heard from JN (White, *Selkirk's Diary*, 26 February 1804, 245–6). For more on Handsome Lake from JN, see Headley, "Account," 12 March 1805, NYSL; "H.W.," "Original Account of a Meeting or Talk of Indians," 709–15.

55 JN to Robert Barclay, 26 November 1805, NL, MS654, 19; JN, Speech, 19 February 1807, ibid., 98–101.

56 [Loskiel], *Moravian Mission*, 305. For another account of JN's promotion of the faith, see Charles Gotthold Reichel, Memorandum, 3 September 1809, "Teyoninhokarawen

Bolstered with gifts, financial support, his Mohawk-language Gospel, and the warm wishes of his British friends, John Norton boarded HMS *Mercury* in August 1805 as a guest of Captain Charles Pelly, who had been ordered to escort a merchant convoy to Canada due to the war with France. The First Lord of the Admiralty and well-known abolitionist, Lord Barham (Charles Middleton), had arranged his passage. Teyoninhokarawen enjoyed Captain Pelly's hospitality and commented favourably on the management and culture aboard the Royal Navy vessel. Coming ashore at Quebec in November, he found that it was too late in the season to travel by water up the St Lawrence. Therefore, he made his way to the Grand River overland, stopping to visit people along the way (while most of the things he had acquired in Britain were sent separately through the goodness of acquaintances on both sides of the Atlantic). Upon arriving home in January 1806, he found his house in darkness, with its roof missing because of a storm, but soon after discovered his family safely secured at a neighbour's place.[57]

Despite their political defeats in England and in Canada, Joseph Brant and John Norton resumed the struggle against their opponents in hopes of restoring their standing and then achieving their goals in securing indigenous control over the Haldimand Tract. On his return to the Grand, Teyoninhokarawen mailed a copy of the Haldimand Grant to Britain, as the problem of finding it in London had been such a difficulty during his visit.[58] As well, Lieutenant-Governor Peter Hunter had died earlier, in 1805, and Alexander Grant had replaced him as interim administrator of Upper Canada. At first Joseph Brant had been optimistic about the change, writing that "I received some hopes that what respects our land affairs might have been accomplished to our satisfaction in this country." Yet, he continued, "these hopes are now vanished; for appearances give me reason to apprehend that the old council, principally composed of men influenced by an insatiable avarice for lands, have so prejudiced His Excellency against us as to disappoint what otherwise we might have expected from the innate benevolence" of the

---

the Indian Chief," 524–5. JN's letters often expressed a personal responsibility to engage in Christian evangelism (NL, MS654, passim).

57 JN to various people, 17 August 1805 to 25 March 1806, NL, MS654, 1–2, 4–6, 7–9, 10–12, 13–14, 15–19, 22–4, 139–44; S. Gerrard to Robert Barclay, 29 December 1805, ibid., 19–20; Klinck, "Biographical Introduction," in *JMJN*, lvii–lviii.

58 JN to Robert Barclay, 15 January 1806, NL, MS654, 22.

King's representative.[59] The situation did not change with the arrival of
a new lieutenant-governor, Francis Gore, in 1806.[60]

Thayendanegea and Teyoninhokarawen managed to recover their
positions on the Grand in 1806, affirm the legitimacy of Norton's actions
in working dutifully for the community with the support of its chiefs,
and condemn William Claus's discreditable conduct. Speaking on behalf
of the Grand River's leaders that year, Brant, for instance, denounced
the deputy superintendent-general for recruiting American-resident Iroquois to subvert Norton's mission illegitimately, as Claus's actions had
prevented "the equitable discussion" of Six Nations affairs by the British cabinet. Brant also stated that "in no point whatever do we consider
Teyoninhokarawen to have passed the bounds of the authority of a chief
interested in the welfare of our tribes. He endeavoured to do good for
us but injury to none."[61] The people at this meeting dissolved the united
Grand River and Buffalo Creek council, and re-established the primacy
of the one on the Grand for governing the affairs of the Haldimand Tract.
Faced with colonial obstinacy, Brant, Norton, and their allies also sought
assistance from anyone they thought might help them, including opposition politicians in Upper Canada such as Robert Thorpe, a judge and
member of the legislative assembly. Thinking that provincial policies
were oppressive and unconstitutional, Thorpe wrote to officials in England protesting the treatment the Six Nations endured at the hands of
colonial officials. Aligning with such political figures proved to be a problem, however, because Gore, the new lieutenant-governor, suspected
them of disloyalty, and even of seditious tendencies. Given memories of
Thayendanegea's threats to Upper Canadian security in the 1790s, relationships with people like Thorpe confirmed the negative opinions held
by Brant's enemies, which naturally tainted Norton as well.[62]

---

59 Joseph Brant to the second Duke of Northumberland, 4? February 1806, BL,
Northumberland MSS, 64:22–3.

60 For a narrative of the events from JN's return to Canada and Joseph Brant's death
late in 1807, see Kelsay, *Brant*, 642–52.

61 Six Nations Address by Joseph Brant to William Claus, 3 September 1806, BL,
Northumberland MSS, 64:60–9 (quotes on 62–3). For similar sentiments, see Council
Speeches, 28 July 1806, ibid., 64:38–51; Six Nations Address by Brant to Claus, 4
September 1806, ibid., 64:71–2; Council Speeches, 23 July 1806, LAC, RG10, 1:398–
406. See also Talman, "Historical Introduction," in *JMJN*, cvii–cix.

62 For a sense of the opposition views, see Mills, *View of the Political Situation*. That 1809
pamphlet, written by John Jackson Mills, one of Robert Thorpe's key supporters,

While allied on most subjects, Thayendanegea and Teyoninhokarawen disagreed on how to use the money generated by selling and
leasing parts of the Grand River Tract. Norton preferred to deposit the
proceeds conservatively in England, which, he argued, most Iroquois
chiefs favoured, whereas Brant wanted to invest more aggressively in
Canadian mortgages. (The fact that they quarrelled over the funds –
amounting to many thousands of pounds – speaks to the growing complexities of the Haudenosaunee economy in the early 1800s.) For a brief
time, Joseph Brant formed a cautious but more positive relationship
with William Claus, despite their animosities. Thayendanegea hoped
that an understanding between them might allow him to achieve at
least some of his goals of resolving the uncertain state of Grand River
tenure for those parts of the tract that the Iroquois still retained, and
addressing the confused status of the existing sales and leases. Brant's
behaviour exasperated Norton. In contrast, Teyoninhokarawen thought
that Thayendanegea's actions might undermine efforts to prevent Claus
from promoting provincial and personal interests over those of the Six
Nations. Therefore, he wrote to Francis Gore on behalf of forty chiefs
and warriors in November 1806, claiming that Brant's initiatives did
not enjoy widespread support, and demanded that decisions be made
by the Six Nations in council (presumably in place of less scrutinized
actions by either Brant or Claus). While Norton's position affirmed
traditional consensus values, his ability to muster so many leaders in
opposition to his powerful patron is striking, and indicates that he had
achieved an impressive degree of influence in his own right beyond his
associations with the older man. It also demonstrates that he possessed
confidence in his abilities within the intricacies of Haudenosaunee
politics. Rumours circulated that Thayendanegea had profited unfairly
from land transactions, which made people doubt his commitment to
Six Nations concerns. (He did provide favours to people who could
assist him, and received land and other benefits for his efforts in disposing of parts of the tract).[63] In contrast, John Norton never seems to have

---

circulated in England and Canada. It condemned the administration of the province,
and included a section on native affairs (20–3) and recorded speeches from 1806 and
1807 by Joseph Brant defending JN's work and denouncing the behaviour of William
Claus (70–6).

63 JN to (Robert?) Barclay, 20 October 1806, NL, MS654, 74–81; JN, Speech, 19 February
1807, ibid., 105; Council Minutes, 9 November 1806, LAC, RG10, 27:15669–76; Kelsay,
Brant, 646–7; Good, "Crown-Directed Colonization," 218–21.

been accused of impropriety in attending to Six Nations affairs, beyond the falsehoods hurled at him by Claus and his supporters. Teyoninho-karawen worried that Brant may have become corrupt, while also being troubled by Thayendanegea's drinking and deteriorating health. Thus, Norton recommended that financial affairs be "confided to trusty people of the nation," who would work "under the direction of the general council," and would provide a yearly "account of their proceedings" while being subject to replacement on an annual basis.[64] His phrase, "of the nation," presumably excluded outsiders like Claus. Joseph Brant suspected that his protégé wanted to replace him as the main figure in managing land issues. As well, Thayendanegea wondered if Norton had aligned with Lieutenant-Governor Gore, because both men preferred to invest Grand River monies in England rather than in Canada. There is no evidence that there was a Norton-Gore alliance, however, even though they shared similar views on the subject of Haudeno-saunee funds. Tellingly, it was Claus who brought Teyoninhokarawen's views to Brant's attention, and he may have planted the notion of a conspiracy in Thayendanegea's mind in hopes of severing the relationship between the two chiefs. The troubles between Norton and Brant did not last long, as they resolved their differences and realized that the deputy superintendent-general had worked to divide them.[65]

As they continued to resist colonial authorities, Brant and Norton obtained authorization from the Grand River council in 1807 to undertake another mission to England to try to confirm ownership of the Six Nations lands, since they could not obtain justice in Canada. Achieving Haudenosaunee goals, Teyoninhokarawen wrote, would "be a benefit to many and an injury to no honest man," noting that the people could not be expected to improve their lands on the Haldimand Tract until they could "rest assured of the enjoyment of the fruits of their labours" through having their ownership of them confirmed.[66] Regrettably, they were not able to make the journey: they did not have enough money to go, and they worried that it would be dangerous to leave the Six Nations at a time when their opponents could use their absence to undermine them and victimize the people of the Grand. Therefore, Brant and Norton gave the Duke of Northumberland power of attorney

---

64 JN, Speech, 19 February 1807, NL, MS654, 105.
65 Joseph Brant to William Claus, 2 July 1807, TPL, Powell Papers; Kelsay, *Brant*, 647.
66 JN to Lord Teignmouth, 24 January 1807, BFBSA, F3/Shore.

to do what he could on their behalf. Norton also wrote to the secretary of state for war and the colonies, seeking his assistance in attending to Six Nations concerns.[67] People in England exercised sufficient influence on behalf of the Haudenosaunee that the British government began to address land issues favourably for the Six Nations before the War of 1812. For example, in 1809, Viscount Castlereagh (Robert Stewart) wrote to Sir James Craig, governor-in-chief of British North America, expressing doubt about John Norton's character because of what he had heard from the Indian Department, but noting that his claims had merit. Therefore, he ordered Sir James to investigate the situation with a view toward giving the Iroquois the ability to hold their land freely and then lease or alienate parts if they wished to do so, with Teyoninho-karawen possibly being involved in the process. The letter has a some-what grudging quality, but Castlereagh clearly expected the solution to respect the Six Nations position. (The tone of the letter may have been intended to assuage Craig's feelings in order to facilitate action, rather than reflect its author's views.) The letter also suggested that Castlereagh's decisions stemmed partly from pressure exerted by the influential friends of the Iroquois in the United Kingdom.[68] Neverthe-less, Canadian officials argued against the idea and employed bureau-cratic intransigence, aided by time, distance, and the crisis of the War of 1812, to avoid dealing with these matters until Norton could resume the struggle after the return of peace.[69] Thus, the fundamental question

---

67 JN to the second Duke of Northumberland, 4 February 1807, BL, Northumberland MSS, 64:25b; Council Minutes, 21 February 1807, ibid., 64:78; Joseph Brant to Northumberland, 27 May 1807, ibid., 64:75; JN to William Windham, 27 May 1807, ibid., 64:81–1; JN to Northumberland, 27 May 1807, ibid., 64:84–6. (JN thought at the time he wrote to Windham that he still was the secretary of war and the colonies, not knowing that Lord Castlereagh had succeeded him.)

68 Lord Castlereagh to Sir James Craig, 8 April 1809, LAC, RG10, 3:975–9.

69 For Lieutenant-Governor Francis Gore's response to Lord Castlereagh, see Talman, "Historical Introduction," in *JMJN*, ciii–civ. Gore's arguments against giving the Haudenosaunee fee simple ownership included fears that the change would make them into voters who would elect seditious people to the Upper Canadian legislative assembly, or would associate with disloyal and greedy land jobbers who would exploit them and turn them against the Crown. He also said that giving them the ability to sell land would see their population disperse, thus weakening them as military allies in time of war. As well, he believed that giving them the ability to manage their land freely would prevent colonial authorities from punishing them if their conduct offended imperial interests.

of control of the Grand River Tract kept on corroding Anglo-
Haudenosaunee relations during a period of growing tensions between
Great Britain and the United States, when improving the bond between
the Six Nations and the Crown ought to have been a priority for provincial authorities, beyond their obligations to behave honourably towards
the indigenous people within the colony.

Aside from promoting dissension between Brant and Norton and
thwarting Six Nations aspirations, William Claus persisted in his attacks
on Teyoninhokarawen in hopes of crippling his ability to serve as an
effective leader. One of these assaults took place at the annual distribution of government presents to the Six Nations in 1807, at which he also
dispensed hundreds of pounds in interest from their investments. Thus,
when people were especially conscious of the government's role in their
well-being and the Indian Department's ability to distribute favours,
Claus again denounced Norton's journey to England. The deputy
superintendent-general claimed that Teyoninhokarawen "had endeavoured to bring trouble to you, confusion in your affairs, and disunion
among the nations by making representations of Indian affairs without
the knowledge and consent of the principal chiefs." After censuring him
further, Claus proclaimed that he no longer would "take notice of any
sort of communication in which Norton is concerned."[70] That, of course,
was a strong statement, coming from the Crown's primary representative to the Grand River community. Later, Norton expressed frustration over the "dirty intrigues practised to sow dissention between" him
and Brant, asserting that it was "the determination of the government
in Upper Canada to throw everything respecting our people into the
hands of Mr Claus and the Indian Department," to control the people
of the Grand in conformity to the desires of the colonial leadership.[71]

On 24 November 1807, Joseph Brant, aged sixty-four, passed away.
According to nineteenth-century historian William Stone, the dying
Thayendanegea asked John Norton to "have pity on the poor Indians:
if you can get any influence with the great, endeavour to do them all
the good you can."[72] In May 1808, after people had had six months to

---

70 Minutes of the Six Nations Council Meeting, 28 September 1807, quoted in Good,
   "Crown-Directed Colonization," 228.
71 JN to Joseph-Geneviève de Puisaye, Comte de Puisaye, 20 December 1810, LAC,
   MG21–Add.MSS–8075, 113.
72 Putative Joseph Brant Statement, 24? November 1807, quoted in Stone, *Brant*, 2:499.
   For JN on Brant, see *JMJN*, 261–75.

reflect on their circumstances following Brant's passing, Teyoninho-karawen, then aged thirty-seven, was called to a "general meeting of the chiefs and principal warriors" at the council house at the Onon-daga village on the Grand. He recorded that the speaker, on behalf of the assembly, said that "formerly they had appointed me jointly with the deceased Colonel Brant to be at the head of their affairs," but "the satisfaction they had received from me" induced them to appoint him "solely to be at the head of their councils."[73] This did not mean that the assembled leaders had abandoned their traditional political struc-tures or given him powers beyond those that chiefs normally exer-cised, but it demonstrated that they wanted him to continue Brant's work, particularly as it related to representing the Six Nations on questions of land tenure, political independence, and relations with the Crown. The Haudenosaunee accepted a degree of divergence from normal leadership structures during this period, based on the talents or limitations, and skills or weaknesses, of people available to meet community needs. The desire for Teyoninhokarawen to persevere in a role akin to the one Brant had fulfilled serves as another demon-stration of his acceptance among them, as well as their recognition of the contributions he had made since the 1790s. As an additional measure of their confidence, the chiefs made their decision despite the Indian Department's deep objections to Norton. As expected, Upper Canadian officials and those members of the Six Nations who had opposed Norton and Brant and their supporters persisted in their enmity, which Teyoninhokarawen undoubtedly found debilitating, and which likely contributed to his decision to leave his home and travel to the Cherokee country a year later, despite the responsibilities conferred on him.[74] In fact, he earlier had suggested that Haudeno-saunee attempts to resolve their problems with colonial authorities might be more successful if he withdrew from public life, because of colonial antagonism to him.[75]

---

73 JN to John Owen, 10 August 1808, NL, MS654, 128. Sometimes people referred to
    Joseph Brant as "colonel," due to an honour bestowed by King George III in 1779,
    although his Indian Department rank was captain.
74 Examples of ongoing opposition to JN centred on the Claus faction include
    Alexander McDonell to Lord Selkirk, 18 March 1808, published in Johnston, Six
    Nations, 170–2; McDonell to Selkirk, 28 November 1808, published in ibid., 173–8.
75 JN to John Owen, 28 January 1807, NL, MS654, 83.

As we saw earlier, two of Norton's reasons for making his journey in 1809–10 were to honour the grave of his father and to promote Christianity to the native people in the American south. It also is clear, considering his life as a whole, that he found inspiration in adventure. Beyond these factors, he wrote that he wished "to enquire into the situation of our brethren the Cherokees, of whom the tribes of the north had received no satisfactory accounts for many years"; and "in the next place, that my father having been taken, a boy, from Kuwoki, when that village was burnt by the English, could any of their old chiefs trace the family, his relatives, it would give me pleasure to take them by the hand."[76] While he returned to the Grand from his travels, he did not expect to remain among the Six Nations, as we shall explore below. Yet, with the approach of hostilities in 1812, he changed his mind and agreed to serve as he had before, and to take on the role of a war chief among those men who chose to follow him into battle during the three years of the conflict. As we also shall examine, his prominence within the indigenous world of the lower Great Lakes would extend beyond the Haudenosaunee of the Grand River to incorporate people from more westerly regions, where he had established connections earlier in his life.

---

76 *JMJN*, 35–6. The town where British troops captured his father likely was a different place from the one JN mentioned, being Little or New Keowee instead (Benn, "Missed Opportunities," 266). For more on the journey, see Klinck, "Biographical Introduction," in *JMJN*, lxv–lxvii; *JMJN*, 5–85, 109–90 (in which JN also wrote about related histories); Morgan, *Travellers through Empire*, 39–45.

A Mohawk Memoir
from the War of 1812

BY

JOHN NORTON — TEYONINHOKARAWEN

1

Uncertainties, Diplomacy, and the Outbreak of War, 1811–12

We begin our exploration of John Norton's memoir during the months before the American declaration of war in June 1812, when Teyoninhokarawen planned to leave the Six Nations Haudenosaunee of the Grand River despite his prominent role there. He changed his mind once Major-General Isaac Brock assumed responsibility for both civil and military affairs in Upper Canada in October 1811, as colonial officials prepared the province to resist an invasion from the United States. Norton thought the British army, as represented by Brock, would be more sympathetic to native wishes than the civil authorities, against whom he and Joseph Brant had struggled for so many years. As the threat of hostilities grew, Teyoninhokarawen hoped that the military's expanding influence would allow the Iroquois to confirm clear title over the land granted to them by Frederick Haldimand in 1784 and win freedom from unwelcome outside interference in their affairs. Yet, as the international situation deteriorated, he set these issues aside for the moment at Brock's request. This was a striking decision when we recall how vigorously he had worked since the 1790s to achieve independent ownership of the Grand River tract for the Haudenosaunee and assert native control of their own affairs. Two considerations generated his decision. The first was Norton's belief that the United States posed such a profound threat to indigenous societies that opposing the republic's aggressions had to take precedence over other matters. The second was his confidence that a forceful demonstration of Six Nations combat support for the Crown would strengthen their arguments in achieving their goals once the crisis had passed. He therefore encouraged the people of the Grand to embrace a British alliance fully. In doing so, he drew upon his ability to persuade, his appeal as a charismatic individual, his integrity, and the standing he had earned through his pre-war service. Conversely, both he and Isaac Brock hoped that support from the British military and the resources it could provide would influence people to agree with him. In June 1812, Norton received a captaincy in the Indian Department to facilitate the process.[1] *(As noted earlier, the department employed officers and translators who were either First Nations men or people of mixed native-white ancestry.) Yet Teyoninhokarawen risked alienating elements of the Grand River community, as people might conclude that his responsibilities to them could be compromised by his connections to the army. Furthermore, political divisions limited the number of the tract's residents willing to listen to his arguments, because of their opposition to the old Brant-Norton party that he now led. Beyond these constraints, cultural factors restricted the hopes of anyone wishing to fulfil a chiefly role, including a general wariness of individuals who might become more prominent than was thought to be wise. In addition, the Indian Department, especially through its deputy superintendent-general, William Claus, remained virulently hostile to Teyoninhokarawen and those associated with him. Thus, Claus conspired to subvert him and his supporters in order to limit their influence and advance the interests of his friends and allies along the Grand, even though his behaviour conflicted with military plans and even though both Claus and Norton otherwise promoted a British-Haudenosaunee alliance against the United States and would oppose the American army with vigour in the coming war. Teyoninhokarawen tended to be circumspect in writing about this conflict; therefore, we will see some of his frustration expressed below in his memoir, but will need to turn to the annotations for more details.*

The spectre of war had troubled the minds of natives and newcomers throughout the Great Lakes region for some years. If there were to be a conflict, would it occur south and west of Lake Erie in the Old Northwest (mainly comprising today's Ohio, Michigan, Indiana, Illinois, and Wisconsin), where a portion of the region's First Nations would fight to defend their societies against American oppression, and which might or might not see violence spread to Canada? Alternatively, would there be a broader confrontation between Great Britain and the United States over a range of problems between the two powers? If that were to occur, how might indigenous people within and beyond the Old Northwest be involved or affected? From an aboriginal perspective, the possibility of a major armed conflict might be dated to about 1805. That year, the famous Shawnee half-brothers Tecumseh and Tenskwatawa began to form the Western Tribal Confederacy. Like others, they feared for the survival of native societies, and they dreamt of uniting people across much of eastern North America to harness the temporal and spiritual strength

---

1 Francis de Rottenburg to Noah Freer, 31 July 1813, LAC, RG8, 257:109.

needed to protect the First Nations against newcomer abuse. Especially worrisome were questions arising from aggressive efforts by Americans to take away their lands, destroy their communities, and even extirpate indigenous populations entirely. The confederacy's leaders saw an answer to their fears through securing autonomous homelands within a large part of the Old Northwest, where native societies could evolve on their own terms, in their own time, and with enough territory to promote the social stability and economic viability they needed to survive into the future. The region's white population was small enough in its westerly and northerly portions that Tecumseh and Tenskwatawa could envision achieving a degree of independence greater than that which the Haudenosaunee living farther east might imagine was possible in their own territories, where Euro-Americans had far more power to intervene into their lives than they did in the west.

With support drawn from many Shawnees, Potawatomis, Chippewas, Mingos, and others, the half-brothers tried to recruit more people from wider areas, but experienced only limited success outside of the eastern and southern parts of the Old Northwest. Even within their areas of influence, a large percentage of those who were hostile to the expanding republic nevertheless were uncomfortable with, or opposed to, Tecumseh and Tenskwatawa. Their attitudes arose in reaction to the radical nature of these men's views, such as holding land across tribal divisions rather than nation by nation, and their rough, even violent, treatment of traditional leaders who the two Shawnees thought had not done enough to protect indigenous interests. Other people within the territory where the Western Tribal Confederacy gathered most of its support – including many Shawnees – sought shelter from the turmoil of the period through neutrality. Some even were willing to align with the United States militarily in hopes of securing protection through friendship with its government. Farther west, a large portion of the Sauk, Mesquakie, and neighbouring tribes of the upper Mississippi River wanted to resist the Americans, using force if necessary, but they generally stayed outside of the confederacy. Unlike most of the confederates, they had not been deeply engaged in the treaties associated with westward expansion or the war for the Ohio country of the 1780s and 1790s, and the settler menace for them did not come as strongly from the east. Instead, their land losses and newcomer troubles arose from the south, centred out of St Louis, as Americans moved northwards up the Mississippi.

Haudenosaunee communities in New York, Pennsylvania, and Upper and Lower Canada generally expressed support for the nativist movement but did not join the confederates, aside from some individuals who travelled west on their own initiative to participate in the struggle for aboriginal liberty. Most Iroquois south of the Anglo-American border, whatever their perspectives, thought they had little choice but to remain neutral in a conflict for the Old Northwest – as most of them had during the Ohio war – or even to ally with the United States should Britain engage in hostilities in the Great Lakes region. Their hold on their reservations, surrounded by overwhelming numbers of settlers, was tenuous enough without taking up arms against the hostile trinity of government officials, land speculators, and ordinary citizens who strove to acquire their remnant territories (while many Oneidas and Tuscaroras had a history of fighting against King George III during the American Revolution of 1775–83). Six Nations people also reflected on their history, in which participation in Euro-American conflicts had brought about the loss of freedom and land, and had inflicted misery, privation, and death on their ancestors and their older relatives. Among a sizable portion of those who thought about that legacy, neutrality seemed to be the best option. Pacifist attitudes enjoyed added strength among people who had accepted the religious messages of the Seneca prophet Handsome Lake, which included demands to stay out of white wars in response to the baleful consequences such conflicts had had on the Haudenosaunee over the two centuries since they first engaged the newcomers in combat.

Some of the Iroquois living within the United States felt they needed to persuade their relatives north of the border to refrain from allying with Great Britain in the event of an Anglo-American conflict, which John Norton's text below records in some detail. Aside from preserving the lives and well-being of their families and friends in Canada, they thought promoting neutrality might demonstrate goodwill towards the United States, and thereby inhibit Americans from finding excuses to oppress them. Many thought that an alliance with King George would be pointless anyway, because common opinion across the Great Lakes region held that his forces were bound to lose a war with the republic. They understood how Britain's titanic struggles against France in Europe, on the high seas, and elsewhere across the globe precluded sending large numbers of troops across the Atlantic Ocean, and they believed that British North America simply did not have the internal resources to resist an invasion. In 1812, for instance, almost eight million people lived in the United States, a figure sixteen times greater than the population of the British colonies to the north. The most vulnerable of them – Upper Canada – had only seventy thousand settlers, a figure equivalent to the number of natives spread throughout the Great Lakes region. In contrast, Ohio alone had upwards of a quarter of a million white inhabitants. Moreover, aboriginal people knew that the majority of settlers in the province were non-loyalist American immigrants and their children and, like many observers, assumed that they would not be willing to oppose an invasion. (In the end, these people would prove to be more reliable between 1812 and 1814 than anyone had expected, despite support for the American cause or attempts to avoid military service among a portion of them.) In 1807, at the start of the slide towards an Anglo-American war (in contrast to a native-newcomer conflict in the Old Northwest), Norton, for instance, noted that "little dependence can be placed on the militia of many districts" in Upper Canada, because its members mainly came from the United States, and many opposed "the royal interest."[2] Therefore, resisting the expanding United States seemed futile, as a retrospective assessment of the outcomes of the American Revolution and the war for the Ohio country would suggest. Beyond the question of the extraordinary disparity in power, many indigenous people doubted the value of an alliance with Great Britain because they believed that Crown officials had ignored their concerns in diplomatic negotiations related to ending the American Revolution and during the tensions of the Ohio war. Other reasons also undermined native willingness to support the King. The ongoing and frustrating attempts by the Iroquois of the Grand River to secure control over their territory remained unresolved, while similar problems and corresponding anger associated with colonial intransigence disheartened indigenous communities throughout Upper Canada. Even individuals willing to fight because of their hostility to the United States and their ties to the Crown felt constrained by fear of the consequences of an American annexation of the colony. Others even adopted a pro-American stance, and strove to weaken pro-British sentiment, although these people formed the smallest political grouping among the indigenous population in the province. During the time of these anxieties, John Norton held a minority view as the leader of one of the Grand's militant pro-British parties (although he enjoyed wider but not universal support for his efforts to secure title to the Grand River tract for the Six Nations).

In the end, three interrelated wars broke out across the Great Lakes. In November 1811, the Americans sent an army to disperse the Western Tribes, culminating in the battle of Tippecanoe in the Indiana Territory, which escalated simmering hostilities in the easterly portions of the Old Northwest into a major conflict that would rage until late 1813. Farther west, violence erupted along the upper Mississippi River between natives and newcomers at about the same time, in a largely separate conflict, because the aboriginal people in that region did not align formally with the Western Tribal Confederacy. Their struggle continued well into 1815. (We should remember, however, that boundaries were porous and that people sometimes travelled far from their homes to support their allies, as hundreds of upper Mississippi warriors, for instance, did on the Detroit front in 1813.) Then, in mid-June

---

2 JN to John Owen, 19 August 1807, NL, MS654, 126.

*1812, the United States declared war on Great Britain and, a month later,
invaded Upper Canada. That conflict, which came to an end early in 1815,
naturally led the peoples of the upper Mississippi, the warriors of the Western Tribes, and the British across the border to come together against their
common enemy. Most of the people of the Grand River, like a large percentage of other indigenous people in Upper Canada and elsewhere, however,
remained neutral during the early stages of these three conflicts. Some maintained that stance until the return of peace, and of those who took up arms, a
minority fought alongside the Americans.*[3]

[In the spring of 1812], several private messages were sent from the
American side advising the Five Nations [of the Grand River] to remain
neutral, adding that all resistance against the power of the United States
would be ineffectual; that in Canada there was only a handful of British troops (at the same time that the bulk of the inhabitants of Upper
Canada were Americans and would therefore rather assist than oppose
an invading army from that quarter); that as soon as war should be
declared they would invade the country with an immense force and
overwhelm with ruin whoever dared to oppose them.[4]

In the [previous] autumn Major-General Brock arrived at York to
take the command of the troops in the upper province, and also assume
the civil government under the title of "president" at the same time
that Francis Gore, Esquire, lieutenant-governor, took his departure for

---

3 Literature on indigenous participation in the war is extensive, but for a concise study
  see Benn, "Aboriginal Peoples and Their Multiple Wars of 1812." For summaries
  and timelines focused on First Nations participation, see Benn, *Native Memoirs*,
  1–24; Tanner, *Atlas of Great Lakes Indian History*, 105–21. For the Haudenosaunee, see
  Benn, *Iroquois in the War of 1812*. A short but broad overview of the conflict is Benn,
  War of 1812. The best extensive single volume general study of the war is Stagg, *Mr
  Madison's War*. Solid general histories are Hickey, *War of 1812* and Hitsman, *Incredible
  War* (revised by Graves), which includes a list of indigenous military strength (Benn,
  Appendix 5 in Hitsman, 302–3).
4 The messages came from Iroquois in New York to their relatives on the Grand River.
  The word "private" reveals attempts to prevent white officials from hearing about
  them, although the Crown's agents did learn about these interactions. It was difficult
  to keep secrets within Haudenosaunee society, because its competing political parties
  had alignments and friendships with a range of natives and newcomers. JN used
  "neuter" instead of "neutral" here and on other occasions.

England.[5] This change was very well-received throughout the province. The decisive manner in which General Brock always spoke and acted was a very favourable feature in his military character, and filled with confidence every true loyalist who was determined to defend the country to the last, whilst his discernment, candour, and rectitude entirely confounded the spirit of party and exposed the mystery of calumny.

I was then prepared to retire to the southwest to prepare an establishment where we might live undisturbed by factious disputes, and had even fixed the day for my departure when, hearing of his arrival, I thought I would inform him before I quitted the province (not liking to sneak away when an attack was expected).[6] I heard from him that he desired to see me at York. On meeting him there, he immediately entered into conversation on the situation of the people of the Grand River, expressing a readiness to accede to every reasonable request. I told him that the title to their lands, having been disputed, was that which required to be ascertained in order to satisfy all parties and completely eradicate the seeds of discontent; and offered, if he required it, to call the people together on my return and inform them of the

---

5 When Major-General Isaac Brock assumed responsibility over civil affairs in Upper Canada in the absence of Lieutenant-Governor Francis Gore, he became "President of the Council" in reference to the province's executive council (which functioned in a manner similar to a cabinet).

6 Informing Isaac Brock made sense because of JN's prominence in Anglo-Haudenosaunee affairs. As we saw in the Introduction, some people considered moving or had moved southwest of Lake Erie to escape the machinations of the Indian Department, the uncertainties of the Six Nations' land tenure on the Grand River, and unwanted Euro-American influences, although the chances of finding freedom from whites in Ohio were diminishing rapidly with newcomer settlement in the state. JN already knew the region well and had established relationships there in the 1790s, and it is possible that this was the "southwest" to which he planned to move. Rather than Ohio, however, he may have thought of settling among the Cherokees. He had told missionaries during his 1809–10 journey that he might return at the request of his Cherokee relatives if his family on the Grand agreed to do so. Some Cherokees had moved to the west of the Mississippi since that time, however, so we cannot be certain what he meant by "southwest" (Anna Rosina Gambold?, April 1810, quoted in McClinton, *Mission to the Cherokees*, 1:355). JN found Haudenosaunee politics and his conflict with the Indian Department to be enormously frustrating, felt that his work on behalf of the Six Nations came at significant personal cost, and wanted to retire from public life. Nevertheless, he generally believed that he had to respect the community's desires to serve its interests (e.g., JN to John Owen, 20 October 1806, NL, MS654, 83).

favourable disposition he expressed towards them. On returning home, I immediately sent a message to call the principal people together. They assembled with great alacrity, and expressed great satisfaction at being informed of the favourable disposition expressed by the general. They deliberated and framed a speech, comprising the substance of all they required (the land on the Grand River was the main object).[7] I forwarded this to York. And a short time after, the deputy superintendent-general of Indian affairs [William Claus] arrived at Ancaster with the interest of money lodged in the funds and other monies arising from the sale of land made by the late Colonel Brant, when I received a letter from the secretary of Major-General Brock expressive of his disposition to favour their requests.[8] After the money was delivered and the deputy superintendent-general had taken his departure, it surprised me to hear from one of his confidential Mohawk friends that he had advised them strongly to omit or retract that part relative to lands contained in the speech which I had forwarded to York. His advice, however, was at this time without effect. In the winter [of 1811–12], while I was yet amusing myself with hunting in the woods, the deputy superintendent-general came to the council fire at the Onondaga village where a council was called under the pretence of repeating or confirming the speech which had been sent to York. I never heard exactly what passed at this meeting;

---

7 Securing control over the Haldimand Grant for the Six Nations in fee simple was the fundamental issue, but there were other matters that the Haudenosaunee wanted to have resolved, including removing squatters and solving issues associated with problems arising from the alienation of part of the tract. They voiced their confidence in Isaac Brock, saying: "Your words have spread general satisfaction among us. They express the benevolence of your heart and your generous desire to dispel the clouds of uneasiness that have for some time hovered over our abode. You thereby appear ready to grant every request consistent with justice that may be necessary to secure our interests or to promote our welfare" (Council Minutes, 31 October 1811, LAC, RG10, 27:16320–2, quote on 16320).

8 Council Minutes, 14 November 1811, ibid., 27:16328–31. Some Haudenosaunee proceeds from previous land sales had been invested to generate revenue. Delivering payment at that point was a gesture of goodwill but did not address the issue of title to the Grand River Tract. This document also called upon William Claus to get along with JN: "Peace is a most desirable object, and we anticipate much pleasure and advantage to ourselves from the appearance we see of a good understanding between you and our friend Mr Norton, and we hope that no further differences will occur between you" (Echo or Raweanarase, Speech, ibid., 27:16330). Isaac Brock took some additional measures to deal with Six Nations concerns over settler encroachments on the Grand (e.g., Brock, Proclamation, 1 February 1812, ibid., 28:16342–3).

the greater part of the people, not understanding English, said that they only confirmed what had been said in the autumn.[9]

In the May following [in 1812], General Brock, accompanied by his staff and the deputy superintendent-general of Indian affairs, visited the Mohawk village on the Grand River; and to receive him all the tribes living on it were assembled at that place.[10] The Mohawks were divided into two parties, and the other tribes kept rather aloof, disgusted at their contentions.[11] When the usual salutations had passed, General Brock, addressing them in an expressive speech, informed them of the increasing appearances of hostility [from the United States]. And, showing the necessity of being prepared to meet any sudden attacks, he expressed his confidence in their readiness to cooperate with His Majesty's troops, and proposed that they might divide the men fit to bear arms into three

---

9 As explored in the Introduction, William Claus's actions here were consistent with his pre-war efforts to prevent the Six Nations from gaining fee simple or equivalent ownership of the Haldimand Tract. The Onondaga village on the Grand River (in the modern Caledonia area) was near the site of the Six Nations council house. The "confidential Mohawk friend" was George Martin (Shononhsese), a veteran of the American Revolution, who worked as an interpreter for the Indian Department and who collaborated with Claus against JN for many years. Despite his hostility to JN, Martin shared similarities in enjoying political prominence on the Grand, promoting Anglicanism, defending Six Nations interests against external pressures, and fighting against the Americans in the War of 1812 (although he initially seems to have opposed belligerency in the weeks before the capture of Detroit in August 1812).

10 The Mohawk village (in modern Brantford) sat at an important ford across the Grand.

11 While both Mohawk parties wanted the Haudenosaunee to hold the Grand River lands in an arrangement that guaranteed Six Nations ownership and autonomy, one faction mainly was pro-British while the other was pro-American (and other groups within the tribe were neutralist). Further complicating the situation, membership in these divisions was fluid, and individuals associated with them held diverse and opposing views. As well, family and other relationships along the Grand and across the wider Iroquois world affected people's perspectives and alignments. While Mohawks dominated the two groups, others also participated in their affairs. Several factors motivated the American party (and the neutralists). Some arose from relationships with disloyal white settlers and a degree of dependency on receiving annuities from the United States for land alienated there after the American Revolution. Other reasons included disgust with the behaviour of Canadian authorities, hostility to the way Crown officials had treated indigenous concerns in negotiations with the United States in the 1780s and 1790s, and desires to avoid having the Americans seize their lands if the Haudenosaunee were to support the British in what seemed likely to be a hopeless cause.

divisions, one of which [was] to be always on the frontier, and relieved monthly, so that all might have an equal opportunity of participating in the defence of their country and of attending to the cultivation of their fields. Unanimity could not be effected. Much the most numerous party appeared discontented because they had received no satisfactory answer to the speech which they had made in the autumn respecting their lands. They sat together, and the Echo (or Raweanarase), as their speaker, arose, and in a very long oration, urged the necessity of their minds being satisfied as to the lands they held ere they should be involved in the confusion of war – it being uncertain who might survive the conflict – and they desired to see the interests of their posterity well secured before they engaged in it. [He] enquired how long the horizon would be darkened by the clouds of war, and when it should again be enlightened by the bright rays of peace, [and] in what situation they would find themselves (alluding metaphorically to the peace of 1783 in which their country fell into the power of the Americans). They also asked, "Should the Americans defer declaring war against the King, and persist in making encroachments on our brethren of the west, will you give them assistance?" General Brock answered frankly, "It is out of my power while we are at peace to interfere. They dwell beyond our limits, in consequence of which I have advised them, through the medium of the Indian Department, to endeavour to live at peace with their neighbours. Should the people of the United States invade our territories [however], I will then feel myself authorized to oppose them with force, and trusting in God and the justice of our cause, have no doubts of the result of our exertions."[12]

General Brock had further informed me in conversation that, should he promise anything respecting their lands, he could have no prospect of the performance unless by petitioning the ministry (which might involve him in a labyrinth of difficulties out of the line of his profession); that he therefore thought it improper to make any further promises than what came within his power to fulfil; [and] that as to the true intent and

---

12 Raweanarase (also known as Young Clear Sky or Echo) was an Onondaga chief who opposed the Brant-Norton party. He used the exchange with Isaac Brock to express bitterness over Britain's decision to ignore native interests at the end of the American Revolution and to suggest that the King's government had behaved duplicitously by withholding support from the Western Tribes who had gone to war with the United States in 1811 independently of Anglo-American troubles. His words put Brock at a diplomatic disadvantage, because the general's reply was a truthful statement of British policy at the time but essentially confirmed Raweanarase's charges.

meaning of General Haldimand's grant, he thought it sufficiently clear grounds on which to hold their lands.[13] From the time that he made this candid avowal, I became opposed to insisting any further on the land matters until we should see the end of the expected hostilities. And in support of these sentiments, I stated that to remain quiet and allow the Americans to overrun the country would disgrace us by showing us both deficient in courage and in a loyal affection to the King, whilst we could expect no favourable result from such conduct, for their disposition was too well-known to admit of any hope should we fall under their power. Therefore, to espouse the cause of the King with alacrity was not only the most honourable course to be pursued, but also the most agreeable, as it might afford an immediate opportunity of taking revenge upon the common enemies of all the aboriginal race, and if the Great Spirit should favour our efforts, might preserve our country from desolation and our families from insult and distress. But they [i.e., many people of the Six Nations] seemed determined in the resolution which they had taken, excepting a small party of the Mohawks, and even these, seeing so great a majority of a different opinion, hesitated to make the speech which they had prepared for the occasion. Encouraging them by observing that whatever might be the real sentiments of their hearts, they should speak without disguise, an aged blind warrior then arose, and addressing himself to the general, said, "Brother: when our ancestors first saw the English, they took each other by the hand, and became friends. Since that time, they have risked in every war, and many have fallen. We are now much reduced in number, but we are, notwithstanding, determined to conquer or fall in espousing the same cause for which our ancestors have fought and bled."[14]

---

13 JN's prose suggests that he met privately with Major-General Isaac Brock, possibly with a few of his associates, rather than at a public assembly. Such meetings around councils were common, and often it was at these discussions that people made important decisions; but participants in these gatherings risked offending those who were not involved in them or who saw their concerns compromised because of these conversations. Brock realized that resolving the question of the Haldimand Grant was more complex than he had thought it would be when he said earlier that he would try to secure Haudenosaunee title; and, with hostilities with the United States looming, he did not have the time (or the ability) to pursue the matter with the government in England.

14 The meaning of "speaking without disguise" suggests that JN thought some people had been intimidated or otherwise felt they had to be careful about expressing their views. The blind warrior's identity is unknown, but at that time he and JN belonged to a minority willing to fight alongside the British.

In June 1812, a deputation of the younger chiefs from the Senecas, Onondagas, and Cayugas living within the American boundary came to the council fire at the Grand River. They avowed their motive was to commune with their brethren that they might avoid involving themselves in the difficulties attendant on war.[15] The chiefs and warriors of the Grand River assembled, and on the first day, the Senecas opening the council after the usual salutations, Billy, as speaker for the deputation, arose and spoke to this purport: "Brother: we have come from our homes to warn you, that you may preserve yourselves and families from distress. We discover that the British and the Americans are on the eve of a war. They are in dispute respecting some rights on the sea, with which we are unacquainted.[16] Should it end in a contest, let us keep

15 The Haudenosaunee delegation from western New York visited the Grand River early in June 1812, before the United States declared war on Great Britain but after the Americans had entered hostilities with the Western Tribes in 1811. They wanted the meeting to be secret, but British officials learned about it, with JN playing a role in providing information to the colonial authorities (Jean-Baptiste Rousseaux to William Claus, 7 June 1812, published in Johnston, *Six Nations*, 193–4). Rousseaux noted that the chiefs carried a message from Red Jacket (Sagayewatha), and his description of its content aligned with those recorded by JN. Thus, this older leader had his views communicated through these "younger chiefs." At the time, Red Jacket preferred neutrality, but later entered hostilities as an American ally. Rousseaux also recorded that the delegates from New York had told JN that they did not all agree, and that a few of them held pro-British views. Often in native diplomacy, opponents of one party accompanied the delegates of another to councils to monitor discussions, limit the other group's influence, and create opportunities for alternative outcomes.

16 The words about "rights on the sea" reflect the public pronouncements of the American government, and perhaps the republic's officials had suggested the delegates use them. Yet it was clear to anyone who thought about international relations that the reasons for the approaching war were more complex. Nevertheless, Britain used its navy to control trade in the quest to defeat Napoleonic France and its allies, and those measures hurt American commercial interests, even though the republic's overall trade expanded before 1812 because of wartime opportunities. Outside of these immediate challenges, the United States wanted to open trading opportunities beyond those it enjoyed in peacetime, contrary to British restrictions. In addition, the Royal Navy searched for deserters from its ships in hopes of maintaining the fighting capacity of its under-strength crews, and conscripted or "impressed" sailors into the service, some of whom were Americans who had no connection to Britain or its navy. That practice insulted the dignity and sovereignty of the United States (although the number of people involved was much smaller than commonly asserted, and many of those seized,

aloof. Why should we again fight and call upon ourselves the resentment of the conquerors? We know that neither of these powers have any regard for us. In the former war, we espoused the cause of the King. We thought it the most honourable (all our former treaties having been made with his representatives). After contending seven years without ever listening to the pacific overtures sent from the enemy, we found that peace was concluded across the sea, and that our enemy claimed our territory in consequence of the boundary line then acceded to. We found none to assist us to obtain justice. We were compelled to rely on ourselves and make the best of it. Experience has convinced us of their neglect except when they want us. Why then should we endanger the

---

despite their American citizenship, were in fact deserters from the King's service and legally obliged to return to the fleet). Faced with the potential of hostilities with its former colonies, George III's ministers tried to restore harmony, including altering economic restrictions, offering trade opportunities, and returning illegally impressed sailors. The administration in Washington, however, did not respond positively to these initiatives and failed to use them to negotiate a resolution of tensions between the two powers. For its part, the government in London could not make many concessions if it hoped to defeat Napoleon Bonaparte and prevent the island kingdom from becoming a French vassal state. Beyond maritime issues, people in the United States wanted to conquer all or part of Britain's North American possessions. Their reasons included nationalistic dreams, anglophobia, economic opportunism, and desires to punish the United Kingdom for its practices on the high seas. Furthermore, the administration of President James Madison wanted to deprive the former mother country of North American resources outside of Washington's control, thereby enabling the United States to dictate its will internationally by threatening to withhold essential military and commercial goods from Great Britain. As well, southern expansionists dreamt of annexing Spanish colonies, and thought the conquest of Canada would help their cause. Other factors – such as overcoming internal threats to the hold on power exercised by Madison and his Democratic-Republican party – contributed to the American declaration of war, with conquest being the primary goal of its armed forces. Beyond these varied factors, Americans justified their belligerency by accusing the British of inciting the Western Tribes to resist settler expansion within the boundaries of the republic. The reality, however, was that officials in Canada had tried to prevent native-newcomer violence in the Old Northwest before the outbreak of the Anglo-American war in order to discourage Washington from finding an excuse to invade the colonies. Yet at the same time, the Indian Department's agents realized that they would need help from the First Nations in American territory (along with the support they could obtain from the aboriginal population in Canada) if the United States were to declare war. Therefore, they tried to manage the need to prevent indigenous hostility as long as peace continued, but provided sufficient help and friendship so that the tribes would ally with the King if Anglo-American hostilities were to break out.

comfort, even the existence of our families, to enjoy their smiles only for the day in which they need us? The American agent who lives in our neighbourhood has told us that the United States does not require our assistance, that their number is endless and adequate to every emergency of war. This entirely meets our sentiments. We are in their power, but we do not wish to join them in war. Brother: we entreat that you also sit still in your habitations, regardless of the tempest of battle. You may thus escape unhurt and unobserved by the enraged combatants. Let us now pledge ourselves to each other to observe a strict neutrality. We may then meet again with our hearts unclouded by disagreeable circumstances when the storm of war shall have blown over and left the sky clear without a threatening cloud. We hope our words may penetrate your hearts. Take this wampum in token of our sincerity."[17]

Taking the wampum, the people of the Grand River withdrew to deliberate.[18] At this time, there was a party among the Mohawks strongly inclined to pursue the line of conduct recommended by the deputation from the other side and ambitious to inculcate similar sentiments into the minds of all the people of the Grand River. This called forth more strongly the exertions of the firm and loyal to render steady such as wavered from the apprehension of the great number and power of the Americans, so strongly vaunted by themselves and in the various

---

17 Little Billy (Jishkaaga) was a respected Seneca leader who had fought in the American Revolution as a Crown ally but served alongside the republic's forces in the War of 1812. While JN spoke about the delegation from New York comprising "younger chiefs," Billy was an older man. Much of Jishkaaga's presentation focused on the betrayal felt by the Haudenosaunee after fighting as allies of white forces in the revolution. The agent he mentioned was Erastus Granger. Like many people, Granger believed that the conquest of Canada would not be difficult; therefore, he said that the United States would not need First Nations assistance. He also shared a common view that encouraging the Iroquois to embrace neutrality was the best that the Americans could expect, because the republic's relations with the Six Nations were so bad that it would not be reasonable to think that the tribes would support it in war (although that view would prove to be unduly pessimistic). Granger was so doubtful of indigenous intentions that he threatened those who lived in New York and Pennsylvania with extinction should they ally with the British (Benn, *Iroquois in the War of 1812*, 30). On another occasion, when describing pre-war meetings, JN noted that "it would have been highly impolite" of the Americans "to have asked openly for any assistance, considering the detestation in which they are held by the tribes of aborigines in general" (*JMJN*, 274).

18 By presenting a string or belt of wampum, Little Billy demonstrated that his words represented his delegation's authoritative position.

rumours circulating through Upper Canada. It took up two days before an answer could be made for the Senecas.[19] In that time, two of their most respectable chiefs, calling upon me, entered into conversation to this effect: "Friend: we view you with apprehension and suspicion. We think you so zealously disposed to serve the King that you are inclined to draw after you all these people without considering the difficulties in which you may thereby involve them. Perhaps you also imagine that we come here entirely under the influence of the American agent, only prepared to rehearse the lesson he may have given us. We may both be mistaken. To convince you that we act from a disinterested love to our people and to ensure their welfare and preservation, we shall lay before you the reasons which induced us to recommend a neutrality. The gloomy day, foretold by our ancients, has at last arrived. The independence and glory of the Five Nations has departed from us. We find ourselves in the hands of two powerful nations who can crush us when they please. They are the same in every respect, although they are now preparing to contend. We are ignorant of the real motives which urge them to arm, but we are well assured that we have no interest therein, and that neither one nor other has any affection towards us. We know that our blood, shed in their battles, will not even ensure their compassion to our widows and orphans, nor respect to our tribes weakened in their contests. Has not our nation partaken in every war in which the English have been engaged since they first joined hands (for then the English and Americans were one)? In standing between them and the French, many a valiant warrior has fallen. But although we have thus been weakened and deprived of our independence, it has not been by the victories of a conqueror. It has been [by] the neglect or unkindness of our friends. Seeing, therefore, that no good can be derived from war, we think we should only seek the surest means of averting its attendant evils. We are of opinion that we should follow the example of some of their people who never bear arms in war, and deprecate the principle of hostility."[20]

---

19 Taking two days to reply to a visiting delegation was normal within Haudenosaunee council protocols.

20 We do not know who the "respectable chiefs" were. The discussions that occurred were private conversations outside of the official council. While such encounters were important, we rarely have records of what people said in them. JN represented this speech, as well as Billy's, with sympathy, and presumably accuracy, despite his opposing views. He regularly commented with fairness upon the opinions and actions of those with whom he disagreed. In terms of the history the Senecas

I answered, "What you have now said is certainly applicable to you who remain on the other side. The Americans have gained possession of all your country, excepting the small part which you have reserved. They have enveloped you. It is out of your power to assist us, because in doing so you would hazard the destruction of your families. You can, however, have no motive to assist them. The King does not want to take your lands nor to injure you, and the Americans will not give you more for assisting them. Even should your actions or courage merit a glorious report, they will hardly allow you that which they bargain for themselves. It is, therefore, both your interest and your duty to remain peaceable at home. Our situation is very different. You know that the preference to live under the protection of the King rather than fall under the power or influence of the Americans induced us to fix our habitations at this place. If the King is attacked, we must support him. We are sure that such conduct is honourable. But how profitable it might be to submit to these 'mighty men' without resistance we can by no means ascertain. We know that we would feel it highly disgraceful, and we remember what has been the fate of those who have thought that a passive, inoffensive demeanour would be a sufficient protection. Witness the peaceful people of Conestoga butchered at Lancaster, the harmless Moravian Delawares murdered at their own village on Muskingum, and many other instances that clearly demonstrate a manly resistance to be the strongest security against armed enemies like them, who invade us with their host of new-made soldiers, only confident of awing by the pomp of military parade and numbers. We know them to have always been the enemies of the aboriginal nations. Last autumn, they commenced their grand military achievements, and marched against the village of Tippecanoe. Astonished at the resistance of a few warriors whom they found there, they returned home to meditate on a more easy method of conquering."[21]

---

recited, their ancestors and others from the Six Nations had allied with the French during some of the struggles for control of North America before 1759. Therefore, the comment that implied that they were British allies was overstated; however, the overall sentiments captured widely held views based on understanding native-newcomer relations over previous decades, especially in relation to the land losses that had occurred through fraud and diplomacy independently of military events. JN inserted a footnote to identify the people who never bear arms as "the Quakers." At the time, these pacifist Christians operated missions among the Senecas in New York.

21 During the Pontiac War in 1763 white vigilantes in Pennsylvania, known as the Paxton Boys, killed 20 peaceful Conestogas or Susquehannocks. In 1782, towards

These men spoke openly their minds. There were others who, I discovered, had been spreading dreadful alarms of the immense preparations of the Americans: that they would cross the line with a great force from Detroit, from Presque Isle to Long Point, from Black Rock to Fort Erie, and that another army would invade Lower Canada whilst the country people in many places would espouse the cause of the enemy.[22] These reports alarmed the women, and indeed seemed to cause many others to waver. An apparent majority, however, unanimously determined to give the following answer, whilst the wavering retired: "Brothers: we thank you for this further proof of your affection, which you have now shown us in coming to forewarn us of impending danger.[23] We lament with you the situation in which we are now placed by being separated. You have fallen under the power of those who were once our enemies, and are likely to become so again. They have encompassed you, and as we cannot extricate you from the difficulties in which you are involved, we recommend to you peace, and request that you restrain all your young men from becoming subservient to the Americans. We would be ashamed of our tribes should any be found among the common enemy of our race. They have said that they require no assistance. Keep them to their word. In the former war, they held the same language to the Oneidas, but when they had them in their power, they insisted on

---

the end of the American Revolution, rebel militia murdered 96 pacifist Delawares at the Moravian mission of Gnadenhutten in Ohio on a tributary of the Muskingum River. The reference to the "village of Tippecanoe" was to the battle of that name outside Prophetstown on 7 November 1811. In the fighting, 1,000 Americans suffered high casualties but held the field against 500 warriors, and then burned the native settlement after its residents abandoned it (but they rebuilt it afterwards). Note JN's dismissal of the American army's competence, largely comprising "new-made" (and thus not well-trained) soldiers recruited during the approach of war. Nevertheless, the size of the republic's military resources was worrisome in comparison to British forces in North America.

22 The government in Washington had planned a multi-pronged invasion of Canadian territory to achieve a quick conquest by dividing the outnumbered British defenders, but was not able to coordinate such a campaign. JN's "country people" were settlers, the majority of whom were economic immigrants from the United States and their children.

23 With people retiring from the council, the visitors from New York and the representatives of the British Indian Department on the scene realized that the content of the speech possessed only limited support. JN seems to have acknowledged this through his use of "apparent majority."

their joining, and you know we found them in arms combined with our enemies, and many of them have fallen by our hands.[24] Brothers: our forefathers, when they first took the English by the hand, agreed to risk with them. When those who had surrounded our villages under the name of brothers raised their arm against our father the King, we all joined him because he was our father. At the peace, we removed here to live under his protection, and if he is now attacked, we will risk with him. We are not alarmed at the boasted numbers of the Americans, for it is he who dwells above that will decide on our fate. We cannot lie down at ease when our father is threatened. He has not yet given us the hatchet, but should the enemy invade us suddenly, we hope to find something wherewith to strike. Brothers: we will never consider you as belonging to them. We will caution all our western brethren not to hurt you in striking at the Americans who dwell around you. May the Great Spirit preserve you in peace!"[25] Many of these people [from the visiting delegation] expressed the most earnest desire that the peace might continue without interruption. They appeared very sensible of the awkward situation in which they were placed, and notwithstanding the pacific language of the Americans, they apprehended that they might entice some of their thoughtless young men to join them.

A few days after the departure of these people, we gained notice of the declaration of war. It was then all bustle throughout the country, calling together the militia and making every preparation to meet the

---

24 As noted earlier, most Oneidas (and Tuscaroras) had allied with the rebels during the American Revolution. Once the United States won its independence, they found themselves forced to alienate land in New York as much as those who had fought beside Crown forces. At the time JN spoke these words, the Americans had told natives within their borders that they did not need their help, but they changed their minds soon afterwards.

25 The "western brethren" mainly were non-Haudenosaunee natives, such as the Shawnees in the Western Tribal Confederacy, but the phrase captures a sense of solidarity across indigenous communities, at least in spirit if not in reality. JN inserted a footnote after the word "hatchet": "Implying that they had not yet been called upon to take up arms." When native people used the term "father" in reference to a head of state or his representative, they conceptualized it in indigenous terms as someone who cared for his "children" and had obligations towards them, but who did not exercise control over them. That difference from Euro-American concepts generated confusion among contemporary observers and later scholars. Someone other than JN probably gave the speech, judging from the personal nature of the description of historical events in which he had not participated.

attack expected.[26] The people of the Grand River met again in council, although I had supposed that already they had decided on the part they would take. A small party only repaired to Niagara, and many of these not the most steady men. General Brock, however, received me with that pleasing affability so natural to him, and appeared as well satisfied as if there had been with me a thousand men. He asked me, "Can you confide in the people of the Grand River? Do you think that they will be faithful to you? Tell me without reserve." I replied, "They are unfortunately divided into parties, and there are some plausible men who succeed in retarding their coming forth; but when they engage, I have no doubts they are not so depraved as to be faithless. It will be necessary, however, in order to render them steady and permanently serviceable, to allow them a regular stipend for their support. Otherwise, want will oblige them to return to their usual occupations for the support of their families, their present situation being now very different from what it was when they possessed an extensive country, abounding in game, wide ranges for cattle, and were protected from the sudden assaults of the enemy by a desert frontier." He answered that he saw clearly the propriety of my remark, at the same time adding that he thought goods might answer the purpose better than money.[27]

---

26 The Anglo-American conflict began when President James Madison signed the war bill in Washington on 18 June 1812. People along the Grand River probably learned about the outbreak within a day or so of word reaching the Niagara Peninsula on 25 June.

27 Isaac Brock's headquarters were at Fort George near the mouth of the Niagara River. At the end of June or beginning of July, 100 Grand River men went there, representing a respectable portion of the tract's 400 warriors, although JN's comment suggests that few of them were committed to fighting. Presumably, some went to evaluate the situation along the border and to acquire weapons and supplies as gifts from the Crown, as had occurred in previous conflicts. While JN was impressed with Brock, the major-general distrusted the Six Nations. He knew that some contemplated allying with the Americans and realized that most of the community favoured neutrality at that moment. The situation along the Grand worried him because he believed that Haudenosaunee help was critical for the preservation of Upper Canada. Not only would their warriors significantly augment his small professional military force of 1,600, but the response of other natives in the colony would be based partly on Iroquois decisions. Brock also feared that militiamen in the Lake Erie region would not muster if they thought the Six Nations might remain neutral or join the invaders. Brock agreed with JN that he might need to provide payments to improve relations with the warriors and their families, but there was a severe shortage of specie in Upper Canada, which would make it almost impossible

From what passed within our observation on the opposite side of the [Niagara] River, it appeared that the enemy had not as yet collected any considerable force there. With us, the militia of the adjacent country had assembled and made a formidable appearance. A proportion of them, called the flank companies, were retained to do duty with the [regular] troops, and the main body was permitted to return home [so] that the agriculture might not be too much neglected.[28]

At this time, the commander on the American side wrote a letter to General Brock, intimating that some chiefs of the Senecas, desiring to communicate with their brethren on the Canadian shore, had required him to ask permission for them to come over to meet them. He acceded to their proposition and requested me to meet them with some chiefs at Queenston, as it would not be prudent to admit them into the country where they might have ascertained the quality and quantity of our force. At Queenston, we met the Senecas, or Ondowaga. The principal man was named Arosa. (One of his ancestors of the same name was a celebrated warrior in the French war, remarkable for his fidelity to the English, by whom he was called Silverheels.)[29] They were saluted with much cordiality. They seemed strongly impressed with the importance of their mission, and after having been seated for a few minutes, Arosa

---

to do so. Therefore, he offered presents, as had been traditional when white powers met native material needs. The Crown also regularly provided accommodation, transportation, food, and other assistance to support war parties and their families during campaigns. (The military did provide cash from time to time, such as to pay warriors for prisoners or to cover travel costs.) Gift-giving, aside from providing straightforward economic benefits, helped compensate people for losses sustained by not pursuing their usual activities, and also represented tangible expressions of alliance, affection, and respect for native communities.

28 The Upper Canadian militia flank companies during the early part of the war consisted of volunteers who received more training than the rest of the militia (who comprised most of the military-aged male civilians in the province). They were different from the flank companies – the elite grenadiers and the light infantry – of regular line infantry battalions, which, along with eight line or battalion companies, typically formed an infantry battalion with a collective strength of 500–800 men (but the number of soldiers could be greater or smaller). On the American side, as in Canada, obligations to serve in the militia were close to universal, although many men joined "volunteer" regiments or other units drawn from the militia to participate more actively in the war.

29 Arosa (George Silverheels) was a Seneca leader. His ancestor was a prominent chief during the Seven Years' War and participated on the British side in the Cherokee War of 1759–61, in which JN's father came under the care of Scottish soldiers.

stood forth, holding some wampum in his hand. He thus began, "Brothers: feeling that tender anxiety for your welfare, which should always influence people of the same blood and kindred, we have come to you to explain the sentiments of our hearts. It was our intention to have abode with you some days [on the Grand River], to gratify our eyes with a sight of our brethren, but the gathering clouds of war, covering the earth with the gloom of darkness, forbid us passing this place. We shall, therefore, deliver immediately what moves within our breasts. Brothers: our hearts overflow with tenderness when we look upon you. We lament that you are on the eve of being plunged into the miseries of war, and we beseech you to avert them by remaining peaceably at home, unmindful of the din of arms. We know that war is destructive, its conclusion may be ruinous, and it is well ascertained that misery is its constant attendant. Brothers: the people of the great King are our old friends, and the Americans are our neighbours. We grieve to see them prepare to imbrue their hands in the blood of each other. We have determined not to interfere; for how could we spill the blood of the English or of our brethren? We entreat you, therefore, to imitate our determination. For, remember, we are in the power of the Americans, and perhaps when you shall have spread destruction through their ranks, they will change their language, and insist upon us to join them. They may compel our young men to fight against their kindred, and like devoted animals, we shall be brought to destroy each other."[30]

After deliberating a few minutes, an Onondaga chief arose, and as speaker for the people of the Grand River, answered in their behalf, "Brothers: we have heard your words with pleasure, because we know they proceed from the goodness of your heart. We regret that we are separated, for if we had been living together we would have been of one mind. Brothers: you know that we removed from the country of

---

30 The meeting at the border village of Queenston occurred on 12 July. As well as Senecas, some Onondagas formed part of the mission from New York. Another record of this council – which aligns well with JN's – noted that Arosa spoke on behalf of the "chief warriors" and that someone else spoke for the women (Council Minutes, 12 July 1812, AO, F1015, Correspondence 1812–14, 1–3). The Americans already had begun to change their mind about employing Haudenosaunee warriors alongside their troops. A few days earlier, the Indian agent, Erastus Granger, had stated that the United States did not need native support; nevertheless, 150–200 warriors could join the Americans (Granger, Speech, 6 July 1812, Public Speeches, 17–18).

our ancestors when overhung by the power of the Americans in order to place ourselves under the protection of the King. He does not desire to invade the Americans, but if they follow us here to attack our father, we cannot be passive spectators. We must share the same fate with him. We shall participate in the shout of victory – or in the grave – whichever he who rules may allot us. Brothers: we commend your resolution not to join in the approaching contest. You can have no interest therein; but we regret that we shall be separated. May he to whom we look for aid protect you!"[31]

Arosa stood forth again, and spoke thus: "Brothers: we see our words have no effect, but we are easy. We have done what we judged our duty, and we perceive you have made your election. Therefore, we shall yet further exhort you. As you will join with Europeans in their wars, imitate their example in humanely treating your prisoners. Let the warrior's rage only be felt in combat by his armed opponents. Let the unoffending cultivator of the ground and his helpless family never be alarmed by your onset, nor injured by your depredation. And you, Teyoninhokarawen: we exhort you that, as the Five Nations listen to your words, you will help them and endeavour to make them happy in the favour of the great King, and should you pass through the chance of war, be to them a protector. May he who dwells above the clouds avert every evil from your heads, and lead you by the hand!" He ended, bidding us adieu in a manner truly affecting, while every feature expressed the sensibility of his heart, and they recrossed the river.[32]

---

31 This person's identity is unclear. While JN noted that he was a chief, speakers often were not, being instead people who could represent the views of their community with eloquence.

32 The reference to European warfare's restrictions were overstated, but one of the great problems the Haudenosaunee in New York faced was the hatred Americans expressed towards them, which white society used partly as an excuse to exploit them. That hostility arose in partial response to the traumas (often exaggerated) of settlers who suffered when war parties in the American Revolution destroyed farms and villages and inflicted casualties on civilians in order to defend native land and to reduce the ability of the rebels to feed their armies.

2

Opening Moves, Disunion, and the Capture Of Detroit, 1812

John Norton continued his narrative with the story of his small band of followers from the Six Nations engaging a reconnaissance mission on the American side of the Niagara border in mid-July 1812. He then shifted his story to the west. First, he stopped at the Grand River, where the majority of people remained unwilling to participate in the conflict, which he blamed partly on the behaviour of the Indian Department. Then, late in the month, he began an overland journey through the native and white communities of southwestern Upper Canada as he made his way to the Detroit River boundary between Upper Canada and the Michigan Territory. In opposition to the broad consensus among the Six Nations at that point, which favoured neutrality, he joined efforts to repel the first American army to cross into British territory, which had invaded in mid-July. As we saw earlier, the province's defensive posture appeared to be grim. The King's forces were outnumbered, the militia seemed unreliable, and most native people within Canada chose neutrality, as did many to the south, including most of those who lived along the Detroit River and had not joined the Western Tribal Confederacy around Tecumseh and Tenskwatawa at that time.

Major-General Isaac Brock responded to the American threat and the prevailing gloom with boldness, not only to defeat the invaders but also to convince people that the situation was not hopeless. In August, he travelled to the Detroit front with reinforcements from Niagara and elsewhere, and allied with Tecumseh, whose warriors had moved north to the border to take part in the impending confrontation. As the two forces prepared to oppose their common American enemy, news arrived from the head of Lake Michigan that Fort Mackinac had fallen to the British in mid-July. That event encouraged some of the neutralists and the wavering, both native and newcomer, to rally

*against the United States as the Detroit campaign progressed to its denoue-
ment in mid-August.*

⁓ᥱᢣᠪᥱ⁓

At this time abundant and various were the rumours of preparations-
making by the enemy on the opposite shore [of the Niagara River]
wherewith to assail us, and the rear of the Grand Island [within New
York] was one of the points particularly suspected because it was concealed from our view.[1] Some of the counsellors of Canada proposed
that the Indians should encamp on the island as a party of observation.
General Brock objected to remaining stationary there, as the enemy
might lay a plan for cutting them off, while the want of boats would
put it out of his power to render them immediate succour. He only
required us to make every possible observation on the opposite shore.
We examined every recess without making any discovery, and after
returning to the mainland, we heard that an express had arrived from
Amherstburg with the information that General Hull, with an army of
some thousand men, had crossed from Detroit and had taken possession of Sandwich.[2]

The want of unanimity among the Five Nations and the small number that acted with any degree of steadiness at this time afforded no
promising prospect of their service redounding much to their credit.
I, therefore, hearing of this invasion, thought it a fit time to make an
essay, and if I could not succeed [in gathering Grand River support],
I intended to have left them and the Indian Department together, and,

---

1 JN's text says "Grand River" rather than "Grand Island," but that was an error.
2 Brigadier-General William Hull, governor of the Michigan Territory, crossed the
   Detroit River and seized Sandwich (in today's Windsor) with somewhat more than
   half of the 2,000 men under his command. At the time, Detroit, with 700 civilians, was
   the largest Euro-American community in that area, protected by a fort and smaller
   defensive works. At Amherstburg, 16 miles south of Sandwich, the British had a fort
   with more than 300 regulars when Hull invaded. It served as a garrison and depot,
   supported the Indian Department's operations, and commanded the waterway
   between Lake Erie and points north. The British, who maintained a naval station near
   the fort, had a stronger waterborne presence in the area than their opponents (and
   captured the one American vessel in the region on 2 July). Many of the Canadian
   militia, however, either deserted or refused to muster during the early weeks of the
   conflict.

with my friends, to have acted as volunteers wherever occasion might offer. With this intention, I called upon General Brock and proposed to go with whatever number of men I could collect, and taking post at the mouth of the River Tranche or Thames, endeavour to prevent the American army from obtaining any supplies from that quarter and observe their movements.[3] He appeared to approve of the proposal, and required me to come to an early breakfast next morning. I found his mind prepared, and that it was arranged that a detachment of the Long Point Militia and a party of picked men of the 41st Regiment under Major Chambers should also take the same destination.[4] The general said, as we were about to part, "Be united in whatever you undertake, and communicate freely your sentiments on whatever suggestions may arise from the discoveries you make."

We set out on different roads because I had to pass by the lower village on the Grand River and from thence ascend.[5] Arriving there, I found the people all [had] gone to the Onondaga village to council, and heard that since we had been on the lines they had sent a message to the tribes about Detroit to enquire of them if their intention was to take an active part in the war or not, and had got an answer, for deliberating on which they were assembled. On my way to that place, I met numbers coming away, and perceived that the answer from the westward had been expressed decidedly in favour of neutrality, and that these were the sentiments they had generally imbibed.[6]

I had sent a confidential and faithful chief before me to the council fire.[7] On arriving there, he informed me that in consequence of the news

---

3 The Thames River (formerly La Tranche), flowing through southwestern Upper Canada to Lake St Clair, was an important communications corridor north of Lake Erie. This meeting between JN and Isaac Brock occurred around 20 July.

4 As was common practice, Captain Peter Chambers (of the 41st Regiment of Foot) held the local rank of major so that he, as a regular officer, would outrank less-experienced militia officers of similar status. His detachment of 50 soldiers was part of the general movement of men and resources to the Detroit front.

5 The lowest native village on the Grand River was a small Seneca community near a ford in the river.

6 JN arrived at the Grand around 22 July, where he learned that the natives in the Detroit region overwhelmingly had decided to remain neutral, not yet having joined the Western Tribes. Their stance helped to influence the majority of Haudenosaunee to do the same. JN seems to have sent a letter to Isaac Brock informing him of the situation (Brock to Sir George Prevost, 26 July 1812, LAC, RG8, 676:208).

7 This person's identity is unclear.

which they had heard, they unanimously had determined to take no
part in the war; and that one of the messengers (an Oneida), leaving the
Wyandot village in a state of intoxication and passing along the main
road, had been taken hold of by the Americans and brought before General Hull, who had sent by him a proclamation expressing his pacific
disposition towards the Five Nations and the inhabitants of the country
in general, providing they should not, by resistance, draw upon themselves his resentment, promising to confirm to them every right and
privilege to which they were entitled, and boasting in the most exalted
strain of the irresistible power of the formidable army he led, to whom
it would be madness to oppose resistance. From the impression which I
perceived this had made upon their minds, it seemed useless to lose any
time with them. I therefore determined to pass without delay, observing that I was ashamed to find that the words of the enemy were so
eagerly received and so sincerely obeyed, although it was well-known
to all who reflected on the past that it was his usual method to gain
victories rather by deceitful speeches than by hard fighting, and that his
impudence in offering terms and threatening with his resentment those
who resisted him – as if he had really been our master – was enough to
fill the heart of every honest warrior with indignation, and impel him
to inflict due punishment on the vain boaster; but as numbers did not
always ensure victory, so the lack of mine should never dishearten me
from trying the enemy when a good cause encouraged me to trust in
him above who decides the event of battles.[8]

---

8 The identity of the Oneida is unknown, but JN probably meant to discredit him by
   commenting on his intoxication. We do not know in which Wyandot village the
   meeting occurred, but Brownstown (or Big Rock) in Michigan was the main council
   site in the region. William Hull's proclamation to the Six Nations stated: "The
   powerful army under my command is now in possession of Canada. To you who
   are friendly it will afford safety and protection. All your lands and all your rights of
   every kind will be guaranteed to you if you will take no part against us. I salute you
   in friendship, and hope you will now act such a part as will promote your interests,
   your safety, and happiness. May the Great Spirit guide you in person" (Hull to the
   Iroquois, 12 July 1812, published in Wood, *British Documents*, 1:359). Hull seemed
   to have known about Haudenosaunee fears of American power and their concerns
   to preserve their lands and freedoms. The general also issued a proclamation to the
   province's settlers, offering protection if they did not take up arms, but declared that
   "no white man found fighting on the side of an Indian will be taken prisoner. Instant
   destruction will be his lot" (Hull to the Inhabitants of Canada, 13 July 1812, ibid.,
   357). Hull's words to the white population undermined the sincerity of his message

At the Mohawk village, I expected to have been readily joined, from their great professions of loyalty, but I was disappointed.[9] I found them only disposed to council, in which they were joined by the people from below who had followed me, and were very cautious [about] what they said to the disparagement of the message that had been received from the west.[10] Tekarihogen, one of their village chiefs, had the impudence to make a speech setting forth the power and moderation of the Americans, and the probability of Amherstburg having already fallen before them. He was, however, so severely retorted upon that he withdrew.[11] The war hatchet was taken up and the war song sung by the warriors.[12]

---

to the native people, because it implied both hatred of, and threats to, indigenous communities, and thus subsequently helped influence the Haudenosaunee to oppose the Americans once they reflected on the nature of the two messages, and once the British and Western Tribes achieved some victories. Isaac Brock countered with a declaration linking the white and indigenous populations in a common cause. He asked by what "new principle" did Hull think the natives were "to be prohibited from defending their property," noting that "they are men, and have equal rights with all other men to defend themselves and their property when invaded, more especially when they find in the enemy's camp a ferocious and mortal foe, using the same warfare which the American commander affects to reprobate" (Brock to the People of Upper Canada, 22 July 1812, published in Tupper, *Brock*, 190–1).

9 This comment suggests that even individuals within the pro-British Mohawk party would not take up arms.

10 The "people from below" lived along the Grand River south of the Mohawk settlement.

11 The British fort at Amherstburg had not fallen. Henry Tekarihogen had fought against the rebels in the American Revolution, had been instrumental along with Joseph Brant in founding the Grand River community in the 1780s, had promoted the modernization of the Iroquois economy as Brant and JN did, and had been a member of their party, although the association between him and JN had ended before the war. In 1811, Tekarihogen had been "dehorned," or removed from his role as the most prominent Mohawk hereditary confederacy chief, when people became angry over his attempt to sell some Six Nations land to his white son-in-law. He interpreted for the British Indian Department and worked with its officials, but the department's efforts to thwart his desires regarding Haudenosaunee land tenure undermined his support for the Crown. With the coming of war, Tekarihogen became a leader in the tract's pro-American party. He also may have been one of a number of people who provided intelligence to the Americans on the state of Iroquois affairs. Soon after the incident described here, he moved to New York, but later returned to Canada, re-embraced the British alliance, and fought at Beaver Dams.

12 War songs, dances, prayers, and other religious acts were important in honouring and harnessing spiritual power to aid people embarking on campaign. For these themes related to war described by or recorded from JN, see, *JMJN*, 111–13, 152–3;

A Mohawk (a confidential interpreter of the deputy superintendent-general of Indian affairs) then said on his behalf that he had requested they would not weaken themselves too much at home, but retain a sufficient number to watch the mouth of the [Grand] River. In consequence of this request, the people from below engaged to perform the part of a lookout at the mouth of the river.[13] A spirited young warrior of the Cayugas (the son of Karhagohha or Hawk) exclaimed, "I will go to the west, where I am assured I shall meet an enemy; but why should I go to the mouth of the river, unless to catch fish? The enemy will not cross the lake so wide while the ships of the great King hold the command."[14]

A considerable party promised to be ready in two days. Indeed, so much occupied were many in [the] harvest that I could not rely upon them in less than a week.[15] I determined, therefore, to join Major

---

Boyce, "Iroquois Cultural History"; Headley, "Account," 12 March 1805, NYSL. See also Benn, *Iroquois in the War of 1812*, 87–8. JN demonstrated a war dance in England, startling his audience with the "violence of his gesticulations indicative of defiance or combat preparatory to a last desperate leap, when he inflicted the deathblow on his adversary" (Shore, *Reminiscences*, 1:6).

13 The "confidential interpreter" was George Martin (JN to J.B. Glegg, 11 August 1812, LAC, RG10, 487:4454). If we can assume that the Indian Department did not share Martin's views, his words would indicate that his primary loyalty was to his people, despite claiming to speak on the department's behalf.

14 The name of the son of Karhagohha is unknown. Watching the mouth of the Grand River was pointless from a strategic perspective, because the Americans did not have vessels to cross Lake Erie in strength at that time. Assembling at the river's mouth, however, reflected a consensus within the divided Six Nations. It served as a gesture of alliance towards the British, who had the ability to punish them should they decide that the Haudenosaunee were not friendly, but it kept warriors safe from harm until they knew how the coming contest between Isaac Brock and William Hull would conclude. Once that occurred, the people of the Grand could decide how best to respond. They could disperse their force as a demonstration of neutrality if Hull won, or they could ally with the British if Brock triumphed, or they even could fall upon the King's forces as they retreated in the face of an American victory in order to put the invaders in their debt, as General Brock feared they might. One knowledgeable observer thought that the Iroquois that summer were "preparing to join the enemy who had invaded us with a much stronger force than we could bring against them; not that they preferred the enemy, but they considered our case desperate and they thought that by joining the Americans early they might preserve their lands" (John Strachan to William Wilberforce, 1 November 1812, published in Spragge, *Strachan Letter Book*, 21–2).

15 While this sentence seems to contradict the earlier statement that few would take up arms, JN meant a smaller number than we might assume by the word

Chambers at Oxford with those that were ready (promising to wait another two days for such as followed), as the body of militia expected to join him from Long Point had refused to undertake the expedition, and he was there with a handful of troops, exposed to an attack should the scouts of the enemy be as enterprising as had been reported. When I came there, I found Major Chambers and his little party of the 41st without having received any reinforcements from the militia to encourage him to proceed.[16] Those of the Five Nations who had promised to follow me did not come at the time appointed, and I perceived the confidential Mohawk interpreter was using his utmost endeavours to induce the others to turn back.[17] Therefore, to put him to the test, I directed

---

"considerable." At least a portion of those who intended to go to the Detroit River rejected the community's consensus that favoured neutrality, but Haudenosaunee freedoms allowed individuals to take actions that other societies would not have accepted in terms of foreign relations. JN's decision to fight placed him in a minority position at that moment. Around the end of July JN told someone that he thought 40–50 men represented the largest number of Grand River warriors who would join him on the campaign (Thomas Talbot to Isaac Brock, 27 July 1812, published in Cruikshank, *Documents Related to the Invasion of Canada*, 94).

16 Most militia from Long Point on Lake Erie refused to muster, partly because they were suspicious of Six Nations intentions and did not want to leave their families unprotected in case the warriors should join the Americans. The militia's inaction was a blow to Isaac Brock, who needed to assemble as many men as possible to augment his small professional force. Brock was so concerned about the situation that he thought it might be necessary to move the Haudenosaunee of the Grand away from their tract at some point (although JN did not seem to know this).

17 JN arrived in Oxford around 28–30 July with 12 or 14 warriors (Charles Askin Journal, 30 July 1812, published in Quaife, *Askin Papers*, 2:713). As many as 60 men had accompanied him beforehand but most had returned to the Grand, inspired partly by George Martin, the "confidential interpreter." Some who travelled with JN went along without intending to fight but to dissuade others from continuing on the campaign. When JN arrived on the Detroit River, taking longer than expected to get there, he wrote: "I am sorry that by being necessitated to look for men along the road, I have not had it my power to be expeditious as intended. At the Grand River, they completely deceived me. For, although in council I overcame the machinations of the Teharihogen and General Hull, yet those who promised to follow us have not come, and of these who did set out with me, Mr George Martin and three others returned, discontented for no other reason than because I had neither the means nor the inclination to furnish them with as much whisky as they wanted. But notwithstanding these disappointments I hope God will yet enable us to hurt the enemies of our King and Country" (JN to J.B. Clegg, 11 August 1812, LAC, RG10, 487:4454–5). The comment about the absence of whisky affecting some men's behaviour may have reflected JN's frustration at the moment he penned that letter, in contrast to the more reflective analysis in *JMJN*.

him to take a dispatch to Colonel Procter at Amherstburg.[18] He set out
with three companions, and about half an hour after their departure a
dispatch arrived with the agreeable intelligence of the capture of Michilimackinac from the Americans.[19] A dragoon was sent after him to call
him back that he might take with him this additional good news for the
encouragement of the people of Amherstburg, but he then objected to
go, and the next morning returned to the Grand River.

    Major Chambers receiving orders to repair to Long Point to embark
with more troops and militia, we proceeded alone on the original route
without having been joined by any reinforcement. At Delaware Township we found the militia of that place embodied at the house of a man
called Andrew Westbrook, who having been taken up on suspicion of
favouring the enemy had escaped from custody and gone to them.[20]
Here they were regaling themselves on the store of whisky which he
had left at his house. A party of Chippewas, coming from hunting,
joined us here in the evening. The next day we proceeded to their village, which was only a little out of the main road. It was inhabited by
Munsees and Chippewas.[21] We acquainted them with our business and
urged them to combine with us. They required that evening to prepare,

---

18 Lieutenant-Colonel Henry Procter of the 41st Foot became a brevet colonel in 1810
    and a major-general in June 1813. He assumed command on the Detroit front on 26
    July 1812, and continued to lead the King's forces there, aside from the time Isaac
    Brock was present that summer, until defeated at Moraviantown in October 1813.

19 The commandant of the American fort on Mackinac Island at the northern end of
    Lake Michigan surrendered his garrison of 60 men on 17 July without resistance
    to 45 British soldiers accompanied by 600 warriors and fur traders. As a result,
    the British secured control over the native-newcomer trade in the region and
    communications south through Lake Michigan to the upper Mississippi River. That
    event encouraged a good number of indigenous people in northern Upper Canada
    and the American Old Northwest to enter the war alongside the British, such as the
    previously neutral Wyandots of the Detroit River.

20 Andrew Westbrook was a businessman who sided with the Americans in 1812 and
    encouraged settlers to abandon the British. Later, he led destructive raids against
    Canadian settlements before moving permanently to the United States. JN was in
    this area west of modern London in early August.

21 The main road between York and the Detroit River was Dundas Street. Munsee is
    one of the main sub-groups of the Delawares. After the war, JN wrote about them
    and the Chippewas: "I have reason to be grateful to these people. For at a time when
    the whole population of that part of the country was wavering and alarmed at the
    formidable appearance of General Hull with his proclamations, these joined me,
    thereby furnishing the means of executing the orders of Major-General Sir Isaac

promising to accompany us the next morning, which they performed, and we recommenced our journey with great glee, the woods resounding with the war song. That evening we encamped within a few miles of the Moravian town. Early on the next morning we entered that village. The people expressed great joy at our appearance.[22] They informed us that the Americans had been at the [Thames] River and were intending to come there again for the flour they expected to obtain from the mills (where [an] abundance of grain was deposited), and that they apprehended some of them were now stationed at the mouth of the river.[23]

I sent away the dispatch for Colonel Procter with notice that I would await his answer in a convenient place to intercept the enemy should they attempt to revisit the river. The next morning, while the people were preparing, I proceeded with some young men, mounted. We got notice of some Americans, and coming to the place where they had been lodged, we discovered that they had gone that morning. We pursued, and near sundown came abreast of them. They were in a canoe and opposite to us. On seeing us, they immediately jumped ashore and ran. Before we could reach the opposite shore, they had passed through two fields. We were gaining fast on them when they reached the woods. It was then nearly dark, and they completely eluded our search. We returned to the canoe and found their arms there. They were loaded and the bayonets fixed. This was a prize to us at that time as several of

Brock in preventing the enemy from drawing supplies from the River Thames until that [time] we met him at Sandwich preparatory to the attack upon Detroit" (JN to J.F. Addison, 13 February 1817, LAC, RG8, 261:25–6).

22 Moraviantown, or Fairfield, was a Moravian Christian mission to the Delawares, but included other people. Refugees from the Ohio country had established the community north of the Thames River in 1792 (in modern Chatham-Kent). United States forces burned it after the battle of Moraviantown in October 1813. With the return of peace, its people resettled south of the river, at New Fairfield or New Moraviantown. JN was at the mission from 5 to 8 August with 38 Iroquois, Munsee, and Chippewa warriors. They received food and discussed the war with its residents, with JN listening to missionaries who "beseeched him to spare human life, to abstain from murder and plunder, and to show himself as a servant of God going to war" (Fairfield Diary, 5–8 August 1812, published in Sabathy-Judd, *Moravians*, 483–4, quote on 484). He promised to do so; and when he returned to the village after the Detroit campaign, he reported that he had fulfilled his pledge (ibid., 484).

23 Once established in Sandwich, the Americans patrolled inland as far as modern Chatham, gathered supplies, and skirmished with opposing forces. The "mouth" of the river may have referred to McGregor's Creek, which intersects the Thames (in today's Chatham) about 20 miles from Moraviantown.

the men who had joined us were destitute of arms. It did not appear an object to make any further search for the fugitives, so we returned without delay to our party. Our arrival seemed to spread joy and cheerfulness, and trifling as the adventure was, it was received as a favourable omen of our future success. The good people of the village had furnished our warriors with [an] abundance of provisions, and several of them joined the party.[24]

The next morning we proceeded, and in a few miles we were joined by another party of Chippewas, who informed us that the Chippewas of the River St Clair had said that they would immediately take up arms when they should hear from the Five Nations. I therefore sent a messenger to them with a belt of wampum requesting them to meet us at the mouth of the [Thames] River.[25] We stopped near this place to call the militia together to prepare them to assist us in repelling the enemy should they return in search of provisions.[26] We found the royalists in

---

24 JN described this 7 August encounter a few days after it occurred: "Going out in front with three young men and myself, mounted, we heard of four Americans who had obtained papers from General Hull to come to this place and harvest, and ... near sundown, we perceived a canoe with four men in it; but their arms being in the canoe and not perceptible to us, we at first supposed them to be the people of the place until their hastening to the other shore ... caused us to suspect them. We then jumped off our horses, and running to the riverside, called on them to come across, threatening to fire in case of non-compliance. They never answered, but sprang out of the canoe in an instant, and the banks being very low, they were immediately under cover of a cluster of trees, which concealed them from our sight. The time we lost in crossing the river enabled them to distance us so far that, before we came up with them, they got into thick bushy woods, which completely hid them from our search. The ground was hard and [had] little grass, so we could not track them. We ran in a straight line after them until we reached the plains, and proceeded a considerable distance into them. When we returned to the riverbanks, it was near dark. We found their army clothes and shoes in the canoe, which I divided among our people" (JN to J.B. Glegg, 11 August 1812, LAC, RG10, 487:4451–2). While Moravian Christianity preaches pacifism, some members of the community rejected that aspect of the faith.

25 There were a number of Chippewa villages along both sides of the St Clair River between Lakes Huron and St Clair. The decisions of the Six Nations of the Grand were of obvious importance to their inhabitants, and JN's text presumably meant that they awaited word that a respectable number of the Haudenosaunee had entered the war beside the British. The text "with a belt of wampum requesting them" is missing from the published *JMJN*.

26 We do not know exactly where JN was at this time but he seems to have been in or near the area of today's Chatham. History overlooks the facts that native people

good spirits, rather exulting over the wavering and disaffected.[27] The next day we descended the river to the lower township, where we had another meeting of the militia in that quarter and exhorted them in the same manner. But, being engaged in their harvest, I did not call upon them to join me until the enemy might advance towards us or that offensive operations on our part should be undertaken.[28] While we waited with eager expectation for the return of our messenger from the River St Clair, the warriors prepared spears, and we obtained a sufficiency of ammunition from Mr McGregor, a merchant in the neighbourhood.[29] We received notice that a hundred warriors would join us in two days, and at the same time I had a letter from Lieutenant-Colonel Procter requiring us to join him at Sandwich with all possible expedition, at which place he had just arrived in consequence of General Hull having retired to Detroit. Seeing that our presence might be wanted at Sandwich, we left two old men to wait for the reinforcement, and the next morning, early, we began our march for that place where we arrived in the evening, it being hardly forty miles distant.[30]

---

often asked settlers and fur traders to join them on campaign, that some white and native groups lived in close contact with each other, and that there were intercultural military forces. Brant's volunteers during the American Revolution, for instance, contained a large number of Euro-American combatants, while JN noted the presence of 30 whites with the native army at the time of the battle of Fallen Timbers in 1794 (*JMJN*, 178).

27 The inaction of the Americans once they arrived in Sandwich, combined with the capture of Mackinac, helped improve morale among Upper Canadians.

28 While the militia had not been called out to march to the Detroit River because of the harvest, 145 men volunteered to reinforce the native people should the Americans move up the river. JN recorded that their officers were away at Amherstburg, so he took "the liberty to appoint people to take charge of the different companies." That statement begs the question of why they agreed to his arrangements, but they may have responded to his obvious leadership of the warrior contingent and his recent appointment as a captain in the Indian Department (JN to J.B. Glegg, 11 August 1812, LAC, RG10, 487:4452–3).

29 John McGregor was a miller, merchant, politician, and militia officer based in Sandwich who had interests along the Thames River. He fought in the war, losing an arm and much of his property. Muskets and rifles were the primary weapons of First Nations warriors, with tomahawks also being significant, but spears (used mainly for close-quarters thrusting rather than throwing) and other weapons, including knives, clubs, pistols, and bows, were common.

30 JN arrived at Sandwich on 12 August. Beyond his small contingent from Grand River, the warriors with him included Chippewas, Delawares, and Odawas,

There we got particular information of the invasion and subsequent events. Immediately on the declaration of war being notified, the militia assembled as they had done on the Niagara frontier, but when the Americans began to demonstrate their intention of coming across, the whole body made room for them by a timely retreat.[31] So they landed on the Canadian shores without opposition, but their scouts, advancing to reconnoitre Amherstburg, were always checked at the River Canard (three or four miles from that place) by a small detachment of troops and Indians.[32] Another party of these warriors, crossing from Amherstburg to the Big Rock, beset the road from Detroit to the River Raisin. These places are about twelve leagues from each other, and that part opposite to Amherstburg is about midway between them.[33] In one of

---

who brought the strength of his party up to 70 men (JN to J.B Glegg, 11 August 1812, LAC, RG10, 487:4453; JN to Henry Goulburn, 29 January 1816, published in Cruikshank, "Campaigns," 43). Given that the Chippewas planned to meet him at the mouth of the river, and given that he thought the 100 warriors "in two days" would arrive farther inland, JN presumably expected the reinforcement to come primarily from the Grand. On his way to Detroit, Isaac Brock had stopped at the Grand on 7 August. There, he had learned that 60 men would proceed west in addition to those who already had joined JN, and JN presumably had been made aware of this in order for him to send a wampum belt to the Chippewas (mentioned above) to encourage them to enter the campaign. The improvement in morale in Upper Canada following the capture of Mackinac was important in the decision of warriors to move against Detroit. Additionally, the American army had shown weakness when it withdrew from Upper Canada between 7 and 11 August in the face of a widespread rising of the native population after the fall of Mackinac. At the time William Hull retired to Detroit, he thought he needed more men to continue his campaign and worried about the vulnerability of his communications lines.

31 There was a militia force in Sandwich (with a small number of regulars) immediately south of the site of the American landing. Its officers, however, decided they could not resist an attack, and feared that a large percentage of their men would desert, so they withdrew south to Amherstburg to join the main body of British soldiers on 11 July, the night before the American landing.

32 The Canard River empties into the Detroit River five miles north of Amherstburg. Of the several skirmishes in its vicinity between 16 and 26 July, the largest occurred on the 16th, after which the invaders moved to a point three miles from the fort at Amherstburg before withdrawing north. That was the farthest south of Sandwich they ventured during William Hull's brief occupation of Canadian territory.

33 At the beginning of August, British and First Nations forces established themselves on the Michigan side of the Detroit River near the Wyandot village at Brownstown, a short boat ride across from Amherstburg. Their objective was to disrupt American communications on the 35-mile road between Detroit and Frenchtown on the Raisin River to the south.

the American dispatches, General Hull notices [*sic*] of having sent two hundred riflemen to open the communication. These were routed with considerable loss by the Indian warriors.[34] A gallant young Shawnee of the name of Logan was killed in this encounter: eager in pursuit of the routed enemy, he fell under their fire.[35] In consequence of this failure, the enemy determined to attempt to force the passage with a greater portion of their army. They were met by Captain Muir with the grenadiers of the 41st and two or three hundred brave warriors led on by Roundhead (or Stayeghtha), Tecumseh, Sounehhooway, and Myeerah.[36] The loss of the enemy was reported to have been considerable. Both sides claimed the victory, and what is certain, both sides retired, the Americans without

---

34 North of Brownstown on 5 August, Tecumseh and somewhere between 25 and 70 warriors ambushed 200 militia from Detroit. The Americans had marched south with mail and expected to escort supplies back from the River Raisin, but retreated in panic with the loss of 30 dead to one native killed after a short fight. On the same day, warriors also destroyed most of a party of 25 men travelling north with mail in the area south of Brownstown. JN's reference to riflemen reminds us that some British and American infantry, as well as some natives, used rifles instead of smoothbore muskets. Rifles were more accurate and had longer ranges, but took longer to load and suffered from other limitations, which meant that smoothbores were more appropriate for most combatants until technological innovations in the 1840s rendered them obsolete.

35 John Logan, who served as an interpreter, was the only native fatality on 5 August. While not the better-known Captain Logan encountered below, he was well liked along the Detroit River. Afterwards, natives executed two American prisoners to avenge his death. In aboriginal society, prisoners traditionally might be adopted, killed, or tortured, although by 1812 these practices were far less common than they had been in earlier days. Instead, warriors turned over most Euro-American prisoners to their white allies, usually receiving payments or other rewards in return.

36 The officer was Captain Adam Muir of the 41st Foot. Roundhead (Stayeghtha) was a leading Wyandot chief who lived on the Canadian side of the Detroit River in 1812. He supported Tecumseh and Tenskwatawa, and participated actively in hostilities until passing away in 1813. Roundhead's brother Sounehhooway (Thomas Splitlog) also fought the Americans. Myeerah, from the Michigan side of the river, joined Tecumseh and the British, fighting until 1813, when he withdrew from the conflict as the balance of power in the Detroit region shifted to the United States following the battle of Moraviantown in October 1813. JN recorded his own thoughts on the half-brothers Tenskwatawa (the Prophet) and Tecumseh in the pre-war part of his journal in addition to the sections presented in this book. While on his way home from the Cherokee journey in 1810, for instance, he visited a Shawnee village, and noted that "the greater part of the nation, I am told, [now] live at the Wabash, where there is a man who is styled the Prophet. His brother is a very sensible man and brave warrior,

having effected their object of opening the communications whereby to receive their supplies of provisions, and without which their fate was inevitable. In this affair, the Wyandots of Big Rock joined [with] about seventy warriors of the best character.[37] This was the posture of affairs when we joined Lieutenant-Colonel Procter at Sandwich.

The next morning, General Brock arrived with a considerable detachment of the 41st and militia dressed in red coats. He commenced by sending a summons to General Hull to demand the surrender of his army and the place he held. The flag soon returned with a refusal.[38] A battery opposite to Detroit, which had already been begun, was soon completed; and in the evening, a few shots were fired to try the effect, which were returned with great punctilio. The distance across the river at this place was something more than a thousand yards. It was arranged to cross before the dawn of day. The armed vessels moved up the river to cooperate.[39] General Brock made selection of our party to accompany the troops. The warriors from Amherstburg, led

---

of an independent spirit and enthusiastic to preserve the territory and independence of his brethren" (*JMJN*, 168). JN tended to write about the Shawnee leader in distant but positive terms (*JMJN*, 168–9, 289–90, 304, 310, 328, 330–1).

37 The battle of Maguaga occurred south of a village of that name on 9 August, when a First Nations and British force of 500 ambushed 600 Americans who William Hull had ordered to clear the route south from Detroit. In two hours of fighting, the Americans repulsed the attack but did not open the road. The next day elements of that force, along with a boat convoy sent to aid them, came under native harassment and fire from British vessels on the Detroit River. On 11 August, the Americans retired back to Detroit. They suffered 80 killed and wounded over those three days in comparison to 30 among the British and natives, including Tecumseh, who received a leg wound. The comment about the Wyandots was significant in signalling their change from neutrality to belligerency.

38 Isaac Brock arrived on the Detroit River on 13 August (and met Tecumseh for the first time that day). He gave old army tunics to some of the militia to convince the Americans that he commanded more regulars than he in fact did. On 15 August, Isaac Brock sent a letter to William Hull demanding his surrender, which Hull, following normal protocol, refused.

39 The British crossed the border during the night of 15–16 August, landing unopposed a few miles downriver of Detroit. The armed vessels were the 20-gun *Queen Charlotte* and the 10-gun *General Hunter*. The British and First Nations forces on American soil numbered at least 750 regulars and militia, along with 600 warriors, the latter comprising men from a number of groups, such as JN's contingent, the Detroit-region Wyandots, and people associated with Tecumseh (mainly Shawnees, Miamis, Delawares, and Potawatomis). Other men served on the two vessels, the batteries at Sandwich, and elsewhere.

by Stayeghtha, Tecumseh, Tharoutorea, and Myeerah, were to pass in the skirts of the wood and to take the enemy in flank should he come out to give us battle.[40]

In the morning, we crossed at La Belle Fontaine.[41] There had been usually a picket at that place of about one hundred men, but we found none there. The breadth of the river as well as the scarcity of boats caused us some delay ere we were in readiness to advance. All formed, we proceeded.[42] The troops [including the militia] followed in good order so as to give the whole body the appearance of regulars. Our gallant general rode in front of them. The cannon from our batteries [on the Canadian side of the river and on the naval vessels] were firing at the fort, and the enemy making regular answer. When we had approached near, I proposed to the general that, with my party, I might incline to the left to examine some enclosures and a ravine that might conceal an ambuscade. He approved the plan, cautioning us to avoid precipitation in the most affectionate manner. Passing the ravine, we found assembled in it a number of females and children of the French-Canadian inhabitants who had taken shelter there from the probable fire of the expected conflict.[43] When we came within 150 yards of Macomb's enclosure, we perceived the heads of the Americans behind the pickets.[44] [While we were] waiting to be joined by those following, the enemy retired precipitately. We ran to intercept some horsemen entering the fort.[45] They escaped us

---

40 JN's party did not deploy with the main native force. Instead, it provided close support to the British regulars and Canadian militia. These troops, along with JN's men, moved on Detroit from the landing site while most warriors advanced ahead beyond their left flank. This manoeuvre severely restricted William Hull's ability to leave his defences and offer battle south of Detroit. Otherwise, a logical way for him to oppose Isaac Brock was to use the fortifications as fixed positions within a flexible defence in which some of his men would march out to engage the British.

41 La Belle Fontaine was a short distance south of Detroit.

42 The British advance on Detroit began between 7 and 8 a.m.

43 The French had founded Detroit in 1701, and the francophone presence continued to be prominent in the region at the time of the War of 1812. The British and First Nations force did not disturb the women and children hiding at this spot (Knagg's Creek).

44 William McComb's property, immediately downriver of the town, had stockaded fences.

45 In running after the Americans JN presumably knew that fleeing enemies did not represent a serious threat, in comparison to the situation immediately beforehand when they stood behind their defences in an organized manner.

but in making this attempt, we came between the sentry and the camp, and took him prisoner. He belonged to the 4th Regiment and appeared so much alarmed that it was with great difficulty [that] we could get any information from him. I sent him to the general.

The white flag was now hoisted, and we heard that the enemy had entered into a parley to capitulate.[46] The parapet of the fort was crowded with men. Those in the camp outside of it were striking the tents and removing everything precipitately [into the fort], at the same time making pacific signs to prevent attack. The capitulation was concluded. The American general agreed to surrender [his men as] prisoners of war (excepting only the militia, who were to be sent home immediately) and to deliver up the fort to the British troops at twelve o'clock. The arms surrendered of all kinds might amount to between two and three thousand stands, but there were not more than one thousand regular troops.[47] The force that General Brock led on consisted of about six hundred regulars and militia in red coats, and perhaps as many Indian warriors. The latter were increasing in number daily; in a few days more we would have exceeded a thousand. The fort was taken possession of by a part of the 41st Regiment; and the general recommending us to go to Amherstburg, we returned to Sandwich that evening, and the next morning went on to Amherstburg.[48]

---

46 William Hull hung out a white flag on one of the bastions around 10 a.m. to communicate his desire to parlay, without having offered any meaningful resistance to Isaac Brock. He also sent one across the Detroit River, assuming that Brock was in Sandwich rather than on American soil.

47 As well as "stands," which referred to muskets and rifles with their accoutrements, the Americans surrendered their artillery and other military stores. Often warriors and soldiers simply took what they could get from defeated individuals, but there also were formal transfers of property arranged by opposing commanders. When warranted, the British government provided prize money to those who participated in such events. The payments varied by rank. JN was eligible for prize money for the capture of Detroit at least as a chief (given the same rate as that of an ensign or lieutenant), which amounted to 120 pounds, although as an Indian Department captain he presumably was entitled to a higher sum. Bureaucratic errors delayed his award (Great Britain, Adjutant-General, *Regulations and Orders for the Army*, 148; Edward Baynes, Memorandum, 26 July 1813, LAC, RG10, 28:16492; JN to Colley Foster, 25 May 1815, LAC, RG8, 695:81).

48 William Hull surrendered the 2,200 men under his command on 16 August. As his force was dispersed along the Detroit River, and as some men had deserted or were sick, he had only 1,000 effectives at Detroit itself, but he included the other troops in the region in the capitulation. Thus, contrary to numerous histories, Isaac

The Americans can have no pretence for accusing the Indian allies of cruelty in this instance.[49]

Seeing the divided state of the Five Nations on the Grand River, when General Brock rejoined us, I proposed to him to allow me to remain in the west. But he urged me to return to the Niagara frontier, saying that he expected the enemy would, in a very short time, make a serious attempt in that quarter to avenge their present loss, and that he must have me with him. The day after the capture of Detroit, I was joined by a hundred Chippewa warriors from the River St Clair, and before I left Amherstburg, about one hundred men from the Grand River augmented our number. They told me that they had followed us according to promise, but meeting with the confidential interpreter already mentioned as having left us at Oxford, he informed them that orders had been sent after us to return, and believing what he said to be true, they went home again until they heard of the prosecution of the original plan when General Brock passed the village.[50]

An American officer with money for the use of the army had reached the River Raisin when General Hull surrendered. He included him as

---

Brock had more men operating in the immediate vicinity of the town at the moment of surrender than Hull did, although the American general held the significant advantage of holding well-fortified positions. Beyond having strong defences, one of Hull's detached forces, numbering several hundred, lay within a few miles of Brock's rear, but it failed to threaten the British. Most of the American regulars went into captivity, while the militia were paroled and sent home, unable to fight again until "exchanged" (a process for trading prisoners between the opposing sides). There were few casualties that day, mainly caused by British artillery fire directed against the Americans.

49 To a large degree, William Hull capitulated because he worried that civilians otherwise would be rendered vulnerable to violence from indigenous war parties. In demanding Hull's surrender the day before, Isaac Brock had played upon those fears by stating that the natives with him would be uncontrollable once the fighting began. In contrast, in the last sentence of the paragraph, JN showed his sensitivity to ubiquitous and exaggerated American assumptions of aboriginal barbarity, and perhaps hinted at his displeasure when the British exploited those worries (although it was an effective technique in undermining American resolve). Some warriors, however, did loot private property, including taking goods and livestock from Canadians on the east side of the Detroit River. For a modern study of JN's thoughts on indigenous warfare in opposition to common affirmations of brutality, see Glover, "Going to War on the Back of a Turtle."

50 As already noted, Isaac Brock had stopped at the Grand River on 7 August, which provided an opportunity to expose George Martin's misinformation.

well as Colonel McArthur in the capitulation. The latter, who was within some miles of Detroit with a few hundred men, immediately submitted. Mr Elliott was sent to the River Raisin to summon the former to acquiesce in the submission to which his commander had agreed. The officer refused, alleging that as General Hull was a prisoner he had no further command over him. To prevent discovery, he took Mr Elliott part of the way and retreated with all expedition.[51]

---

51 Captain William Elliott of Upper Canada's 1st Regiment of Essex Militia had
   been ordered south from Detroit to help secure the terms of capitulation beyond
   the town. He met Duncan McArthur after travelling a few miles, and told him
   that his command had been included in the American surrender. McArthur, a
   prominent politician and the senior colonel of the volunteers from the Ohio militia
   on the Detroit front, obeyed the order to march his force into captivity. Elliott then
   continued to the River Raisin to bring in the men commanded by Captain Henry
   Brush of the Ohio militia (the "officer with money"), arriving on 17 August. Brush,
   however, claimed that Elliott's documents were forgeries, locked him up, and left
   for Ohio with his troops and the supplies that had been intended for Hull, even
   after learning that the orders to surrender were legitimate and despite the fact that,
   having been included in the capitulation, his force legally could not fight again until
   exchanged. Another American officer released Elliott on 18 August, apologized
   for Brush's behaviour, and surrendered more men. McArthur appears later in JN's
   narrative when he led a raid along the north shore of Lake Erie towards the Six
   Nations settlements in 1814. (He had been exchanged and entered the American
   regular army in 1813.)

3

Niagara and Victory at Queenston Heights, 1812

In the overall struggle across the Old Northwest to the end of August 1812, British and First Nations forces suffered few losses, but killed, wounded, or captured most American troops sent against them. They seized Mackinac at the head of Lake Michigan, destroyed the garrison of Fort Dearborn (in modern Chicago), and took Detroit. At the last, Brigadier-General William Hull surrendered the Michigan Territory to the British. The allies also acquired enormous quantities of desperately needed weapons and supplies from their defeated enemy. Not only were these triumphs important strategically and materially, but they demonstrated the weaknesses of the Americans and the strength of the British and natives despite the numerical imbalance between the opposing sides that ostensibly favoured the republic's forces. In the process, these events encouraged many people in Upper Canada – both natives and newcomers – to think that a successful defence of the colony was possible. Critically, the surrender of Michigan seemed momentous because it raised hopes of securing a separate indigenous homeland in the Old Northwest, thus fulfilling the dreams of the Western Tribes. Not only were the people surrounding Tecumseh and Tenskwatawa inspired by that development, but it also captured the imaginations of natives across the wider Great Lakes region beyond the confederacy's members. These victories possessed additional characteristics that made them meaningful from indigenous perspectives. For those holding traditional beliefs, the events of the summer of 1812 indicated that the allied side had been able to harness substantial spiritual power, and had satisfied the imperative to avenge or otherwise assuage some of the past wrongs committed by a hated foe, especially as these feats had been obtained at so little cost but with awe-inspiring gains in territory, prisoners, and matériel. For Christian natives, a providential theology also allowed people to interpret the outcomes of the summer's campaign in religiously pos-

itive terms. Losing few men was crucial because the numerically small First Nations valued their people greatly and could not afford to sacrifice many of them if they were to maintain social viability; thus, they interpreted high casualties as equivalent to defeat, regardless of the outcome of a confrontation. Moreover, capturing supplies contributed to aboriginal views of success because seizing enemy goods (and receiving gifts and payments from allies) was a customary secondary objective in their warfare.

The summer of 1812 saw a general shift from neutrality to active participation in the conflict by many aboriginal people. Most who were willing to fight aligned with Great Britain, whether they lived in the Canadian provinces of Upper and Lower Canada, or in the American Old Northwest. The change in the strategic situation saw three-quarters of the Six Nations population of the Grand River ally with the Crown at the expense of the agendas of the neutralist and pro-American parties on the tract (although the freedoms inherent in Haudenosaunee military tradition meant that men could come and go on campaign as they pleased). For the inhabitants of the Grand, the issues were different than they were in the Old Northwest. While most of them did not see their future in Upper Canada as including an independent homeland on the same scale or standing that people farther west did, the majority generally concluded that their prospects would be better within the British Empire than they would be if the Americans were to conquer the colony. Many always had thought this way, and felt uncomfortable after the fall of Detroit for not having participated in the campaign. For instance, we saw hints in John Norton's text above that people holding pro-British views were cautious in expressing their feelings at the beginning of the war, logically doubting that the soldiers of the King and the warriors of the Western Tribes could succeed; hence they changed their minds only after the Americans suffered their series of defeats. Moreover, people's reflections on the threat the United States posed as the realities of war became clearer created something of an imperative to join the struggle against the republic so long as success seemed possible. Taking up arms also offered opportunities to realize cultural objectives associated with the warrior identity and perceptions of masculinity. Some people saw participation in mercenary terms, expecting to receive payments in goods, provisions, and money for their services, especially as they could control the depth of their contributions to a campaign, and thus expect to survive the fighting. Some individuals along the Grand that summer, however, interpreted the strength of the British in negative terms. They thought the Crown's power, which they had found oppressive before the war, could be used against the Six Nations if they continued to hold their warriors back while other aboriginal communities entered the struggle against the United States.

Therefore, they believed that they had to demonstrate goodwill towards the colonial order to some degree, whether or not they wanted to do so.

In New York, a small number of Senecas had moved west in 1811 to join the Western Tribal Confederacy, and some Iroquois warriors in the state slipped into Canada to fight alongside their Grand River relatives. Nevertheless, most of the Haudenosaunee south of the border who decided to fight chose to ally with the United States after its officials began to ask for their support. (Some natives elsewhere, such as in Ohio, also aligned with the republic.) Aside from the same cultural motives that inspired their relatives in Canada, some families had fought against the Crown in the past, while others thought their best chance of securing their future would come through supporting the still-dominant white power in North America and by proving that their attitudes towards it differed from those of their pro-British relatives elsewhere. Furthermore, many realized that the Detroit campaign was only the first of the war, and that the Americans, with comparative ease, could replace the forces they had lost. Beyond these general sentiments, there were specific reasons for taking up arms, such as among Senecas in New York, who wanted to defend Grand Island in the Niagara River. They affirmed that it was their territory, but feared losing it after British-allied Mohawks ventured onto the island, whether American forces unaided by the Senecas regained control of it or whether the British wrested it from their white enemy. Iroquois support in New York for the United States in 1812, however, was modest in comparison to the help the British received from the Six Nations of the Grand River.

The changes arising from the victories in the west improved John Norton's standing along the Grand when many people chose to align with the British. At Detroit, only a small group from the community had accompanied him into the Michigan Territory as part of the allied force, but soon afterwards one hundred men went to the Niagara Peninsula to strengthen British defences for a time; and later, in early October, three-quarters of the tract's four hundred warriors encamped along the border, ready to fight. This sweeping development underscores how fluid Six Nations politics could be, and how people made decisions by assessing unfolding events within larger intellectual and cultural settings rather than following those who promoted particular agendas. Naturally, Teyoninhokarawen influenced some; yet it would be a mistake to overestimate his sway, because some who rejected Norton's leadership or simply were not close to him nevertheless wanted to fight the Americans. Not all of the people changed their minds after the fall of Detroit, and while the neutralist and pro-American parties suffered blows to their ability to influence others during the late summer of 1812, they could expect to regain support if shifting conditions led people to reconsider the existential question of how to

meet the needs of their families and communities. With so many Haudeno-
saunee and other aboriginal men joining Teyoninhokarawen along the Niagara
River, he fulfilled greater roles during the late summer and early autumn of
1812 than he had earlier in the war as a diplomatic leader in relations between
the British and First Nations. Then, he proved to be a skilled combatant in the
field as a senior war chief, particularly at the next major confrontation of the
conflict, at Queenston Heights, which he described in striking detail below.

We returned home by the same road we had come, and were received
by the most part with great appearances of satisfaction. A number of
Moravian Delawares, Munsees, and Chippewas joined our party to go
to the Niagara frontier.[1] We stopped only a few days at the Grand River
and found them all ready to accompany us. On the road, we met with
a number [of warriors] on their return from Niagara. They informed
us that a truce having been agreed to by the commander of the forces,
they were going to their homes, but would hold themselves in readiness
to repair to the lines whenever I should see fit to call upon them. We
arrived at Niagara just as the truce had expired.[2] As soon as I had con-
sulted General Brock, I sent to the Grand River to call all the warriors,
and in a few days we had collected between five and six hundred men.
We were generally occupied in moving from Niagara to Fort Erie, wherever an attack was most apprehended. Sometimes we passed round the
Grand Island to observe the opposite shore [to see] if any preparations
were making there to attempt an invasion.[3]

---

1 JN's "Moravian Delawares" and "Munsees" distinguished between the two Delaware
   or Lenni Lenapi communities in southwestern Upper Canada that he had mentioned
   earlier. There also were substantial numbers of Delawares on the Six Nations Tract.
   (See Appendix A.)
2 The "commander of the forces" was the governor-in-chief of British North America,
   Lieutenant-General Sir George Prevost. On 30 July, he received news from London
   that the government, before learning of the American declaration of war, had offered
   concessions to the United States in hopes of avoiding a conflict. Therefore, Prevost
   wanted to restore peace quickly. He negotiated a truce with the senior American
   officer on the border, Major-General Henry Dearborn, on 9 August (but which did
   not include the opposing forces on the Detroit front). The administration of President
   James Madison disavowed the ceasefire, and hostilities resumed on 8 September.
3 JN met with Isaac Brock at Fort George early in September. The warriors from the
   Grand and elsewhere performed reconnaissance duties and acted as a fast-moving

At about this time, a person who came from the other side gave information that, having been stopped on the bridge at Cayuga Creek by the sentry, he had observed, while he stood there, a number of boats. In consequence of this intelligence, General Brock desired that a scout would go to the other side to make observation at that place, which is a few miles above Fort Schlosser at the Falls and a little above the point of the Grand Island.[4] Two men crossed the river in a small canoe, the one perfectly well acquainted with the ground and the other determined to make the strictest research.[5] They landed a few hundred yards below a guard, unconscious of its being there. They drew up their canoe and went on. In a few paces, they crossed the main road, then a field, and passed through the back part on the skirt of the woods to avoid discovery until they had passed the houses in the vicinity. Then, with great circumspection, they continued to the stream [Cayuga Creek], which is about twenty yards over. They examined strictly without making any discovery, passed the bridge, and continued their researches along the shore until they reached a place observable from the Grand Island. From thence, they returned, thinking it of no use to pass further on.

As they had seen nothing that could make it necessary to form any enterprise on that place, they thought it needless to be so extremely cautious of giving alarm. They therefore continued on the road, at the same time keeping a sharp lookout to every house they passed, which they were very well enabled to do from the light of the moon which shone very bright. At a tavern where the range of houses seemed to end, they expected to have found the guard, and approached it very cautiously. When at the door, they imagined they heard a challenge at

---

reserve that Brock could deploy to strengthen any of the fixed positions held by the regulars and militia along the Niagara River.

4 There are two Cayuga Creeks on the New York side of the Niagara Peninsula. This one empties into the Niagara River's east branch by Cayuga Island near the north end of Grand Island, which is not visible from the Canadian shore. It is not the better-known tributary of the Buffalo River farther south (in present-day Buffalo). The British feared that the boats would be used to cross the Niagara River, and when the Americans did invade at Queenston shortly afterwards, they used bateaux that had been hidden in this area. Fort Schlosser (in today's Niagara Falls, New York) was a military depot that guarded the southern end of the American portage around the Falls. British forces destroyed the fort in July 1813. The northern end of the portage was at Lewiston. The Canadian portage ran between Chippawa and Queenston.

5 JN was one of these two men. This was one of the occasions in the memoir when he referred to himself in the third person.

a little distance, but the clattering of geese at the same time confused the sound and rendered it uncertain. They passed. Suddenly, a sentry started from behind a tree and called, "Who's there?" The foremost answered, "It is I," advancing at the same time till they met. The guard-room was within ten paces. "You cannot pass," said the sentry, "without a passport or countersign."

"Don't bother me about your passes," he replied, "at this time of night you cannot read them" (going at the same time to seize him). The sentry started back a few paces, called upon the guard, and cocked his gun. The other kept so close to him that he could not bring it to bear upon him nor strike him with the bayonet, and just as the guard was coming out of the door, he [i.e., the sentry] fell at his feet, calling out, "He has killed me." Apparently, they [i.e., the Americans] had not their arms, for they re-entered, and he walked off to his canoe. When he arrived there, they fired several shots. He began to reload, and his comrade (who had jumped over a fence and had taken a circuitous route) then rejoined him. They embarked in the canoe and reached the opposite shore a few hours before day. Subsequently a report was sent to Niagara that the enemy was about to make a lodgement in the Grand Island. We returned to that quarter and ranged over the island as before; and all we could discover were a few tracks, and boats going down from Black Rock with troops and others apparently laden with stores.[6]

---

6 JN and his unidentified companion crossed the Niagara River near Navy Island, upriver of Fort Schlosser, on 24 September, landing on the New York mainland. JN almost certainly was the man who killed the guard because the text makes it clear that the senior of the two scouts did it. An American account reads: "On Thursday night last, Lewis Nyles, a sentinel from Lieutenant-Colonel [Silas] Hopkins's regiment [of New York militia], posted near Field's Tavern on the Niagara Road, about 17 miles below this place, was shot dead on his post by some person who, being hailed by the sentinel, replied that he had not got the countersign but a written pass, which he would show him. On being permitted to approach to the point of the bayonet, he drew a pistol, and shot the sentinel and made his escape. The report of the pistol and the cries of the sentinel gave an immediate alarm, and it was thought the person made his escape across the river to Grand Island, as a boat was soon after heard upon the river" (Buffalo Gazette, 29 September 1812). Over a year later, another American paper presented a propagandized version of the event, which is interesting because it indicates that JN had gained some notoriety in the United States. It read: "As everything that is British is to be extolled by the English 'writers' in America, the following notice has run its round in our papers. 'Norton, the Indian chief, frequently spoken of during the present war in Upper Canada, is a man of education, has travelled in Europe, and been received with distinguished attention

At this time, there was [a] great appearance of the enemy having [assembled] a considerable force on the lines, and these indications were equally obvious in the vicinity of Black Rock, the Cataract, and

---

for his talent and amenity. While in England in 1804, he translated the Gospel of Saint John into the Mohawk language, which was printed at the expense of the Bible Society. His Indian name is *Teyoninhokarawen*.' Now, this *Norton* must be a very devout, 'religious,' and magnanimous man. He fights for *England* and *that* shows his devotion to 'liberty.' But why did not the knaves tell us that this *pious* 'translator of the Gospel of Saint John,' crossed the Niagara River in the dead of the night for the purpose of shooting an *American* sentinel in cold blood! *Holy Norton!* – ALLY OF ENGLAND! MIDNIGHT MURDERER!" (*Niles' Weekly Register*, 18 December 1813; the quote beginning, "Norton, the Indian chief," may be seen, for instance, in the *Daily National Intelligencer*, 27 October 1813). The author of that piece reacted in part to the numerous examples of JN appearing in the press, which included an official British army document that praised his behaviour at the battle of Queenston Heights, and which a number of American papers republished (as indicated by a search through the Readex online database, "America's Historical Newspapers"). Teyoninhokarawen also had received favourable attention for his piety and biblical translation (e.g., *The Olio*, 23 October 1813, and other newspapers). That same article on JN's godliness produced a brutal response in another newspaper that incorporated some of the common tropes applied by white Americans towards indigenous people. It stated: "This same Norton, this savage of defined education, during the last year's campaign, crossed the Niagara River, in the dead of night, for the magnanimous purpose of shooting an American sentinel in cold blood; and we have no doubt the fellow, with all his education, is as barbarous and unrelenting a monster as any of the tawny race who tread the wilds of Michigan or Missouri. Not one of them, we dare say, could dash out the brains of an innocent, smiling infant, or take off the scalp of an unprotected and unoffending mother, with more barbarous *sang froid* than this polished and enlightened European traveller – this learned and pious translator of the Gospel of Saint John!" (*American and Commercial Daily Advertiser*, 5 December 1813 and other papers). After the Americans captured Fort George in May 1813, pro-American settlers in Upper Canada fled to the post to seek shelter from reprisals by loyal people in the colony. An anonymous document from the fort declared: "There is a number of Yankees here from the Grand River. They come to obtain paroles [from serving in the Canadian militia] and say that if our army leaves them, they dare not return to their homes for fear of the Indians. Norton and other Scotch chiefs have lists of suspected Yankees whom they will plunder and murder without remorse" (Letter, 9 June 1813, quoted in Cruikshank, "Study or Disaffection," 32). There is, of course, no evidence in JN's history to suggest he would engage in such activities. JN even was the subject of a bad poem celebrating the American naval victory on Lake Erie in 1813: "The thunder of the battle's roar, / Was heard to Erie's farthest shore: / The Western warriors trembled. / SPLITLOG – TECUMSEH – *old chief* Norton / Such dreadful fighting ne'er had thought on. / And ill their fears dissembled" (Wilkes-Barre *Gleaner*, 5 November 1813). One periodical in England carried a letter to the

Lewiston, in the rear of which a great smoke showed to us the encampment.[7] Thus the point of attack being uncertain, it behooved us to be equally vigilant in every part. From Niagara [at the mouth of the river] to Queenston is seven and a half miles, and for the greater part of this distance a passage might be effected, but nowhere with greater facility than at that place [i.e., Queenston], the river being there the most narrow, and the eddies on both sides favouring the traverse. From about a mile above this place to Chippawa, nine miles distant, there is no possibility of crossing by reason of the Cataract and rapids connected with it. Between this place and the lower end of the Grand Island, the traverse is difficult from the breadth of the river and swiftness of the current. From thence to the upper end of the island is about twelve miles, the channel on each side never less than half a mile, and generally more, wide. It forms a triangle, of which the base faces our shore. It is, therefore, several miles across it through thick woods and swamps, excepting at the upper extremity, from whence to the ferry of Black Rock, which is three or four miles [farther south], the passage is no ways difficult except from its breadth, which is from one to three miles, and the intervention of Strawberry and Squaw islands.[8]

On the 9th of October, being at Niagara, an express brought notice that on the preceding night the Americans had surprised and taken off two vessels lying at anchor off Fort Erie; but one of them, in going down the rapids, had been carried by the stream on our side of Squaw Island, where she ran aground. A contest was maintained to destroy or recover her, and in the afternoon we were directed to march up there. It was near sundown before we could set out. We marched a great part of the night and reached the place a little after sunrise. The vessel was now burnt to the water's edge, and General Brock observed that as nothing

---

editor condemning the use of Cossacks in the war against Napoleon and aboriginal warriors in America. It said, "Who knows, but ere long but we may be regaled by the presence of some of our cannibal allies from North America, and that Generals Splitlog, Norton, Scalpemall, and Roundhead may be cheered with 'Hurrahs' in our Royal Exchange as *liberators of America*? I blush for my country and the character of the age" ("Censor" to the Editor, 2 April 1813, *The Monthly Magazine; or British Register* 35 [1813]: 403–4).

7 JN used "Cataract" as a synonym for Niagara Falls.

8 The Senecas claimed Strawberry and Squaw islands, located on the American side of the border between Grand Island and Black Rock. The ferry ran between Black Rock and Frenchman's Creek, four miles north of Fort Erie.

could be done to remedy the evil sustained, we might return at our leisure.[9] That day, we remained there, and observed a number of troops move down the river on the opposite side. In the morning, we returned to Niagara through a tremendous rain, which had fallen on us all the preceding night, and on the way we met the flank companies of the [Royal] Newfoundland Regiment.

We reposed ourselves on the 12th. At this time, the number of my men was considerably reduced. A great part had gone home. The approach of winter made them feel the want of warm clothing, and in constant marching, they had worn out their moccasins. The fall of the leaf – the season for hunting the buck – had arrived, and many had gone to the woods to supply their wants by the chase. Few would have remained had not the love of glory animated their hearts and inspired patience to support them in their sufferings while they awaited the coming of the enemy. There were then hardly three hundred warriors remaining at Niagara.

On the morning of the 13th, a firing was heard from Queenston, although hardly distinguishable from the high wind blowing.[10] When I

---

9 In the early hours of 9 October, 100 American soldiers and sailors crossed the Niagara River in small boats near Fort Erie to cut out the six-gun *Detroit* (which had been taken from the Americans at Detroit) and the three-gun *Caledonia*. Under British fire from shore, the vessels ran aground, the first on Squaw Island and the second at Black Rock. The Americans refloated and saved the *Caledonia* but destroyed the already damaged *Detroit* late that evening after sharp fighting throughout the day. Casualty numbers are uncertain, but both sides seem to have suffered about 20 killed and wounded; the British also lost 60 men taken prisoner, including civilians. The capture of these vessels and their cargoes was a blow for the British cause in the competition to build up naval resources on Lake Erie.

10 The second major thrust into Canada in 1812 centred on the events surrounding the battle of Queenston Heights of 13 October. The Americans assembled 6,700 regulars, militia, and warriors along the Niagara Peninsula in anticipation of the invasion. Of these, 4,600 militia and regulars mustered under Major-General Stephen Van Rensselaer of the New York militia at Lewiston, across the Niagara River from Queenston. Isaac Brock had 2,350 men along the waterway to oppose them. Van Rensselaer, despite leading poorly trained and inadequately equipped soldiers, chose to invade largely because of worsening weather, spreading sickness, and pervasive desertions. He wanted to capture the village of Queenston and the heights that dominated the landscape immediately south of it. His objectives were to restore American honour after the summer's humiliations, undermine Canadian morale, cut British communications between Lakes Ontario and Erie, and secure housing for his men for the forthcoming winter.

arose, I saw General Brock and his staff riding up the road to that place, and heard that he had given orders for the guns of Fort George and the batteries [nearby] to fire upon the American fort of East Niagara.[11] I called upon General Sheaffe.[12] He desired me to get my men in readiness to move on the shortest notice. I had gone only a few hundred yards when I saw the brigade major, Lieutenant-Colonel Evans of the King's [Regiment], riding after me.[13] I stopped till he came up. "The enemy," said he, "are in possession of Queenston. Hasten there as soon as possible. I am now carrying orders to the troops in the garrison to march up."[14] I ran immediately to the camp and delayed no longer than was necessary to see the whole completely equipped with ammunition. The cannonade had commenced, which roused the spirits of the warriors, and shouts re-echoed from one to another. All ran towards

---

11 Forts George and Niagara sat within artillery range of each other. "East Niagara" was the area around Fort Niagara in New York. JN saw Isaac Brock on the River Road that connected Niagara, Queenston, Chippawa, Fort Erie, and smaller centres.

12 Major-General Roger Hale Sheaffe was Isaac Brock's second-in-command, and succeeded him when Brock fell early in the battle of Queenston Heights. He served as commander-in-chief and administrator in Upper Canada until June 1813, when he was replaced following his defeat in the battle of York in April that year. He thought highly of JN (and had married into the Coffin family, which, as we saw in the Introduction, had employed JN's mother as a servant and seems to have played a role in arranging JN's discharge from the army in the 1780s).

13 Major Thomas Evans of the 8th Foot (the King's Regiment) was a brevet lieutenant-colonel. A brigade major was not a rank, instead being the head of a brigade's staff administration. Brigades normally comprised three or four infantry battalions, but people in Canada often used the term loosely to designate smaller multi-unit formations.

14 This conversation may have occurred around 7 a.m. on 13 October. Several hours earlier, when still dark, Stephen Van Rensselaer began sending men across the river· at Queenston in 13 boats (some of which subsequently were lost). Soon afterwards, opposing artillery in the surrounding area opened fire. The British resisted the invaders vigorously, but the Americans established a lodgement on a sheltered beach to the south of the village where the heights intersected the river. As more troops landed, part of the invading force climbed 300 feet up the river side of the heights south of the village. Near sunrise, the British pulled men down from the high ground to support the hard-pressed troops in the village, not realizing that their enemies posed a threat from their immediate south. Back on the heights, the Americans formed a line and advanced northwards down the slope to capture a battery two-thirds of the way up its side around 7 a.m. More men joined them on the high ground soon afterwards.

Queenston. The 41st [Regiment] marched quick time in that regular order which increases confidence.[15]

On the road, General Sheaffe rode past us. We met a few prisoners taken by the 49th [Regiment] out of two boats, which having got into the current, were driven by it under the fire of a battery, which obliged them to surrender.[16] When we were within two miles and a half of Queenston, a rumour was spread that General Brock was killed, and that the enemy were passing through the woods on our right flank. Although I did not believe the last report, knowing these woods to be so encumbered by fallen trees as to be almost impassable, yet it appeared advisable to ascertain the fact in order to give greater confidence, particularly as by taking that circuit [inland] we might ascend the hill undiscovered by the enemy, and assail him in a point he least expected whilst the general might be occupied in collecting his forces.[17]

On entering the woods, which were very thick, we divided into five or six files (the more effectually to make the necessary researches). We discovered only a few [Canadian] militiamen that had escaped from Queenston. They said in excuse for their flight that six thousand Americans had gained possession of Queenston Heights.[18] Some warriors answered, "The more game the better hunting." These reports,

---

15 Opposing batteries along the 35-mile length of the Niagara River fired at each other during part of the day, causing destruction on both sides of the waterway. When Isaac Brock at Fort George heard the firing to the south at the beginning of the battle, he rode to Queenston to assess the situation. Deciding that the American attack there was not a feint, with some other area being the primary target, he sent word to British posts along the river to concentrate a large portion of their troops at Queenston.

16 At dawn, a party of Americans came ashore at the north end of Queenston, at Hamilton Cove (north of their designated landing site), but suffered heavily under British fire and failed to establish a second lodgement.

17 Isaac Brock had been shot leading a charge up the north side of Queenston Heights in an unsuccessful attempt to dislodge the invaders who had captured the battery on the slope. The rumour about American movements on the warriors' right flank was false. (The Niagara River was on JN's left.) The terrain generally was relatively open close to the riverbank, but thick forest predominated farther inland. The unnamed "general" was Roger Sheaffe.

18 After Isaac Brock fell, some militia and regulars engaged the Americans near the top of the heights, enjoyed a degree of success against their more numerous enemies, but were repulsed. By mid-morning, the Americans had 1,300 men on the heights with an artillery piece, held control over the captured battery part way down the slope to the north of their main force, deployed some soldiers near it as skirmishers, posted men to watch the approach from Chippawa to the south, and began constructing

however, had not the same effect upon all. Many were alarmed thereby, and filled with anxiety for the safety of their families (which at that time happened to be at Niagara), we found ourselves much diminished in number by the imperceptible desertion of many. There did not remain together more than eighty men, when, coming to the skirts of the wood, we descried the enemy on the heights.[19] At the sight the warrior's heart burned with indignation, and panted to come in contact with the insolent invaders, yet paused to seek the surest way to hurl destruction on their heads. He then addressed the band: "Comrades and Brothers: be men. Remember the fame of ancient warriors, whose breasts were never daunted by odds of number. You have run from your encampments to this place to meet the enemy. We have found what we came for. Let no anxieties distract your minds. There they are. It only remains to fight. Should others cross below near the lake's shore and threaten your women, they can retire until the contest is ended, and then we will look for them; but my heart strongly forebodes that before the sun shall have sunk behind the western hills, these invading foes shall have fallen before you, or have owed their lives to your mercy. Haste; let us ascend yon path, by which, unperceived, we may gain their rear. Your bullets shall soon spread havoc and dismay among those ranks that form so proudly, exulting in their temporary advantages. Let not their numbers appal you. Look up: it is he above that shall decide our fate. Our gallant friends, the redcoats, will soon support us."[20]

---

field fortifications. Meanwhile, the British had retired out of the village of Queenston and had reassembled at a gun emplacement at Vrooman's Point 2,000 yards north of the American landing site (which enabled some of the invaders to move into the settlement and rob people's homes).

19 The native force left Niagara for Queenston with 160 men as part of the British concentration on Queenston from points to the north and the south, but only 80 warriors ascended the heights a mile inland from (or west) of the village with JN. Although some probably returned to Niagara to protect their families, indigenous societies tolerated decisions by men to leave battles because of bad omens, natural feelings of fear, their assessments of the dangers they faced, and the need to preserve lives in their numerically small societies. The characteristics of aboriginal warfare, with loose fighting formations and without strict command structures, made it easy for people to retire from combat. Other warriors had remained at Fort George in case the Americans should assault it, although some of them subsequently rushed south to fight on the heights.

20 JN likely was the speaker. There was a more formal version of the Mohawk language compared to that of everyday use, and his prose seems to have been an attempt to capture a sense of it.

The warriors ascended the hill in three files, thus prepared for any sudden encounter. Near the road from Chippawa, we met a young gentleman who had narrowly escaped from a party of Americans by dismounting, jumping over a fence, and taking to the woods. He told us they were near at hand. We hastened on. At the road, we met one of our militia officers, well mounted. I entreated him to go with speed to meet the troops and militia from Chippawa to hurry them to our support, and to tell them that we would amuse the enemy in the meantime.[21]

We then came in sight of the enemy at the other end of a field. We doubled our pace to come up with them. They fired and ran, and fired again. We hastened on without losing time, and met two women (whom they had taken by force from their homes) running towards us with tears in their eyes. We assured them in passing that the enemy should soon be repaid for their insolence.[22] We came up with some of the fugitives in front of the main body, which was drawn up in line behind a fence on the skirt of a wood, which bounded the field we had entered. On our left, they advanced into the field. We inclined in that direction to attack them, thinking the flank the most advisable part to assail with our small party. The whole line opened fire on us, but without any effect at that time, a declivity in the ground favouring us. The warriors returned the fire of the enemy with coolness and spirit; and although their fire certainly made the greatest noise (from the number of muskets), yet I believe ours did the most execution. The enemy retired behind the fence, from whence they kept up a heavy fire. We inclined imperceptibly to the extremity on the mountain's brow. From thence, we rushed on with impetuosity, and some were stretched upon

21 The warriors made a broad and circuitous move inland around the American positions, ending up south of them. (When they attacked soon afterwards, the invaders thought they had come from Chippawa rather than Fort George to the north.) JN's descriptions of combat normally conformed to the period's common literary practices (e.g., "amuse the enemy") and did not describe the grotesque horrors of battle. The mounted officer may have been Lieutenant William Hamilton Merritt of the Niagara Light Dragoons (later a captain in the Provincial Dragoons).

22 At around 11 a.m., the warriors engaged their enemy, driving in a detachment of militia riflemen deployed to face the approach from Chippawa. Although the British sent men from both the north and the south towards Queenston to repel the invaders, the 80 warriors with JN and the other chiefs were the only substantial defending force that had reached the heights by that time. The women's identity is unclear but they may have been members of the Chisholm family that lived in the vicinity.

the ground. They rallied among sheds that had been erected there by the troops and militia formerly encamped on that ground.[23]

At this time, we heard some report similar to that of platoons [firing musket volleys] proceeding from the shrapnel shells fired from a field piece under the direction of Captain Holcroft, Royal Artillery, and with which he continued to annoy the enemy with the greatest skill and gallantry.[24] This led us to suppose that the troops were advancing in front of the enemy, which caused us to push with more forwardness than our small number should otherwise have authorized, in order to favour them by distracting the attention of the enemy in giving them a furious onset from our quarter at the same time.

Now undeceived, and seeing the enemy rally in great numbers, the warrior stands meditating how to range with greatest advantage his gallant band when an impatient Seneca warrior called out, "Why stand so mute? Now here is the foe before us." He then replied, "Come on. I never will fail to lead where any warrior can follow," and darting forward, and swiftly, they stand within a javelin's throw of the crowded ranks, when, levelling sure, they discharged the leaden deaths among them (the slight foliage of some slender oak concealed them from hostile view).[25]

---

23 The terrain was a mix of open fields, forests, and brush, interspersed by a few buildings. After the warriors drove in most of their enemy's light infantry screen that had protected their main body of infantry, American officers reformed their line to oppose the Iroquois. Even though the Haudenosaunee were outnumbered significantly, the natives used the terrain and forested areas to screen their movements and protect themselves from their opponents, who generally had much less cover. As they fought, the warriors shifted their position towards the north slope of the heights opposite the right flank of the American line.

24 Captain William Holcroft of the Royal Regiment of Artillery and his men, along with soldiers from the 41st Foot, entered the village of Queenston around 11 a.m. and pushed the American skirmishers and looters back up the heights. By about noon the British artillery, located on high ground in the village, recommenced firing on the boats ferrying invaders between New York and Upper Canada. Their fire included shrapnel shells, or spherical case (hollow balls containing gunpowder and small balls, which exploded above the heads of enemies to rain destruction down upon them). To JN's ears, shrapnel explosions sounded like musket fire. With these developments, along with the sight of wounded men being carried back to Lewiston and rumours of the presence of warriors on the opposite shore, most of the Americans still on their side of the border refused to cross and support their comrades on the heights. Thus, the course of the battle began to shift in favour of the defenders about this time.

25 The Seneca's identity is unknown; the warrior likely was JN writing in the third person.

Those, who with more distant assault annoyed the enemy, attracted his attention until the fusil's flash and near report discovered the friends.[26] Then the foe raged like a hive of bees disturbed. Volleys of bullets flew towards them [i.e., the warriors], but all passed harmless over. Viewing each other with a smile, they acknowledged it rather too hot, and retired towards the more numerous body. In a few paces, they turned again upon the advancing foe, and met them with their well-aimed balls. The latter hesitated, and again fired a volley. The warriors reloaded and plied them well, when seeing the cloud of enemies thickening fast, and their more cautious friends keeping aloof, they ran swiftly along the mountain's side, and the hostile bullets passed harmless through the air, or rather among the branches. Enraged and thus retiring, they turned again to inflict more wounds upon the insulting foe.[27]

Having returned to those in the rear who lurked secure in a deep ravine, they thus endeavoured to arouse them: "Where are now those fierce spirits that at the village feast were wont to boast of their prowess? Why now so calm? Come forward whoever holds a manly heart!"[28] Some Delaware warriors from the summit of the hill met the advancing enemy.[29] The guns cracked, the bullets whistled through the air, the warriors rushed forward, closed, and drove back the foe.

---

26 This sentence suggests that while JN's party moved close to the Americans another war party distracted the invaders until his men opened fire, revealing their location.

27 The Americans advanced against the warriors to drive them off, but the move faltered and the invaders withdrew closer to the edge of the heights to increase the distance between their line and the forest and brush where the natives found shelter. The Americans had part of their force face north towards the village of Queenston and the rest look diagonally west and south across the top of the heights (with their right flank being located further inland than the left). Firing high, which the Americans did at this and other battles, was a sign of poor musketry training, but the warriors also took advantage of the terrain to conceal their movements and stay close to the ground. Years later, a Canadian militia officer remembered watching this part of the battle, writing, "It was most interesting ... to see Norton, young [John] Brant, and [William Johnson] Kerr, with about 50 Indians, driving in the outposts of the enemy on the edge of the heights above us. They [the Americans] being reinforced, obliged the Indians to retire. This happened several times, and as there was a clear sky beyond, it became quite a picture to witness the evolutions" (James Crooks, "Recollections of the War of 1812," c.1853, 35).

28 As noted earlier, warriors participated in spiritual ceremonies before going on campaign, which included affirmations of personal daring and audacity.

29 It is unclear whether the Delawares were part of the Six Nations contingent from the Grand, came from elsewhere in southwestern Upper Canada, or were a mix of both.

At this time a heavy fire commenced on our right. Supposing it to proceed from those of our people [i.e., the warriors] who were bringing up the rear having fallen upon the centre of the enemy, we ran there to extricate them from the difficulty in which they might have got involved from the great superiority of the foe. We found them retiring, and carrying away some wounded men, with a party of the enemy following, which we compelled to retire upon the main body. There had been only about twenty of them that had imprudently fallen upon the centre instead of joining us in a more advantageous position. They behaved with much gallantry, but were entirely put to flight with a severe loss: two chiefs and a warrior killed, and many wounded.[30]

In regaining our position on the flank of the enemy, we found numbers [of warriors] gone to the rear to a place that had been named as a rendezvous. A message was immediately sent after them, expressing that no place of rendezvous was acknowledged for that day unless it should be within sight of the enemy, and that wherever the cracking of guns was greatest, there they might be assured of finding us. We came in time to repulse the enemy, who had again advanced as far as the bakehouse, from which we had driven them at the first onset.[31]

We now saw with joyful hearts the troops and militia passing obliquely through the fields at the foot of the mountain to ascend it by the path where we had passed.[32] The enemy again sounded the charge,

---

30 The action on JN's right indicates that there were several distinct war parties in the field, each with their own chiefs, although they supported each other and were capable of decisive collective manoeuvres. It was normal in indigenous combat for there to be one or more senior individuals to direct the action at a higher level. JN served as the foremost leader that day within the loose character of native military structures. He later named eight men from Grand River wounded at Queenston Heights from the Cayuga, Mohawk, and Onondaga nations. That document includes information on men wounded elsewhere, although he did not always indicate the action where they suffered their wounds. It also provides additional detail, such as noting that some of the people who fought in 1812–14 were veterans of the American Revolution (JN to J.F. Addison, 13 February 1817, LAC, RG8, 261:25–33).

31 The bakehouse likely was at the British army's cantonment on top of the heights near its north side.

32 Instead of advancing up the heights from the village of Queenston in the face of American opposition, Roger Sheaffe's forces from Fort George marched a mile inland to gain the top of the escarpment out of range of their enemy and to join other men arriving from the south from Chippawa before moving against the invaders across flat ground.

but they advanced towards us with reluctant pace. They stopped and fired their cannon, loaded with grape, which rattled around.[33] We returned the fire with more effect. They soon retired; and now, although the enemy left the ground on which we first assailed them with many of their fallen friends lying around, we also had to lament the loss of some brave warriors, which served to whet the warriors' rage to renew the combat. We now awaited with impatience the arrival of the troops to fill the space on our right, that we might then push the enemy to the precipice without being enveloped.[34]

The ground on which we had fought was well adapted to favour a small number against a stronger force. On our left, the steep descent of Queenston Mountain, along which, and [across] the meadows beneath, we had an uninterrupted view; on our right, an extensive field that reached to the Niagara River, which exposed to our sight any body of the enemy that might advance in that direction to pass our flank. The space between the field and the brink of the mountain was clear of wood and about twenty paces in breadth, until within sixty paces of the sheds or cabins, when a copse of oak wood expanded so much as to render it impracticable to press the enemy any further with our small number unless we had been supported on the right.

General Sheaffe and the troops having now ascended the hill, I sent [someone] to inform him of our position. (The advantage I expected to derive from it made me very tenacious of leaving it myself.) The general sent to me Lieutenant Kerr of the Glengarry [Light Infantry Fencibles] to enquire more particularly into our situation and the

---

33 The Americans charged the natives on the heights, not Sheaffe's force below. Grape shot was an anti-personnel artillery projectile, normally consisting of a round disk for a base, a metal rod attached to the disk, and iron balls surrounding the rod, tied together in a cloth bag with cord (looking like a bunch of large grapes as the balls typically were about two inches in diameter). When fired, the component parts flew apart in a wide arc, like an enormous shotgun blast. It was less common than canister, which was a metal container (which looked similar to a food tin) that functioned the same way but contained smaller balls.

34 JN's men manoeuvred on the British left/American right flanks near the north slope of Queenston Heights. The "precipice" was the steep area on the riverside of the heights towards the east. In another document, he said that at this point "I concentrated my men in a ravine and desisted from assaulting the enemy until the troops could form on our right" (JN to Henry Goulburn, 29 January 1816, published in Cruikshank, "Campaigns," 44).

strength of the enemy.[35] I told him that we were ready to rush on as soon as the troops should form on our right, so as to draw the attention of the enemy to that quarter and to be in readiness to support us. He said that the general awaited the arrival of the grenadiers and militia from Chippawa, who were expected every minute. As soon as he had rejoined the general, a reinforcement of light infantry of one hundred men under Lieutenant McIntyre of the 41st were sent to us.[36] They were accompanied by Mr Clench and Mr Willcocks as volunteers.[37] At the same time, we were also strengthened by a number of Cayuga warriors who had been detained at Niagara from the

---

35 Roger Sheaffe's men ascended the heights inland from the river around 2 p.m. but still were some distance from the warriors at that point. Lieutenant Walter Kerr's mother was Elizabeth Johnson, daughter of Molly (Margaret or Gonwatsijayenni) Brant and Sir William Johnson, and thus he represented some of the complexities that terms such as "natives" and "newcomers" fail to articulate. His brother, Captain William Johnson Kerr, also fought at Queenston Heights, but with JN as an Indian Department officer, and spent most of the war with the Haudenosaunee. His wife was Joseph and Catherine Brant's daughter, Elizabeth. Fencibles were professional soldiers raised for service in a particular region, such as British North America, and could not be sent outside of it without their permission.

36 This was Lieutenant Angus McIntyre of the 41st Foot. These and other reinforcements helped to fill in the space between the rest of Roger Sheaffe's force and the warriors on the left of the British line. Light infantry were specialists in reconnaissance, skirmishing, ambushing, and guarding a larger force's front, flanks, and rear, as well as fighting in a more independent fashion from the rest of the infantry. In contrast, the main function of line infantry was to fire the massed destructive volleys at the enemy that normally determined the outcome of a battle (although light troops could do that as well). Effective infantry formations needed a balance of light and line infantry. In another document, JN wrote that General Sheaffe "sent Lieutenant [Walter] Kerr to enquire [about] our situation and the strength of the enemy, to whom I fully explained the advantage I expected to derive in assailing them from the quarter we occupied as soon as the troops should advance on our right. The general then sent me a further reinforcement" (JN to Henry Goulburn, 29 January 1816, published in Cruikshank, "Campaigns," 44).

37 Ralph Clench was head of an influential Niagara family. Joseph Willcocks was a politician and newspaper publisher who opposed Upper Canadian government policies, including those of the Indian Department. His views gave him some stature among the Six Nations of the Grand, which led a group within the tract to appoint him as their agent against the wishes of others along the river (Council Minutes, 31 October 1812, LAC, RG10, 27:16320–1). Isaac Brock employed him early in the war to try to encourage the Haudenosaunee to help defend British territory. Willcocks later deserted to the Americans and led a small gang of Canadian traitors from mid-1813 until he was killed at Fort Erie in 1814.

apprehension of its being also attacked. We were thus more than doubly strengthened.[38]

We arranged ourselves on the extremity of the left, the light infantry taking post on our right, next to the main body. When we saw the right wing enter the field, we rushed forward. The enemy fired. We closed, and they ran. From the side of a hill where they lay, they fired again. We came in upon them swiftly. They left their cannon; and we raised the shout of victory. Whilst our cannon fired on the right, we were in rear of their centre (which lined the skirts of the field through which our right wing was advancing). It fell into confusion. They [i.e., the Americans] ran in disorder, many falling on the way. They then took post behind the bank from whence they fired, as well-covered as from behind a breastwork. We rushed forward, and saw the grenadiers led by Lieutenant Bullock coming from the right along the bank of the river.[39] The enemy disappeared under the bank, many plunging into the river. The inconsiderate still continued to fire at them until checked by repeated commands of "Stop fire!" The white flag from the American general then met General Sheaffe, proposing to surrender at discretion the remainder of those who had invaded us.[40] The prisoners amounted to about nine hundred. Among these were General

---

38 At this point, the Americans remained confined to a narrow area on top of Queenston Heights with the steep downward slopes at their backs. They were short of ammunition and weakened by harassment from the warriors on the heights and from the British in the village below. Large numbers of demoralized soldiers hid away from their line or deserted back to the American shore if they could find a boat to take them. In subtracting the large number of shirkers, prisoners, and casualties, the invaders probably had only 500 effective men on the heights by this point. Once Roger Sheaffe reached the heights from the north, he deployed his men in preparation to advance against the American position. He had 900 men under his command by the time he was ready to move.

39 .This was Lieutenant Richard Bullock of the 41st Foot (not to be confused with his father, a captain with the same name in the regiment).

40 Just after 3 p.m., the British advanced against the Americans, and the two sides fired volleys at each other. The British closed and fought at close quarters as the invaders' line disintegrated and many of its soldiers plunged down the cliff towards the Niagara River before surrendering, which they did with some difficulty in the confusion of the fighting across rough terrain. The shooting ended at about 4 p.m., followed by efforts to secure prisoners and attend to the wounded. Elsewhere JN wrote: "As soon as all was in readiness and the cannon began, we rushed upon them and broke the flank, pursuing them with considerable slaughter till we raised the shout in the rear of the centre, which seemed to throw the whole into confusion,

Wadsworth, Colonels Scott [and] Chrystie, and many others.[41] They
had no reason to complain of cruelty this day.[42] In this last assault, the
41st lost only two men, and the militia the same number. The flank
companies of the 49th as well as our party suffered more severely. Their
encounter early in the morning prior to our arrival, I shall endeavour
to report as correctly as possible.

From their [i.e., the 49th's] accustomed vigilance, they discovered the
enemy at their first landing, and opened such a heavy fire upon them
as completely checked their advance for a considerable time.[43] General
Brock joined them in the battery, and while he was exhorting them to
hold a determined countenance to the enemy in front, a detachment
from the latter, who had gained the eminence in ascending the bank
of the river by a fisherman's path, attacked them in the rear, and compelled them to retire from the battery.[44] General Brock, attempting to
rally them under cover of a wall at the bottom of the hill, received a
ball in the breast, of which he instantly expired. His body was carried
into a house, and this gallant band, enraged at the loss of their brave
commander, inclined to the right, and having ascended the hill again,
attacked the enemy until the great odds of number rendering their
efforts hopeless, they were compelled to retire. Captains Dennis and

---

when, in less than half an hour, we had them down the precipice to the river" (JN to
Henry Goulburn, 29 January 1816, published in Cruikshank, "Campaigns," 44).

41 These were Brigadier-General William Wadsworth of the New York militia, and
regular army officers Lieutenant-Colonel Winfield Scott of the 2nd Regiment of
Artillery and Lieutenant-Colonel John Chrystie of the 13th Regiment of Infantry.
The overall American commander at the battle, Stephen Van Rensselaer, had been
on Canadian soil for only part of the battle, and had returned to the American side
before the surrender.

42 A few warriors may have killed or wounded Americans trying to surrender. One
also killed a Canadian militiaman mistaken for an American. As we have seen
above, JN was sensitive to the common but exaggerated view that indigenous people
committed atrocities. Yet his comment here seems out of character with his general
reliability as a witness to the events of the war, although his use of "inconsiderate"
might have been an acknowledgment of the problem in the confusion that marked
the end of the battle.

43 This section describes events prior to the arrival of the warriors on the battlefield,
which took place mainly around the village of Queenston on the north side of the
heights. As noted earlier, the first wave of American boats approached the Canadian
shore under fire.

44 This was the battery part way up the north side of Queenston Heights.

Williams of the 49th grenadiers and light infantry were both wounded, and Lieutenant-Colonel Macdonell of the militia – the inseparable follower of our brave commander – here received his mortal wound. The militia flank companies attached to the troops were commanded by Captains Hatt, Durand, and Chisholm.[45] The length of time they maintained their position against the formidable body of the enemy which attacked them is the strongest encomium on both the officers and men engaged.

To ascertain the number that the enemy lost this day is not in our power. We know that they transported to their side of the river many of the wounded, and we have just reason to suppose that they did the same by the dead (which the dispatch of General Van Rensselaer confirms).[46] A letter was shown [to] me that had been found on some of the American officers of General Winchester's army, which computed their loss at Queenston at eighteen hundred men, and it was generally allowed that twenty-two hundred men had crossed the river. It was reported that four thousand men, including militia, had been in readiness at Lewiston; but that the militia in the rear, becoming disheartened at the incessant attacks upon those who had already passed to the Canadian shore, and the havoc made among them (which they perceived by the return of the dead and wounded in the boats intended for their transportation), they refused to embark. And it was to remove this panic that General Van Rensselaer returned to Lewiston, but all his endeavours were ineffectual. Prior to our final assault, many of the enemy had recrossed![47]

---

45 These officers from the 49th Foot were Captain James Dennis of the grenadier company and Captain John Williams of the light company. Lieutenant-Colonel John Macdonell, on the general staff of the Upper Canadian militia, was Isaac Brock's provincial aide-de-camp, and also served as the colony's attorney-general and a member of the legislative assembly. He assumed command in the vicinity of Queenston after Brock fell and moved inland a short distance before attempting to ascend the heights, but was shot, which brought the British counterattack to a halt for the time being. He passed away the next day. Captains Samuel Hatt and James Durand commanded flank companies in the 5th Lincoln Militia, and James Chisholm led a flank company of the 2nd York Militia.

46 This is a reference to the American commander, Stephen Van Rensselaer. Newspapers regularly published official dispatches, which other papers reprinted, and thus information became commonly known across the Anglo-American divide.

47 As we shall see below, American Brigadier-General James Winchester suffered defeat and capture early in 1813 at the second battle of Frenchtown. His papers fell

The grief caused by the loss of General Brock threw a gloom over the sensations which this brilliant success might have raised. The dead of the enemy were buried, and we collected the remains of our gallant friends. They were interred with the due honours. At the funeral of General Brock [at Fort George], a great proportion of the militia of the country attended (having been called upon to assemble) and a general salute was also given from the cannon in the enemy's garrison [at Fort Niagara] immediately after our cannon had fired.[48] In a council, General Sheaffe expressed to the Five Nations, in the warmest manner, his thanks for their spirited exertions.[49] A truce was agreed upon, and all

---

into British hands. At Queenston, the Americans lost as many as 500 men killed and wounded, along with 925 taken prisoner. Another 800–1,000 on the New York side of the border deserted during the week following the battle. The invaders also lost a large quantity of weapons and equipment. The defenders had 25 killed (including two Cayugas, two Oneidas, and one Onondaga) and 92 wounded (of whom between seven and nine were natives, although JN's account may be read to suggest that there were more indigenous casualties). The British also had a small number of prisoners taken, including a Haudenosaunee chief, but they were exchanged quickly.

48 The gunfire represented a decision by the Americans to show respect for Isaac Brock. Along with the regulars and militia, warriors participated in the funeral on 16 October, forming a guard of honour and subsequently conducting a traditional condolence ceremony, with JN present (Council Minutes, 6 November 1812, LAC, RG8, 256:194–6). Brock and his aide-de-camp, John Macdonell, were buried in a bastion at Fort George until moved to a monument at Queenston Heights in the 1820s (replaced by the current monument in the 1850s, built in part with funds donated by the Grand River Haudenosaunee).

49 Much of the success in the battle of Queenston Heights stemmed from the contributions of the Six Nations (and the troops below the heights), who prevented the Americans from consolidating their position and then wore down the invaders until Roger Sheaffe brought his forces together in strength for the final portion of the fighting. Sheaffe reported that the warriors merited "the highest praise for their good order and spirit" and singled out "Chief Norton, who was wounded" (General Order, 21 October 1812, LAC, RG8, 1168:325). JN's wound was slight (Sheaffe to Sir George Prevost, 13 October 1812, published in Sheaffe, "Letter Book," 277). Writing on the day of the victory, the general noted that his ability to concentrate men from the north and south of the heights was "chiefly to be ascribed to the judicious position taken by Norton and the Indians with him on the woody brow of the high ground above Queenston" (Sheaffe to Prevost, 13 October 1812, ibid., 275). After the war, he recommended that JN (along with a small number of officers) be given a medal for Queenston Heights, but one was not issued (Sheaffe to Unknown, 7 June 1815, ibid., 378–9). Another record, by a Canadian officer, recorded that "I was sent in the night [12–13 October] with a party to prevent the enemy coming down the mountain [i.e.,

the militia taken in the late conflict were allowed to return home in the same manner as had been done in the capture of General Hull. Only the regular troops taken prisoners were sent to Quebec.[50]

We observed that the Americans were occupied in drawing bateaux from the old fort of Niagara towards the Falls, and we got notice that General Smyth had collected at Black Rock and the vicinity about eight thousand men, including the militia.[51] As the boats were all taken to that part, it was thought that Fort Erie was the part menaced; and for its security General Sheaffe stationed in that quarter a great proportion of the militia, besides a strong detachment of the 41st, 49th, and two flank companies of the Newfoundland.

Near the end of November, notice was given that the truce was to expire in three days.[52] Preparations were made at our batteries to open upon them with a cannonade, and the general went up the river towards Fort Erie to see that the necessary arrangement should be made for the defence of that quarter. At the dawn of day [at Fort George], the mortar battery commenced, and was followed by the others, six or seven guns all together. Of these, two 24-pounders taken from General Hull seemed to make the greatest impression. Some of the shells fell in the great house [at Fort Niagara], on which they had erected a battery, and might have done them some mischief. They returned our fire with great punctuality, completely riddled the houses of the town of Newark [or Niagara], and killed two men, a soldier of the 49th and Captain Frey, a half-pay officer of the American loyalists of the Revolutionary War. This

---

the north slope of the heights]. Captain Norton with 70 Indians were before me. He crossed the fields, gained the mountain, drove in their flank parties, and attacked their main body. He was repulsed with some loss, having so few men" (William Hamilton Merritt, Journal, n.d., published in Sutherland, *Desire of Serving*, 3).

50 After the battle of Queenston Heights, Roger Sheaffe and Stephen Van Rensselaer negotiated a truce. Aside from the need to bury the dead and care for the wounded, General Sheaffe had to secure the large number of prisoners in his care while Van Rensselaer worried that he could not resist an assault into New York. The militia prisoners were paroled but most of the regulars were not.

51 Stephen Van Rensselaer resigned shortly after his defeat at Queenston. Brigadier-General Alexander Smyth of the United States Army negotiated an extension of the truce, which allowed Roger Sheaffe to let a portion of the militia and warriors go home, with the result that the native contingent with JN on the border was small towards the end of 1812. Smyth's forces seem to have numbered 5,000 rather than JN's estimate of 8,000.

52 Alexander Smyth cancelled the armistice on 20 November.

was all the loss we sustained from a cannonade of at least eight hours, and from about six or seven pieces of ordnance. The mess house of the 41st was burnt by a red-hot shot, and a house under the enemy's fort of about the same dimensions was burnt by a shot from our batteries. It was reported that the fire of our artillery had been more destructive to them than their fire had been to us.[53]

A few days subsequent to this event, an express from Fort Erie informed us that the enemy had crossed there. We marched up the river. At Chippawa, we joined the flank companies of the 49th, and meeting General Sir Roger Hale Sheaffe at the same time, he caused us to stop there, the affair above being ended. A mixed detachment of sailors and soldiers under a Captain King had come over in the night, and having surprised the militia stationed at the ferry, they proceeded to the battery, which they also gained (it being open in the rear). Another party had landed near the quarters of a detachment of the 49th. They killed the sentry; and falling upon them suddenly in the house, the officer was badly wounded and some of the men were killed and wounded. The 49th from Fort Erie coming to their succour, a part of the enemy retired across the river, and Captain King with a small party that remained with him were taken prisoners. The loss of the enemy on this occasion was perhaps equal to our own, but we had to regret the death of a worthy young man, Lieutenant King of the Royal Artillery, who was wounded at his gun and taken off prisoner to the enemy's shore, where he died after lingering a long time. It was said that it had been arranged for the

---

53　The events of this paragraph occurred during an artillery exchange on 21 November between Forts George and Niagara and their external batteries. The British lost one wounded and two killed (the private mentioned by JN and Barent Frey, a retired officer from Butler's Rangers). The Americans suffered 11 killed and wounded. Mortars normally fired exploding shot (or shells) on high trajectories, which often allowed their crews to drop projectiles into enemy defences. Exploding shot consisted of a hollow iron ball filled with gunpowder, equipped with a timed fuse so that the shell exploded at or above the target. Artillery guns, in contrast, normally fired on a much lower 0–5 degree trajectory, and were rated by the size of solid shot they fired; thus JN's 24-pounders fired iron balls (round shot) of that size. Round shot did not explode but smashed into or through its target (and hence needed to fire on a low trajectory to maximize the impact). Round shot could be heated to red-hot temperatures to set buildings and vessels on fire. The "great house" was a large (still extant) building at Fort Niagara dating from the 1720s. At the time, the Americans had dismantled the roof so that the upper floor could serve as an artillery battery to help compensate for the fact that Fort George had the advantage of sitting on higher ground than their post did. The "mess house" was Navy Hall outside Fort George.

army of General Smyth to have followed this detachment immediately, which might be considered as the forlorn hope. This far, however, is certain: that the American army were embarked and some of the boats came nearly halfway over the river when the militia, which lined the Canadian shore, began to fire, and they retired. The whole then disembarked and returned, the regulars to their encampment and the militia to their homes. We heard that the latter were so much enraged at their general that they came little short of shooting him.[54]

Every few days, we gained some intelligence through the means of deserters that were constantly coming to us. We got Smyth's proclamation, which even exceeded Hull's. In it he offers a reward of forty dollars for the despoils of every Indian warrior.[55] We heard that a disorder, apparently epidemic, raged in the camps of the enemy, of which many died, and subsequent to the battle of Queenston, we felt some tokens of it prevailing among ourselves. The symptoms resembled much the

---

54 Before dawn on 28 November, Alexander Smyth (who was deeply unpopular among his soldiers) launched a two-pronged assault across the Niagara River. More than 400 men landed downstream of Fort Erie with the objective of facilitating the success of a larger attack against the fort, while others ferried troops across the river or participated in the operation near the end of the battle of Frenchman's Creek. Over 600 regulars, militia, and warriors on the British side repelled the Americans, killing, wounding, or capturing 130 of them, while suffering 100 killed, wounded, and taken prisoner of their own. Next, after sunrise, Smyth tried to embark 3,000 men to attack Fort Erie, but abandoned the effort after the lack of success in the first assault, logistical problems, and bad weather. He made another attempt two days later but cancelled it as well. The reference to "Sir Roger" recorded the fact that General Sheaffe received a knighthood for his victory at Queenston Heights in January 1813. The first "King" mentioned by JN was an American, Captain William King of the 13th Infantry, who was wounded slightly and then captured; the other was Lieutenant Charles King of the Royal Artillery, who was wounded in action and subsequently died while imprisoned in Buffalo. (JN also referred to Brock as "Sir Isaac." He had been knighted for his success at Detroit, but did not live to hear about the honour.)

55 JN inserted a footnote to define despoils as: "the scalp," which is how people then and historians since have interpreted Alexander Smyth's words. The relevant part of the proclamation read, "I ... will order 40 dollars to be paid for the arms and spoils of each savage warrior who shall be killed" – an amount equal to five months' pay for a private (Smyth to the Soldiers of the Army of the Centre, 17 November 1812, published in Cruikshank, *Documentary History*, 4:216). There was some hypocrisy on the American side regarding scalping, because some combatants in the republic either took scalps or hoped to do so, while the press and society in general condemned warriors for scalping dead enemies. For Euro-Americans, scalping was little more than trophy hunting, but in native society there was a widespread belief that spiritual power was concentrated in the scalp, and thus it could be "adopted"

pleurisy. Those attacked complained of violent pains in the breast, and sometimes in the loins and head. It was more generally fatal to the aged and to children.[56]

From Chippawa, we proceeded to Fort Erie where we remained until near Christmas, when the apparent impracticability of the enemy making any further attempt to invade us for that season allowed us to retire. At this place, we lost a valuable chief of the Cayugas. He was descended from the celebrated chief of that nation so much esteemed by Monsieur de Frontenac. He was about sixty years of age, but in the late engagement he seemed to show the vigour of youth. He died of four days' illness, his complaint in the breast and head.[57]

General Sir Roger H. Sheaffe gave us a hearty welcome, and the lines being free from any further apprehension of attack until the spring, he cordially approved of the warriors returning to their homes. Previous to their going, they had received all the goods in the Indian store, which nearly amounted to a suit for each person. They had also required of him some provisions for the use of their families (their crops of corn having greatly failed on account of the harvest having been neglected from their attention to the service). He immediately complied, at the same time desiring the deputy superintendent-general [of the Indian Department] to make an estimate of the quantity necessary to supply their deficiency. Sometime after I had returned to the Grand River, I learnt that two Mohawks had visited the different villages and had made their report of the deficiencies.

---

into a family and thereby strengthen the family spiritually (whereas adopting a prisoner was beneficial both spiritually and temporally). Scalping was rare among British and Canadian forces, and some natives opposed scalping, such as Mohawk warrior John Smoke Johnson (Sakayengwaraton), who fought alongside JN at Queenston Heights and who rose to prominence on the Grand in later years. Scalps were taken from the dead, although at times wounded people thought to be dead were scalped (and sometimes survived).

56 Sickness was a major problem for armies at the time, but the Americans suffered particularly badly, in part because of shockingly poor sanitary conditions in their camps and garrisons, even by the period's standards.

57 This man's identity is unclear, but his ancestor likely was Ourehouare, who JN mentioned in his description of Franco-Haudenosaunee diplomacy when Louis de Buade, Comte de Frontenac, governed New France from 1689 to 1698 (*JMJN*, 230–3). JN added a footnote regarding "descended": "That is, of the same branch or family and holding the same rank in the nation."

4

Ambiguity and Frustration on the Detroit Front, 1813

Beyond the victories in the Old Northwest in 1812, the successful defence of the Niagara Peninsula – due partly to the efforts of the Six Nations – helped secure Upper Canada for the following winter, when the weather restricted military operations to some degree. Farther east, an American effort directed against Montreal collapsed in the latter part of November. Thus, Lower Canada also survived the first year of the conflict, keeping open the only viable supply line into the upper province from Great Britain. The government in London managed to send reinforcements late in 1812 and continued to do so into 1813, and officials within the colonies improved the defensive posture of the Canadas for the next campaigning season. Yet not everything unfolded to the advantage of the allies, especially because the United States increased its war-making capabilities at a faster pace than its opponents could. For example, its shipbuilding efforts on Lake Ontario would shift the balance of power to the republic on that strategic waterway for much of 1813. The Americans also enjoyed some successes before the end of the year, although not on the scale of their adversaries' victories at Detroit and Queenston. In September 1812, for instance, its soldiers repulsed indigenous attacks against Forts Wayne and Madison in the Indiana and Missouri territories, and burned a number of aboriginal villages across the Old Northwest. Consequently, affairs had not swung as decisively against the republic as often has been asserted. Although limited, American resilience undermined the prospects of creating independent indigenous homelands in this region, despite the surrender of Michigan during the summer.

Isaac Brock's successor, Major-General Roger Sheaffe, followed orders from the governor-in-chief of British North America, Sir George Prevost, to appoint Teyoninhokarawen "Captain of the Confederate Indians" shortly after the battle of Queenston Heights.[1] *That distinction stood above his captaincy in the Indian Department and was the same honour that Joseph Brant had held during the American Revolution. His abilities in English and various First Nations languages, combined with the depth of his knowledge of white and aboriginal societies, his military talents, and his obvious commitment to Canadian defence, made him an obvious choice in Prevost's mind to mediate native-newcomer relations effectively. From the army's perspective, his energetic support for the British alliance was important, as exemplified in a letter General Sheaffe wrote in 1813, in which he declared, with some exaggeration, that Teyoninhokarawen "is the only leader of Indians that I can repose confidence in or expect much assistance from."*[2]

After returning home to the Grand River from the Niagara Peninsula at Christmas 1812, John Norton travelled to the Detroit River early in 1813. He did this because British commanders thought he might assume a principal leadership role among its native population on a temporary basis at a critical moment, especially because the military authorities did not believe that local Indian Department officials were competent.[3] *Sir George Prevost wanted to eliminate American threats that might overturn the successes of 1812 in the Old Northwest. With few troops to spare, he believed that much of the burden would have to be carried by the First Nations who stood to gain the most if Michigan and neighbouring territories could become autonomous homelands for them. Therefore, he appointed a prominent fur trader, Robert Dickson, to be the Indian Department's superintendent for native affairs on the upper Mississippi River, and ordered him to recruit warriors from the region's western and northern reaches during the winter of 1813 and bring them to the Detroit front for the spring campaign to increase the size of indigenous forces that could be deployed in that theatre. Meanwhile, he wanted John Norton*

---

1 JN to James Fulton, 26 June 1813, LAC, RG8, 257:93; Francis de Rottenburg to Noah Freer, 31 July 1813, ibid., 257:109. An 1814 letter noted that Sir George Prevost had given JN "a commission as captain and leader of the Five Nations Grand River Indians or confederates," which indicates that Sheaffe acted on Prevost's orders (Noah Freer to Gordon Drummond, 1 March 1814, LAC, RG10, 28:16704).

2 Roger Sheaffe to Henry Procter, 20 April 1813, published in Sheaffe, "Letter Book," 377. Before the war, people sometimes referred to JN as "Captain Norton," but in those cases "captain" seems to have been used informally in the way it commonly was applied to indigenous leaders (e.g., Sir Evan Nepean, "Sketch of Captain Norton's Claim," 1805?, Bodleian Library, Wilberforce Papers, C.4, Fol. 109).

3 Noah Freer? to Roger Sheaffe, 14 January 1813, LAC, RG8, 257:15; Antal, *Wampum Denied*, 115.

and the Wyandot chief, Roundhead, to gather eight hundred men around the Detroit border area and march on American positions in northwestern Ohio, accompanied by any soldiers who could be spared to help. Prevost thought the mixed native-newcomer force could support Tecumseh's warriors, concentrated in Indiana, and harass their opponents' communications lines and otherwise weaken them so that the American army would become "an easy prey" when Dickson arrived with reinforcements.[4]

For his part, the local commander on Upper Canada's southwestern border, Henry Procter, looked forward to having John Norton back in that theatre.[5] *This is one of several hints we have that the British considered Norton for an important position earlier in the conflict. They presumably intended his captaincy in the Indian Department to help facilitate his efforts by providing him with an income, status in the white world, and access to resources to distribute to his followers.*[6] *(At the same time, we see indications in his memoir that army officers and Prevost issued direct orders to Norton, but these came outside of the department's structure. His commission did place him within the colonial hierarchy, and, like other aboriginal people in Crown service, his loyalties could be pulled in different directions. There is no indication, however, that he experienced a personal conflict in serving both the British and the native causes, despite occasions when he acted contrary to the wishes of the Indian Department and expressed his frustrations over his relationships with different people, whether native or newcomer.) Moravian missionaries in 1812 had thought he might command an "army of Northwestern Indians," presumably comprising people from Upper Canada and the Detroit River region but drawn from outside of the membership of the Western Tribal Confederacy.*[7] *Another indication of his potential derives from Norton's narrative of his travels through southwestern Upper Canada in 1812, in which he had tried to coordinate the operations of the St Clair area Chippewas and some of the local militia with his own war party. It also is difficult to imagine that he did not engage in meaningful discussions with British officers, Tecumseh, and other leaders during the 1812 Detroit campaign on how to*

---

4 Sir George Prevost to Lord Bathurst, 27 February 1813, published in American and British Claims Arbitration Tribunal, *Cayuga Indians*, 1:465–6 (quote on 466). For more on Dickson's efforts, as recorded by Sauk chief Black Hawk (Makataimeshekiakiak), see Benn, *Native Memoirs*, 47–53.

5 Henry Procter to Isaac Brock, 11 August 1812, LAC, RG8, 677:18.

6 JN's pay as a captain in the Indian Department was five shillings per diem, along with rations and forage.

7 Fairfield Diary, 5 August 1812, published in Sabathy-Judd, *Moravians*, 483–4.

prosecute the war to achieve native objectives, especially as he had thought deeply about finding lands beyond white control in the pre-war years. As well, his memoir seems to indicate that he had been regarded as something of a pan-tribal leader when non-Haudenosaunee warriors made their way east to the Niagara River after the fall of Detroit and took their place on the lines alongside him and the Six Nations (as would occur at other times as well). Thus, as hostilities entered their second year, his place among the natives of the Great Lakes transcended his adopted status as a Mohawk; his ethnicity as a Cherokee; his political, diplomatic, and social roles within the Six Nations; and his captaincy in the Indian Department, to include links to indigenous people elsewhere. We can see these connections throughout his memoir, as he regularly mentioned diverse peoples who joined his war parties or otherwise accepted his leadership, although the number of individuals who aligned with him varied from a handful to several hundred, depending upon circumstances. He was not the only person to engage in such cross-national roles, of course. Tecumseh and Tenskwatawa were the most famous examples from the period, while the Sauk chief Black Hawk, or Makataimeshekiakiak, was another well-known example; but our understanding of that role is limited by history's general failure to study cross-cultural leadership in indigenous affairs throughout the colonial-era conflicts of the Great Lakes.

Remarkably, Teyoninhokarawen's narrative is comparatively quiet about exercising such a prominent role in 1812 and unclear about his attempts to do so during the early months of 1813, despite allusions to people from various communities joining him and exchanges he had with important individuals beyond the Grand River. While his autobiography has a modest quality when speaking of his own behaviour, we should remember that he normally avoided addressing issues and events that he did not like rather than tell untruths. As we shall see, those grand plans for a pan-tribal alliance, as they involved John Norton, did not come to fruition. Given that he did not accomplish much during the winter of 1813, and that people criticized him for his failures (as documentary records included in the annotations below indicate), we might assume that he did not want to discuss his attempts to serve as an important multinational figure at the time. His lack of success ought not to surprise us. Sir George Prevost's expectations seem to have been unrealistic within the usual traditions of aboriginal leadership, where people always had been suspicious of power being concentrated in one individual, especially if Euro-American society imposed a person on them, whether native, white, or mixed. In addition, he was something of an outsider to most of the people of the Old Northwest, which presumably limited his capacity to play a major role. Furthermore, Prevost's patronage of Norton could be expected to generate a hostile response from Indian Department personnel who were concerned to subvert any efforts to shift control of Britain's relationships with the First Nations away from themselves, especially given Teyoninhokarawen's history of opposition to their agenda to restrict indigenous freedoms.

During the period covered in this section, the United States sent an army west in an attempt to regain control of the Michigan Territory. That force seized Frenchtown (now Monroe, Michigan) from its opponents in January 1813, but then experienced defeat in a second battle in the village shortly afterwards, which stalled American efforts for some months. While Norton arrived on the Detroit front too late to participate in the fighting, his journal preserves his insights on the wider campaign beyond his own experiences. It was after that battle that Norton tried unsuccessfully to fulfil Sir George's wishes. As noted, his narrative is vague on the subject, merely stating that while he wanted to move against the Americans with warriors unaccompanied by soldiers, another leader wanted the British to come with them (with the consequence that the expedition did not occur, although the weather and other factors also contributed to cancelling it). For his part, Tecumseh did not campaign against the Americans that winter. Instead, he devoted his energies in the area around Prophetstown to strengthen support for his confederacy and recover from a leg wound he had suffered at the battle of Maguaga in 1812.

As spring approached, Teyoninhokarawen returned to the central parts of Upper Canada. There, he found that the Indian Department had undermined the alliance with the Grand River people in its quarrels against both him and the army. He also travelled to York to meet General Sheaffe to defend his actions in the west and discuss indigenous affairs. He expected to return to the Detroit region, presumably to try again to contribute to operations there, but did not do so. Unfolding events kept him in the Niagara area, where he would see considerable action through the summer of 1813, which we will examine later in his memoir. In addition to describing his movements, this part of the narrative presents second-hand information on various events in 1812 and 1813, including descriptions of the battle of York and the siege of Fort Meigs.

About the beginning of February, having received an order from the commander of the forces [Sir George Prevost] to attend a council of the tribes near Amherstburg, where Mr Robert Dickson had his directions to deliver a speech, I set out in company with that gentleman, taking with me three young warriors.[8] On the road, we met the officers and men of General Winchester's army, who had been taken prisoners at Frenchtown, and were now on their way to Niagara to be sent over the river that they might return to their homes.[9] Within a few miles of Delaware Town, we met an express. On enquiring, "What news?" we received for [an] answer, "Bad enough: General Harrison's army has been seen advancing to the River Raisin within a few miles of that place."[10] It being now past midnight and the roads in advance very bad, we remained that evening at Delaware Town. At this place, we met Hoyatategh, a Mingo or Seneca warrior, together with his son, a youth of fifteen years of age, returning to the Grand River to see their relations living there.[11] They had been in the [first] battle of Frenchtown, River Raisin, and the father gratified our curiosity by relating the part which he had observed in this encounter. He said that he, with about twenty of his nation and a party of Potawatomis (not very considerable), had been in advance of the River Raisin three or four days prior to the general action. That then the Americans first

---

8 The speech Dickson carried presented Sir George Prevost's thoughts to the tribes. It discussed American misbehaviour, rehearsed the history and benefits of the British alliance, and called upon the First Nations to continue fighting with the objective of restoring the 1795 Greenville Treaty line, a boundary that would have put northwestern Ohio and most of the rest of the Old Northwest under indigenous control and undone extensive land surrenders (Prevost, Speech, 18 January 1813, quoted in Allen, *Indian Allies*, 223–4; for a map of the post-1795 land losses, see *First Nations of the Old Northwest and Adjoining Regions*, in Benn, *Native Memoirs*, xvi). After meeting Sir George in Quebec, Dickson travelled west with JN between the Grand River and Amherstburg, which gave them time to discuss Sir George's expectations. Beyond JN's potentials as a leader, Prevost also did not have much confidence in the region's Indian Department personnel (Robert Dickson, Memorandum, 23 December 1812, LAC, RG8, 256:228; Dickson to Prevost?, 15 February 1813, ibid., 257:52; Prevost to Sir Roger Sheaffe, 27 March 1813, ibid., 1707:154–67; Sheaffe to Henry Procter, 3 February 1813, published in Sheaffe, "Letter Book," 336–7). We do not know who the "three young warriors" were.

9 On 22 January, an American force under Brigadier-General James Winchester suffered defeat at the second battle of Frenchtown, which JN described later in his narrative.

10 This was a force commanded by Major-General William Henry Harrison, the senior American officer south of Lake Erie, which had been charged with retaking Detroit.

11 JN believed that Hoyatategh deserved recognition for his service as a warrior in the Niagara and Detroit theatres (JN to J.F. Addison, 13 February 1817, LAC, RG8, 261:28). That letter suggests that Hoyatategh lived at Grand River after the war, but in 1813, he may have been associated primarily with the Mingos in the Ohio country.

arrived, and that a [British] field piece having been stationed there, they attached themselves to it in order to prevent it from falling into their hands, which involved them in a fight with some hundred riflemen. They fought, retiring through the plains until evening, when they reached the woods and the enemy returned to the River Raisin. They lost several men, and the sergeant of artillery, who conducted the gun with great gallantry, died shortly after from a hurt which he then received.[12]

In the evening of the 21st January, General Procter came up with several hundred of the 41st Regiment and the Newfoundland, and about five hundred warriors, principally Potawatomis, Chippewas, and Odawas, excepting about seventy Wyandots, the same number of Delawares, [and] the party of Mingos already mentioned. They marched towards the enemy in time to enable them to arrive there before the dawn of day. In forming for the attack, the regular troops took the centre; the Wyandots, the Mingos, and Delawares were on the right; and the Potawatomis and Chippewas composed the left wing. The troops advanced against that part of the enemy that were under cover of a stockaded garden fence, which was a sufficient cover from musketry, and opened a fire upon them with great spirit. But in returning it, the enemy had a great advantage because they were completely secure themselves and our troops [were] entirely exposed, [with] the adjoining grounds forming a complete plain. At this time, the warriors of the right wing, advancing rapidly, attacked a body of five or six hundred men, principally regulars, who had formed on the plain. The Wyandots were mostly mounted. They assailed them with such fury that the assault and defeat were almost at the same instant, and the pursuit was continued with such earnestness that very few escaped. They were all killed or taken. Among the latter was General Winchester himself, who had commanded this division in person. As soon as he was brought in [as a] prisoner, the Kentucky militia, who had defended the stockaded garden fence, surrendered [as] prisoners of war (and they were those already mentioned which we had met

---

12 In the first battle of Frenchtown on 18 January, 650 American militiamen (mainly volunteers) drove 250 First Nations warriors and Canadian militia out of the village in a three-hour struggle. Losses on the British side are unclear, but conflicting numbers range from four to 20 or more; there were 67 American casualties. The "sergeant" was Bombardier James Kitson of the Royal Artillery (the only regular with the British force), in charge of a 3-pounder militia gun crew.

along the road). He spoke highly of the gallantry of the British troops, and lamented their great loss.[13]

The next morning, early, we proceeded. On the way, we met a few of my friends, the Munsees, going to their village. I sent a message by them to their people and the Chippewas of the same village requesting the warriors to follow us. I did this because, from the information taken down by the express, I had reason to believe that Amherstburg was yet menaced with an attack from General Harrison.[14] At the Moravian town, we remained half an hour with the worthy missionary. I found that the son of the chief of this village had received two wounds in the late conflict, one in the mouth, the other in the breast. He was, however, in a fair way to recover.[15] We passed on to a tavern, where we met a number of teamsters and others returning with their sledges.[16] Early in the morning, we recommenced our journey, and that evening we arrived at Sandwich, having travelled upwards of sixty miles that day.[17] On the road,

---

13 This paragraph describes the second battle of Frenchtown on 22 January. After the Americans secured the village on the 18th, Brigadier-General James Winchester arrived with more men at the head of one component of William Henry Harrison's army as part of a move to march northwards and push the British out of the Detroit region. Henry Procter and Roundhead led 1,200 regulars, militia, warriors, and others against Winchester's 1,000 regulars and militia. The five-hour confrontation cost the Americans 900 killed, wounded, and captured; the British and First Nations side had 200 losses. Although many natives owned horses, fighting on horseback was uncommon among them in the lower Great Lakes region. The mounted men used long-handled tomahawks as their primary edged weapon in the charge.

14 Although James Winchester had been defeated at Frenchtown, the British worried about the movements of the main portion of the American army under William Henry Harrison; however, the allied success in battle, combined with other problems facing Harrison, brought American offensive efforts against the Detroit region to a halt for the time being.

15 The wounded man was a war chief, Joseph (Josephus) Jacobs. His father was Jacob (Gendaskund) and his mother was Christiana. Although JN refers to Joseph as a son, he was not a young man. He may not have intended to fight because a document noted that some men had gone to Amherstburg for clothing (presumably supplied by Indian Department officials) and "could not avoid taking part in a battle on the Raisin River." It also recorded that the bullet wounds "were not fatal" (Fairfield Diary, 20 January 1813, published in Sabathy-Judd, *Moravians*, 488–9).

16 Henry Procter transported wounded men part of the way from Frenchtown to Amherstburg on sleighs.

17 In order to travel so far in one day, JN's party probably was on horseback or in horse-drawn sleighs.

we met a number of the American inhabitants of Detroit, sent away by General Procter in consequence of a discovery having been made by a conspiracy for cooperating with the invading army of the enemy.[18]

On calling upon him the next day, he informed us that he had been misled as to the subject of the express we had met, from the too great precipitation of those who had brought the intelligence from the River Raisin. We learnt that the remainder, or rather the division of the enemy's army under General Harrison, consisting of seventeen hundred men, had retired to the Carrying River, or La Rivière du Portage (eighteen miles southeast from the rapids of the Miami [Maumee] River).[19] In consequence of this information, it was proposed to march there without delay and attack them before they could receive any reinforcements. The general approved of the plan, but expected the Indians to undertake the expedition alone, thinking it imprudent to hazard the loss of any of the troops under his command, already too weak to defend the position allotted to them to hold. I thought with him that the warriors of the different tribes then assembled were in sufficient force to defeat the enemy, and at the same time were more capable of performing the expedition with secrecy and dispatch when alone than when accompanied by troops. We had, however, the council and too many ceremonies to go through.[20] Roundhead (or Stayeghtha), Sounehhooway, and a few Wyandots went to reconnoitre.[21] They returned with intelligence that the enemy had assumed a position at the foot of the rapids [on the] Miami River, about forty-five miles from Amherstburg.[22] One delay succeeded

18 As the American army advanced before the battles of Frenchtown, some people in Detroit threatened to rise against the British garrison, while residents of the River Raisin region helped the republic's forces, and others aggressively protested the Crown's administration of the occupied territory. Henry Procter responded by declaring martial law in Michigan and removing some of the individuals whom he thought threatened British security.
19 William Henry Harrison had upwards of 3,000 men, although a large portion of the volunteers were eligible to leave before the end of February. At the beginning of that month, he withdrew to the area of modern Woodville, Ohio on the Carrying River.
20 Councils, other meetings, and post-battle condolence ceremonies incorporated a range of protocols and ritual elements that participants needed to respect.
21 JN rendered the name as "Karonteoreas," which seems to have been a variation of "Tharoutorea," a name for Thomas Splitlog, whose native name more commonly was rendered "Sounehhooway."
22 The Americans began constructing Fort Meigs (in today's Perrysburg, Ohio) in February. Roundhead's reconnaissance discovered it in March. Its purposes were to

another until a thaw commenced, after which we knew the ice could not hold long, and when it should break up, the succeeding floods would not only impede our journey, but render our passage across the Miami River almost impracticable. Myeerah then made a speech in council, expressive of their resolution not to go without being joined by the troops. The season now began to [be] opposed to our undertaking, [with] obstacles more difficult to surmount than all he could say.[23]

While in the neighbourhood of Detroit and Amherstburg, some of the Americans accused of having been concerned in the conspiracy fabricated many stories of the cruelties exercised by the Indians on the prisoners taken at Frenchtown. That there may not have been some instances of this kind, it is difficult to say, but [that] no such instances of cruelty have been general or public, we can with all confidence affirm. General Winchester and many other officers were personally taken by the Indians. The former was delivered by Stayeghtha to General Procter; and others, who had been retained for some time and not delivered up until after repeated intercession on their behalf by the British officers, made no complaint of cruelty. A young officer of the American regulars, whom the Potawatomis had wished to retain (but at the intercession of the British commander, had released), spoke in high terms of the kindness with which he was treated. Indeed, the wandering Indians of the

---

guard the approaches to Ohio from Detroit and serve as a staging point for offensive operations towards Michigan.

23 These events seem to have undermined JN's credibility for a time, as Robert Dickson received orders "to explain to Norton and Roundhead in the most distinct terms the service the King expects from his faithful allies, the Indians" (Noah Freer to Dickson, 1 March 1813, LAC, RG8, 1220:209). Aside from the letter's insensitivity towards indigenous autonomy, the British were frustrated because the natives had not taken the active measures against William Henry Harrison that they had wanted them to perform. Had they done so, they presumably would have degraded the fighting capacity of American forces by the time Robert Dickson returned from farther west with more men in the spring (Sir George Prevost to Lord Bathurst, 27 February 1813, ibid., 1220:204–6; Prevost to the Prince Frederick, Duke of York and Albany, 20 March 1813, ibid., 1220:238–9). JN subsequently explained himself satisfactorily (Sir Roger Sheaffe to Prevost, 5? April 1813, published in Sheaffe, "Letter Book," 362). Later, the governor-in-chief thought it necessary to encourage JN after the controversy surrounding his performance on the Detroit front, saying that "with very great satisfaction ... I have heard from different quarters the high commendations which have been passed upon your courage and activity since the commencement of the war" (Prevost to JN, 24 May 1813, LAC, RG8, 1221:90).

vicinity of Detroit had become much contaminated since that place had been in the possession of the Americans. They had been debauched and impoverished by their own drunkenness and the knavery of their neighbours to such a degree that tenderness or delicacy of feeling could not be expected to fall to their share. The Wyandots were the principal exception in that neighbourhood. Their morality had been more firmly established by the precepts of Christianity and [they] were not, therefore, so suddenly changed. It would be useless as well as endless to repeat the number of cruelties that had been asserted, and as bluntly contradicted, without proofs to substantiate either on one side or the other; and as the Americans are fond of complaining of cruelty without just cause, I should be more inclined to believe the contradiction than the assertion.[24]

While I was at this place, I received two letters to return to the Niagara frontier. At the same time, in compliance with a request of General Procter, Sir George Prevost assented to my remaining there, of which I was informed by his aide-de-camp, Lieutenant-Colonel McDouall; but there existing no possibility of any active operations at that time, I returned home with my party, promising to endeavour to rejoin him

---

24 The "conspiracy" referred to efforts by Americans in Michigan to subvert British control of the territory. After defeating James Winchester at the second battle of Frenchtown, Henry Procter withdrew north to safeguard his forces because he thought William Henry Harrison might counterattack. Since he did not have enough sleighs to transport all of the injured, he left 50–80 (mainly wounded) American prisoners in the village under the care of captured medical staff and a small party of British Indian Department officials. He did not leave more men to guard them because he expected Harrison to arrive in the community within a short time and thus did not want to weaken his forces more than necessary. On 23 January, 50 warriors, apparently angered at brutalities committed against natives earlier, and having drunk heavily, murdered some of the Americans in an event known as the Raisin River Massacre. The number killed is unclear, but it seems to have been about 30. JN affirmed that whites used alcohol to degrade, impoverish, and exploit indigenous people, a view that was common within the First Nations world during this period. Through exaggerated propaganda in the United States, the killings reinforced long-held American prejudices against the First Nations and their British allies, which helped to unite people behind the war effort in the badly divided republic. JN seems to have been tainted by that event even though he was not present, as one bitterly ironic newspaper comment spoke of "'Yield to our mercy,' which has shone so conspicuously in the transactions of Tecumseh, Procter, Chief Norton, and others of His Majesty's worthies" (*The Chronicle, or Harrisburg Visitor*, 12 July 1813).

in the spring.[25] I was much troubled at perceiving in the Indian Department of this neighbourhood a strong dislike of the general, apprehending that by the insinuations which their ill nature might urge them to throw out, they might seriously injure the service.[26]

While I remained at this place, I saw two or three persons from the village called the Prophet's Town on the Wabash (inhabited by Tecumseh) with a party of Shawnees, Kickapoos, Potawatomis, and Sauks, in all amounting to about four hundred men. At this time, a message was sent to call these people to Amherstburg.[27] The operations which took place in this neighbourhood since the capture of General Hull [in 1812] were also related to me. All the warriors that could be collected in the neighbourhood, together with the Indian Department, accompanied Major Muir with a small party of troops. Their object is said to have been the capture of Kekionga or Fort Wayne, a small fortress situated at the portage between the Miami of the Lake [Maumee River] and the Wabash. They left Amherstburg towards the end of September, and advanced as far as the Auglaize, or main forks of the Miami. Here a scout fell in with a party of Americans and took them prisoners. They thereby gained intelligence that a numerous body of the enemy were advancing. After some deliberation, they retreated, and the enemy either remained stationary or advanced very slowly.[28]

---

25 Robert McDouall was a captain in the 8th Foot at that time. He became a major in the Glengarry Light Infantry in June 1813 and a brevet lieutenant-colonel in July.

26 Although Henry Procter won the second battle of Frenchtown, his casualties may have been higher than necessary because he opened the battle with an artillery bombardment, which gave his opponents time to assemble and fight better than they may have done had he made a surprise assault. He also was the subject of broad criticisms for his management of operations at the time. JN's comment seems to have been motivated in part by desires to note how Indian Department behaviour undermined the war effort, in contrast to the army's leadership, in which he had more confidence.

27 Tecumseh returned to the Detroit front early in April after spending the winter in the Prophetstown area.

28 Captain Adam Muir (mentioned earlier) received the local rank of major in August 1812. A native force of 500 besieged 100 men at Fort Wayne in the Indiana Territory between 5 and 12 September 1812 (near the site of the Miami village of Kekionga, 160 miles southwest of Detroit). Henry Procter learned about the investment, and on 14 September dispatched Muir with 250 regulars and militia along with 800 warriors to help take the post, not knowing that the siege had ended. On 25 September, 45 miles from Fort Wayne (near today's Defiance, Ohio), Muir heard that 3,000 Americans were operating close to him. Outnumbered and short of

In the October [of 1812] following, Lieutenant-Colonel Elliott, with his Indian Department (of Amherstburg) and a few hundred warriors, being at the foot of the rapids [on the] Miami River, they saw the Americans on the opposite bank. But they did not come in contact with each other, excepting about twenty or thirty Indian warriors that passed the river and exchanged a few shots with the enemy, which I believe furnished the subject of a very long dispatch from the American commander.[29] About this time, Mr Clark of the Indian Department having been sent on a scout, he was taken prisoner by the enemy, who treated him with great severity.[30] [In another incident] Mr Elliott, the son of Lieutenant-Colonel Elliott by a Shawnee mother – a very promising young man – having gone on a reconnoitring party with a Potawatomi chief and three warriors, about twenty-five miles up the river from the foot of the rapids, they met three Shawnees from Wapakoneta and asked them where they were going. They replied, "To see their father," meaning Lieutenant-Colonel Elliott. They belonged to the same tribe with young Elliott, who said to them, "Then you shall go with us." The Potawatomi chief and a Tuscarora [in Elliott's party] went in front. The three Shawnees followed them. Elliott and two warriors brought up the rear. They had stopped to pick some haws from a tree near the

---

supplies, he nevertheless prepared to fight, but the native contingent suffered from internal divisions, which led many of its men to leave the expedition, so that only 350 warriors remained by 28 September. Therefore, having engaged only in minor skirmishing, the allied force returned to the Detroit River. For the next few months, the Americans concentrated their efforts on securing their territories and raiding native villages in Indiana and Illinois rather than threatening the British in Detroit.

29 Lieutenant-Colonel Matthew Elliott of the 1st Essex Militia was the superintendent of the Indian Department at Amherstburg. On 29 October, to ease the pressure on limited British food stores, he took 250 natives towards the Miami (Maumee) River rapids, where there were crops to harvest and where the Americans had abandoned stocks of provisions following their earlier defeats. He arrived on 7 November but withdrew after some minor skirmishing with a larger opposing force. We do not know what JN meant by the "dispatch" but the American press covered the campaigning in this region, and a newspaper article that reprinted an official report likely had come to his attention.

30 Andrew Clark, a white person who grew up with the Shawnees, worked as an interpreter for the Indian Department and was close to Tecumseh. He fell into American hands while hunting near Matthew Elliott's force. His captors threatened to kill him in order to extract intelligence about British deployments in the region. He later returned to the British lines, and died of wounds received at the October 1813 battle of Moraviantown.

path when they heard the report of guns, and at the same instant saw that the Shawnees had shot the chief and the Tuscarora. Immediately after, Mr Elliott received a mortal wound. Exhorting the young man to fight, he fell dead from his horse. They returned the fire with great precision, wounding two Shawnees, one of whom, named Logan, died of the wound. The body of the youth was taken to the unfortunate father, who late in November embarked in a vessel to return to Amherstburg, where he arrived after having been driven about by adverse winds. The whole party returned to that place, and nothing more was heard of the enemy until the advance of Winchester in January, as already related.[31]

We returned from Sandwich [to Amherstburg], and so did more than a hundred militia that had come from the neighbourhood of Long Point in consequence of the late alarm, which had arisen from nothing more than this: an inconsiderable party of Wyandots, having collected together a drove of the cattle and hogs belonging to the army under General Winchester (and which had been scattered in the action), were discovered approaching the River Raisin on the ice by the militia on the lookout. Apprehension, or the reflection of the sun, changing the rear appearance of the objects, the hogs were mistaken for infantry, the horned cattle for the cavalry, and the Wyandots, who were mounted and were observed to be constantly riding from one extremity of the line to the other, were allowed to be General Harrison and his staff (as they appeared to be

---

31 Alexander Elliott's Shawnee mother was Marie Louise Sanschagrin. He had been educated as a lawyer in Montreal, recently had been called to the bar, and was a captain in the Indian Department. Wapakoneta (in today's Auglaize County, Ohio) was a predominantly Shawnee town whose residents allied with the United States. On 22 November 1812, Elliott's party captured three Shawnee cousins from that community who were scouting for the Americans. Included among them was the famous Captain (or Johnny) Logan (Spemicalawba). It seems that the people in both parties knew each other. The British-allied group let the other individuals travel with them unbound, and possibly with their weapons. The prisoners either grabbed their captors' guns or used their own, and shot five of the seven people in Elliott's party, including Alexander, and then escaped (although Logan received a mortal wound in the fight). The men with Logan were Bright Horn (Waskweela/Wathethewela), who recovered from his wounds, and Big Captain Johnny (known as Moluntha after his father) who was not hurt. The Potawatomi chief killed was Winamac (one of two chiefs of that name at the time, the other being pro-American). The identities of the other people are unclear. In December, when Matthew Elliott retired from the Miami River rapids, he brought his son's body home for burial, but his schooner became trapped in ice while crossing to Amherstburg.

occupied in preserving regularity in the line of march). On arriving at Frenchtown, all appeared in their proper characters, but the express had been dispatched by the zealous and vigilant observer, and he to whom it was entrusted travelled with such diligence that the *éclaircissement* never overtook him.[32]

I had only been three or four days at the Grand River [after returning from the Detroit River] when I was called to the [Niagara] frontier and required to take a party of warriors with me. I went myself but I could not at that time collect any number of men. They had begun to make preparations for the making of maple sugar, and were not very well pleased at not having yet received the assistance in provisions which they had required for their families.[33] They therefore preferred remaining at home to provide for them by following their usual occupations to going to the lines at that inclement season of the year, where they would suffer seriously from remaining in an uncomfortable situation, while the islands of ice floating down the current of the Niagara threw so many impediments in the way of invasion as rendered the attempt very improbable and the execution almost impracticable. Irregulars, who at home have to work or hunt for the support of their families, ought not to be called too often, else perhaps in the time of want they may answer to the call in such a reluctant manner as not to render very efficient service. Worn out with fatigue, unadorned with glory, the very best men retire to their homes with disgust to alleviate, as much as possible, the poverty and distress into which their families may have been involved from their absence.

Arriving at Niagara, I found that General Sir Roger H. Sheaffe had not yet returned from York, where he had been called in a civil capacity as president of the province. In his absence, General Vincent held the command of the troops stationed on the frontier.[34] We gained information

---

32 This story relates to the period after the second battle of Frenchtown of January.

33 These events likely occurred early in March 1813. JN's text indicates that the Indian Department had failed to obey Sir Roger Sheaffe's orders because of its opposition to his support for JN. With JN away in the west, the department was in a good position to work against him among the Six Nations of the Grand, such as by distributing supplies to its friends and withholding them from his supporters (Sir George Prevost to Sheaffe, 27 March 1813, LAC, RG8, 1707:163–4).

34 Lieutenant-Colonel John Vincent was a brigadier-general as of February 1813 (which at that time was a temporary position in the British army, not a formal rank). Promoted to major-general later in 1813, he commanded at the battles of Fort George

from some deserters from the enemy that their force from the other side [of the Niagara River] did not exceed thirteen hundred men, that the main body of their army had concentrated at Sackett's Harbour, and that the militia had returned home. It was also reported that an attack upon Fort Erie or the batteries in that neighbourhood was in contemplation on the 17th of March, and we made all the preparation in our power to receive them. It, however, ended in a cannonade of no great execution on our side, and what damage the fire of our cannon did to them, we could not ascertain.[35]

I received a letter from General Procter calling upon me to join him [on the Detroit front]. At the same time, at Niagara, I was required to remain on that frontier. It surprised me that no intimation had been made to the officers commanding in this quarter regarding the directions Sir George Prevost had given that I should assist in acting against General Harrison. I then thought that, as we had certain indications that the enemy was preparing two armies in two different and distant points (to attack us at Niagara and Detroit at the same time), and thereby effectually preventing us from rendering assistance to either, that it was most advisable to act offensively in the part where he might yet be the least defensible. At Detroit and that neighbourhood, where the greatest number of native warriors might be collected, it appeared weakness to allow General Harrison to establish a position within forty miles of Amherstburg and 150 miles in advance of the American settlements [farther east] from whence he was necessitated to get all his supplies of provisions. I therefore felt desirous to participate in an attempt against that place, that if we should succeed in annihilating the force which threatened that quarter, we might then concentrate the greater

---

and Stoney Creek, and then served under Major-General Francis de Rottenburg on the Niagara front until late in the year. On one occasion he wrote that JN's "anxiety and zeal for the public service" was "constantly conspicuous" (Vincent to Sir George Prevost, 19 May 1813, ibid., 678:303). In contrast, JN's journal presents several softly stated criticisms of Vincent. First, the previous paragraph seems to refer to his decision to call the warriors to the front lines earlier than necessary; second, readers will note references to Vincent below often include subtle hints that JN did not agree with that officer's decisions. JN's words contrast with his typical comments on the senior army leadership, which normally were positive.

35 The artillery duel on 17 March generated light casualties and limited damage. St Patrick's Day was a holiday celebrated with enthusiasm by the American military at the time.

part of our troops and warriors for the defence of the Niagara frontier, which would be adequate to repel any army they could bring against us that campaign.[36]

I went to wait upon General Sir Roger H. Sheaffe at York, and found him occupied in fortifying the place and mounting every gun that could be found, hastening the building of a ship then on the stocks, and forwarding the troops as they came up [overland from Kingston] to the Niagara frontier. The first division of the King's or 8th had just arrived there.[37] He expressed great surprise that the people of the Grand River had not yet received the provisions which they had required, and immediately gave directions to write to the deputy superintendent-general of Indian affairs on the subject. He told me that he was fully assured from the information which he had received that either York, Niagara, or Kingston would be attacked, that he was anxious to get the ship upon the stocks completed as soon as possible, and that he had already sent one which had wintered there to join the fleet at Kingston.[38] He allowed

---

36 William Henry Harrison's "position" was Fort Meigs in northwestern Ohio. As discussed earlier, the Americans, with greater resources, often thought of launching two or more simultaneous attacks to prevent the British from concentrating their limited forces to repel a single thrust against Upper and Lower Canada. Logistical and administrative challenges within the republic's military establishment, however, made it difficult to coordinate two large deployments at once. The British realized that a pre-emptive attack against their enemies in one quarter might allow them to muster in strength in another, but they had few troops for such operations. They did besiege Fort Meigs in the spring of 1813 as a forestalling move, however, as we shall see below.

37 These soldiers arrived on 25 April, two days before the battle of York, which means that JN left the provincial capital to go back to the Grand River that day or early enough the next to miss the news of the approach of the American Lake Ontario squadron, spotted by lookouts towards the evening of the 26th. He had arrived in York at least by 19 April (Sir Roger Sheaffe to Sir George Prevost, 19 April 1813, LAC, RG8, 678:170). The 8th Foot formed part of the reinforcements sent to Upper Canada. JN used "division" informally to signify part of a battalion of infantry rather than the larger military formation, or even the period's definition of a division within a battalion.

38 The British knew the Americans were assembling troops at Sackett's Harbour for the spring campaign, but did not know where they would attack first. Logically, Kingston should have been the primary target, because it sheltered the Royal Navy's Lake Ontario squadron, the loss of which would have been fatal for Upper Canadian defence; however, the Americans decided to attack the weakly defended provincial capital of York instead. They overestimated Kingston's fortifications, and they needed a victory to help sway voters in New York to support pro-war candidates

me to go to assist General Procter, as I had promised to the warriors of
the west to rejoin them, but with strong injunctions to return as soon
as possible. Indeed, I would have been sorry to have left him on any
other occasion than in the hopes of promoting the good of the service
by destroying that portion of the enemy's force which threatened the
west, so that the tribes in that quarter being freed from all apprehension with respect to themselves, the warriors would have come forward
with greater alacrity to assist in repelling the more formidable attack of
the enemy on the Niagara frontier.[39]

I parted with my good friend Sir Roger H. Sheaffe in hopes that his
forebodings of an attack would not take place till I should have rejoined
him or till he had received reinforcements sufficiently powerful to repel
any attempt of the enemy. Having reached the Grand River and called
upon the warriors who had engaged to follow me to the west, we were
informed that a heavy cannonade had been heard in the direction of York.
In consequence of this information, I hastened to the lake [Ontario]. There
it was ascertained, by the arrival of some soldiers in a boat, that York had
been assailed by a formidable fleet and army, and that it had in all probability fallen.[40] I immediately sent to the Grand River to call together all

---

in the state elections scheduled for late April. At the time JN met General Sheaffe in
York, the British were building a 30-gun frigate, the *Sir Isaac Brock*, which Sheaffe
wanted to finish and send to Kingston. The other vessel mentioned, which had
sailed to Kingston, was the 12-gun *Prince Regent*. Not being aware that the *Prince
Regent* had left York, American commanders thought that seizing both it and the
Brock would give them a decisive advantage on Lake Ontario without having to
capture Kingston.

39 Sir Roger Sheaffe wrote: "Captain Norton is here and is so urgent for my assent to
his going back to Detroit, pleading that he had engaged his word to the Indians
there for his speedy return, that I cannot withhold it. He promises not to stay long
away from me" (Sheaffe to Sir George Prevost, 19 April 1813, LAC, RG8, 678:172).
After the war, JN described this meeting, writing, "I did not think fit to leave our
own frontiers [i.e., Niagara and western Lake Ontario] without the assent of Sir R.H.
Sheaffe, which he at first declined giving, alleging that he soon expected an attack.
Being desirous to overcome General Harrison that we might concentrate to repel
the attack hanging over us, I persisted, and he acquiesced. However, it was of no
effect, for a few days after, while I was yet collecting my party to go, we heard that
the enemy had attacked York" (JN to Henry Goulburn, 29 January 1816, published in
Cruikshank, "Campaigns," 45).

40 The sound of cannonading carried long distances in a world that was much
quieter than today's, and people heard the battle at least as far away as Niagara.
Confirmation of the 27 April fall of York reached the British at Fort George two

the warriors able to come. There were soon collected between three or four hundred men from the Grand River. Having sent forward a scout with a letter to the general, I followed with the main body. At the Head of the Lake Ontario, we learnt that the Americans had re-embarked and that General Sir R.H. Sheaffe had retired upon Kingston.[41] I at the same time received letters from Niagara, which required me to repair to that place. I could not, however, prevail upon my people to accept of this last invitation. Had the enemy yet been onshore at York, they were willing to go and attack them, but they could not reconcile themselves to leave their families to starve while they should remain stationary at Niagara, particularly as the present season was that of preparing their fields for planting the maize. They also murmured at seeing no move whatever among the militia, as the latter certainly had as much interest in defending the country as they could have. Many who were even personally attached to me yet returned home to prepare their cornfields before they should commence the campaign. So, I proceeded towards Niagara with a very small party.[42]

---

days later. The battle was the first major American victory in the war. The United States Navy's squadron of 14 vessels, carrying 2,550 soldiers and sailors, sailed to a point west of York's defences. Its leaders sent men ashore under the protection of the squadron's guns. The British force of 800 soldiers, militiamen, warriors, and others fought from the landing site eastwards along the waterfront but recognized they could not hold the town. Therefore, Major-General Sir Roger Sheaffe withdrew from his primary defensive works (at the site of today's Fort York) and set a fuse to blow up its gunpowder magazine. The explosion caused heavy casualties among the Americans and halted their advance long enough for Sheaffe to burn the frigate being built in York that the Americans had hoped to capture, along with naval stores, and then retreat overland to Kingston with his professional troops at the end of the six-hour battle. The warriors also withdrew but the militia remained to surrender the town and stay with their families. Casualties numbered 320 killed and wounded on the American side, and 160 on the British, along with the surrender of the militia and some of the other troops in York who did not escape with Sheaffe.

41 The text is unclear as to whether the "general" was Sir Roger Sheaffe, assumed to be near York, or John Vincent in the Niagara region. The Head of the Lake was the region around today's Hamilton, Coote's Paradise, and neighbouring areas. After the Americans captured York on 27 April, they boarded their vessels to leave on 2 May but had to remain in the harbour for six days due to adverse weather conditions. JN arrived at the Head of the Lake about 3 May. The warriors had assembled as part of a potential effort to march on York, launch surprise attacks on the Americans, or otherwise take action as circumstances allowed.

42 About 100 Grand River warriors went to Fort George, although most later returned home. JN's "very small party" reminds us of the limits of his military leadership

On arriving there, we heard accounts of the unfortunate affair of York; and as is common whenever the result is disastrous, little merit was given to the defence.[43] It appears that at the attack on York on the 27th of April, there were with General Sir R.H. Sheaffe the grenadiers of the King's and a detachment of the Glengarry [Light] Infantry and of other regiments (about three hundred men). The number of militia in arms, I have never been able to ascertain, and those who only appeared upon paper could not with propriety be classed among the defenders of the place. There were also sixty Mississaugas and Chippewas. The enemy approached with a favourable wind in fourteen armed vessels (one carrying twenty-eight guns, the *Oneida* sixteen guns, [while] the others were of inferior force). The [shore] batteries opened a spirited fire upon them, but [were] unavailing against so great a superiority. During the cannonade, a small magazine at one of the batteries exploded, and killed and wounded several men.[44] When the enemy demonstrated his intention to land, the grenadiers of the King's were detached to oppose them. The Mississaugas and Chippewas were also sent in the same direction. Before the grenadiers could reach the place of landing (which is more than a mile west from the batteries), the enemy had disembarked and filled the woods with an immense number of riflemen. Against these this heroic band opposed a most undaunted resistance until they lost their much-lamented Captain McNeale and the greater part of them were killed or wounded.[45] They then retired. The Mississaugas also cooperated in opposing the enemy until a number of them were killed or wounded, and [further] resistance was unavailing. They

---

even among like-minded people, as was typical in the Haudenosaunee world. At some battles and other major confrontations, he served as a senior leader with sizeable war parties (e.g., Queenston Heights and Chippawa) but not at others (e.g., Stoney Creek and Fort Erie).

43 Some of York's prominent citizens and other people criticized Sir Roger Sheaffe for losing the battle, which led to his removal from the civil and military leadership of Upper Canada.

44 This was a small gunpowder magazine at a defensive work known as the Western Battery, located about one kilometre west of Fort York at the mouth of the harbour. It blew up accidentally late in the battle after the Americans had established themselves onshore, killing and wounding men and overturning one of its two artillery pieces.

45 Although grossly outnumbered, Captain Neal McNeale led his grenadier company of the 8th Foot in a charge to drive the Americans from their landing spot west of the Western Battery early in the fighting. At first, he enjoyed some success, but then fell prey to superior numbers of enemy soldiers.

then moved off as quickly as possible to take care of their women and children. Some few of the inhabitants of York joined the grenadiers, and of these, a Mr McLean was killed.[46]

The enemy having thus effected his landing, and advancing with an immense force in the rear of the batteries, any further resistance was thought useless.[47] The general, therefore, gave orders for a retreat, first making arrangements for the complete destruction of the King's stores [and] of the ship building there.[48] The explosion of the magazine took place when the enemy were within a small distance of the place. It killed General Pike and many more, and threw the whole army into such consternation as gave ample time for the destruction of the ship and retreat of the troops.[49] At the River Don, they met the light company of the King's running to their assistance. They had come many miles that morning, the report of the firing sometimes inciting them to a trot, eager to arrive in time to participate with their friends in the contest.[50] The force of the enemy is said to have amounted to between two and three thousand men. Major Allan of the militia capitulated with them for the town.[51] General

---

46 The warriors were the first to oppose the American landing, but the invaders drove them off. The grenadiers mentioned prior to this in fact arrived next. Donald McLean, the clerk of the Upper Canadian House of Assembly, volunteered to serve with the soldiers that day.

47 The Americans pushed along the waterfront and did not gain the rear of the British batteries, but their movements threatened to do so, which helped demonstrate the futility of further resistance after the Western Battery had been damaged by the explosion mentioned above.

48 While burning the *Sir Isaac Brock* deprived the Americans of the frigate that they had expected to seize, its destruction and the loss of naval supplies was a blow to British naval aspirations on the Great Lakes.

49 American Brigadier-General Zebulon Montgomery Pike died because of injuries from the explosion of the garrison's main gunpowder magazine, which occurred after the explosion at the Western Battery. He had led the invaders onshore while overall command of the expedition rested with Major-General Henry Dearborn, who remained on board the squadron. Commodore Isaac Chauncey commanded the naval forces.

50 The Don River marked the eastern edge of York. The light company of the 8th Foot had been marching towards the town from the east when its men realized it had come under attack, and therefore they hurried to help. They arrived too late to participate in the battle beyond screening the retreat (although the Americans did not pursue the British).

51 Major William Allen of the 3rd York Militia, a businessman and political figure, negotiated the capitulation along with his superior officer, Lieutenant-Colonel William Chewett of the same regiment, and the town's Anglican rector, the Reverend John Strachan.

Sir R.H. Sheaffe proceeded with the remnant of his force to Kingston to protect that post and the ship that was building there, which, if the enemy had been able to destroy, would have entirely prevented our fleet from making its appearance on the lake that campaign.[52]

At Fort Niagara, we observed the enemy constantly engaged in forming additional redoubts, strengthening the old works, and collecting troops in the neighbourhood, which formed several encampments. The [American] fleet from York landed there all the troops which had been on that expedition. At other times, we perceived boats arrive laden with troops. The fleet returned to Sackett's Harbour, and we remained in expectation of an attack whenever it should revisit our neighbourhood with another cargo of soldiers.[53]

In the meantime, an express arrived from the west, which informed us of the success of the troops and Indians under the command of General Procter at the rapids of the Miami. We fired a salute in exultation for the good news; and shortly after, the Americans did the same, and on the same occasion. I shall therefore relate the particulars of that affair as we heard them from such as were present. At the beginning of May, General Procter moved from Detroit with two or three hundred regulars of the 41st, upwards of a thousand Indian warriors of the different tribes, and some of the Detroit militia. He came to the foot of the rapids [on the] Miami River, and finding General Harrison too strongly fortified [in Fort Meigs] to hope for success from a *coup de main*, he invested him. Batteries were erected on both sides of the river, but the artillery was too light to make much impression.[54] The warriors behaved with great intrepidity, taking advantage of every slight cover that the

---

52 The ship at Kingston was the 22-gun HMS *Wolfe*, completed about the time of the battle of York.

53 Following the capture of York, the Americans concentrated troops in and around Fort Niagara for the second phase of their campaign, an attack on Fort George, which came in late May. The United States Navy landed troops who had participated in operations at York a few miles from Fort Niagara on 8 May, and then sailed to Sackett's Harbour to bring back more men for the assault.

54 Henry Procter, Tecumseh, and other indigenous chiefs, at the head of 2,200 men, wanted to launch a quick assault against Fort Meigs on the Miami River; however, with 1,200 Americans entrenched behind stout defences under the command of William Henry Harrison, they could not do so. Therefore, they besieged the post from 28 April to 9 May, using artillery to weaken it in hopes either of forcing the defenders to surrender or of opening gaps in the fortifications for an assault. The "Detroit militia" mainly came from the border regions of Upper Canada.

natural face of the ground afforded. They advanced daily to within a small space of the parapet, from behind which none of the enemy could show their heads with safety. They formed two divisions. The one was stationed on the southeast [or right] bank of the river, where the enemy had taken position and fortified; the other remained on the northwest [or left] bank.

The enemy, having notice of the advance of more than a thousand militia to their assistance, made a sally from their fortification on the redoubt next to them [on the right bank]. They overpowered the party of the 41st which held it, took Lieutenant McIntyre with some prisoners, and pursued the remnant.[55] At this time, Tecumseh came up with a body of Indian warriors, retook the batteries, and drove the enemy into his fortifications with great loss. On the northwest [or left] side of the river, the reinforcement of the enemy landed, and there they had also a temporary advantage, but the vigorous cooperation of the warriors of the different tribes with the troops soon overcame all resistance. Those who were not killed surrendered [as] prisoners.[56]

An act of cruelty was here perpetrated so suddenly as to prevent the interference of the humane. A worthless Chippewa of Detroit, having with him a number of wretches like himself, who had not the courage to kill their enemies while in arms, but yet were desirous of obtaining the repute of having killed them, they assailed the unfortunate prisoners and killed a sentry of the 41st that stood forth in their defence. They had made great havoc before their ungenerous fury could be restrained. The remainder of the prisoners, to the number

---

55 This was Lieutenant Angus McIntyre of the 41st Foot.

56 The attackers erected their main gun emplacements on the left bank of the Miami River across from the fort to bombard the post. On 5 May 1813, a 1,200-man American relief force came down the river. Of these, 800 soldiers under Lieutenant-Colonel William Dudley landed on the left bank upriver of the British positions, and then assaulted the British and natives opposite the fort, driving them some distance; however, they then suffered a costly defeat in a British and First Nations counterattack. The other members of the relief force moved directly to Fort Meigs on the right bank. At about the same time, William Henry Harrison sent troops out from his post for a short period to attack both the natives and the British gun emplacements on the right bank. Casualties throughout the siege totalled 80 killed and wounded among the allies. The Americans lost 350 killed or wounded and 600 captured. At a tactical level, Henry Procter and Tecumseh did well, but strategically the siege was an American success, which accounts for both of the opposing sides on the Niagara River firing a salute to honour the performance of their combatants.

of several hundreds, were sent to Cleveland (or Cuyahoga) to return to their homes.[57]

Finding that the guns [of Procter's artillery] made little or no impression on the fortifications of the enemy [after defeating the American relief force and those who sortied from the fort], and the Indian warriors, according to their ancient custom thinking themselves free from any further engagement [on] this expedition, as they had now struck a blow, began to return to their homes. General Procter retired from the investment and marched back to Amherstburg.[58]

---

57 The "worthless Chippewa" was Splitnose (Normee), a chief from the Detroit region. The murdered sentry was Private Paddy Russell of the 41st Foot. The number of prisoners who lost their lives is uncertain, but it seems to have been about 25, although most estimates suggest 40. Many of the warriors present opposed the murders. Tecumseh, other natives, Indian Department officials, and British soldiers came to the prisoners' rescue and brought the killings to a halt. Procter released the captured men on parole largely to protect them from the potential of further violence.

58 Towards the end of the siege, Henry Procter and Tecumseh withdrew north after the majority of warriors and a large percentage of the militia left the army, placing them in the untenable position of besieging a force secure within its fortification that outnumbered them. For many warriors, going home after participating in one engagement was normal, and in this case, they left the area with considerable quantities of seized materials and some prisoners (most of whom they turned over to the British). In describing Iroquoian Cherokee warfare, but within the context of a broad assessment of aboriginal combat, JN wrote, "One rencounter is all that is sought for in an expedition, and when it is met with, they say, 'This is the fortune the Great Spirit had prepared for us'" (JMJN, 124).

5

The Fall of Fort George, Desperate Moments, and the Battle of Stoney Creek, 1813

Teyoninhokarawen next saw action at the mouth of the Niagara River, where he fought in the unsuccessful defence of Fort George in late May 1813. Defeated, the British retreated not only from that post, but also from Fort Erie and other positions along the waterway to reassemble at Burlington Heights (in today's Hamilton). At about the same time, the Americans repulsed an attack on their Lake Ontario naval base at Sackett's Harbour. With the republic's forces in the ascendant, the Six Nations Tract seemed vulnerable to a direct assault by the invaders who now occupied both sides of the Niagara River, especially as many believed that the British soon would abandon all of Upper Canada west of Kingston. That prospect threw the Haudenosaunee of the Grand River into crisis, especially as they remembered the devastation inflicted upon them a few decades earlier during the American Revolution, when rebel armies burned their villages, destroyed their crops, and impelled them to seek shelter in squalid refugee camps surrounding Fort Niagara (then held by Crown forces). Naturally, they wondered if all of the rebuilding of their world that had consumed their energies since arriving in Canada in the 1780s might be undone through American retribution for their alliance with King George III. Consequently, many of them withdrew from their homes to hide in safe places, while some thought they might need to purchase American forgiveness by falling on the vulnerable British camped in and around Burlington Heights. Thus, as the Americans followed up their success at Fort George by marching troops through the Niagara Peninsula along the shore of Lake Ontario towards the British positions in early June, a sizeable number of warriors assembled near the heights with uncertain intentions, while rejecting requests to send men to help the colony's defenders in the coming confrontation. Would they fall on the British army or the settler population if the invaders were to win another battle? That was the vital question

*on the minds of the King's officers and in John Norton's thoughts at that
moment. These developments troubled him deeply, and we will see his distress
expressed through elusive and incomplete descriptions of the situation at the
time. As a vigorous proponent of the Anglo-Haudenosaunee connection during this troubled period, Teyoninhokarawen lost most of the support he had
enjoyed earlier, and found himself reduced to leading a small war party as the
crisis moved towards its conclusion. With deep anxieties over the security
of the province and the safety of its inhabitants, the British made a fraught
decision to launch a surprise night attack at Stoney Creek against the much
larger American force, accompanied by John Norton's small band of followers.
It was a desperate move, but if they were to win the battle, they then could
begin the difficult process of re-establishing dominance in the Niagara region
to preserve their hold over the colony.*

The warriors of the Grand River were very dilatory in coming down
to Niagara this spring. I heard of their making preparations, but none
came. I had only about sixty or seventy effective men when the enemy's fleet reappeared. We saw troops landing [on the American side
of the border] from the ships, and deserters gave us information that
there was a numerous army assembled on the opposite shore. Our force
was scattered along the lines from Fort George to Fort Erie (a distance
[of] more than thirty miles). At the former post the greater proportion
remained. The enemy sent a detachment to the Head of Lake Ontario,
burnt the Government House, [and] landed near the house of the late
Colonel Brant. His widow having retired with her family, they broke the
windows and returned to their ships triumphant.[1]

An attempt to put boats into the water at the Five Mile Meadows on
the American shore called forth the fire of one of our batteries opposite,
which was returned by the enemy along the lines until it reached Fort
Niagara, when a general cannonade ensued, which ended in the burning of the barracks and wooden works contained in Fort George. We

---

1 Two American schooners carried 100 soldiers to the beach area at the Head of Lake
, Ontario on 11 May. The 60 Canadian militiamen on the scene withdrew without
offering resistance. The attackers burned the Government House, or King's Head Inn
(used as a military depot and assembly point), and vandalized the home of Catherine
Brant (Ohtowakehson/Adonwentishon). They withdrew when the militiamen
returned with reinforcements.

did not suffer much in killed, but the pickets were mostly burnt down, which left the rear of the fort open.[2] It was now evident from every move of the enemy that they meditated to fall upon Fort George and the neighbourhood with all their force. The concentration therefore of our troops in one point to oppose them with effect appeared to be the best measure to extricate ourselves, as we had no tenable fortification on the whole line. The general [John Vincent] sent to Fort Erie for two companies, and he sent into our rear a depot of ammunition in case of a reverse.

Between the Two Mile Run and Mississauga Point [in Niagara, half a mile downriver of Fort George], we expected the enemy to land; and the better to be in readiness to oppose them, I had placed our camp a little space in the rear of that place in a wood so as not to come within their observation.[3] Every night we watched with the most persevering vigilance that they might not take us by surprise. On the night of the 26th of May, we heard at the garrison opposite a great bustle.[4] All were under arms. A detachment of the King's of about three hundred men under Colonel Ogilvie formed the centre division occupying the town of Newark. A division of the 49th of about the same number occupied Fort George [on the right]; and on the left, near to our station, were posted two companies of the Glengarry (Captains Liddell and Roxburgh) and the grenadiers of the Newfoundland under Captain Winter, the whole about 130 men.[5]

---

2 Five Mile Meadows on the New York side of the Niagara River derive their name from the distance between them and Fort Niagara. They consist of low ground close to the water's edge, in contrast to the higher riverside elevations surrounding them. On 25 May, the Americans wanted to move their boats from there to the area around Fort Niagara to help carry troops for an amphibious attack at the mouth of the river. The British opened fire when it still was dark after hearing them being launched. As the day progressed, the two sides fought an artillery duel (which included the guns of Fort Niagara and the American naval squadron), which largely destroyed the barracks and fortifications at Fort George by the early afternoon.

3 Two Mile Run (or Creek) empties into Lake Ontario west of the Niagara River. Mississauga Point was beside the mouth of the Niagara River (on the site of today's Fort Mississauga, built in 1814).

4 American soldiers in and around Fort Niagara began boarding their boats about 4 a.m. on 27 May.

5 The British had 1,400 regulars, fencibles, militia, and warriors to oppose the assault by 4,700 Americans supported by both the United States Navy and men stationed at the military works across the Niagara River. Major James Ogilvie of the 8th Foot was a brevet lieutenant-colonel at the time. Alexander Roxburgh of the Glengarry Light

At the dawn, the horizon was covered by a thick fog.[6] The alarm appeared to subside, when the sound of voices on the lake again called our attention and we hastened to fill our stations. The cannon from Fort Niagara ranged the open plain near the lighthouse.[7] We collected as many of our warriors as we could at the Two Mile Run. We lay near the bank of the lake at the extremity of the right [of the British left flank].[8] The fleet of the enemy moved on with a gentle breeze (which began to chase away the fog) and anchored opposite to us. Some murmured that the position was too much exposed to the fire from the ships. The warrior replied, "We are here to do our duty, not to seek security. Those who desire *that* only should remain at home. The warrior knows no anxiety for his safety. He only hopes to be truly so when his body is under ground and his soul is gone above."[9]

While the [vessels in the] flotilla of the enemy were putting themselves in order, at about three or four hundred paces from the shore, the boats, filled with men, remained at some distance behind them. Our batteries at this time observing the strictest neutrality, and no reinforcement coming to the support of our little party, many of our men seemed to lose confidence and expressed that appearances gave no indication of any resistance being intended. I went to the nearest battery, about one hundred paces on our left, to enquire the cause, and there I met an officer who was giving injunctions not to fire till the boats full of troops should approach the shore. As I returned he passed on to our position. I told him that unless we received support, I felt assured that in a little time I would be left with only a few of the bravest warriors, and that the others were already beginning to show much unsteadiness. Immediately after he had passed, the enemy opened a heavy cannonade from

---

Infantry and William Winter of the Royal Newfoundland Regiment both suffered wounds in the ensuing battle of Fort George. Andrew Liddell of the Glengarry Light Infantry died there.

6 This was 27 May, the day of the battle of Fort George. The fog screened American movements as they organized more than 130 small craft for the landing and the 16 vessels of the squadron that would cover them.

7 The lighthouse was at Mississauga Point. Fort Niagara's guns began firing at daybreak.

8 Being on the "right" refers to JN's position in the immediate area, but his and the other forces deployed near the Lake Ontario shore at Niagara formed the overall British left flank.

9 This quote may be another example of JN speaking of himself in the third person.

seventeen vessels anchored along the shore. They fired very close, but the bank of the ravine afforded some cover when we stooped low.[10] The fire continued, and my forebodings were verified. The wavering had retired. Some, yet hesitating between shame and apprehension, said, "Where is it best for us to go?" I replied, "If you don't like to stay here – you see it is the place I have chosen and I have not changed my mind – I shall direct you to a safe place. It is the ravine on our left, about a quarter of a mile distant, but I am assured that they will land here. Therefore, as soon as you see the boats pass the ships, hasten to our assistance." I then remained with only about twenty warriors.

The cannonade had now continued for an hour. The battery on our right was deserted. The boats of the enemy moved towards the shore. A young Mohawk, Joseph Claus, then came to me and said that General Vincent had sent him to call me, and that he awaited me at Secord's, a house half a mile in the rear.[11] We ran there, completely exposed to the shot of the enemy, for I did not require the men to remain behind, apprehending that the plan of operations had been changed, and that no opposition was to be made to the enemy's landing. On arriving at Secord's, the general was gone, but he had desired Major Merritt to inform me that on board of the *Madison*, the enemy wore *red coats*.[12] I felt disappointed at having been called from my position to gain such intelligence. I then saw Captain Brock of the 49th.[13] He told me that the Glengarry had advanced to the shore of the lake, which made me hasten to return, desirous to take to their succour as many as I could. I required young Claus to run and call

10 Between the squadron, Fort Niagara, and other batteries, the Americans had 76 artillery pieces engaged in comparison to 16 on the British side. The defenders had two small batteries on their left flank where JN fought. The barrage from the American squadron started later than that of the land batteries, beginning after 8 a.m. and continuing until the invaders came ashore on Canadian soil, and then recommenced as opportunity allowed.

11 Joseph Claus was an adopted or natural son of William Claus. The home mentioned was John Secord's, near Two Mile Creek, 500 yards from the waterfront.

12 Major Thomas Merritt was a militia officer and sheriff of the Niagara District. The rumour about red coats was false, although American drummers wore red uniforms with blue facings in contrast to the blue coats and red facings of the bulk of the infantry. As well, the 22nd Infantry wore brown coats (due to a shortage of blue cloth), which may have been mistaken for red. The USS *Madison* was a 24-gun ship.

13 Paymaster James Brock of the 49th Foot was related to Isaac Brock. His captaincy likely was a local rank or an error by JN.

those who had sought shelter from the cannon. He complained of lameness. I sent another, and he advanced with me towards the shore with the most active zeal. We heard the fire of small arms, and my little band hastened their speed.[14]

We directed our course towards the heaviest fire and crossed a muddy brook. The fire was very hot. Between the Glengarry and the Newfoundland, we came to the lake. They were standing within about twenty paces of the bank, from behind which the enemy kept up a heavy fire. Lieutenant-Colonel Myers was already badly wounded; his horse lay dead on the bank.[15] Poor Joseph Claus soon fell, and the ranks were quickly thinned. The enemy seldom showed their heads above the bank but fired incessantly. We advanced to get a fair view of them. We met them rising [up] the bank a few paces to our right and brought some of them to the ground.[16] We returned to our line, the right of which [at the right side of the British left flank] began to yield to superior numbers. For a while, however, a stubborn valour supported the little band. At last, pressed both in front and flank, we retired under a tremendous fire from our enemy. In about one hundred paces, we met the King's advancing to our assistance in the most gallant manner. There were in this division only 280 muskets. Had there come forward eight hundred in such a manner the enemy would certainly have been compelled to take to the water. These brave fellows advanced courageously against a heavy fire of grape in front, and what was more galling and destructive, a sharp crossfire of musketry and rifles from the flank. They staggered the enemy for some time notwithstanding the odds of numbers. Here they lost several brave officers, among them the adjutant, Mr Lloyd, and they did not retire until they were diminished half their number in killed and wounded, and were nearly enveloped. They then fell back

---

14 The small arms fire occurred as American soldiers began to come ashore around 9 a.m. near One Mile Creek.

15 Major Christopher Myers was a brevet lieutenant-colonel, a local colonel, acting deputy quartermaster-general to the forces in the Canadas, and John Vincent's second-in-command at the battle of Fort George. Wounded five times during the battle, he became a prisoner in its aftermath. Later exchanged, he rejoined the army on the Niagara Peninsula to fight again in 1814. As well as the regiments JN mentioned, Canadian militia engaged the invaders.

16 The steep bank by the narrow beach was 15–20 feet high. Grape shot hit Joseph Claus in the forehead (William Claus, Account, 4 December 1813, published in Cruikshank, "Campaigns," 26).

and retired through a ravine.[17] There now remained with me only fifteen warriors. We came to where the [men of the] 49th (who had been kept in the reserve) were formed. The Americans were then advancing through the common in good order. As soon as the general gave orders for a charge, this gallant body of men, although not more than three or four hundred, ran forward to meet this formidable column of several thousands. We accompanied them. The enemy seemed to pause, when we received orders to return, the other part of the army having been too much reduced to support us. We then retired to the rear of some barracks and stores nearly out of reach of the enemy's shot. The latter were advancing to the tune of *Yankee Doodle*.[18] The poor Glengarry had few remaining unhurt. Captain Liddell and Mr McLean were killed, the two Kerrs badly wounded. Captain Roxburgh, who was slightly wounded, brought off the remaining few.[19] The grenadiers of the Newfoundland were also greatly reduced.

A principal staff officer came to me at this time, requesting that I would go with my party to discover if the enemy were making any move with his riflemen through the woods in order to envelope our little army, the main body [of] which had been advancing towards us having stopped in the town of Newark. I took a circuit to where we had been encamped and found that none had yet ventured into the woods. We then hastened to rejoin our friends in a direct line through the field of Mr Butler. On ascending the hill, we heard a shout, and quickened our pace, thinking that the fight had recommenced. We had nearly entered among the enemy, who were concealed in the bushes when we discovered them, and then saw that our friends had retired. We followed their example.[20]

---

17 Lieutenant Thomas Lloyd of the 8th Foot died in the battle. The opposing lines exchanged musket fire at ranges as close as six to ten yards for a quarter of an hour until the numerical superiority of the Americans forced the defenders back.

18 This phase of the battle occurred around 10 a.m.

19 Lieutenant Walter Kerr (already mentioned) and Ensign Robert Joseph Kerr were the sons of a prominent Niagara doctor, Robert Kerr (who also served in the Indian Department) and his wife Elizabeth Johnson, who was the daughter of Sir William Johnson and Joseph Brant's sister or half-sister, Molly. Robert Jr was captured after being wounded, escaped while in Philadelphia, rejoined his regiment, and was wounded again at Lundy's Lane in 1814. Ensign William McLean was a Canadian, killed in his first action.

20 After the British withdrew from the landing site just northwest of the town, their field artillery stopped the American advance for half an hour late in the morning

A young man, mounted, having just arrived from the Grand River with notice that a number of warriors from that place were on the march to join us, I sent him with injunctions to make the greatest speed until he should meet them, and then to exhort them not to be influenced by those who had made so much haste to retreat, and to tell them all that I expected to find them at the Twelve Mile Creek when I should come there. He faithfully performed the errand: I found nearly two hundred men at the Twelve Mile Creek. It was then late in the day; we were all wearied and hungry. We heard that the [British] army had reached the depot of ammunition on the mountain about three miles from us.[21] I thought that, as this was the only road by which the enemy could pass, we might cut off their retreat, and that to keep this position for the night would be rendering more service than to join our friends.[22] I therefore

---

(near the site of St Andrew's Presbyterian Church in today's Niagara-on-the-Lake). In response, the invaders sent riflemen to outflank the guns. Butler's property was southwest of the site of the field guns. Subsequently, the defenders withdrew to the landward side of Fort George south of the town. Their officers thought of continuing the fight; however, after suffering 430 casualties (to 160 Americans) and hearing reports that the Americans threatened their flanks and rear, John Vincent withdrew from Niagara just after 12 o'clock in order to preserve his remaining force. He gave orders to destroy stores at Fort George and spike the artillery pieces that the British could not take with them. Native casualties in the battle consisted of two Mohawks killed and a number of men wounded. "Mr Butler" probably was the late Thomas Butler, a loyalist officer in the American Revolution.

21 Word had been sent to the Grand River for reinforcements at the time of the bombardment on 25 May, before the amphibious attack two days later. JN met these people below the Niagara Escarpment by Lake Ontario. The area largely was settled in 1813 (unlike the area on the high ground), although there still was a significant amount of forest on the lowland. The distance between the lake and the steep slope of the escarpment (JN's "mountain") varies from less than a mile at some places to seven or more at others. While JN retreated along lowland towards the lakeshore, John Vincent with the main British force marched south towards Queenston and St Davids, and then inland to a depot at John DeCew's mills and farm on top of the Niagara Escarpment (in modern Thorold). Thus, at the end of the day, JN stopped near the mouth of Twelve Mile Creek (in modern St Catharines) a few miles downstream from Vincent. After the battle, the Americans did not pursue the British with any spirit.

22 JN's text, in relation to his location near the mouth of Twelve Mile Creek, suggests that he meant that the enemy might come along the Lake Road on the lower ground of the Niagara Peninsula. The Queenston (or York) Road, however, ran parallel to it further inland, but also below the escarpment, and was in better condition, so JN's text is not clear.

placed a sufficient party on lookout and retired to rest with the intention of joining the army in the morning, of which intention I sent notice by the light infantry of the King's, which met us at this place and in the evening ascended the mountain.

The next morning, when preparing to move, a dragoon came with the intelligence that the [British] army had continued its march towards the Forty Mile Creek. I then desired the people to follow, and returned with one man along the road [that] we had passed in order to discover if the enemy had undertaken to pursue us.[23] Going a few miles, I met an officer of the militia, an inhabitant of the Four Mile [Creek], who had just left his home, well mounted. He told us that the enemy had not ventured out as far as his house. We therefore returned to follow our retreating friends, and that night slept at Mr Kerr's at the Twenty Mile Creek.[24] The next morning, early, we proceeded, and found that a report had been brought of the enemy having commenced a pursuit, and in consequence of this information the first [people] we overtook were occupied in damaging a bridge and in throwing ammunition into the water. I told them that they laboured in vain in both respects. First, that all the injury they did [to] the roads the enemy could repair while the horses were taking breath; and what they did with the ammunition was uselessly distressing themselves, for that the enemy was lying still at Fort George.[25] Proceeding a little farther, I overtook General Vincent and his staff, and soon came up with the whole body of the army, for it now began to have that appearance. A division of the 41st, a strong detachment of the 49th, some of the Newfoundland, and others had now joined from Fort Erie, Chippawa, and Queenston. Lieutenant-Colonel Bisshopp, who commanded at these places, having heard of our disaster at Fort George and consequent retreat, ordered the batteries in the neighbourhood of the former post to be opened upon the enemy, and having left a sufficient number of men to work the guns, he retired

---

23 This movement by John Vincent's forces occurred on 28 May, and JN directed the warriors to join them while he scouted towards Niagara. Forty Mile Creek empties into Lake Ontario (at today's Grimsby). The narrow width of the ground between the lakeshore and the rise of the escarpment at this point made it a good location to deploy for battle against the Americans.

24 This likely was the home of Captain William Johnson Kerr of the Indian Department. Twenty Mile Creek empties into Lake Ontario at Jordan.

25 The rumour that the Americans were in pursuit was false. As well as destroying bridges, soldiers cut down trees across the roadways to impede the invaders.

with all the troops under his command, unperceived by the enemy, and joined General Vincent without interruption.[26]

At the battle of Fort George I related hitherto only as much as had fallen within my own observation, the place where we engaged being covered with bushes, we could not see what was going on at a distance. I heard that the militia were on our right, although in very small number, and that the 24-pounder battery under the charge of Captain Powell of the militia artillery was deserted without firing a single gun.[27] This was much to be regretted, as it completely ranged the beach on which the Americans had landed and formed, and from which under cover of the bank they thinned our ranks with a galling fire of rifles and muskets. The small battery near to which we fought was entirely exposed, being no more than a platform. Therefore, the men could not stand at the gun after the flotilla of the enemy had commenced a cannonade.

I was rejoiced to find that the general agreed to stop at the Forty Mile Creek with the whole army, as I yet had hopes that God would favour us with an opportunity to avenge ourselves upon our enemy for the blood of our friends that had fallen on the plains of Fort George, on whose lifeless bodies we had turned our backs. The position here gave me the most flattering prospect of a glorious issue to a contest should the enemy have overtaken us. On our right, the mountain hung over us [and] a steep inaccessible ravine cut through it for a great distance. To gain it, the enemy would have been obliged to make a circuit of six or seven miles through woods almost impenetrable. From thence [i.e., the edge of the mountain or escarpment] to the lake, rather more than half a mile, ran a ravine, in front of which the ground was clear of wood for a considerable distance. We had now enough men to fill

---

26 Lieutenant Cecil Bisshopp of the elite 1st Regiment of Foot Guards served as a brevet lieutenant-colonel and inspecting field officer of the militia. He rendezvoused with John Vincent at the depot at John DeCew's property noted earlier with his soldiers and field artillery, mainly from Chippawa and Fort Erie, who, with other men along the Lake Ontario shore, brought Vincent's immediate command up to 1,600. To mask his withdrawal, Bisshopp had detached some militiamen at and near Fort Erie to fire on the opposite shore until the morning of 28 May, and then destroy the guns and the defences while others destroyed stores along the border that they could not move inland. Shortly after the British abandoned Fort Erie, American soldiers crossed the Niagara River and occupied its ruins for about two weeks.

27 This officer was Captain John Powell of the 1st Lincoln Militia. He fired one shot before intense enemy fire drove his gunners away. JN's memory of Powell's behaviour, as he said, did not derive from personal observation.

this space, and while our flank was secure, they never could penetrate our line in front. We had a good park of artillery, which in the open ground through which they had to advance would have given fair scope to the ability of the gallant officers and men of that corps to have dealt destruction through their ranks. But we did not hold this position long. In two days, we moved on to Burlington [Heights].[28] The lower part of the Grand River becoming more exposed to the enemy by this retrograde movement, the warriors all left me to place their families in a place of security.[29] There only remained with me

---

28 On 31 May, John Vincent arrived at Burlington Heights, a fortified depot on high ground (where the 1830s Dundurn Castle now stands in Hamilton). JN often referred to this place simply as "Burlington," but his use ought not to be confused with the site of the nearby modern city of that name. JN seems to have disagreed with Vincent's decision, judging by his enthusiasm for defending the camp they had established at Forty Mile Creek.

29 The American victory and British withdrawal from the Niagara River gave the invaders control over communications between Lakes Ontario and Erie, thus posing a grave danger to the security of much of Upper Canada, including the Grand River. At that point, there was little to prevent the invaders from dispatching troops from Buffalo or other Niagara River locations to assault Haudenosaunee villages and farms along the Grand. As it was, the British had halted at Burlington Heights rather than York or Kingston partly because of fear over how the Iroquois would respond to a retreat farther east, but the decision did not provide much comfort to the Six Nations. Furthermore, the Americans drove off a British attack on the United States Navy's base at Sackett's Harbour on 29 May, and news of that failure reached the Niagara region soon afterwards, further depressing morale after the defeats at York and Fort George. In responding to these deteriorating and worrisome conditions, people along the Grand drove away their livestock, while women, children, and vulnerable individuals hid in the forests in expectation that the Americans would send a punitive expedition against them. As it was, the government in Washington had told its senior officer on the Canadian front, Henry Dearborn, that, if he enjoyed success, he was to destroy "all Indian establishments" (John Armstrong to Dearborn, n.d. [1813], quoted in Cruikshank, "Blockade," 21). The Americans, occupying the ruins of Fort George, knew about Haudenosaunee fears because individuals from the tract had opened communications with them, which led Dearborn, free from any significant indigenous harassment, to note that they were "quiet for fear of losing their valuable tract of land on Grand River" (Dearborn to Armstrong, 8 June 1813, ibid., 23). We do not know whether JN thought his actions on behalf of the Anglo-Iroquois alliance endangered the Six Nations or if people on the tract thought so, correctly or not, and we also do not have useful information on the Indian Department's role in the discussions of that moment. Yet, a day after the British army retired to Burlington Heights, JN wrote a letter to the governor-in-chief, Sir George Prevost, asking to be given the freedom to reward Six Nations

my young Cherokee cousin, a few Delawares, some Chippewas, one Mohawk, and a Cayuga.[30]

We gained information that the enemy had followed us to the Forty Mile Creek.[31] With the few men that yet remained with me, we returned to observe their motions. Near to that place, we observed the glistening of the arms of mounted men. We left the road to pass through a wood in order to gain their rear imperceptibly and intercept their return. We had gone rather more than half a mile when we saw them abreast of us advancing on the road. The Mohawk at that time exposed himself to their view. Seeing them take the alarm, and apprehending that they might entirely escape us, we ran directly for them, and although the field we had to pass was three hundred paces wide, they began to fire their muskets. When within about eighty paces, they fired their pistols.

---

people for their participation in the fighting independently of his adversaries in the department, who he felt undermined his efforts to assemble warriors to oppose the invaders. He argued that without the ability to distribute presents he was limited to attracting people who were "induced from personal affection or the love of glory" to join him. If changing the management of indigenous affairs were not possible, he hoped to leave the Niagara region and join the First Nations fighting in the west because of his determination "to exert myself to the utmost to annoy the enemy" in a context where government largess carried "less weight" as a motivating factor in encouraging warriors (JN to Prevost, 1 June 1813, LAC, RG8, 257:81–3).

30 JN's enumeration of his war party underscores how much his influence among the Six Nations had declined after the retreat from Fort George (although it would recover to a respectable degree afterwards). His "Cherokee cousin" was John Charles Wolateagh. He had been born about 1794 and "served faithfully through the war" (JN to J.F. Addison, 13 February 1817, ibid., 261:32). His mother was JN's first cousin, Tahneh or Naomi (who he had met during his pre-war travels to his father's people). Missionaries described her as "a full-blooded Cherokee, the daughter of a considerable chief and warrior" ("Journal at Dwight," 1828, 311; see also Benn, "Missed Opportunities," 270; Klinck, "Biographical Introduction," in *JMJN*, xxxv–xxxvi; *JMJN*, 146–7). The Chippewas likely came from southwestern Upper Canada. The Delawares may have been from Six Nations or another community in the colony. We do not know who the Cayuga was, but the Mohawk seems to have been John Smoke Johnson.

31 On 1 June, the Americans began to march through the Niagara Peninsula from Fort George towards Burlington Heights, where John Vincent had assembled 1,800 men. By 5 June, they had two brigades at Forty Mile Creek, 18 miles from the British camp. They intended to continue through the peninsula and then bypass the defenders' position by proceeding along the beach area near the Head of the Lake and thereby cut John Vincent's line of retreat and force a battle. The British assumed instead that their enemy would make a direct assault against Burlington Heights.

We then fired. One of them fell, and another, with difficulty, recovered his seat. They rode away, and being well mounted, soon distanced us.[32] After dark, we returned to Burlington. The next day, I expected with great anxiety the return of our people from the Grand River, and happened to be absent when the first report reached headquarters of the enemy having advanced to Stoney Creek (five miles from Burlington) and having attacked a picket of the 49th stationed there.[33] About sunset, having received notice, I went on the advance with the few men I could collect, and in about a mile and a half I met Lieutenant-Colonel Harvey returning from reconnoitring the enemy.[34] I observed to him that I had come forward in hopes that it was in contemplation to attack the enemy by surprise while secure and confident from his recent success, that I

---

32 On 4 June, JN skirmished with a scouting party of American dragoons somewhere between Forty Mile and Stoney creeks along the Queenston Road below the Niagara Escarpment. (The Americans fired at almost twice the effective range for each type of weapon mentioned, suggesting poor training or discipline.) That small event created the spectre in the minds of the invaders that there were significant numbers of warriors threatening them, even though few were active at that time and even though Major-General Henry Dearborn thought the Grand River people did not pose much of a threat. An early history of the war published in the United States in 1817 presented a completely inaccurate account of the skirmish, claiming, for instance, that JN had 200 men under his command ("A," "Sketch of the Life of Lieutenant-Colonel Towson," 219).

33 Note how little JN says about the possibility that part of his community might turn against the British in the phrase "I expected with great anxiety the return of our people." One American source recorded that there were 200 Six Nations warriors camped 14 miles from Burlington Heights (Anonymous Letter, 5 June 1813, *New York Statesman*, 21 June 1813). British efforts to have a portion of these men join them to oppose the Americans failed, and we might wonder if JN went to the camp to see if he could persuade them to fight.

34 On 5 June, the American army camped at the hamlet of Stoney Creek alongside the Queenston Road (in today's community of the same name, now part of Hamilton). The site was about 40 miles from Fort George and seven from Burlington Heights. The main camp occupied farmland protected on its north side (towards Lake Ontario) by a swamp, on its south by the rise of the Niagara Escarpment, and on its west by a small creek valley facing the road from Burlington Heights. Major John Harvey of the 6th Garrison Battalion was a brevet lieutenant-colonel. He scouted the invaders' camp and discussed their position with other officers and JN. Harvey thought that in spite of its good location, his opponents had laid out their camp poorly to withstand an assault, had posted inadequate pickets to guard against surprise, and had deployed a large portion of their force too far away to come to the aid of the main body should the British make a surprise night attack. Accordingly, he convinced John Vincent to strike in the early hours of 6 June.

regretted not having yet been joined by a sufficient number of men to take a more considerable part in such an enterprise, but that the enemy now compelled us to make our election of either fighting or retiring. He said, "Wait here until I go to the general. I shall rejoin you as soon as possible." We remained there in company with the light infantry of the 49th until one or two o'clock in the morning, when the King's, commanded by Lieutenant-Colonel Ogilvie, and the 49th, under Lieutenant-Colonel Plenderleath, came up with the general, Lieutenant-Colonel Harvey, and the staff.[35] As neither of the regiments was entire, the whole amounted to no more than seven hundred men.[36] The 41st, Glengarry, and Newfoundland remained in their quarters near Burlington.

The orders given were to advance upon the enemy without firing. We marched on with a cannon. We came to a Methodist meeting house in which the picket of the enemy was stationed. They gave the first alarm.[37] We then could discern the encampment of the enemy by the fires on both sides of the road. The 49th entered the field on the left; the King's advanced in the road.[38] After passing a lane, which led to the encampment of the enemy on the left, they opened fire upon us, both from the division on the right and from their artillery in front, at about a hundred yards' distant. This was returned by the troops notwithstanding the orders [not to fire but to use their bayonets instead in

---

35 Lieutenant-Colonel Charles Plenderleath would play a decisive role in the upcoming battle; the "general" was John Vincent. JN's small war party, resting at an advanced position held by the light company of the 49th Foot, was 2.5 miles in advance of Burlington Heights when the bulk of the British force approached. (The light troops had skirmished with the Americans close to Stoney Creek earlier that day.) Although not mentioned, the light company of the 8th Foot also was present.

36 The two regiments deployed 700 lower ranks, but adding in the officers, a detachment from the Royal Artillery, some militia, and other men, the British force numbered 765. The two American brigades around Stoney Creek had 3,000 soldiers.

37 The Methodist chapel was 500 yards in advance of the main camp on the west side of the creek that cut across the road from Burlington Heights. The British had bayoneted or captured several American guards further away to preserve secrecy. Most of the large guard of soldiers in the chapel were asleep when the British arrived, and they too were bayoneted or captured; however, some firing and shouting at this point alerted the troops in the main camp of the attack.

38 The fires of the American camp were on the east side of the creek, the Queenston Road divided the camp into north and south sections, and the British left was north of the road. The fires generally burned in advance of the main area where the Americans had their camp, which made the attackers miscalculate their objective, thinking it was closer than it was.

hopes of surprising the Americans]. However, after a short time passed in firing, they rushed on with loud huzzahs.[39] The enemy fled, leaving four pieces of cannon, Generals Chandler and Winder, and about one hundred of their men prisoners.[40] The day (the 6th of June) now began to dawn and we marched away to our former position, the soldiers exulting with patriotic joy at having retaliated on the enemy [for] the affair of Fort George, and, indeed, they had just reason. For here, with seven hundred men, the British army came off victorious from an attack upon four thousand men, whereas on the plains of Fort George, seven thousand Americans, with some difficulty, had compelled a handful of British troops to retire.

We brought away two of the guns, not having horses to draw the other two. The drivers were sent for them afterwards, when they perceived that the enemy had returned to the ground. In the morning, we imagined our loss to have been very considerable from the great number that had been bewildered by the darkness of the night; but on exact examination, we found that it only amounted to twenty men killed, a few taken prisoners, and a great number wounded. Among the former were two officers, one of the King's, the other of the 49th. Lieutenant-Colonels Ogilvie and Plenderleath, Major Clerk, and several other officers were among the wounded. We had reason to suppose the loss of

---

39 This part of the battle began after 2 a.m., with the fighting continuing for an hour. The Americans were able to recover from the initial shock of the assault and the tremendous confusion caused by the dark to defend their lines, and many British soldiers began to fall back on their own initiative. Charles Plenderleath of the 49th Foot, however, led a charge with a few dozen men that captured the American artillery on the Queenston Road at the centre of his enemy's line. That event helped spur most of the Americans engaged in the fighting to panic and fall back eastwards as part of a general withdrawal of soldiers who, like their opponents, often sought shelter from the fighting on their own initiative rather than within the confines of orders from their officers. Subsequently, the British retired to Burlington Heights while the Americans withdrew a mile to the east to establish a new position in case of renewed combat.

40 The highest-ranking senior American officers were John Chandler (who was injured in falling from his horse), followed by William Winder, both of whom were brigadier-generals. They stumbled among the British who had captured the American artillery. These officers later were exchanged. Winder commanded the American army at the battle of Bladensburg in 1814, where the British routed their opponents and captured Washington. (On the British side, John Vincent lost his way in the dark and disappeared until the next day; however, John Harvey exercised command during the attack.)

the enemy to have been more considerable.[41] Immediately after we had left the field, they were reinforced by Colonel Chrystie with fifteen hundred men, who the preceding night had lain encamped on the lakeshore within two miles of Stoney Creek.[42] But having lost their generals, and the remaining officers differing in opinion as to what was more expedient to be done, they returned to the Forty Mile Creek, there to await orders from the general at Niagara.[43]

---

41 The British suffered 220 killed, wounded, missing, and captured from the skirmishing on 5 June and in the battle on the 6th. American losses at Stoney Creek are unclear due to conscious efforts by their officers to mask the cost of the battle, but killed, wounded, missing, and taken prisoner probably numbered more than 300. Captain Alexander Clerk of the 49th Foot held the rank of brevet major. Captured at Stoney Creek, but later exchanged, Clerk subsequently saw service with the Glengarry Light Infantry. A contemporary report of the battle stated: "About 500 regulars under General Vincent, and some Indians under Chief Norton, unperceived, broke into the American camp, took possession of seven pieces of cannon, which they turned against their foes" (Smith, *Geographical View*, 110). While this is not entirely accurate, it is noteworthy that JN received recognition.

42 This was the same John Chrystie JN mentioned at Queenston Heights and who had been promoted from lieutenant-colonel to colonel. His presence on campaign seems to have violated his parole because he had not been exchanged yet, as also was the case with Winfield Scott and other officers on the Niagara Peninsula in 1813. At the time of the battle of Stoney Creek, Chrystie commanded 800 men by the shores of Lake Ontario north of the fighting (having been assigned to guard the army's baggage bateaux). At dawn, he planned to advance in hopes of cutting off the British retreat, but cancelled the move when summoned to join the main body of soldiers east of Stoney Creek; but he took prisoners among soldiers lost in the forest and gathered equipment and some of the wounded from the battlefield.

43 The Americans retired to Forty Mile Creek to reorganize and replenish their ammunition and other supplies, as well as to await orders from Fort George, not being sure how to act after the loss of their senior officers. JN's assessment of the "differing" opinion of the American leadership conforms to the period's records from the invading force, which he may have learned through intelligence gathered at the time or afterwards from newspapers and other sources. The "general at Niagara" was Henry Dearborn.

1 John Norton – Teyoninhokarawen sat for this watercolour on ivory miniature during his journey to Great Britain in 1804–5. As was common among native people, his dress included silver jewellery and a blanket used as an outer garment. One person who met him during the visit wrote that he was "tall, muscular, and well-proportioned; his countenance fine and intelligent, illuminated with 'an eye like Mars to threaten and command.'"

2 This c.1762 print shows Cherokee chiefs from the American south who visited London at the end of the Anglo-Cherokee War of 1759–61. Norton's father, a young Cherokee, fell into British hands during that conflict. Unlike other captured non-combatants, the army did not return him to his people, apparently because the injuries he had suffered made it impossible to do so. He recovered, entered the army, and journeyed to England with his regiment but then left and moved to Scotland. There, he married or entered a relationship with Christian Anderson, which led to the birth of John Norton in 1770. He eventually returned to the Cherokees. His son visited the tribe in 1809–10 and again in the 1820s.

3 Fort Niagara was one of the "Western Posts" in American territory that the British occupied until 1796. In Britain, John Norton and his Cherokee father joined the 65th Regiment of Foot, likely to gain passage to North America, as was not uncommon. They were posted to Fort Niagara in 1787. Young John deserted later that year and found a new home within the First Nations, primarily with the Haudenosaunee in New York. Much later, in 1813, he participated in capturing the fort from the Americans. This watercolour dates to c.1780.

4 After living with natives on the American side of the Great Lakes in the late 1780s, John Norton served as a teacher among the Mohawks of Tyendinaga, located in British territory on Lake Ontario, in 1790 and/or 1791, likely in a room similar to the Mohawk school represented in this print from the 1780s.

5 This print of an Ohio country Shawnee from 1805 derives from a drawing created in the 1790s. Norton went to that region in 1791 to help defend indigenous lands against the Americans in the war between the tribes and the United States. He fought in the battle of the Wabash, where warriors from different First Nations united against their common enemy.

6 In 1796, John Norton moved to Niagara (or Newark) to serve as an interpreter for the British Indian Department, after the war for the Ohio country had ended the previous year in an American success over the tribes. This 1804 watercolour shows the Canadian town of Niagara in the right background, the American Fort Niagara in the lower right, Fort George towards the left rear, and Navy Hall below the British post. (The artist has truncated distances somewhat.)

These details show Fort George and Niagara.

7 The famous Mohawk chief, Joseph Brant, met John Norton during the Ohio war and was impressed with his potential to serve native interests. He adopted Norton as his nephew in the late 1790s. Norton left the Indian Department, moved to the Grand River, and rose to become a war and alliance chief among the Six Nations Haudenosaunee of the Grand in Upper Canada. They comprised the Mohawks, Oneidas, Onondagas, Cayugas, Senecas, and Tuscaroras, along with other people (such as Delawares and Nanticokes) who lived with them. It was at the time of his appointment to chiefly status that Norton received the name Teyoninhokarawen. He succeeded Brant as the leader of one of the political groupings on the Grand after the older man's passing in 1807 (about the same time this oil painting was created).

8 This c.1795 drawing on birchbark shows the Mohawk village on the Grand River. Norton first visited the community a few years earlier. The steeple of the still-extant Anglican church may be seen towards the right. The building with the flag is Joseph Brant's home. The Crown had provided the land to the Haudenosaunee after the American Revolution for those who sought to leave the new United States and live within British territory; however, the nature of Iroquois tenure was unclear, causing tremendous challenges for Brant, Norton, and others in asserting indigenous ownership and control over the tract.

9 This watercolour from 1804 depicts a Mohawk at a council in the village above. Note the silver, including his "nose bob." He also wears a sun-shaped gorget and a crucifix, symbols of traditional and newcomer religions. Between them is a chief's medal, a symbol of the Anglo-Haudenosaunee alliance. Cut and stretched ears traditionally indicated that someone was a veteran warrior. Body paint was common, with different colours having distinct meanings.

10 This print, published in 1807, offers a sense of lower Great Lakes indigenous dress during Norton's time. Clothing was a mix of native and newcomer fashion, made largely from Euro-American textiles (and even included imported feathers). Interactions between settler society and the First Nations generated debate over how aboriginal communities might evolve in response to changing circumstances. Norton, Brant, and others advocated modernizing the Haudenosaunee economy. They thought such a change would generate the prosperity needed to provide comfortable lives and enable natives to resist unwanted intrusions from colonial society, which often used indigenous poverty as a weapon to impose its will on aboriginal peoples.

11 This late 1700s watercolour of an Iroquoian woman and baby shows dress in more detail than the print above (and was apparently a source for the print). Information on Norton's private life is elusive, although we know he had three marriages or similar relationships. The first was with a Mohawk woman, the second was with an Onondaga, and the third was with a Delaware. The names of the first two women have been lost to history. His third wife was Catherine or Karighwaycagh, whom he married in an Anglican ceremony in 1813. The other two relationships likely followed indigenous marriage customs.

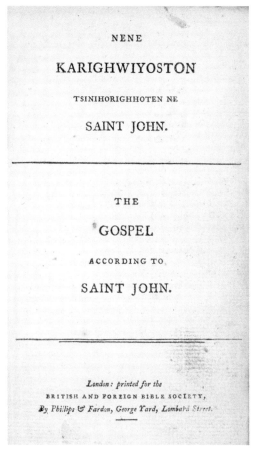

NENE

KARIGHWIYOSTON

TSINIHORIGHHOTEN NE

SAINT JOHN.

THE

GOSPEL

ACCORDING TO

SAINT JOHN.

London: printed for the
BRITISH AND FOREIGN BIBLE SOCIETY,
By Phillips & Fardon, George Yard, Lombard Street.

12 (top left) John Norton visited the United Kingdom in 1804–5, where he produced or completed a translation of the Gospel of Saint John into Mohawk. His primary concern during his time in the United Kingdom, however, focused on asking the imperial government to confirm unrestricted Haudenosaunee ownership of the Grand River Tract to manage as the natives thought best, in conformity with their understanding of the grant made to them in 1784. He made good progress until Canadian officials, who opposed Six Nations independence, sent word to London denouncing his mission, which largely ended his efforts at that time.

13 (top right) During his attempts to resolve Six Nations land and other claims, Teyoninhokarawen received help from influential individuals, including Joseph Brant's old acquaintance from the American Revolution, the second Duke of Northumberland. His Grace sent this pipe tomahawk to Brant via Norton as a gift. The inscription reads: "Given to my friend Joseph Brant from the Duke of Northumberland 1805."

14 William Claus (depicted in this c.1792 watercolour on ivory miniature) was the deputy superintendent-general of the Indian Department in Upper Canada. Claus opposed John Norton's and Joseph Brant's attempts to secure unrestricted tenure of the Six Nations Tract on the Grand River for the Haudenosaunee and otherwise undermined their efforts to assert independence from colonial control. He did not hesitate to lie and otherwise use aggressive and unjust tactics to achieve his goals, such as claiming that Norton's 1804–5 mission to the United Kingdom was "fraudulent" and that Teyoninhokarawen was an "imposter."

15 This c.1810 oil portrait depicts Sir George Prevost, the governor-in-chief of British North America during the War of 1812. Prevost thought the Indian Department was corrupt and incompetent. In contrast, he believed that John Norton could play a major role in maintaining the alliance between the Crown and the First Nations. For his part, Teyoninhokarawen countered the department's actions to subvert his endeavours to protect Haudenosaunee interests by obtaining support from the army and from Sir George.

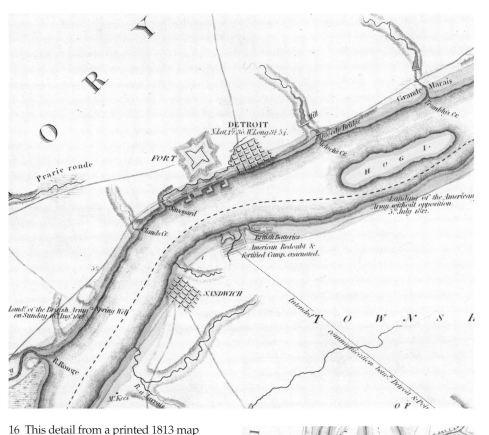

16 This detail from a printed 1813 map of the Detroit River shows operations in 1812. In July, the Americans crossed the border at Sandwich and engaged in some minor fighting with British forces but later withdrew to their side of the river. In August, British forces – including warriors with John Norton – crossed into Michigan and moved against their opponents' positions at Detroit but before much fighting could occur the Americans surrendered.

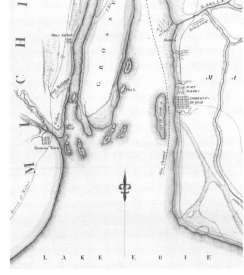

This detail from the same map shows the mouth of the Detroit River, where several actions that Norton described occurred before the capture of Detroit in 1812.

17 Created in 1816, this print of Queenston Heights presents the observations of a veteran of the battle, depicting major events in the British victory in October 1812 in one scene. John Norton and the warriors with him fought on the top of the heights, where they kept the Americans confined to an exposed position for several hours until reinforcements assembled to defeat the invaders. While Teyoninhokarawen fought at more battles and small actions than almost anyone else in the war, he is remembered best for his leadership at this battle, which impressed British army officers, who supported and favoured him during most of the war to the frustration of his opponents in the Indian Department.

18 The British post at Amherstburg, shown in this 1813 watercolour, served as a garrison, naval station, and centre for Indian Department operations. It controlled the main channel of the Detroit River at its southern end and provided a base for British and First Nations forces to operate against the Americans in Michigan, Ohio, and Indiana. John Norton visited it in 1812 and 1813, before it fell into American hands. He and British officials thought that he might serve in a major diplomatic and military role in Anglo-First Nations affairs in the region, beyond his work among the Haudenosaunee of the Grand River. While that did not happen, some natives from southwestern Upper Canada and the American Old Northwest aligned with him.

This detail shows the dress of Algonquian men and women. One man holds a bottle. Although Norton did not oppose the consumption of alcohol, he condemned the way white society used it to exploit indigenous people.

19 This watercolour from 1815 shows a group of Chippewas (Ojibwas/Anishinabek) from within Upper Canada with a captured American drum. Teyoninhokarawen had frequent contact with them and other Algonquian speakers. Although he did not become a major military leader on the Detroit front, as had been hoped, many Chippewa and other warriors from the region chose to fight alongside him during the conflict, in addition to the Haudenosaunee men who took up arms within his war parties. Two people in this scene suggest that they have at least some white and black ancestry, which reminds us that indigenous societies in Norton's day comprised people of diverse origins. This image, like many that depict native peoples in the period, is naïve, being the work of an amateur artist, and is undermined by a variety of limitations; but, like many others, it nevertheless possesses documentary value and offers insights into material culture and other factors that otherwise are elusive.

21 (facing page bottom) Norton chronicled the April–May 1813 siege of Fort Meigs on the Miami (or Maumee) River in Ohio, even though he was not present. British and native forces inflicted heavy losses on their enemies but failed to take the post. This 1840s printed map reproduces a less readable 1813 drawing.

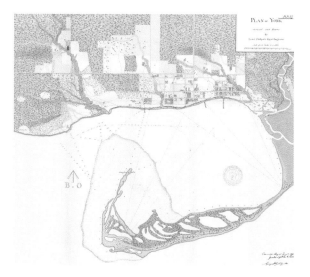

20 Beyond describing the battles in which he engaged the Americans, Norton's memoir includes detailed accounts of some events he heard about second-hand. One was the American attack on York, Upper Canada in April 1813. Their Lake Ontario squadron sent troops ashore to the west of the town (beyond this 1818/1823 manuscript map's left edge) and then supported them as they advanced east along the waterfront towards the British defences near the mouth of the harbour, winning their first major battle of the war on the Canadian front.

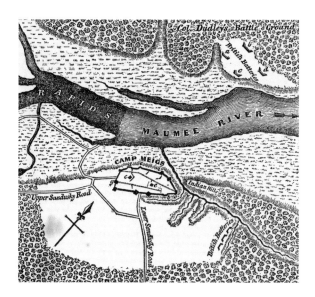

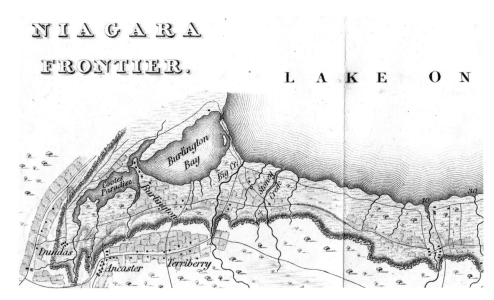

22 This detail shows areas where John Norton saw considerable action in 1813. He fought at the battle of Fort George in May, the battle of Stoney Creek in June, the blockade of Fort George through the summer, the capture of Fort Niagara in December, and a number of skirmishes, particularly along the lowlands between the lake and the Niagara Escarpment. (Note the names of the numbered creeks indicated at their mouths.)

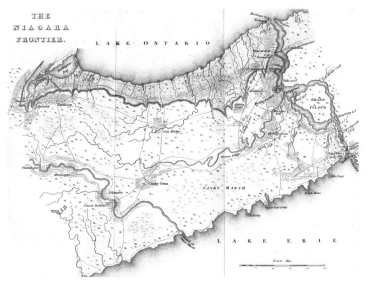

On this complete printed map from 1818, note the proximity of the Six Nations of the Grand to the Niagara River, which was the most heavily fought-over region in the war.

This detail shows the area near Fort Erie. In 1812, Norton patrolled on the American (right) side of the Niagara River and deployed warriors around Fort Erie at the time it came under threat late in the year. In 1814 he scouted and skirmished in this area and fought at the battles of Chippawa and Lundy's Lane (or Bridgewater on the map detail above) and the blockade of Fort Erie.

23 This print from 1817 offers an impression of the May 1813 battle of Fort George. Fort Niagara is on the left side of the river; Fort George is on the right side. Norton's warriors opposed the American landing (to the right of image) and then fought a running retreat through the woods and past the Presbyterian church (to the right of the lighthouse), before withdrawing with the rest of the British forces once the invaders gained the ascendancy.

24 This detail from an 1810 manuscript map shows the town of Niagara between Two Mile Creek and the Niagara River, including the site of the May 1813 battle of Fort George and the summer and autumn 1813 blockade of the fort. At the latter, Norton fought in various actions and skirmishes designed to prevent the Americans from penetrating inland. American defences also included a camp they had built between the fort and the Anglican church (to the left of the fort) and pickets they established beyond their main positions.

25 This period print depicts the American victory in October 1813 at Moraviantown, on the Thames River in southwestern Upper Canada. Norton was not present but described the fighting in which the famous Shawnee leader, Tecumseh, died.

26 Late in life Joseph Brant moved into a fine house at the Head of the Lake in modern Burlington, depicted in this 1804 watercolour. His widow, Catherine, continued to live there. In May 1813, Americans vandalized her home during a raid. After the battle of Moraviantown, refugees from the Western Tribes, the Grand River, and elsewhere camped in and around this area behind British lines in comparative safety, from a military perspective, but suffered the privations of living through winter weather without adequate supplies or food.

27 In early 1814, John Norton went to Quebec (shown in this 1807 print) to seek help from the governor-in-chief, Sir George Prevost, after enduring ongoing hostility from the Indian Department. As part of their desires to exercise control over the Haudenosaunee, its personnel had tried to undermine Teyoninhokarawen's standing among the Six Nations and the British army, despite his importance to the war effort. Prevost ordered officials to support Norton and gave him considerable freedom to manage relations between the Crown and the First Nations but his opponents in Upper Canada nevertheless did their best to thwart Prevost's decisions.

28 In March 1814, representatives of the upper Mississippi River people met Sir George Prevost in Quebec, with Teyoninhokarawen in attendance. This watercolour dates from that council. Later that year, some of these people fought as British allies on the Niagara Peninsula, including a portion that aligned with Norton.

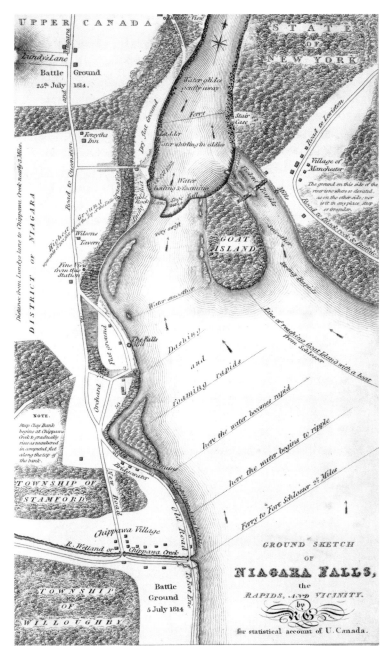

29 The battlefields of Chippawa and Lundy's Lane, where the opposing forces clashed in July 1814, may be seen on this printed map from 1822.

30 This 1807 print shows Burch's Mills near Niagara Falls prior to the war, before American forces burned it in 1814 (a fate common to civilian property on both sides of the river). John Norton knew this landscape well, had a camp with several hundred people in this vicinity at the beginning of the 1814 campaign, and skirmished over it early in the day of the battle of Lundy's Lane.

31 The largest battle on the Canadian front in the war was Lundy's Lane, in July 1814, which occurred largely at night. This 1815 print shows how close the armies stood as they inflicted devastating volleys on each other. At one point, Norton found himself in the open between the opposing lines. After the Americans fired a volley at the British, Teyoninhokarawen wrote, "our troops behind me" were preparing "to return the compliment," so "I hastened to regain the line."

32 After the battle of Lundy's Lane, the Americans withdrew to Fort Erie (which they enlarged and strengthened, as shown in this print from 1816). Their position consisted of the original fort on the right, a strong position at Snake Hill on the left, and a fortified camp in the centre. The garrison could be supplied and reinforced from the New York side of the border. The British put the fort under a siege-like blockade and their lines may be seen on the right of the image. Not many warriors from the Grand River participated in that event, although John Norton fought in several actions during the blockade.

33 This drawing from 1815 shows British infantrymen of the war years. One of the many contributions of Norton's journal to historical understanding includes his detailed description of how effectively British troops and First Nations warriors cooperated closely with each other in combat against American forces.

34 This print shows London at the time John Norton visited Great Britain in 1815 and 1816. Following the successful defence of Canada, he once again attempted to have the imperial government confirm the Grand River Tract to the Haudenosaunee according to their understanding of the 1784 grant. This time, Canadian officials were not able to undermine him in England, and the authorities in the British capital sent orders across the Atlantic to meet Six Nations demands. Nevertheless, colonial officials in Upper Canada stalled and otherwise took action to prevent a resolution of the matter (although Norton continued to oppose provincial authorities during his remaining years among the Haudenosaunee). Teyoninhokarawen also completed his journal while in Britain and hoped it would be printed. That did not happen, and it did not become widely available until the first published version appeared in 1970. After his visit to the United Kingdom, he lived at the Grand River until 1823, when he mortally wounded a man in a duel. In the aftermath, he travelled to the Cherokees in the American south and also journeyed through Mexican territory. He died in 1827 in or near a Cherokee mission in the Arkansas Territory.

6

The Blockade of Fort George,
Intrigue, and the Capture
of Fort Niagara, 1813

Within three days of the battle of Stoney Creek in early June, the American army retreated precipitously to Fort George and abandoned its other positions on the Canadian side of the Niagara Peninsula. Their opponents advanced from Burlington Heights, camped at Forty Mile Creek by the shores of Lake Ontario, and reoccupied Fort Erie and other posts along the border. British forces and First Nations warriors then established forward positions to monitor and harass their enemy between Forty Mile Creek and the mouth of the Niagara River. Thus, shortly after the beginning of this section of Teyoninhokarawen's autobiography, the Americans only occupied the area in and around Fort George, where they strengthened the old earthworks and erected additional defences to protect their troops, who could be supported by the United States Navy's Lake Ontario squadron along with Fort Niagara and other nearby works in New York. Nevertheless, the initiative had passed to the British. With this change in the strategic situation, a large proportion of the people from the Grand River rejoined the struggle against the invaders, although they did so warily immediately after the battle of Stoney Creek.

While British soldiers, Canadian militiamen, and First Nations warriors gained a tenuous ascendency, they did not attempt to expel the Americans from Fort George because their adversaries outnumbered them significantly. Instead, they directed their efforts towards confining the invaders within their works, thereby preventing them from posing a broader threat to the province. Most of the fighting on the Niagara Peninsula during the blockade between June and October took place on a smaller scale than the earlier confrontations of Queenston, Fort George, and Stoney Creek; yet it occurred on an almost-constant rather than periodic basis. During this time Haudenosaunee warriors from New York crossed the border as allies of the United States, where they occasionally deployed against indigenous people aligned to the British, including their relatives from the Grand River. Their efforts represented a troubling escalation from the year before when they had played only minor roles as American allies, and brought to fruition the fears they had expressed during councils with representatives from Canada in 1812. Other Iroquois people saw action on a more intense level than they had during the previous year, with the participation of warriors from Akwesasne, Kanesatake, and Kahnawake, along the Ottawa and St Lawrence rivers, on the Niagara front in late June being particularly striking. Beyond the Six Nations, warriors from various native communities, primarily within Upper Canada, also deployed alongside their British allies in this theatre during the last half of 1813.

Following the victory at Stoney Creek, John Norton recovered a substantial amount of influence, as indicated by the number of men who joined him in operations against the Americans in the weeks that followed. In late August or early September, however, he withdrew from the campaign until the end of the year due to illness and possibly other problems. While fighting the invaders, Norton also had to contend with the hostility of the Indian Department and members of the Grand River community who either aligned with it or otherwise opposed him, whether they were pro-British or not. For their part, the army's leadership and the governor-in-chief, Sir George Prevost, thought the department and its senior local official, William Claus, were inefficient and self-serving, but tried to reconcile Claus and Norton for the benefit of the overall war effort. They were not successful, and not all of the blame lay with the deputy superintendent-general, his department, or the people who aligned against Norton. As before, Teyoninhokarawen's memoir says little about his political tribulations, so explorations of these themes occur mainly in the notes.

Due to supply shortages, the weather, and American successes in the west, the British lifted their blockade of Fort George in October and retired from other positions along the Niagara River for a time, to concentrate at Burlington Heights. They even contemplated withdrawing farther as they had thought of doing earlier in the year, to York or Kingston, allowing the Grand's small pro-American party to enjoy a brief period of increased influence, as it had before the battle of Stoney Creek. These developments gave the Americans a chance to assert power over the area; nevertheless, nothing came of that opportunity. Then, in December, the invaders withdrew from Canadian territory, destroying the civilian communities of Niagara and Queenston in the process. Before the end of the year the British returned to Fort George and their other posts, captured Fort Niagara, and, with native help, drove their enemies from the New York side of the Niagara River, burning most of the American border settlements, which had been used to support military operations against Canada. At the same time, American forces retreating from Buffalo looted their Six Nations allies at Tonawanda. That transgression added to the stress and impoverishment of the non-combatant population along the border – both native and newcomer – who faced the rest of the winter without adequate shelter or sustenance, and who often had to seek protection from the elements and the privations of the front lines many miles from their now-desolated homes.

While Norton's journal provides substantial detail from June through August, it records little first-hand information for much of the rest of the year until mid-December, when he participated in the British thrust into the New York side of the Niagara Peninsula. Instead, he presents his readers with a general survey on the course of the war as he had heard and read about it second-hand, which is interesting in filling in the details of the campaigning and in giving us a good sense of how he and his contemporaries understood the period's events. His memoir tells us that he was unwell through much of the latter part of the campaign, which likely was true, because sickness was a substantial problem on the Niagara Peninsula that year and because his journal subsequently indicates that he suffered from recurring health problems, as was common at the time. Yet his narrative – centred on his public life – also says nothing about an important personal event that summer: his wedding in late July within a few miles of the American lines. He was forty-two; his bride, Catherine or Karighwaycagh, was much younger, perhaps only sixteen. It seems unlikely that such an event had no effect on his willingness to serve. Furthermore, it seems most doubtful that the Indian Department's campaign against him had no impact on his capability to attract a following or his enthusiasm for the war effort, as the story explored in the notes suggests. Moreover, Teyoninhokarawen's withdrawal from an active role due to illness or other factors undoubtedly diminished his ability to maintain support among the warriors, who drifted away or attached themselves to other leaders.

The British and their First Nations allies achieved their objectives on the Niagara Peninsula in 1813. They also won important battles at Châteauguay and Crysler's Farm farther east (thus saving Montreal and preserving communications lines into the upper province). Yet the Americans enjoyed their only successful campaign of the war against the Canadas, in the Detroit River region. First, the British and Western Tribes failed to capture their opponents' forts in northwestern Ohio in the spring and summer (as we saw in part earlier with Norton's description of the first siege of Fort Meigs, and as we will encounter again below). Then, the United States Navy won the battle of Lake Erie in early September. Having lost water communications, the allies abandoned southwestern Upper Canada. Many withdrew towards

Burlington, primarily because the British could not supply the troops, war-
riors, and their dependents with food or other necessities following that
defeat. The senior American officer in the region, William Henry Harrison,
next led his army across the border, pursued the retreating forces, and won
the battle of Moraviantown (near modern Chatham) early in October, at
which Tecumseh died. As the invaders enjoyed their triumphs, the Western
Tribal Confederacy collapsed, and a large portion of its member communities
signed peace treaties with the United States late that year and during 1814,
although sizeable numbers of its warriors kept on fighting, mainly alongside
British forces within Upper Canada. Tecumseh's half-brother, Tenskwatawa,
fled to the Niagara region after Moraviantown, where he found that most of
his influence evaporated. For the Six Nations of the Grand River, the very
difficult year of 1813 ended in fear and despondency. Following the defeat at
Moraviantown, their villages and farms again sat exposed to a direct assault,
this time from the west. That threat, combined with stories of atrocities com-
mitted by Americans against the First Nations, drove more than fifteen hun-
dred people from their homes to shelter behind the British lines along with
hundreds of other native refugees from the west. Most of them camped around
the Head of the Lake behind Burlington Heights, where they faced the coming
winter enduring the scarcities and privations of living as refugees in a man-
ner that reminded them of the disasters of the American Revolution, and the
miserable consequences that had followed the end of that war.

On the return from Stoney Creek, we met many of the Five Nations
from the Grand River who had stopped the night on the road, and were
now coming to look for us.[1] As soon as I had reposed a few hours at Burlington, seeing the number of our warriors increase, I proposed to them
to follow the enemy along the summit of the mountain, thereby avoiding even the possibility of falling into ambuscade, and reconnoitring
from time to time his march or position, so that whenever a favourable
opportunity for attacking him should occur, we might make the most
of it.[2] The warriors joined in the plan with alacrity, but before we had
got ready to proceed, some of the Mohawks had received a suggestion

---

1 JN met these people during the day on 6 June, a few hours after the battle. The "road"
  likely was Dundas Street.
2 Presumably JN meant "possibility" rather than "probability" in this sentence, but the
  latter appears in the fair copy of his manuscript.

from a certain quarter, and in consequence thereof, proposed a council. In this, several difficulties were stated, among others, [that] the troops were required to accompany them. Thinking it imprudent to make this request in the present situation of affairs, when I knew there existed so great a disparity of force [between the opposing sides], and [recognizing] that the troops had neither agility nor skill to take advantage of the natural face of the country as our warriors [did], should they find the enemy fully prepared to take every advantage from his great number, I therefore thought that to take them would be risking too much, while the plan I proposed would be without any hazard whatever, as we had all been accustomed to hunt through the very woods by which we intended to pass. We might therefore have challenged them to have followed us without any risk of its acceptance should we not find it advantageous to attack them. For this reason I urged, as a point of honour, that we should now attempt something alone, as in the last two battles we had aided our father's troops with a very few warriors indeed. However, while I was endeavouring to get the better of this cabal, I had sent a party of twelve young men, Onondagas and Senecas, to reconnoitre the motions of the enemy.[3]

---

3 Words like "cabal" in JN's text suggest serious contention between his supporters and other people at a time when the strategic situation was unclear: the Americans appeared to be in retreat, but the outnumbered King's forces had lost many men at Stoney Creek. Thus, some indigenous people thought of re-entering the war on the British side, but others advocated caution or wanted to retain the options of either avoiding combat or joining the Americans in order to protect their communities from retribution should the invaders regain the ascendancy. JN's desire to have the warriors operate separately from the army may have been motivated by hopes of avoiding a clash between the allies. In contrast, other people may have wanted some soldiers to be deployed with them to become hostages if such a decision would serve Haudenosaunee interests during the troubled times between the battle of Stoney Creek and the collapse of American vigour on the Niagara front shortly afterwards. Wanting troops to accompany them also may have been a response to a similar request from the British before the battle to send some Six Nations men to fight alongside the army, who also could have been seized as hostages if the Grand River people had decided to turn on the Crown's forces. JN's argument that troops could not operate in the terrain of the Niagara Escarpment seems forced, because light troops fought effectively alongside warriors over rough ground, as his memoir regularly demonstrates. His suggested deployment on top of the escarpment may have been an attempt to achieve a compromise, because the movements he proposed not only would allow the natives to fight effectively should opportunities arise, but would provide an easy way to withdraw from the area without the Americans

At this time, a fleet appearing on the lake, it gave us great joy to learn that it was Sir James Yeo with seven sail, among which was the new-built ship, the *Wolfe*, of twenty-four guns. He sailed on towards the Forty Mile Creek.[4] In the evening, our party returned. They related that, within a few miles of the encampment of the enemy, discovering a party of horse advancing towards them, they ranged themselves in ambuscade on the side of the road until the enemy had passed. They then attacked them, killing one and dismounting another. The rest, twelve in number, took to flight as fast as their horses could carry them; and

---

necessarily being aware of their presence in the first place. The character of JN's prose here suggests that he had not fully worked through his story to address the challenges of that point in the history of the war. Presumably he wanted to be truthful in terms of what he wrote (in keeping with his general approach to his autobiography), but did not want to reveal details that might offend a white audience or undermine broader Iroquois interests such as securing title to the Grand River lands, which, as we have seen, was a fundamental motivating factor for his participation in the war. Aside from JN's text, there are few documents relating to this time, as we would expect from people who generally did not write and where the actions they may have contemplated were dangerous. Nevertheless, it does seem that the pro-American party enjoyed a moment of prominence, because a portion of the Grand River population considered abandoning the British alliance in favour of one with the invaders in hopes of preserving their homes and people from disaster. We do not know how many individuals seriously considered this change, but a document signed by 15 chiefs (but not by JN) some months later, which referred to this time, said 105 people from 12 families had "acted in an unbecoming manner towards their great father, the King, by endeavouring to discourage the warriors, and refusing themselves to fight the King's enemies" (Memorandum, 9 January 1814, published in Johnston, *Six Nations*, 219). As written, that text suggests that the number of affected people was greater than 105, but that the chiefs thought only members of these particular families ought to be penalized by not receiving presents from the Crown. Given the nature of Iroquois politics, it seems likely that another portion of the Grand's inhabitants moved from a pro-British to a neutralist stance around that time. There is an oral tradition from the Six Nations (written down in modern times) that captures a sense of considerable stress surrounding the period of the battle of Stoney Creek, as it sounds like the "redemption" half of a "fall and redemption" story in recording an event that happened shortly after the battle (Roy Buck's Interpretation, 1982, quoted in Hill, *War Clubs and Wampum Belts*, 49). The crisis soon passed as significant numbers of Grand River warriors came into action against the Americans.

4 At a distance, it was difficult to distinguish American from British vessels. Commodore Sir James Lucas Yeo was the senior Royal Navy officer on the lake. He sailed from Kingston on 3 June with six ships and schooners. (The American squadron had returned to Sackett's Harbour on 2 June following the capture of Fort George, and thus was not in the vicinity to challenge him.)

finding themselves intercepted on the direct road by which they had come, they took a circuitous route, which ascended to, and passed along the summit of the mountain. In this flight our young warriors pursued them until they had reached the camp, when, in resentment for their escape, they fired among the crowd whilst at the same time our fleet approached very near [to] the shore, which, to the enemy, appeared [to be] a regular cooperation.[5]

The next day, we gained information that the enemy had retired from the Forty Mile Creek precipitately, leaving their tents standing.[6] All then moved on with great alacrity. No exhortations were wanting. No council retarded their advance.[7] In following the enemy, we

---

5 After skirmishing with American dragoons on the Queenston Road, a dozen Onondagas and Senecas fired into the American camp at Forty Mile Creek at about the same time that the Royal Navy fired upon the invaders early on 8 June. Although the warriors' numbers were small, and they had to retreat when driven off by some infantry, their efforts, in conjunction with those of the squadron, led the invaders to decide to retire to Fort George, which they did hurriedly from fear that the British would land troops between them and the Niagara River to cut off their retreat. At the same time, the Americans heard rumours that large numbers of warriors were arriving to bolster the British force. At that moment, the invaders at and near their camp numbered 4,000, having been reinforced after the battle of Stoney Creek.

6 "The next day" was 9 June. During the previous evening, after the naval attack earlier in the day, British forces came ashore at Forty Mile Creek to discover that the Americans had abandoned 500 tents along with large quantities of other equipment. They also had burned much of their baggage in their haste to withdraw to Fort George.

7 These short sentences refer to the easing of the tensions JN described immediately prior to these developments when he spoke of the "cabal." Other accounts of this period noted that significant numbers of warriors pursued the Americans once the invaders lost the initiative (e.g., William Hamilton Merritt, Journal, n.d., published in Sutherland, *Desire of Serving*, 7). The natives operated within a broader context that saw them, along with regulars, militia, and naval forces, harass the invaders in their retreat, with one result being the capture or destruction of immense quantities of American equipment and supplies along the route from Stoney Creek to Fort George. Indigenous forces acquired a portion of the spoils (such as 180 tents). One report stated that "the fugitives were pursued in every direction by a numerous body of Indians under the Chief Norton" (General Order, 8 June 1813, *Niles' Weekly Register*, 26 June 1813, reprinted from the *Kingston Gazette*). In attempting to subvert JN's leadership and reputation, William Claus later lied, "Captain Norton is complimented for the handsome manner in which he followed up the enemy with his warriors, when not an Indian advanced until after our troops came in, and they only went to the field for plunder" (Claus, Account, 4 December 1813, published in Cruikshank, "Campaigns," 26–7).

picked up a few stragglers only of those who had left the Forty Mile Creek in boats, and being alarmed by the fire from our shipping, had disembarked and taken to the woods.[8] About ten o'clock in the morning we came to a deep hollow through which ran a small stream. Here we found that the heavy artillery of the enemy had remained the preceding night.[9] A mile and half further on, the main body had encamped. We went on two miles more to the Twelve Mile Creek. There we received information that the enemy had continued their retreat without intermission and that they were by that time securely lodged in Fort George.[10] We heard also that a detachment of three hundred men were returning to this place for the purpose of collecting and protecting the stragglers already mentioned, and that they were near at hand. We therefore prepared an ambuscade for them and waited a few hours till we were notified of their having been recalled.[11] We then returned to the Forty Mile, which had now become headquarters for the army.

---

8 The Royal Navy seized 17 or 18 bateaux on 8 June as their crews tried to return to Niagara from Forty Mile Creek. When the British vessels chased these boats ashore, the men on board fled and the warriors with JN captured some of them, the number of which is not known, but the Americans lost 80 men taken prisoner during the retreat from Forty Mile Creek on 8 and 9 June. Sir James Yeo's squadron subsequently cruised along the New York shore of Lake Ontario, where it seized more vessels and stores, which the British desperately needed to help sustain themselves and their allies.

9 JN arrived at the hollow on 9 June. With the bridge over the low point of the ravine destroyed, attempts to move artillery through the water and mud failed, so the Americans left most of the guns behind after they sank into the mire. The location likely was on the Queenston Road at Sixteen Mile Creek, although there are other possibilities, such as Twenty Mile Creek.

10 The Americans completed their withdrawal to Fort George from the Lake Ontario shoreline and posts along the Niagara River by 9 June.

11 Another account of this incident, which seems to have occurred on 11 June, notes that there were 30 natives with JN and Captain William Johnson Kerr of the Indian Department. They laid the ambush in cooperation with the Provincial Dragoons, but because of "bad management" it was not successful (William Hamilton Merritt, Journal, n.d., Sutherland, published in *Desire of Serving*, 7). That document is confusing, but it seems that the cavalrymen and warriors had trouble coordinating their movements and tracking the opposing force of 100 riflemen accompanied by some cavalry. The natives may have left the ambush site too early, and a subsequent effort they made to get behind the Americans failed, but in doing so JN watched his opponents' movements and thought they posed a threat to a militia force in the neighbourhood, which withdrew upon hearing his warning.

A chosen band picked from the soldiers of the 49th was put under the command of Lieutenant Fitzgibbon, an officer of peculiar merit and activity, to accompany the Indian warriors on the advance. With this small detachment and a considerable body of the Five Nations, we advanced to the Twelve Mile Creek, intending from thence to have attempted a surprise upon some of the outposts of the enemy, but an inhabitant in the neighbourhood deserting inclined us to change our plan. We moved up the mountain to a stone house in the vicinity of the Beaver Dams. At this time, excepting about sixty warriors, all the Indians had returned to headquarters.[12] The whole party therefore, including soldiers, amounted to little more than one hundred men. On the evening of the second day, a loyal inhabitant brought information that the enemy intended to attack us that night with six hundred men. We therefore moved from our quarters and dressed an ambuscade on the side of the road by which the enemy had to pass, but this precaution proved to be premature. (He had not sufficiently prepared to assail us.) The people testified so strong a desire to return, excepting a very few, that it appeared useless to make any further attempt to retain them. In the hopes of collecting a more formidable party, I was inclined to follow, only awaiting the return of some of my young warriors who were on the lookout.[13] Lieutenant-Colonel Clark of the militia arrived

---

12 The officer was Lieutenant James Fitzgibbon of the 49th Foot. The "stone house" where he established a depot in mid-June was John DeCew's, mentioned earlier. It sat near Beaver Dams Creek (a tributary of Twelve Mile Creek in modern Thorold). With 50 men from his regiment, along with some dragoons and native warriors, his patrolling and skirmishing helped to undermine the invaders' morale and inhibited their ability to contest control of the region following their earlier reverses. The "headquarters" to which 240 warriors retired was at Forty Mile Creek, where the main British force had camped, although the majority of natives returned to the Grand by 20 June. Patrols moved between and in advance of these posts, as well as along the Niagara Peninsula as a whole. Meanwhile, the invaders sent out parties beyond their foothold at Fort George, particularly along the Niagara River, while other Americans crossed from the New York side of the border to undertake similar operations.

13 The "loyal inhabitant" seems to refer to Laura Secord and her famous effort to warn the British of a surprise attack on James Fitzgibbon's depot at John DeCew's property after she overheard a conversation among American officers who had commandeered her home in Queenston. Years later, Fitzgibbon wrote that Secord informed him of the invaders' approach, and "in consequence of this information I placed the Indians under Norton together with my own detachment in a situation to intercept the American detachment, and we occupied it during the night of the 22nd" of June, but the Americans did not appear at that time (Fitzgibbon, Memorandum, 11 May 1827, quoted in Zaslow, *Defended Border*, 313).

at this time with a letter from General Vincent requesting us to proceed to Chippawa to cover the transportation of provisions and stores that had been left in the neighbourhood.[14] I therefore determined to accompany Lieutenant Fitzgibbon and his party with the few young men who yet remained with me. We marched all night, and at the dawn of day arrived near the place of destination. Scouts were sent out, and people set about transporting the articles mentioned while the party remained concealed. In the evening we removed, and by retired roads moved on towards the enemy until we had reached the descent near the village of St Davids. There, we took repose until the morning.[15]

The object of this excursion having been accomplished, we took leave of our friend Lieutenant Fitzgibbon, who expressed his intention of making the stone house his permanent quarters. In the afternoon, within a few miles of the Forty Mile Creek, we met a considerable body of Kahnawakes, Chippewas, and some of the people of the Grand River. Not seeing many of the latter, I continued my route in the hopes of collecting more and rejoining them before any encounter might take place. In expectation of being joined by a considerable party from the west, I remained two days at Burlington, and then returned to the Forty Mile Creek, where I arrived in the evening. The general having expressed a desire to have a conversation with me before I should pass, I called upon him in the morning.[16] About noon, we had notice that six hundred of the enemy, with two pieces of artillery, had surrendered prisoners of war. The same day the prisoners were brought forward

---

14 Lieutenant-Colonel Thomas Clark served in the 2nd Lincoln Militia.

15 St Davids was a village at the base of the Niagara Escarpment on Four Mile Creek on the Queenston Road. JN's movements that day had been on the high ground towards the south. The reason why only a few men remained with him is unclear, although it seems that William Claus was active at this point in trying to undermine JN, as we shall see below.

16 War parties totalling 340 men from the Haudenosaunee-dominated communities of Kahnawake, Kanesatake, and Akwesasne on the St Lawrence and Ottawa rivers arrived around 20 June (which led the British to establish a strong forward position at Ten Mile Creek). More men came to the lines afterwards and by early July several hundred Algonquian warriors "from the west" – including Chippewas, Mississaugas, and Odawas – also assembled on the Niagara Peninsula in addition to the Iroquois. The "general" was John Vincent; the "conversation" likely occurred on 25 June if JN remembered the sequencing of his narrative correctly.

accompanied by many of the warriors, who gave a narrative of the encounter.

A young man of the Kahnawakes, who had accompanied one of the scouts that had been sent from the Twelve Mile Creek immediately after their arrival at that place, having been missing, a party went in search of him towards St Davids. At that village, a road passes which leads direct to the Beaver Dams and the storehouse already mentioned. The party just came in sight of it while the Americans were passing. The men hastened to give information to their chiefs and brother warriors, who marched instantly in the straightest possible direction to intercept the enemy's line of march. The enemy had just reached the conjunction of the roads, about two miles from the position occupied by Lieutenant Fitzgibbon and forty-five [men] of the 49th.[17] When the warriors came in sight, they moved on to attack him [i.e., the American force under its commanding officer], and he immediately put himself in a posture of defence. Placing the cannon on a commanding situation, they checked the approach of the more cautious part of the warriors, but the truly brave advanced with ardour through the wheat fields, defying the fire of the enemy's cannon and musketry. They invested him on all sides. Many of the loyal militia, hearing the report of the fire, ran and joined with the Indian warriors. The road by which the enemy had passed was crowded with fierce warriors. He despaired of forcing his passage, and was galled by their fire from every quarter. The white flag was hoisted, but the ignorant disregarded this token of submission. Two or three hours after the commencement, Lieutenant Fitzgibbon arrived with forty-five men of the 49th, some militia volunteers, and others. He commenced a parley with Colonel Boerstler (the enemy's commandant), who capitulated for about six hundred men with two pieces of cannon. In this, the account of the Indians differs from that of the 49th. The latter say that the white flag was not hoisted by the enemy until they arrived, the former insist that it was and that resistance had ceased, but both concur that only the Indians (with a few scattered militiamen) had been

---

17 On the evening of 23 June, Henry Dearborn sent 600 soldiers towards Queenston from Fort George with orders to attack James Fitzgibbon's post at John DeCew's home, which led to the American defeat at Beaver Dams the next morning. Early on the 24th, the Americans marched up the Mountain Road to the top of the Niagara Escarpment en route to DeCew's property. They killed a warrior near St Davids, became aware that their movements had been discovered – which had been meant to be secret – but nevertheless decided to continue.

engaged. The number amounted to 280 men from the villages of Kahn-awake, Kanesatake, and St Regis [Akwesasne], about one hundred from the Grand River, and about sixty Chippewas and Mississaugas. There were five killed and many wounded. The enemy had thirty killed.[18]

The avidity of the Indian warriors in seizing the horses and plunder of this detachment of the enemy displeased the general [John Vincent]. It was urged that they had no right, as the enemy had capitulated; and [in response] they insisted that had they not fought the enemy he would never have been reduced to that situation, and alleged as an apology their receiving no pay. Therefore, the poverty brought upon them by war impelled them to seize with eagerness the booty of a fallen enemy. The Kahnawakes seemed to think that their service had been prized too lightly, and hastened to return to their homes. They all stated that their families would suffer in their absence for want of their support. The general now expressed a disposition to advance and take post at the Twelve Mile Creek, but the Indians who had fought at the Beaver Dams were not disposed to return immediately to that place. According to the ordinary custom whenever the seat of action is not very far

---

18 At the battle of Beaver Dams on 24 June, Lieutenant-Colonel Charles Boerstler of the 14th Infantry commanded 600 American infantry, artillery, and cavalry. A native force of 180 Seven Nations, 200 Grand River, and 80 other warriors, with some militia and Indian Department officers, ambushed their enemy on the Mountain Road (in modern Thorold). Forest dominated one side of the site, where most of the natives deployed. Low-lying fields and swamp formed the other. Early in the fighting, Grand River warriors assaulted the rear of the column on the road, but withdrew in the face of artillery and infantry fire after dispersing American cavalry sent against them. Other parts of the indigenous force remained, and after more than two hours of sharp fighting, Boerstler (who was wounded) tried to surrender, but his opponents kept firing until Fitzgibbon arrived with the first wave of British reinforcements (who had been watching other routes). After another hour of less intense combat, Fitzgibbon negotiated the capitulation. The number of native casualties is not certain, but there may have been as many as 20 killed and upwards of 30 wounded. The Americans lost their artillery and other equipment, along with 30 killed. The 70 wounded men and 500 other soldiers became prisoners. Warriors killed one or more Americans after the surrender and at least one prisoner found himself adopted by a Mohawk chief. Beaver Dams was the largest battle of the war in which the Iroquois (and other natives with them) defeated an enemy without significant participation by white troops at their side. It also was a rare event in Haudenosaunee history, with Grand River and Seven Nations warriors serving together in the field. The number of Six Nations men present indicates that a portion of those who had left the Niagara Peninsula a few days earlier, as mentioned by JN, had returned, and fought independently of him, as he was not present.

distant, they returned home to revisit their families before they would prepare for another enterprise; and the greater part of the Kahnawakes returned home, saying that if they were not at home by haying time and harvest that they would lose the means of sustenance for their families and cattle.[19]

I followed the general immediately myself with a party which increased daily.[20] The first thing we undertook was to reconnoitre the position of the enemy. We found them entrenched in their encampment, which was yet flanked and commanded by Fort George. They had six

---

19 Despite a provision in the capitulation that American officers could keep their possessions, warriors robbed them and the other prisoners – as did some whites – and many of the Grand River people who had left during the battle returned after the surrender and took what they could. Looting the living and stripping the dead were common practices on both sides of the white–native divide on the period's battlefields. The aboriginal combatants also wanted payment for the prisoners they turned in, and they needed additional supplies to maintain themselves. The departure of the majority of Seven Nations warriors was a blow to the British on the Niagara Peninsula, but the army faced enormous difficulties feeding and equipping the warriors and its own troops (with, for instance, such essential things as footwear being inadequate). Additionally, the military suffered from a lack of money to help alleviate these challenges. The British tried to assuage their allies' disappointment through issuing such goods and provisions as they could, arranging payments for prisoners and American supplies that the warriors brought in, offering support and pensions to the wounded and the families of the killed, and taking other actions along with honouring the warriors' achievements. Beyond these issues, the people from Kahnawake, Kanesatake, and Akwesasne had just won an important battle, thus fulfilling a fundamental objective in going to war, which, in indigenous tradition, obviated the need to remain on campaign if it was not necessary to do so. At the same time, people also wanted to return home for reasons related to their economy and the need to celebrate their successes and mourn their dead. Thus, most of the Seven Nations people travelled back to the St Lawrence and Ottawa rivers. JN's text seems to indicate that the Six Nations who had fought at Beaver Dams also went home for a time, as we would expect them to do in respecting wartime customs. As his journal indicates, JN was not at the battle; but shortly afterwards he apparently joked, "the Kahnawake Indians fought the battle, the Mohawks or Six Nations got the plunder, and Fitzgibbon got the credit" (William Hamilton Merritt, Journal, n.d., published in Sutherland, Desire of Serving, 8). James Fitzgibbon, however, reported that the warriors "beat the American detachment into a state of terror," and only claimed credit for "taking advantage of a favourable moment to offer ... [the Americans] protection from the tomahawk and scalping knife" (Fitzgibbon to William J. Kerr, 31 March 1818, LAC, RG10, 781:185).

20 After the battle of Beaver Dams, the British advanced closer to Fort George, from Forty Mile to Twelve Mile Creek.

pickets in front, extending in a line from Lake Ontario to the Niagara River, a distance of a mile and a half. We supposed these pickets to consist of something between sixty or a hundred men each.[21] Major-General de Rottenburg arrived to take the head command, and all the troops composing this division of the army were now in advance: Colonel Stewart, with the flank companies, occupied the village of St Davids; the King's, under Colonel Young, lay at the Ten Mile Creek; and our body, amounting to five or six hundred men, held the same position.[22] A detachment of the 104th Regiment and eight [companies] of the 41st lay on the same stream where it crosses the Lake Road. The artillery and main division of the army remained at headquarters on the Twelve Mile Creek.

Thus situated, on the evening of the 7th of July, I sent a note to an officer at headquarters for communication to the general, expressing a desire that the whole body of Indian warriors, followed by the flank companies, might approach the enemy and provoke him to detach a part of his force to engage them, and thus, by the discomfiture of this party, enrage him to send out other detachments so as to afford us an opportunity of defeating him in detail without incurring the risk in which a *coup de main* on his entrenchments might involve us.[23] To this

---

21 The main American force camped beside Fort George and the town of Niagara behind newly built defences. As they faced inland from the Niagara River, the fort anchored their left flank with their camp extending to the right as far as the town's still-extant St Mark's Anglican Church, while pickets stood in advance of these positions.

22 Major-General Francis de Rottenburg, Baron de Rottenburg, served as commander-in-chief and administrator of Upper Canada between June and December 1813. John Vincent, who had been leading British efforts in the Niagara region, became subordinate to de Rottenburg upon his arrival on the peninsula on 29 June. Lieutenant-Colonel Archibald Stewart of the 1st Foot was a brevet colonel. He moved to St Davids on 1 July to prevent the Americans from foraging for provisions and to watch for potential enemy movements in that vicinity. Lieutenant-Colonel Robert Young of the 8th Foot (the King's Regiment) was a brevet colonel. "Our body" seems to refer to the warrior contingent from a range of nations. They held an advanced position at Four Mile Creek and deployed pickets close to the American lines in Niagara.

23 JN's plan, in which he wanted the Americans to sally out from their defences and fall into a trap, differed from a *coup de main* where the British would try to break through their enemy's positions in a surprise attack. JN's decision to make his suggestion indicates that he felt confident in terms of his relations with the military leadership and the number of warriors who would fight with him at that point in the campaign.

proposal no direct answer was given. But a short time before the dawn, Mr Brant came to me and told me that the deputy superintendent-general [of] Indian affairs, the Honourable William Claus, had sent him to let me know that the general had directed that I should proceed with a hundred warriors as a covering party to a wagon that was to be sent for the medicine chest (which had been concealed in the neighbourhood of Fort George at the time of the retreat on the 27th of May).[24] I replied, "We shall go in front, and as many wagons as they please may follow in security." When I called upon the warriors, I found the Indian Department industrious in their endeavours to prevent any more going than the number mentioned, for which I could see no just reason, as the enemy was only in front [and did not threaten the flanks]. I therefore encouraged my friends to exceed the number rather than remain behind me.[25] At the Four Mile Creek, a boy, the son of Mr Law, met us. We found that he had escaped from a party of Americans about a mile further on. We hastened forward, but they had retired before we came to the spot.[26]

Having received information that the enemy [at Fort George] sent out a party of two or three hundred men every day to look out for Indians, we were desirous that they should not be disappointed again.[27]

---

24 The British had buried the medicine chest on a farm southwest of Niagara near a branch of Four Mile Creek. "Mr Brant" was Joseph's son, John (Ahyonweaghs), a lieutenant in the Indian Department, who had fought at Queenston Heights and Beaver Dams. Brant was 19 years old at this time. He later succeeded to the title of Tekarihogen, becoming a leading figure on the Grand River until his premature death during the cholera epidemic of 1832.

25 As JN was a captain in the Indian Department, calling men to follow him beyond the authorized number could be regarded as insubordination, but as a Six Nations war chief, he was free to act independently of white authorities. The conflicting perspective of how many warriors to deploy captures a sense of the tension between JN and William Claus.

26 The boy was 13-year-old John Lawe, son of Captain George Lawe of the 1st Lincoln Militia. George then was an American prisoner, having been wounded at the battle of Fort George. John's elder brother, George Jr, a private in the 1st Lincoln, had been killed at the time his father received his wounds. John joined the native forces in the skirmishing on the outskirts of Niagara on 8 July until his mother, Elizabeth (or Eliza) McGrath Lawe, ventured onto the battlefield "and took him away in her arms by force" (William Hamilton Merritt, Journal, n.d., Sutherland, published in *Desire of Serving*, 10).

27 The Americans sent out these large patrols to push back the soldiers and warriors harassing their pickets. This section of JN's text describes a sizable skirmish on 8 July

We approached near their centre picket and there dressed an ambuscade with the design of allowing them to pass before we should assail them. I then sent messengers to call those who had remained with the wagon, and dispatched scouts to the pickets on our right and on our left to observe the motions of the enemy (it being uncertain by which road he might advance). From the right I was notified that a party was there formed, apparently in readiness to advance by that road. At the same time, the scout from the left came in and said that the enemy was actually advancing in that road in some force. It was, therefore, immediately proposed to hasten there and begin with them first. On arriving there, we found that the [American] party had returned. I used my utmost endeavour to conceal the greater part of my men, for it was out of my power to conceal the whole (many of them, as they passed, firing on the picket).[28] Returning to the road on which we had prepared the ambuscade, we perceived the enemy ranged in order to advance in that direction. It then appeared most advisable, as we were discovered, to endeavour to entice them out as far as possible that they might have more difficulty in effecting their escape. For this purpose, the greater part of the men retired unperceived on the side of the road, and I only remained with a few in sight of the advancing enemy. At this time, Captain Merritt with a dragoon came up, and the latter was dispatched to give notice to the commandant at St Davids [to come to the warriors' aid].[29]

The enemy came on to the amount of about two hundred men until we had reached the border of a wood. Then perceiving that they would advance no further, we jumped over a fence and moved up to them. They had ranged themselves behind a fence and opened a heavy fire upon us; but running upon them briskly, their balls passed over our heads. A brave young man, a Chippewa Canadian of the name of Langlade, was slightly wounded in the arm.[30] They ran. We followed

---

associated with retrieving the medicine chest mentioned earlier, which the British were able to recover.

28 The firing by the warriors subverted the attempt to surprise the Americans. JN's inability to "conceal the whole" indicates that various war parties cooperated in the affair but manoeuvred with some autonomy from each other.

29 JN's opinions of Captain William Hamilton Merritt at this action resulted in this officer receiving favourable official recognition (District General Order, 9 July 1813, published in Cruikshank, *Documentary History*, 6:208).

30 Lieutenant Charles de Langlade Jr of the Indian Department was the son of a French-Odawa man and an Odawa woman. Some sources mistake him for Lieutenant Louis Langlade (associated with the Seven Nations).

swiftly, firing at them incessantly from the fields on each side of the road. They fired on us without effect. There is a piece of wood between this field and the post of the enemy. We suspected an ambuscade might have been prepared there to assail us unexpectedly in the hurry of pursuit. We inclined to the right and passed through it while a few only followed the main body in the road. There were enough, however, to draw the attention of the ambuscade, which was in reality as we had suspected, and consisted of about ninety men under Joseph Eldridge, so that we were just on their backs when they perceived us.[31] They fell into such confusion that they were instantly routed and pursued in all directions. The wood favoured the escape of many, for the thick foliage drove every object from our sight at thirty yards' distance. When we reached the more numerous body of the enemy, there were few of us together, and we retired under cover of the consternation into which this affair had thrown them.[32] Langlade rejoined me and told me that he saw one of my young warriors shot by an officer with a pistol while he seemed to be standing unsuspicious of harm. The warriors who followed instantly killed the officer and two soldiers who were in his company. We passed by the place and found the bodies of the Americans lying there, but our young man was carried off.[33]

---

31 The officer was Lieutenant Joseph Eldridge of the 13th Infantry. JN called him "Eldridge Livingston."

32 From mid-morning to mid-afternoon on 8 July, various war parties, totalling 160 combatants (accompanied by a few white men), engaged a larger but uncertain number of American infantry and cavalry across the farms, forests, and roads west of the town of Niagara, centred on property owned by the Butler family. JN and the Odawa leader, Blackbird (Jean-Baptiste Assiginack), played conspicuous roles in this action, which consisted of a number of small- and modest-scale encounters of some intensity separated by quieter periods. At one point, the Americans recognized an attempt to ambush them, so they moved cautiously, and the two sides formed opposing lines to fight. Cavalry then charged the warriors, but the natives repulsed them with small arms fire. Next, infantry commenced shooting at almost 300 yards, far beyond effective range, so the warriors, perceiving the poor fire discipline, attacked. Their assessment was correct as most bullets flew over their heads. Their opponents fell back into a wooded area, but the natives followed them. The Americans next tried to set a trap, but the warriors were not deceived, so some of them moved into a position behind the opposing infantry while another part of the indigenous contingent drew their opponents' fire and attention. Those in the rear then attacked, killing and capturing a large number of Americans.

33 The young warrior was Joseph Crawford, also known as Big Arrow (Kahishorowanen), an Onondaga (JN to J.F. Addison, 13 February 1817, LAC, RG8, 261:30). Joseph

It was proposed to the whole body to assemble at the Four Mile Creek to be prepared should another division of the enemy come out. Whilst I was taking some refreshment that was brought to me on the road, I saw the enemy again advance in much greater number than before. They came to where we had begun the preceding encounter, extending their line into the fields. After giving them a shout, we retired to where we had expected to have found all our men reassembled, but to my surprise and regret, I found no more than twenty. The Chippewas had all passed on, and many of our own had carried away my young man who had been dangerously wounded. Others had conducted the prisoners to headquarters. We now saw coming on the road from St Davids a body of horsemen and infantry. It was Colonel Stewart and his detachment hastening to our assistance, but it did not appear advisable to make any further attempt, it being late in the afternoon and the greater part of my party having left me. The colonel went forward to the ground to which I had seen the enemy advance and found that they had retired.[34]

After dark, we reached our camp at the Ten Mile Creek. There I found the wounded youth. He told me that when he had overtaken the officer and the two soldiers, on his pointing his gun at the former, he dropped his hand holding the pistol, making signs of submission. That then, as he turned his eyes to the soldiers, he received his fire, which brought him to the ground, and the other warriors coming up at the instant dispatched all three without delay. The young man had received a bullet in the side and a buckshot in the shoulder.[35] The party engaged in

---

Eldridge, armed with a pistol, made a gesture of surrender by lowering his arm, but when Crawford turned his attention to the two soldiers with him, the officer raised his weapon, fired, and wounded him. Other natives arrived just in time to witness the incident and immediately killed the three Americans. Although Kahishorowanen was associated with JN's party, the people who killed Eldridge seemed to have been with Blackbird, whose account of the incident accords with JN's: "the officer ... fired and wounded one of our colour; another [warrior] fired at him and killed him. We wished to take him prisoner, but the officer said, 'God damn,' and fired, when he was shot" (Blackbird, Speech, 15 July 1813, published in Sutherland, *Desire of Serving*, 32n255. See JN's comments two paragraphs later in his memoir).

34 The Americans may have had as many as 1,000 men in the field at this point. Archibald Stewart's soldiers were the British reinforcements from St Davids, eight miles away, which the natives had asked for earlier in the engagement.

35 Americans often put a bullet (ball) plus one, two, or three small buckshot in their firearms. Buckshot normally caused small, non-serious wounds but could be disabling. Adding it, however, degraded a weapon's accuracy.

this affair amounted to fifty Delawares, thirty Onondagas and Cayugas with a few Mohawks, thirty Odawas from Michilimackinac, and about thirty or forty Chippewas and Mississaugas. The enemy lost sixty or seventy; of these fourteen were taken prisoners.[36]

---

36 JN's figures for native participants and American losses seem to be accurate. Casualties on the aboriginal side were two warriors and an interpreter wounded. Francis de Rottenburg noted that "Captain Norton commanded the Indian warriors ... with great spirit" (de Rottenburg to Sir George Prevost, 9 July 1813, LAC, RG8, 679:211). In contrast, William Claus complained, "All credit again [was] given to Norton, when [three interpreters] ... were the men who encouraged the Indians. The lavished praise on Norton caused jealousy" (Claus, Account, 4 December 1813, published in Cruikshank, "Campaigns," 29). Claus regularly said things that were untrue, but post-battle praise by senior officers often could not mention everyone who deserved recognition, so it is difficult to assess Claus's words. Among his many complaints about JN, the Indian Department's deputy superintendent-general said that JN had accused him of ordering interpreters not to help him when dealing with the western natives whose languages he did not speak, which British army officers seemed to think was true, but which Claus claimed was false (ibid.). Earlier, we saw that JN had recruited more men to join him at the recovery of the medicine chest than Claus had authorized. JN complained that "the Six Nations themselves appointed me a leading [non-hereditary] chief" (in 1808, as discussed in the Introduction), and that the British had made him "commander of the warriors of the Five Nations" (in 1812). Thus, having received authority from both partners in the Anglo-Haudenosaunee alliance, he argued that "I must consider any interference between ... [the Indian Department] and me as an injustice and an attempt to degrade me. With respect to Colonel Claus, I consider him to be the deputy of Sir John Johnson [superintendent-general of Indian Affairs in Lower Canada], equally connected with the different stations and branches of the Indian Department, but in no manner particularly attached to the Five Nations or any other tribe. And whatever control it might please the commander of the forces to give him over myself, I cannot admit that he should have any right to interfere with the people that I am to lead, or countenance any of them that endeavour to counteract me in the different arrangements which circumstances may require me to make" (JN to James Fulton, 26 June 1813, LAC, RG8, 257:93–4). Along with other matters, JN wanted the warriors kept together as a large force in order to be more efficient than they would be if divided into smaller parties. He also requested resources so he could distribute rewards, and asked that assistance be given to the wounded and to the orphans and widows of the fallen (ibid.) William Claus protested that JN had distributed unnecessarily large quantities of goods, and decided he needed to authorize JN's requisitions, but Major-General de Rottenburg overruled him after JN objected. In fact, the army issued an order early in August restricting Claus's authority by limiting decisions on providing supplies and rewards to those people who led men in battle, as JN did. Colonel Claus generally could not fight with the warriors because of his obligations as a militia officer in addition to his administrative responsibilities in the Indian Department. He thought the

It appeared now to be in contemplation to move forward and to take post more approximate to the enemy. At the same time, a proposal was made to join Lieutenant-Colonel Bisshopp with my party in an enterprise for taking or destroying some stores belonging to the enemy at Black Rock. But when I proposed it to the general, he positively objected to engaging our warriors in any enterprise on the other side, observing that, as the enemy was always making a great outcry of the perpetration of cruelties by His Majesty's allies, whether any were committed or not,

---

army's decision was wrong and would undermine British efforts to manage native allies (Claus to de Rottenburg, 13 August 1813, ibid., 257:117–25; General Order, 7 August 1813, LAC, RG10, 28:16498–9). In commenting on JN, Claus argued that "the government was deceived in the high opinion it had of that man," stating that "both in public and private did the Indians speak of" him "in a most despicable manner." That likely was true for a portion of them, given the divisions that existed within the Six Nations, but was false in terms of all. The exchanges recorded in these documents, however, suggest that JN aspired to exercise a degree of military leadership across a large segment of the warriors on the Niagara Peninsula that exceeded the level of authority that indigenous people normally would accord to someone. In his highly coloured account of this controversy, William Claus wrote that Francis de Rottenburg felt it necessary to hold a council after the events surrounding the recovery of the medicine chest to tell the chiefs and warriors that "no one was to command them" outside of their normal leadership structures (Claus, Account, 4 December 1813, published in Cruikshank, "Campaigns," 30–1). In the same document he made claims that warriors would not follow JN, but the historical evidence for the fighting around Niagara contradicts him. The deputy superintendent-general spoke of the anti-JN groups and other people who simply operated separately from him as if they were the whole of the aboriginal force on the Niagara Peninsula (ibid., 31–2). In contrast, de Rottenburg wrote that JN's "personal services are the most efficient of any in that department, as he is the only one who personally led Indians into action" (de Rottenburg to E.B. Brinton, 22 July 1813, LAC, RG8, 257:102). The general attempted to reconcile the two men, but failed (de Rottenburg to Brinton, 11 July 1813, ibid., 679:214; de Rottenburg to Edward Baynes, 15 August 1813, ibid., 257:116). In that second letter just cited, the general acknowledged JN's power and independence when he wrote in both admiration and anxiety that he was "certainly a great intriguer but is a fighting man, and may do a great deal of mischief if not supported." Such a view presumably accounts partly for de Rottenburg's decision to give JN freer control over distributing presents to warriors and their families. The general did not say what he thought the mischief might be. Logically, he might have worried that if JN became frustrated, he would withdraw from the campaign and take warriors with him, or that he might move west to fight on the Detroit front; in either instance, this would weaken de Rottenburg's capacity to resist the Americans locally (Claus, Account, 4 December 1813, published in Cruikshank, "Campaigns," 33).

he was resolved to give them no grounds for such complaints on their side of the river among the peaceable inhabitants. Lieutenant-Colonel Bisshopp, with a detachment of the 41st Regiment and a party of militia, passed over to the American side. There, after taking and dispersing the guard, he seized upon a quantity of stores and provisions. Before these were entirely transported to the Canadian shore, he was attacked by a superior number of the enemy, by which he suffered some loss and was himself badly wounded. Captain Saunders of the 41st Regiment was dangerously wounded and taken prisoner with a few of his men. The main body made good their retreat; but in a few days, we had to lament the death of Lieutenant-Colonel Bisshopp, a valuable officer and an amiable man.[37] The day appointed for his interment, the 17th of July, the whole army moved forward at sunrise to take position along the Four Mile Creek from St Davids to the lakeshore, which prevented me from attending to show the last tokens of regard to the remains of our worthy friend.[38]

Having joined the light division under Colonel Stewart at the crossroads (formed by the centre road through the swamp and the road along the stream from St Davids to the Four Mile Creek on the lake) late in the afternoon, we heard firing in front.[39] We hastened there with

---

37 On 11 July, 250 British regulars and Canadian militiamen crossed the Niagara River to disperse the garrison at Black Rock. They captured significant quantities of stores, and destroyed artillery, boats, and equipment, as well as set fire to a schooner and military facilities. As they prepared to leave after two or three hours in New York, 250 Americans and 40 Senecas counterattacked. American and Seneca casualties totalled 16 killed, wounded, and captured compared to 46 on the British side. Later exchanged, Captain William Saunders returned to Britain (although some sources assumed he died in captivity). Cecil Bisshopp died of wounds received in the action. (Later in the year, a new British commander proved willing to deploy warriors on the American side of the Niagara River.)

38 On 17 July, Francis de Rottenburg moved his lines to Four Mile Creek, establishing camps between St Davids and Lake Ontario and posting pickets in advance of this line and elsewhere. He also strengthened Burlington Heights in his rear, and sent native and white patrols along the Canadian side of the Niagara River farther south to watch for any American movements that might pose a danger to his positions. Anglo–First Nations forces also harassed their opponents at Fort George on a continuous basis.

39 The "light division" was a battalion-sized formation drawn from several regular, fencible, and militia units. The crossroads (today's intersection of Niagara Regional Roads 55 and 100 in Virgil) sat southwest of Niagara where the Black Swamp

a few warriors, desiring the whole to follow. On approaching nearer, I perceived the firing to be stationary. We therefore inclined to the left that we might pass the flank of the enemy unperceived by him. They broke, and fell back on another party, where they rallied, and made a resistance of a few minutes when we effectually put them to flight, pursuing them till they took shelter behind the cannon and crowded ranks of a division of their army. They left many dead on the ground, the exact number we never ascertained. But the main body of Indian warriors not coming forward to our assistance, we retired after having fired a few rounds in compliment to the fire of their cannon. When we came within four hundred yards of our advanced picket, which, although a mile distant from the advance of the enemy, was yet in full view, they, having remarked our removal from where we had fired upon them, now turned their guns towards it, taking the range of a wide-open road. With this fire of round shot, we lost a worthy young man of the Cayuga dialect.[40] Subsequent to this skirmish, the enemy remained tranquil within their lines, and we never made any serious attempt upon them. All that passed among us was the bustle of the Indian Department. This, and the sickness caused by the badness of the water, continued to diminish our numbers every day, for whoever became either sick or discontented generally went home.[41]

Road intersected a route that ran along the east side of Four Mile Creek. This location formed the centre of the British line facing the Americans in Fort George and Niagara three miles away. The firing – on 17 July – began when 200 soldiers advanced towards Niagara from Four Mile Creek to harass American pickets.

40 With the British probing the American lines on 17 July, 500 or more soldiers moved out against them, at which point JN and other warriors came into action. A strong force of British infantry and artillery followed the warriors and helped drive their opponents back behind their pickets. The number of men deployed during the one-hour engagement probably totalled over 1,000 on each side. Casualties apparently numbered 13 Americans and perhaps only two on the British side. John Le Couteur of the 104th Foot recorded that the commanding officer of the American force, "a fine man on a grey charger ... was killed by Norton or one of his Indians" (Diary, 18 July 1813, published in Graves, *Merry Hearts*, 130–1). Another participant recorded that JN and Blackbird commanded the two native contingents, and said that the (unidentified) Cayuga had his arm and side carried away by a round shot (Thomas G. Ridout to Thomas Ridout, 20 July 1813, published in Edgar, *Ten Years in Upper Canada*, 204).

41 Note JN's terse criticism of Indian Department officials: "all that passed among us was the bustle of the Indian Department." During the latter part of July, the British found it increasingly difficult to maintain an effective blockade against Fort

On the 17th of August, early in the morning, we heard that the enemy had begun to advance. Being unwell, I dispatched a young man to ascertain the fact. He returned with a report that a strong detachment showed themselves in front of our advanced picket.[42] We then hastened to the place. Arriving there, we saw a body of the enemy's cavalry in front of us at the distance of six hundred paces, and on their left a body of infantry. Parties of our warriors were detached in various directions by our Indian Department so that few remained in a body.[43] At this time, an officer of the 19th [Light] Dragoons, with two troopers, going

George. The Americans regularly outnumbered their opponents (4,000 to 2,000 at this point in JN's narrative), and also enjoyed the periodic support of their Lake Ontario squadron, but the invaders generally remained cautious and so did not take advantage of their strength to try and break out of Niagara. A major problem for the British was a lack of *matériel*, food, and money for both their own men and their indigenous allies. Worrisome numbers of soldiers deserted, some warriors went home, and both natives and newcomers resorted to stealing from civilians to meet their needs. In addition, widespread illness became a problem in the hot, humid summer. It was during this time – probably on 27 July – that the Reverend Robert Addison baptized a Grand River Delaware, Catherine (Karighwaycagh), and then joined her to JN "the Mohawk chief" in marriage (Addison Parish Registers, 27 July, 2 May 1813, published in Carnochan, "Early Records of St Mark's," 27, 59). Presumably his wedding distracted JN, leading him to make an error in his text when he said that "we never made any serious attempt on" the American lines. For instance, a major demonstration occurred on 31 July, which drove in the invaders' pickets and allowed the British to undertake a close examination of the American positions (Francis de Rottenburg to Noah Freer, 1 August 1813, published in Cruikshank, *Documentary History*, 6:297). The ever-cantankerous William Claus wrote: "He has ... connected himself with a Delaware family, and has married the granddaughter of an old man or rather the daughter of a deserter from the Queen's Rangers and a common woman. Had the family been of any weight or the least consequence I should not have been surprised, but they are the poorest and least influenced [*sic*] among their people. Indeed, they are seldom with their nation, being among the whites making brooms and baskets, and the mother and daughter amusing themselves. Mr Addison married them ... since which ... [JN] has done nothing but ride about the country with madam and a posse of his connections" (Claus, Account, 4 December 1813, quoted in Cruikshank, "Campaigns," 33–4; see also Benn, *Iroquois in the War of 1812*, 143).

42 The picket occupied the area of Ball's Farm outside Niagara, between Two and Four Mile creeks along the Black Swamp Road.

43 William Claus obeyed orders to send warriors to protect the right and left flanks, which made sense tactically, although he objected to the decision (Claus, Account, 4 December 1813, published in Cruikshank, "Campaigns," 34). As we saw in an earlier note, JN also thought native forces should be kept together.

forward to reconnoitre, I attempted to collect a party to advance; but before this was in readiness, we heard the cracking of firearms. A few of us then ran to the spot from whence the sound had come, the deputy superintendent-general of Indian affairs and others of the department following us. Having yet in sight the enemy's cavalry, I was seized with a desire of getting imperceptibly round their flank to intercept their return; and to effect this, we were inclining to the [British] left through a hollow in the field when we perceived a party of Chippewas with their interpreter in the woods in the rear.[44] He called out that a sufficient number of them had already gone to circumvent the enemy, who might retire before they could gain his rear should he perceive us. About this time, a scout of the enemy's was discovered. (The long grass had hitherto concealed him.) He arose and ran; we pursued ineffectually. Some fired at him, and he fell within twenty paces of the woods in front. He again got up, and running a few paces, fell to rise no more.

We now saw a body of warriors approaching us in full run from the wood in that direction. On first view, I supposed them to have been the detachment of Chippewas mentioned by the interpreter, retiring in consequence of having seen a band of enemies too formidable to attack; but their appearance soon undeceived me. I suspected them to be the Indians of the opposite side of the water who had now undertaken to support the enemy.[45] I was about to challenge them, when I saw them level to fire. There were no more than six or seven men near me. We returned their fire and retreated on a more advantageous position about one hundred paces in our rear. There, I called upon all that I saw scattered through the field and woods to join, but few obeyed, and we had to take [to] the woods. From thence, we gave them another fire after having taken several shots from them. Those who had directly followed us retired, but it was loudly reported that a great number of the enemy were passing on our left. I called out to face about to meet them. It was then rumoured that the picket on our right was retreating. I now thought it improper to persevere any further, seeing that the men were rendered unsteady from the uncertainty of receiving any support, and

---

44 JN's "Chippewas" in this instance encompassed men from other tribes as well. *JMJN* errs in stating the officer was from the 49th Light Dragoons rather than the 19th. (There was no regiment named the 49th Light Dragoons in the British army.)

45 American-resident Haudenosaunee had crossed the border on 7 August to participate in a demonstration along the Niagara River north of Fort Erie; 200 of them (mainly Senecas) then took up picket duty around Fort George in mid-August.

having only thirty or forty of them to oppose a much greater number of the enemy. I proposed to join the picket immediately. Some of the Chippewas who had been detached were killed, and several Kahnawakes, separating from us, were taken prisoners. On returning to our encampment, we found that the enemy's Indians had been within a hundred paces of it, and had taken prisoner the man of a house adjoining. It was fortunate for us that the enemy did not support this sally of their Indians. Several Delawares that had been detached in a different direction were also taken this day.[46]

This was the first time that we had met in war that part of the Five Nations which remain within the boundary of the United States, and their cooperation with the enemy spread no small dismay among the warriors attached to the British army. The most alarmed were those of the Chippewa nation. Respecting the Nottawagees [or Haudenosaunee] for their ancient celebrity in arms, as well as for their number, they did not meet their attack with the firmness that might have been expected from the gallantry and lively courage they had formerly evinced in repeated combats with the Americans. But the distracted state into which the whole had been thrown made me despair of being able to bring the warriors to act collectively and consistently against the enemy so as to ensure success. On this account, I desired to communicate to

---

46 These events on the morning of 17 August occurred during a large-scale skirmish where Haudenosaunee men allied to the opposing armies fought each other. An American force of more than 500 warriors, militia, and regulars moved against the British on the Black Swamp Road. Their regulars, however, held back at a critical point in the fighting, thus crippling the attack, although they managed to burn a farm and its crops. Both sides sent reinforcements later in the engagement after most of the warriors had retired, and then returned to their former positions as the struggle came to an inconclusive end. Casualty numbers are unclear, but there were five natives killed, three wounded, and 10 taken prisoner on the British side (independent of a small number of Euro-American losses), while the warriors from New York seem to have suffered two killed and several wounded, and the white troops with them may have lost 30 or more killed, wounded, and captured. According to one newspaper, a senior American officer reported that "many of the enemy's dead were left on the field, among whom is supposed to be the famous Chief Norton" (John P. Boyd to William Armstrong, 17 August 1813, *The War*, 31 August 1813). The British did not have "many" dead, and of course JN survived. William Claus's account of the events that day suggests that the withdrawal of the warriors was both unnecessary and JN's fault, but so many aspects of his narrative lack credibility that we cannot be confident in his assertions (Claus, Account, 4 December 1813, published in Cruikshank, "Campaigns," 34).

the general [Francis de Rottenburg] my opinion that he might not be deceived by too great a reliance on their support.[47]

An alarm that the enemy was again making approaches called my attention. On examination, I found it to be premature. In returning, I met the deputy superintendent-general [of] Indian affairs followed by the whole of the department and a considerable body of Chippewas and Five Nations going in the direction from whence I had just come. Having been delayed an hour by the arrival of a party of Delawares, I had only just mounted to go to St Davids when I heard a firing in front. I then called upon them to follow, hastening towards the place. On the road we met numbers of the Indians retiring, and some ranging through the woods a mile in rear of the point attacked on pretence that the enemy [consisting of a group of warriors] had passed our flank and was getting in our rear. I observed that I could not wait for the enemy at so great a distance in rear of the party engaged on the apprehension of his making a move so very complicated that it could only operate against himself unless we should be so weak as to allow ourselves to be thereby intimidated. I therefore exhorted my companions to advance without regarding these manoeuvres. We ran on and soon joined with the enemy [comprising a mixed group of warriors and militia]. They retired but soon came on again to attack with great spirit, the Americans [i.e., regular troops] all the time remaining aloof. At last, they withdrew, leaving a few dead on the ground that we had gained. A brother to the chief Kayengwiroghtongh [from New York] was wounded and taken prisoner. He informed us that the Americans had decoyed them to that place under the pretence of holding a conference with the tribes attached to the British, and that since their arrival they had used every intrigue to engage them, which they finally effected, [and] that yesterday they had lost two warriors killed, and that several had been wounded. Of the former, one had emigrated from the Grand River in 1809. His name

---

47 "Nottawagee" and variants of the word were common among the non-Haudenosaunee populations in naming the Six Nations. After the fighting on 17 August, some of the Chippewas and other western warriors withdrew 10 miles from the front lines, while at the same time relations between the British-allied Six Nations and other indigenous people deteriorated. Given that natives had been leaving the front lines for some time, these events hurt Francis de Rottenburg's efforts to keep the Americans confined to Fort George and its outer defences. Note how JN thought General de Rottenburg might not have realized how aboriginal attitudes had changed without anyone telling him about it.

was Tekeantawea, and had always been much respected for his probity and good sense. This day we also lamented to recognize, in one that had fallen before us, a warrior who had in the former war particularly distinguished himself in fighting against the enemy. He had also removed from the Grand River in 1809. On our side, the troops fought with the Indian warriors, but on the American side, they did not move forward with their Indian associates; [instead], they remained several hundred paces in rear of them.[48]

No further hostility occurred until the 24th of August when Sir George Prevost, having arrived, advanced with the whole division, driving in the enemy's pickets until he had gained a position from whence he made a full reconnaissance of the enemy's position. I was not present at this affair, having been obliged to retire for indisposition the day prior to his arrival.[49] My illness having been in some degree alleviated, I returned to the lines a few hours before Sir George had taken his departure for

---

48 This two- or three-hour skirmish on 18 August unfolded much like the one a day earlier, beginning with an attack by a combined white and native force on the British pickets at Ball's Farm on the Black Swamp Road. As before, the American regulars did not provide close support to the warriors and militia. The Anglo–First Nations side lost seven killed (including four warriors), one wounded, and 15 taken prisoner. The Americans and their allies had four warriors killed, one captured, and an unknown number wounded. JN's account of the action underscores how porous the border was for the Six Nations, how relatives could fight against each other, and how individuals made alliance decisions based on their understanding of events, threats, and opportunities. The identities of the "brother to the chief Kayengwiroghtongh," "Tekeantawea," and the "one that had fallen" are unclear, as is JN's reason for intending to ride to St Davids. Claus's description of the day's events criticized JN for not engaging in the fighting for the first 90 minutes of the action (Claus, Account, 4 December 1813, published in Cruikshank, "Campaigns," 35).

49 The governor-in-chief, Sir George Prevost, arrived in Niagara on 21 August to examine conditions on that front. On the morning of the 24th, he led a demonstration in strength (which included warriors) against the American defences, to determine whether the British could change their objective from confining their enemy in Fort George to recapturing the post (or possibly encourage their adversaries to come out and fight in the open). At daybreak, the British advanced, drove in five of the six forward American pickets (guarded by 300 men), entered the town of Niagara, captured 50–70 soldiers, and killed and wounded 32 more while suffering 10 losses themselves. The Americans did not take up the challenge to march out and engage in battle. After using the opportunity to examine their opponents' positions in detail, Sir George and his officers concluded that they did not have the resources to break through the enemy's lines, and thus would have to continue the blockade.

Kingston. It was the first time I had ever seen him. He met me with that frank and warm expression of regard that carried with it the full proof of his sincerity. General de Rottenburg inviting me to dine with him, I passed the remaining hour with him, and was highly gratified with the candour that shone throughout his conversation.[50]

We heard by deserters that immediately after the 18th August, the Indians on the side of the Americans, having been disgusted, had retired to their homes.[51] In September, sickness quite overcame me. I was forced to keep [to] my bed and was reduced to the most enfeebled state. The want of the necessary comforts induced me after a week's ill-ness to remove to the Head of Lake Ontario. After my departure, I heard that a few skirmishes had taken place, but that which was accompanied by the most serious effects appears to have been the *événement* which had marked the operations of the Right Division of the army under the command of General Procter [in southwestern Upper Canada], and which I can only describe from report, which I shall endeavour to do from such as carry with them the general testimony.[52]

---

50 JN's visit with Sir George Prevost and Francis de Rottenburg signifies his importance (and possibly these officers' anxieties). Contrary to JN's positive reflection on the meeting, William Claus claimed that Sir George spoke to JN "very seriously, which I understood from an officer at headquarters was not well received," because the deputy superintendent-general had complained about JN to the governor-in-chief (Claus, Account, 4 December 1813, published in Cruikshank, "Campaigns," 37). While Prevost likely represented the need for JN to behave in ways that did not undermine the war effort in his relations with the Indian Department, it seems doubtful that he expressed himself as harshly as Claus alleged, given the need to preserve JN's support as a major indigenous leader.

51 There were a number of reasons behind the decision of most of the Haudenosaunee from New York to cross back over the border (although a good number returned to this front later in the year). American officials had insulted them at various times, such as by telling them that their modes of war were cowardly, and had mismanaged their material needs. During the fighting on 17 and 18 August, American infantry had not provided the support that the warriors had expected, which led many of the Iroquois to think that their allies were willing to sacrifice them unnecessarily. After those events, the Haudenosaunee sent word to those in Upper Canada on 20 August suggesting that they both withdraw from the conflict, but they did not obtain an agreement to do so.

52 The "Right Division" refers to the British forces on the Detroit front (the Centre and Left divisions covered the Niagara and St Lawrence regions respectively). Much of what follows in JN's text until December 1813 consists of stories that he had heard second-hand. During this time, he generally seems to have been inactive behind the

General Procter having been reinforced by a considerable body of Indian warriors collected from the Mississippi, the Green Bay, and Lake Michigan, and brought forward by Mr Robert Dickson, he was induced to attempt the crippling of the force which the enemy was then preparing at the Miami River to march against him or [engage in] the destruction of his magazines. For this purpose, having combined with them the warriors of the neighbourhood of Detroit, the whole amounting to more than three thousand, he led them forth with a detachment of several hundred troops. At [Fort Meigs on] the Miami, it was judged improper to make any serious attempt on account of the great strength of the fortification. It was therefore proposed to pass forward to Sandusky [to Fort Stephenson], there to cut off the supplies or to intercept the reinforcements on their march to complete the army. The greater part of the Indian warriors objected to having an American army at the Miami between them and their families, which remained in the neighbourhood of Amherstburg defenceless and unprotected by the warriors. Among these, the celebrated chief, Tecumseh, took the lead. The main body therefore, returned to Amherstburg. A few hundred warriors with Mr R. Dickson, Colonel Elliott (superintendent [of Indian Affairs] at Amherstburg), and the rest of the Indian Department proceeded with the troops which followed General Procter. They arrived at Sandusky and invested an American fort, which, after having despaired of taking by siege, they attempted to storm, in which they failed, and suffered a considerable loss for the number engaged. In this the Indians did not greatly participate, a few only were wounded and an officer of Mr Dickson's branch of the department was killed.[53]

---

front lines. It might be tempting to assume that JN's illness was an excuse for not participating in the blockade of Fort George due to frustrations or other problems with the Indian Department, and it is difficult to imagine that these issues had no impact on him. Nevertheless, sickness did incapacitate large portions of the opposing forces through the summer and autumn of 1813, and his near-constant involvement in combat may have generated emotional challenges, exhaustion, and other problems, while he also had married that summer, which presumably had some bearing on his conduct. We also know that two children of his from a previous relationship died during the war, and it is possible they passed away at this time during the general sickness of that summer (JN to J.F. Addison, 13 June 1818, LAC, RG10, 489:29364).

53 This paragraph continues the story begun earlier in JN's narrative about the failed siege of Fort Meigs in Ohio in April and May 1813. Henry Procter, Robert Dickson, Matthew Elliott, Tecumseh, and other war chiefs led a second effort against Fort

Here this unfortunate expedition ended, and General Procter returned to Amherstburg where the difficulties of his situation had become peculiarly pressing. The great body of Indians victualled at this place had exhausted the stores. The commissaries said that a sufficient quantity of flour and beef could not be obtained in the country adjoining, and the Americans now made their appearance on the lake [Erie] with a fleet, which they had recently built, equipped, and completely manned.[54] At this time the ships and vessels under the command of Commodore Barclay had not received their complement of seamen, nor the guns necessary for their equipment; but it was required that he should clear the lake of the enemy's flotilla [in order] that provisions might be transported from Long Point.[55] Soldiers were therefore embarked to supply the place of seamen, and the guns on the battery [at Amherstburg] were dismounted to arm the ships. Having thus prepared his force as well as circumstances would admit, this gallant commander proceeded in search of the enemy. Near the islands which extend from Point Pelee on the northern shore of the lake and the point forming Sandusky Bay on the opposite coast, he met the hostile squadron on the 10th September 1813. In the commencement it appears that he obtained the advantage, one of the principal ships of the enemy having been so completely overcome as to strike [its colours]; and he only wanted men to enable him to take possession of her when, a calm having rendered the sailing

---

Meigs from 21–8 July with 2–3,000 men, but lacked the resources to reduce its defences, while an attempt to entice part of the 2,000-man garrison to leave the security of the post and fall into a trap failed. Therefore, the allies moved 30 miles east to attack Fort Stephenson (in modern Fremont, Ohio) on 1–2 August with 500 soldiers and a few hundred warriors. (Meanwhile, Tecumseh and the majority of men with him withdrew to guard the approaches to native villages and camps from a potential strike from Fort Meigs.) Procter did not have artillery heavy enough to breach its walls; therefore, British soldiers assaulted Fort Stephenson, but without native support because the warriors refused to participate. The American garrison of 170 repulsed the attack. At the second attempt to take Fort Meigs, the Americans lost six men killed or captured, while the British and natives had no casualties. At Fort Stephenson, the British suffered 100 men killed, wounded, and captured, compared to eight casualties for the Americans.

54 The United States Navy collected vessels and built others at Erie, Pennsylvania with the objective of winning control of Lake Erie to cut British communications and support the army's operations to recover Michigan and invade Upper Canada.

55 The senior officer of the Lake Erie squadron was Lieutenant Robert Heriot Barclay of the Royal Navy.

vessels unmanageable, a powerful squadron of the enemy's gunboats approached, and opening upon our fleet a very destructive fire, it was reduced to so shattered a condition as to be compelled to surrender after a severe loss of killed and wounded, among the latter the gallant commodore, who had the shoulder of his remaining arm severely shattered by a grape shot.[56]

Not a vessel having escaped, we could not immediately ascertain our misfortune. When it became known at Amherstburg, it appears to have created a general despondency and to have suggested the idea of evacuating that post and retiring to the River au Tranche (or Thames). We remained in anxious expectation of hearing the result. We yet founded our hopes on the powerful body of Indian warriors attached to, or acting with, the Right Division of the army. Their number seemed sufficient to defeat any body of men that General Harrison could bring forward at that time, if we might be allowed to judge of the future by the past.[57]

The greater part of the American army on our frontier had now gone to Sackett's Harbour. This and other movements giving strong indications that he meditated an attack upon Kingston, General de Rottenburg ordered the 49th and 104th regiments to that place, and leaving the remaining troops under the command of General Vincent, he hastened there himself.[58]

---

56 In the battle of Lake Erie on 10 September, the six vessels of the Royal Navy squadron with crews totalling 440 men came close to overcoming the nine ships and schooners of the United States Navy's force of 530, but in the end lost the three-hour fight. The Americans had 125 casualties, the British 134, but the British also surrendered the rest of the ships' crews and their vessels. Robert Barclay, who had lost one arm in action against the French in 1809, received a severe wound to his other arm and had part of his thigh cut away by enemy shot (but he lived until 1837).

57 While the number of warriors who remained with Tecumseh was impressive, the Western Tribal Confederacy began to disintegrate after the battle of Lake Erie when many people went home. They realized that the strategic situation after the battle favoured the Americans and saw that the British could no longer send supplies to the Detroit front. Furthermore, if the King's soldiers were to withdraw east, as expected, and as occurred shortly afterwards, the chances of securing indigenous independence in the Old Northwest – a fundamental motivation for the confederates to fight – would diminish.

58 JN's comment referred to transferring men from Niagara to Sackett's Harbour. His chronology is confused here, as this paragraph more logically should follow the next one. After defeating the British on Lake Erie in September and at Moraviantown

Some who had made great haste [from the west] brought us the account of the defeat of the division of the army [at Moraviantown] under General Procter by the 7th, although it had only taken place on the 5th of October; and from the report made to General Vincent, he was led to believe that General Harrison was in full march for Burlington. Therefore, leaving his position on the frontier [near the Niagara River], he marched to that place to meet him. By attending to this incorrect information, a great quantity of stores and provisions were destroyed or lost. Every report that had reached us respecting the unfortunate affair of the 5th of October being confused and contradictory as to the fate of the Indians who had accompanied the retreat [from Amherstburg], we sometimes supposed them to have been slaughtered indiscriminately by the enraged Americans. At other times, they were reported to have held their ground and compelled the enemy to return to Detroit. This uncertainty determined me to go in search of them. In a few miles, we met many, and learnt that the whole were approaching, and that they had only been retarded so long on the road by the difficulty of bringing on their old people and the little children. We proceeded, however, about thirty miles [along Dundas Street], meeting in the road various bands, and there we found that the rear was not very far distant, and were made acquainted with the following particulars of the late unfortunate events.

On the approach of the enemy, the lieutenant-general proposed to retreat to a place called the forks of the River Tranche (or Thames), [and] there to fortify.[59] The Indians generally opposed retiring without first trying the decision of arms. However, Colonel Elliott and the

---

in October (described below), the Americans transferred men east to join other troops with the objective of seizing Montreal and thereby isolating Upper Canada. The British, however, did not know whether their adversaries intended to attack Kingston or Montreal. Before the invaders made their move against the St Lawrence region, however, there was more skirmishing on the Niagara Peninsula in the late summer and autumn, with Haudenosaunee warriors from both sides of the border taking part and suffering casualties. On 9 October, the British withdrew from their positions in front of Fort George and began to move to Burlington Heights in response to the defeat at Moraviantown. Their enemy made major demonstrations towards the post on two occasions and destroyed military facilities closer to the Niagara River before returning to Fort George without engaging the British in a significant confrontation, although small parties skirmished on a regular basis.

59 JN's forks of the Thames were in today's Chatham, where the Thames River and McGregor's Creek meet, not the main forks in today's London, farther east.

Indian Department at last·prevailed upon Tecumseh and his band, [along with] the Munsees, Wyandots, Odawas, Chippewas, and some Sauks (in all about five or six hundred men) to follow General Procter and the troops in the retreat. But the much greater number expressed their determination to remain, requiring a supply of ammunition wherewith to defend themselves. This, however, was only complied with in a very small degree. Thus, the forts of Amherstburg and Detroit were destroyed and evacuated, and the enemy suffered to approach and land without meeting any opposition. It appeared that various positions had been proposed wherein to await the enemy, which had only retarded the retreat as no regular preparation for resistance had been made at any place. The van of the enemy at last overtook the baggage (which was brought up in boats), and here they captured the scattered soldiers without difficulty, and became acquainted with the distressed situation of the main body, which encouraged them to continue the pursuit.[60]

The general was informed of the speedy approach of the enemy. He prepared to meet them. The Indians, as if anticipating misfortune, hastened to conduct their women and children with the old people out of the reach of the pursuer, and then returned to the position assigned them. About 250 men of the 41st Regiment were drawn up on the left. They were flanked by the [Thames] River, their order rather extended. The Indian warriors took the right, to the amount of three or four hundred men. The Americans made their appearance, and advancing forward rapidly, overwhelmed the troops. The Indians on the right for a little time sustained the assault, but were finally obliged to retire with some loss. Among the killed was the intrepid Tecumseh. He was seen rushing boldly forward upon the hostile ranks when victory seemed to

---

60 The "lieutenant-general" was Major-General Henry Procter. Following the defeat on Lake Erie, he withdrew eastwards from the Detroit River before the Americans began their expected invasion of southwestern Upper Canada. The people of the Western Tribes generally wanted to fight the Americans close to the Detroit River, in the area of greatest meaning to their interests, but in the end a large number reluctantly agreed to retire with the British. Procter then destroyed stores he could not carry with him, along with the fortifications at Detroit and Amherstburg respectively on 24 and 26 September. The British evacuated Amherstburg on the 27th; the United States Navy's squadron landed the American army under William Henry Harrison there later that day. Procter's subsequent withdrawal up the Thames River was slow and disorganized.

incline to their side.[61] Few of the women or children fell into the hands of the enemy notwithstanding the little time they had to effect their escape; but some of these which they took they inhumanely butchered, and they barbarously skinned the body of the gallant Tecumseh.[62]

The poor people arrived in much distress, destitute of every necessary. They passed on to Ancaster and the vicinity; and the people of the Grand River, as if a general retreat had been proposed, left their habitations and their cornfields, moving to the east with their families

---

61 At the battle of Moraviantown on 5 October (between modern Bothwell and Thamesville) 3,000 Americans (with native allies) defeated 950 British soldiers, Canadian militiamen, and First Nations warriors. Henry Procter's infantry had drawn up on the north side of the Thames River in open order rather than closed ranks to meet the enemy attack. That decision made sense to cover the amount of ground they defended to oppose an infantry assault, although such a deployment came at the expense of the firepower they could deliver, as well as their ability to withstand a mounted charge, which the Americans would in fact direct against them, easily breaking through the thin line. The natives with some Canadians mainly took their position in forested and swampy ground on Procter's right, and fought for a somewhat longer period than the regulars did in the 45-minute battle. British losses numbered 30 killed, along with 600 captured or both wounded and captured (including men taken during the retreat before the battle or soon afterwards). The number of First Nations casualties is unknown, but the victors found more than 30 indigenous bodies the day after the fighting ended. The Americans lost 30 men killed and wounded. In the battle's aftermath, a large portion of the remaining people of the Western Tribal Confederacy returned to their villages and negotiated peace with the Americans, but a sizeable number retreated east to the Ancaster-Burlington area to seek shelter behind the British lines rather than go home. Although many on the British side expected William Henry Harrison to continue his march to attack Burlington Heights, he did not do so. Instead, he returned to the Detroit River before many of his men transferred eastwards through American territory to participate in operations against Montreal, being content with his victory and with destroying property in southwestern Upper Canada (including the Delaware community of Moraviantown). Thereafter, the American army in the southwestern part of the province merely established a few outposts east of Sandwich, while the British likewise only maintained a few minor positions west of the Grand River. Afterwards, the two sides engaged in some small-scale skirmishing on that front, and American forces destroyed farms, mills, and other property as well as took food and supplies to meet their needs at their opponents' expense.

62 JN's footnote regarding Tecumseh reads: "This has been asserted by so many that force of testimony compels its acceptance, notwithstanding its atrocity." The fate of Tecumseh's body continues to be debated, with some stories affirming JN's view, and others suggesting that Tecumseh's followers hid his remains (with the Americans skinning another person in error).

and all that they could carry with them. When they came, however, to assemble together, they were generally averse to retiring any further. They said, "If we yet continue to fly from the apprehension of an enemy, our women and our children, should they travel in their present distressed situation, will perish from fatigue and the inclemency of the season. What then will it avail us to live? Would it not be better for us to fall gloriously in combating for victory, which may preserve their lives? Let our father then, have confidence.[63] We will stand by him; but, if he retires, we cannot follow him any further."[64]

Fortunately for us, a retreat did not take place. Colonel Murray, with a part of the 100th Regiment (and generally a party of Indians), occupied the advanced post of Stoney Creek. The Americans advanced sometimes as far as the Forty Mile Creek, and parties from our advanced posts proceeded several miles further, but without having

---

63 JN's footnote regarding "our father" was: "meaning the general" (Major-General John Vincent).

64 Fearing William Henry Harrison's army, the majority of people from the Grand – 1,530 men, women, and children – fled their homes in hopes of finding security around Burlington Heights and the Head of the Lake (Return of the Six Nations and Others from the Grand River at Burlington, 20 October 1813, LAC, RG10, 28:16579). They joined other natives from the west despite the grim challenges of living in refugee conditions over the approaching winter. Owing to the American success at Moraviantown and the consequent vulnerability of both the Niagara area and Burlington Heights, the British contemplated retiring to York or Kingston. JN's comments reflect discussions between them and their native allies about doing so. John Vincent decided to stay at the head of the lake partly because of indigenous influence, as well as worries that settlers might become vulnerable should he move farther east. At the time, with the Haudenosaunee people facing tremendous uncertainties, and with the pro-American and neutralist parties among them exerting increased influence, he told the Six Nations how disappointed he had been in the lack of support they had provided at the battle of Stoney Creek, and that he would need their help should the Americans advance towards him. He concluded his thoughts with the statement that it was his "decided determination to be governed in any future conduct and liberality towards the Six Nations and their families by the support that is offered me by the chiefs and warriors in carrying on the King's service" (Vincent, Speech, 22 October 1813, LAC, RG10, 28:16580–3, quote on 16583). One Upper Canadian recorded that the general was concerned that the aboriginal people – which included a large number from the Western Tribes – "would purchase peace with the enemy by the massacre of the population" (Robert Nichol to Vincent, November 1813, quoted in Benn, *Iroquois in the War of 1812*, 146). Concern over that threat would dissipate within a few weeks once the British reasserted their dominance across the Niagara Peninsula.

any encounter.[65] Some disaffected people in the vicinity of Long Point and other parts took up arms, and had the audacity to seize upon the persons of such as they knew to be active in support of the King's government, and sent several of them over the river as prisoners. Among these, Mr Francis, a justice of the peace, was a particular sufferer; but this banditti did not gain much accession of strength. They were shortly dispersed, and eight or nine of them taken by the Long Point Militia under Captain Bostwick, who received a wound on the occasion.[66]

We heard of the battle of Crysler's Farm and of Châteauguay, but I do not feel myself sufficiently informed on the particulars to attempt the description.[67]

There had been frequent marches and countermarches in advance [of Burlington Heights]. Therefore, as I had received no directions or

---

65 Lieutenant-Colonel John Murray of the 100th Foot was a brevet colonel and inspecting field officer of the militia. The primary objectives for occupying Stoney Creek were to remove the region's harvest to British lines and to rebuild native confidence in the King's forces. Murray's actions also thwarted an attempt by the Americans to have their Haudenosaunee allies communicate with the British-allied Six Nations to try and persuade them to sign a peace treaty with the United States (George McClure to Daniel Tompkins, 21 November 1813, published in Cruikshank, *Documentary History*, 8:222; General Order, 30 November 1813, ibid., 8:244; McClure to Tompkins, 6 December 1813, ibid., 8:253).

66 JN's mention of some of the raiding reflects the general state of affairs on the Niagara Peninsula and along the north shore of Lake Erie late in 1813. The disaffected people tended to be American immigrants to the colony. Some of them seized Thomas Francis and incarcerated him at Fort Niagara (and in 1814 murdered his father, William). Captain John Bostwick of the 1st Norfolk Militia received a slight wound in the face in a skirmish against one gang of such people on 13 November (in today's Port Colborne). The "banditti," as they often were called, also robbed and destroyed Six Nations property along the Grand. The British government later provided compensation to the Haudenosaunee victims as a part of a larger war loss claims process in Upper Canada.

67 The battle of Châteauguay occurred over five hours on 26 October about 30 miles south of Montreal on the Châteauguay River, near the international border. A force of 400 men, mainly Canadians with some British and First Nations support, defeated 3,550 Americans who had entered Lower Canada from New York. Losses were 100 on the American side, 22 on the British. On 11 November at Crysler's Farm, 1,200 combatants (mainly British regulars but with some Canadians and natives) defeated 3,000 Americans on the banks of the St Lawrence in eastern Upper Canada (near today's Morrisburg) in less than three hours at a cost of 200 men, compared to double that number of American casualties.

notifications from General Vincent to prepare for active operations, I observed with perfect apathy the advance of a division of the troops and some Indians, knowing that the enemy had recrossed the [Niagara] River and had entirely evacuated our territory. I supposed the movement [by the British] to be solely for the purpose of obtaining quarters more convenient and comfortable for the troops. Therefore, I made no attempt to collect a party of warriors to follow them. When I heard that boats had been sent forward, that the attack of Fort Niagara was in contemplation, and that Lieutenant-General Drummond (who now assumed the command) had passed on to join the advance, I found that there remained hardly sufficient time for me to reach the field of action so as to partake in the enterprise myself.[68] Therefore, without making any delay, I set out alone to overtake the van of the army. On the road I heard that the Indian Department, with a body of Indians, lay at St Davids; but when I reached the Ten Mile Creek where the road separates – the one leading to that place, the other to Fort George – I preferred the latter because it was the nearest. Expecting that the attack upon the enemy would be made from that point, I calculated upon meeting there whatever body of warriors might be in readiness to participate in the enterprise. At Fort George, I perceived that since the enemy had occupied it, they had greatly improved the state of the fortification without having erected any barracks for the shelter of those destined to defend it. Their garrison had been lodged in tents, encircled with a trench, a wall of sod, and a fire in front.[69] But at this place, I saw no preparation for any enterprise whatever. I only heard a report similar to that which was current all along the road: that a plan was in agitation to storm Fort Niagara. I therefore

---

68 The Americans withdrew from Fort George and crossed into the United States on 10 December; but before doing so, they burned down the civilian town of Niagara. The next day they destroyed much of the village of Queenston with artillery fire. The British reoccupied Niagara on the 12th. Lieutenant-General Gordon Drummond succeeded Francis de Rottenburg as the senior military officer and civil administrator of Upper Canada in December 1813, and continued in these roles until after the return of peace. Drummond arrived on the Niagara Peninsula on 16 December.
69 The meaning of "fire in front" is unclear, although it may have been a provision to light fires in advance of the American lines to illuminate the approaches to them at night. The American commander at Fort George cited the lack of winter shelter as one reason for retiring to the United States, along with having too small a garrison to resist an attack at a time when he believed the British were preparing to retake the post. He left substantial quantities of equipment and supplies behind, along with seven artillery pieces.

passed on towards Queenston. At McFarland's brick house, I found a detachment of the 100th and a party of artillery. The officer of the latter being an acquaintance, and learning that the boats and every other requisite were in readiness, and that the storming party to which they belonged was to cross at a little distance above the house, I remained with them until the hour arrived. We then marched up till we had passed the house of the Comte de Puisaye a few hundred paces [to the south]. We then descended the bank to a narrow beach where the embarkation was made.[70] Here I met Lieutenant-Colonel Harvey, who introduced me to General Drummond and the officers of his staff. He informed me that Sir George [Prevost] had written to me, acceding to my request to visit him in Lower Canada, and also that His Royal Highness had honoured me with the present of a sword and a pair of pistols.[71]

On observing a light about a mile down the river on the opposite shore, I was told that it was our forlorn hope, which had reached that place. Seeing Colonel Murray (who commanded the attack) embark, I followed. Reaching the other shore, we entered a house to await the rear, for having only two or three boats we could not cross many at a time.[72] The inhabitants of the house were an Irish family, lately emigrated into the United States, and the colonel hastened them to pack up their property and go over the river with the returning boats, humanely apprehending

---

70 John McFarland's home was two miles south of Niagara on the road to Queenston. Both sides used it as a hospital at different times, and it was one of the few buildings to escape torching by the Americans, although it suffered serious damage during the war. It also was the site of an artillery battery. Joseph-Geneviève de Puisaye, Comte de Puisaye, was a refugee from the French Revolution who had lived in Upper Canada between 1798 and 1802. Both his and McFarland's houses survive, but de Puisaye's sits 500 yards south of its original location. The riverbank is very high in this area, but there were pathways that descended to the shoreline below from which the British crossed the Niagara River on the night of 18–19 December to attack Fort Niagara.

71 JN's desire to visit Sir George Prevost related to his ongoing conflict with the Indian Department and his aspirations to play a leading role in the Anglo–First Nations alliance, as we shall see in the next section of his autobiography. "His Royal Highness" was the Prince Regent (George IV from 1820 to 1830). He fulfilled the monarch's function because George III was too ill to do so. The gift was the same as one made by the prince to Tenskwatawa (Gordon Drummond to Sir George Prevost, 19 April 1814, LAC, RG8, 257:253). In another instance, the secretary of state for war and the colonies, Lord Bathurst, told Sir George that he was "to express to Captain Norton and the Indians under his command His Royal Highness's gracious acknowledgements of their exertions in the common cause" (Bathurst to Prevost, 5 March 1814, ibid., 682:176).

72 John Murray landed at Five Mile Meadows south of Fort Niagara.

that they might be injured by the Indians from the west, who were in readiness to pass over at daybreak and were not under much subordination, and at the same time were highly irritated against the Americans.

About four hundred men having crossed, a wagon was provided to carry the scaling ladders, and we marched on through a dirty, muddy road, half-frozen, it having begun to freeze since dark. Within about three-quarters of a mile of the garrison, there was a cluster of houses and a battery at which there were some troops, the number I could not ascertain. We came upon them by surprise, and the soldiers who entered the houses, meeting with or imagining resistance, killed some of them. We passed forward immediately. At the burying ground, a few hundred yards from the fort, we separated: Captain Martin leading a detachment round the works to enter from the side next the lake, while the main body, conducted by Colonel Murray and Lieutenant-Colonel Hamilton, was to force the passage by the gate. We entered at the wicket without any resistance. Immediately after, a cannon placed on the top of a stone guardhouse fired two or three times. There was also a small discharge of small arms, but in a very short time all resistance had ceased, and the exulting shouts of the soldiers informed our friends over the river of the success of the enterprise.[73]

We lost a gallant officer of the name of Nowlan and several men killed. Colonel Murray was wounded. We found prisoners in this fort: the men who had been taken from us at the crossroads on the 17th of August, and a Mr Francis, an inhabitant near Long Point whom the banditti in that neighbourhood had taken from his home and conveyed to the enemy as a prisoner. In this fort, we took about three hundred prisoners, twenty-eight pieces of artillery, and stores to a great amount. Our friends whom we found prisoners here told us that the enemy had been on the alert and fully prepared to receive us for several nights, [and]

---

73 After landing, the British advanced north, killed the men of two picket guards at bayonet point at the "cluster of houses" in Youngstown, and then continued on to Fort Niagara. Due to the lack of vigilance by the soldiers of the American garrison, the British entered the fort easily in a three-pronged assault about 5 a.m. on 19 December. The attackers carried the post in 30 minutes, although they met stiff resistance from part of the defenders once inside. JN was the only warrior present. One record noted that he had "volunteered his services and accompanied the troops" in the attack (Gordon Drummond to Sir George Prevost, 20 December 1813, LAC, RG8, 681:256). The officers mentioned were Captain John Martin, a brevet major in the 100th Foot, and Major Christopher Hamilton, who commanded the 100th as a brevet lieutenant-colonel.

that this was the first in which, excepting the guard, the whole garrison had indulged themselves in retiring to rest, apparently relieved from all further apprehension of being disturbed by an attack from our side.[74] The commander, Captain Leonard, who had left the garrison at midnight to visit his family at two miles distance, being alarmed at the report of firing remounted his horse, and coming into the fort just as tranquility had been restored, was made prisoner by the sentry.[75]

Having heard the night before that the army was to proceed after the capture of Fort Niagara to the Cataract and to Buffalo as soon as it was morning, I hastened to Queenston to join them. But when I came there I found that the enterprise had been deferred, and the Indians generally in a state of great inebriety, having indulged at Lewiston in the most extravagant excesses.[76] The next day I was taken very ill, which obliged me to return home and prevented me from accompanying the army in its future operations. Nine or ten days after, the villages of Black Rock and Buffalo were taken and burnt in retaliation for the town of Newark, which had been burnt by the enemy previous to his evacuation of the Canadian shore.[77] The night prior to the assault, a body of troops and

74 The officer who lost his life was Lieutenant Maurice Nowlan of the 100th Foot. The British suffered 11 killed and wounded of their 600 men (comprised almost entirely of regulars). The Americans lost 85 killed and wounded plus an additional 360 captured at the fort and along the British march from the landing site. The attackers acquired huge quantities of clothing, footwear, blankets, and other supplies, along with ammunition, 30 artillery pieces, and 4,000 stands of arms. In other actions that followed along the river, the British seized four armed schooners and additional quantities of desperately needed supplies. The prisoners released at the fort included some Grand River and Kahnawake warriors. The "inhabitant" from the Long Point area was Thomas Francis.

75 The American commandant, Captain Nathaniel Leonard of the 1st Artillery, should not have been away from the fort.

76 The western warriors found alcohol in the houses at Lewiston, and they, along with some regulars and militia, drank enough to fall beyond the control of their leaders. Buildings were robbed and burned, at least one civilian was murdered, and a few of the attackers – white and native – were killed or wounded by their compatriots during the debauchery.

77 An extensive collection of documents published immediately after the war from British, American, and Canadian participants in the events of December 1813 affirms that the King's forces had not intended to burn civilian property when they invaded the New York side of the Niagara River. They changed their minds when they realized that most structures had been requisitioned for military storehouses and barracks (which forced their residents to abandon them or withdraw to small portions of their buildings). These same documents noted that subsequent

Indians passed over near the head of the Grand Island. At the dawn, they advanced towards Black Rock. As they came in contact with the enemy, another division passed the river at the ferry; but unfortunately they were carried down by the current much further than was expected, and coming under a heavy fire of the enemy, they suffered severely before they could effect a landing. But soon after they had disembarked, the vigorous cooperation of both divisions soon routed the enemy, who was pursued to Buffalo with considerable slaughter. This place, which had many shops, was completely pillaged by the Indians, and it contributed not a little to alleviate the distress and poverty into which the war had thrown them. A great quantity of public stores was also destroyed. The enemy's force which opposed the landing consisted of between two or three thousand militia. The concluding [of] the campaign with such *éclat* gave a favourable omen of the good fortune of our commanders and raised the confidence of both of the army and the inhabitants of the country.[78]

---

affirmations that the destruction was a retaliatory act were wrong and were not part of the discussions that occurred among the participants in the events of December 1813 (*Memorial of the Inhabitants of Buffalo*).

78 After the capture of Fort Niagara, native warriors and more British troops crossed the border to drive the Americans from the region and capture or destroy more military facilities and resources. Some of those who resisted them included warriors from Tuscarora and Buffalo Creek. The former community (along with Lewiston, Buffalo, and other villages) were looted and destroyed between 19 and 31 December, while the Senecas of Tonawanda and the white inhabitants of Buffalo also suffered the indignity of having their homes robbed by retreating American forces. Although the Tuscaroras fought against British soldiers and warriors from the west, it was a different party, from the Grand River, that burned their village, having crossed the river after their allies had secured nearby Lewiston and then advanced south along the river. The people from the Grand may have sought to avenge some of the deaths they had suffered from Haudenosaunee in New York during the previous summer. While some of the British-allied warriors behaved badly (as whites did on both sides), popular history in western New York has exaggerated their actions, although some civilians died and a great many lost their property. The numbers of men engaged in the fighting varied through this 11-day period, but at its climax, near Black Rock and Buffalo, the British deployed 1,500 soldiers and warriors against 3,000 Americans (mainly militia, but also including regulars and warriors). Casualty statistics are imprecise, but numbered roughly 500 killed, wounded, and taken prisoner on the American side, and 100 on the British, exclusive of the losses both sides suffered at Fort Niagara. At the end of the campaign, the British, aside from retaining Fort Niagara (which they held until the return of peace), withdrew to the Canadian side of the Niagara River because they did not have the resources to occupy more territory. The Americans began to return to Buffalo and the upper reaches of the waterway a few weeks later.

7

Quebec, Burlington, and the
Battle of Chippawa, 1814

*At the beginning of 1814, the United States had regained control over part
of the Michigan Territory which it had lost in 1812 and occupied a small
part of southwestern Upper Canada near the Detroit River, following its
successes on Lake Erie and at Moraviantown in 1813. Otherwise, the
administration of President James Madison had failed to achieve its goal
of conquering Britain's North American colonies. At the same time, in the
war's far west, native people and a small number of British and Canadian
troops dominated the upper Mississippi River in contrast to the situation
in the more easterly lands occupied by the people who had formed the now-
moribund Western Tribal Confederacy. They were able to maintain their
strength in part because the British kept supply lines open – despite the
loss of Lake Erie – by using fur trade routes that ran across Upper Canada
to Mackinac at the head of Lake Michigan and then continued south to the
Mississippi. Within the province, a substantial percentage of native people
persisted in opposing the United States. Across the ocean, Great Britain's
war against Napoleon Bonaparte was progressing towards a French defeat,
so the government in London was able to devote more resources to ending the Anglo-American conflict, with the first reinforcements landing at
Quebec in May. Furthermore, the changing European situation allowed
the Royal Navy to deploy more than a hundred warships on the western
Atlantic (compared to about twenty in 1812), and ultimately, with the
help of the British Empire's privateers and an effective blockade of American ports, it eliminated nine-tenths of the republic's pre-war international
trade. In addition, the blockade rendered coastal communications along
the Atlantic seaboard dangerous, forcing people to use slow and costly
land routes to move goods from one part of the United States to another.
(American naval and privateering efforts likewise hurt their opponent's*

commerce, but while they captured or destroyed more merchant vessels than their adversaries did, the scale of damage in terms of overall trade was much smaller; in fact, the empire's seaborne economy expanded between 1812 and 1814.) Beyond its own operations, the Royal Navy supported the army in an increasing number of raids against the coastal states, intended to intensify stress on the administration in Washington and relieve pressure on the Canadian front. James Madison found it increasingly difficult to prosecute the war, because the collapse of foreign trade reduced import duties and related revenues that normally funded most government operations. Nevertheless, he hoped to seize as much British territory as possible in 1814 before the British could reinforce their colonies adequately. His objectives were to strengthen the American position in peace negotiations and thereby persuade London to cede a portion of its North American possessions (and create a climate that would foster further cessions in later years). In the end, he erred strategically by dividing his forces on the Canadian front in two, thereby contributing to the failure of each component when they neither retook Mackinac in the upper Great Lakes nor drove the British out of the Niagara Peninsula and the north shores of Lake Ontario and the St Lawrence River.

As John Norton recorded in the previous section, Sir George Prevost had agreed to meet him, and had arranged for the Prince Regent to honour him with a gift of a sword and a brace of pistols. While the royal presents acknowledged the value of Norton's service, they also served as a douceur *to assuage any dissatisfaction he may have felt because of his troubles with the Indian Department and his other political opponents. In early 1814, John Norton visited Sir George in Quebec, the capital of British North America. They considered how to preserve the British alliances with the First Nations in the face of battlefield losses, wartime strains, supply shortages, divisions between the Indian Department and the army, and internal stresses within aboriginal communities (although the memoir says very little about Norton's time in Quebec). The governor-in-chief wanted to reconcile the Mohawk chief and the Indian Department's leaders, but favoured Teyoninhokarawen by ordering the department's agents to communicate with the people of the Grand only through Norton, so that he would serve as the principal intermediary between the two allies. Prevost also strengthened Norton's position by placing warriors from southwestern Upper Canada under his care in their relations with the Crown, beyond his role in Anglo-Haudenosaunee affairs, and the governor allotted three-eighths of the province's entire stock of indigenous gifts for 1814 to him to disperse as he thought appropriate. These decisions were significant, and demonstrated*

Sir George's belief in John Norton's importance.[1] *A few days before Prevost issued these orders, Norton had expressed similar desires for increased authority, writing that "in order to act with propriety according to my appointment at the head of the Five Nations or Confederates, I find it neces-sary to entreat that no interference be allowed from the Indian Department between these tribes and myself." Therefore, he asked that "I may have it in my power to reward the faithful services of the warriors" and "countenance the leading war chiefs who assist in preserving good order."*[2] *Not content with the considerable role assigned to him, Norton attracted people beyond Prevost's authorized bounds when he returned to the Niagara Peninsula in the spring. Some of them came from the Old Northwest, being individuals who had fled to the Burlington area after the battle of Moraviantown. Oth-ers included people from Georgian Bay and Lake Huron.*

Norton's standing and behaviour at the beginning of the 1814 campaign exacerbated tensions between him, the Indian Department, and its allies in native communities. His opponents were in a difficult position. As a captain in the Indian Department, he theoretically was subordinate to senior offi-cers within that quasi-military organization; however, the governor-in-chief had freed him from normal bureaucratic constraints. Sir George recognized that opposition to Teyoninhokarawen had "always been shown by some," but expected that he would demonstrate his value to the allied cause through his "perseverance and usefulness."[3] *Naturally, the governor's directions by themselves would not be enough for indigenous people to follow Norton. The strength of Teyoninhokarawen's personality, his history of protecting indig-enous rights, and his competence and bravery on the battlefield, as we saw ear-lier, also were important factors. Within a context where native people might shift their alignments rapidly, John Norton, after being ill for some months and removed from the fighting for much of late 1813, re-established himself as*

1 Noah Freer to Gordon Drummond, 1 March 1814, LAC, RG8, 1222:57–9; with an annotated copy in LAC, RG10, 28:16704–5. JN continued to be responsible for the Thames River people, although the Indian Department tried to undermine his relationship with them by withholding supplies (JN to Duncan Cameron, 30 March 1815, LAC, RG10, 30:17806–7). One list of people put in the care of JN totalled 841 men, women, and children, enumerated as Munsees (Delawares) from the Thames and Detroit, Moravians from the Thames, and Chippewas from the Thames and Bear Creek in the Lake St Clair area (Statement of the Indians, 1814, Fort Malden National Historic Site, Caldwell Family Papers).

2 JN, Memorandum, 24 February 1814, published in Brymner, *Report on Canadian Archives*, x.

3 Noah Freer to Gordon Drummond, 26 April 1814, LAC, RG8, 1222:111.

*a pan-tribal alliance and war chief by the spring of 1814. That role, of course,
was far more meaningful than his captaincy in the Indian Department on the
colonial side of the Anglo–First Nations partnership.*

*Despite Prevost's desires, the Indian Department continued to oppose
Teyoninhokarawen and disobey the governor. For instance, its officials withheld supplies from Norton and encouraged their supporters within the indigenous world to voice their opposition to him. Beyond the department's machinations, John Norton simply was not able to exert the amount of influence that
he and Sir George had hoped he would. As noted before, this is not surprising,
given the complexities of aboriginal politics and people's concerns to preserve
their freedom not only from their American enemies but also from their British
allies. The sorrows caused by the war and the miseries associated with living
in refugee camps led people to make independent and sometimes desperate
decisions, including, for a substantial number, withdrawing from the conflict
as best they could. Nevertheless, Teyoninhokarawen exercised an impressive
degree of leadership at the beginning of the 1814 campaign among people from
the Grand River and elsewhere. This is especially noteworthy when we recall
how little influence he had wielded between the battles of Fort George and
Stoney Creek, and how his stature likely had suffered during the latter part
of 1813 following the battle of Moraviantown, when the Six Nations thought
their British allies might abandon them by retreating to York or Kingston,
and after he had withdrawn from public life in general. In addition, we should
recall that he was only one of many leaders on the Grand who supported the
British and who fought bravely (but separately from him); hence the revival of
a portion of Norton's previous status in early 1814 is even more remarkable.*

*Upon returning to Burlington Bay at the head of Lake Ontario in the
spring, Norton discovered that a majority of the 1,530 Grand River people
who had fled there in fear of a potential American assault on their tract in
the autumn had returned home. (At the beginning of May, only 380 men,
women, and children remained at Burlington.)*[4] *Food shortages, sickness, and
the attendant loss of life, along with the other privations of the refugee camps,
had led them to risk their safety in order to plant their fields and otherwise
seek sustenance. Others, including many from the west who had sought
shelter near the Head of the Lake after the battle of Moraviantown, remained
there, and prepared to cultivate the soil behind British lines. Later, warriors
returned to the Burlington area in time to participate in the defence of the
Niagara Peninsula when fighting resumed with an American invasion from*

---

4 Return of the Grand River Indians, 1 May 1814, LAC, RG10, 28:16819.

*Buffalo at the beginning of July and the fall of Fort Erie. The republic's forces,
accompanied by hundreds of indigenous allies from New York, next marched
north beside the Niagara River. They met a combined British and aboriginal
army at Chippawa, where Haudenosaunee warriors from each side of the
border killed one another in battle. It was at that tragic event that John Norton led a significant number of warriors for the last time, although he would
fight until the end of the conflict, despite the aggravations of his rivals in the
Indian Department while he tried to preserve the alliances between Great
Britain and the First Nations.*

About three weeks after this affair [i.e., the capture of Fort Niagara], I
had sufficiently recovered [from ill health] to undertake my journey for
Quebec. We experienced a very severe cold on the road, but in every
part, wherever I met my military friends, they honoured me with every
civility and attention. At Quebec, Sir George Prevost expressed, in the
warmest manner, his satisfaction at seeing me. I was ready to return
when we heard that a deputation from the tribes that had followed General Procter from the west were on their way to visit him at Quebec,
and Sir George having expressed a desire that I might remain there till
they should arrive, I deferred taking my departure. They were received
with great parade. They were dismissed, and I also took my departure
from Quebec towards the end of March.[5] Before I could reach Kingston,

---

5 He presumably started his journey about 20 January and arrived in Quebec by
   at least 9 February, accompanied by his wife, Catherine, and some other people
   (Robert Barclay to JN, 24 April 1814, AO, F440; *Quebec Gazette*, 17 March 1814).
   JN visited Masons in the Lower Canadian capital, who gave him an inscribed but
   otherwise plain medal that read "To / Brother Norton / Captain and Leader of /
   the Five Nations / from / Lodge Number 40 at Quebec / AYM [i.e., "Ancient York
   Masons"] / as a token of Remembrance / 19th March / AL [i.e., "Year of Light"] /
   5814 [1814]" (Haldimand County Museum and Archives). He also met Thomas Scott,
   the paymaster of the 70th Regiment and brother to the famous Walter, who wrote an
   admiring – even lurid – letter about JN, which suggests that JN was something of a
   celebrity in Quebec. Scott wrote to his brother, saying, in part, "Yesterday morning
   Captain Norton, the chief of the Five Nations, left. I had the pleasure to be his
   intimate acquaintance, and he is a man who makes you almost wish to be an Indian
   chief. What do you think of a man speaking the language of about twelve Indian
   nations, English, French, German, and Spanish, all well, being in possession of all
   modern literature ... and being at the same time an Indian chief, living as they do

the thaw had destroyed the winter roads and I remained there till the beginning of May. The fleet was then ready to go out of harbour, and Sir Gordon Drummond, with Sir James Yeo, undertook the expedition against Oswego for the purpose of capturing or destroying some naval stores expected at that place, without which the enemy could not equip their largest ship, which was then nearly ready for launching.[6]

On arriving at the Head of Lake Ontario, I found that the people had suffered greatly during the winter from a scarcity of provisions. The greater part, however, of the Five Nations had gone to the Grand River to prepare their cornfields, and to those who yet remained here, I repeated the advice I had given before my departure for Quebec to prepare [for the coming year] by the cultivation of their grounds for the support of their families. It was principally Delawares who yet remained at this place, and they immediately began to move towards the Grand River.[7] The presents allotted to them by the Indian Department were much wanted, and I had to inspect the delivery.[8] While thus occupied,

---

and following all their fashions? For, brother, you ask, doth he paint himself, scalp, etc., etc.? I answer, yea, he doth, and with the most polished manner of civilized life, he would not disdain to partake of the blood of his enemy at the banquet of sacrifice" (Thomas Scott to Walter Scott, March 1814, quoted in Klinck, "Biographical Introduction," in *JMJN*, xxix). The council took place on and around 17 March (Sir George Prevost, Speech, 17 March 1814, LAC, RG10, 12:10309–16). Tecumseh's sister and Catherine Norton ("wife of a ... chief") each received a basket of presents and/or flowers at the meeting from Sir George Prevost's wife, Lady Catherine Ann (*Quebec Gazette*, 24 March 1814; *Reporter*, 16 April 1814; *Western Courier*, 30 May 1814).

6 The British captured Oswego on 5–6 May. Their squadron exchanged fire with the American fort on the first day; then, on the second, they renewed the bombardment and landed 1,150 men, who drove out 475 defenders in an hour's fighting. Losses were 100 Americans, 90 British. The attackers captured artillery, equipment, and food, as well as three schooners, before destroying the fort, a schooner, supplies, and armaments they could not carry away. The "largest ship" was the 58-gun USS *Superior* under construction at Sackett's Harbour. A significant portion of her stores had not arrived in Oswego, and thus were saved to complete the vessel. JN's account seems to indicate that he did not participate in the expedition.

7 Limited American operations in southwestern Upper Canada in the months following the battle of Moraviantown suggested that it might be safer to move back to the Grand River than people had thought it was in late 1813. As well, some of the western natives who aligned with the British set up camps on the river at that time, adding indigenous military strength in that area. As written, JN seems to suggest that the Delawares came from the Grand rather than farther west in Upper Canada.

8 Sir George Prevost's decision to give JN control over Six Nations gifts and provisions, combined with JN's slow return to the Head of the Lake, resulted in Haudenosaunee

I received a letter from Major-General Riall requiring me to bring to the lines two hundred men, as he expected an attack from the enemy by the preparations making in the vicinity of Buffalo Creek.[9] Colonel Elliott, the head of that branch of the Indian Department which had come from Detroit, having died this spring, Colonel Caldwell was appointed to

---

people going without the supplies and food they needed, because Indian Department officials claimed they had received orders not to issue anything until JN arrived. This probably was a bureaucratic ploy to undermine Prevost and JN, even though it occurred at the expense of the well-being of the refugees. Then, when JN returned, these men tried to prevent him from drawing upon their stores, and spread rumours that people who followed him would not get goods and provisions, despite having been directed to comply with Sir George's instructions. Yet JN did manage to acquire what he needed, and one consequence was that 300 warriors and their relatives from outside of the Six Nations contingent joined him at that time. They included some people he had not been authorized to care for but who chose to associate with him on their own volition. More controversy arose once JN began distributing food and presents, because William Claus accused him of being overly generous in an attempt to draw warriors from beyond his approved limits after the natives had received their allotment of gifts from other departmental officers. (As usual, supply was a worrisome challenge for the British, so an unstinting distribution from limited stocks could represent a problem.) JN's liberality, including the distribution of whisky, led one Odawa chief to acknowledge that "some of our young men" had gone to him because "he speaks loud, and has strong milk and big breasts, which yield plentifully. You know, Father [William Caldwell], your children are fond of milk, and he gives when they go to him, and promises them provisions as they want, and goods at discretion. If you will do so Father, they will not go to him, but we cannot keep our young men in our hands" (Nawash, Speech, 14 June 1814, LAC, RG8, 257:303–4). Revealing details of the supply problems and Claus's attempts to disobey Prevost may be followed through: Claus to Robert Loring, 4 May 1814, with Enclosures, LAC, RG10, 3:1349–54; JN to William Jervois, 30 May 1814, ibid., 3:1388–91; J.B. Glegg to James Givins, 2 June 1814, ibid., 28:16940; Noah Freer to Claus, 7 June 1814, ibid., 28:16955; Claus to Loring, 10 June 1814, ibid., 28:16974–5; Claus to Loring, 22 June 1814, ibid., 3:1416–18; Claus to Loring, 23 June 1814, ibid., 3:1425; JN to John Holland, 24 June 1814 with Enclosures, ibid., 3:1444–9. A concentration of related documents that provide additional examples of the conflict or which address general administrative matters in the spring and summer of 1814 may be seen throughout ibid., vols. 3, 28, 29, and LAC, RG8, vol. 257).

9 Major-General Phineas Riall assumed command of British forces in the Niagara region in December 1813 in place of John Vincent, under Gordon Drummond's overall direction in Upper Canada. In late June, JN was in the Ancaster-Burlington region. There were 700 warriors from the Six Nations and other communities with him or at Grand River, of whom 500 were fit for service. (JN to Duncan Cameron, 15? June 1814, LAC, RG10, 28:17014).

take his situation.[10] He had arrived and had received orders to take to Kingston as many of the Indians from the west as were willing to follow to that place. He was preparing to take this direction when he was called to the frontier at Niagara. He repaired to Fort George with the whole body of the Indians from the vicinity of Detroit. Their number amounted to five or six hundred men. I was notified to take position in the neighbourhood of Chippawa. I had with me about three hundred men. I took position at the Falls (or Cataract of Niagara), two miles from Chippawa, on account of the healthiness of the situation and the uncertainty as to the length of time which we might remain there.[11]

---

10 Matthew Elliott died in May 1814 from natural causes. Lieutenant-Colonel William Caldwell became deputy superintendent in the Indian Department for the Western District in his place, although JN apparently wanted the position and thought Caldwell was "most unfit" for the job (JN to Sir John Johnson, 23 June 1814, ibid., 28:17040). The issue was so important to JN that he left the Niagara region to travel to York for a few days to see what he could do about it at the very moment the warriors attached to him were assembling in anticipation of an American invasion (ibid.). When JN attracted warriors away from Caldwell, the new deputy superintendent joined William Claus in opposing JN (Claus to Robert Loring, 22 June 1814, ibid., 3:1416–18). One factor that favoured Caldwell over JN was the former's greater reliability as a proponent of the British side of the Anglo–First Nations alliance, in contrast to JN, whose loyalties lay more heavily on the indigenous side, but of course, other issues, especially JN's insubordination and the department's hostility, were factors in any consideration of promoting him.

11 With people coming and going from the lines almost constantly, there were 200 Grand River and 120 other warriors (mainly Chippewas and Odawas) in JN's camp near Niagara Falls around 20 June. Many of them – perhaps as much as one-third of the force – would not follow his leadership, although we do not know what portion comprised Haudenosaunee people compared to the others (Benn, *Iroquois in the War of 1812*, 157). Part of the problem may have stemmed from the ongoing attempts of the Indian Department to deny supplies, ranging from footwear to weapons (JN to William Claus, 29 June 1814, LAC, RG10, 28:17057–8). Despite periodic shortages and dissension within his camp, JN enjoyed considerable respect at that moment, given the number of warriors who chose to align with him, and when we remember that the ratio of combatants to general population was almost 1:5. Yet, there clearly were tensions between people who preferred JN and those who associated with William Claus. For instance, after affirming his faith in JN, Sir George Prevost heard the distressing news that "three of the Six Nations ... have requested the major-general, Phineas Riall, to represent to Your Excellency their dissatisfaction with the appointment of Captain Norton to be their leader. They say they will not acknowledge him as such, will pay him no respect or obedience, nor look to him for anything they want; that they know him not except as a disturber of the peace and harmony that ought to exist among them. They have a head man

The intelligence which Major-General Riall had received was not sufficiently clear to give us a correct view of the plans of the enemy. It was
therefore required that I should dispatch some men to reconnoitre. But
there being no canoe or light boat adapted to such an enterprise to be
found, and it requiring no common men to make such a reconnaissance
as might be useful in directing our operations or defensive precautions,
I prepared, by causing many canoes to be made for passing with all the
active men of the party which I led, to approach the enemy's encampment so near as to make every observation possible to be made from an
open observer. While this was in operation, the enemy crossed in the
night [and] cut off the retreat of Major Buck and the garrison of Fort
Erie, consisting of about 150 men, who were consequently obliged to
surrender to the very superior force that invested them.[12] As soon as this
intelligence reached Chippawa, Lieutenant-Colonel Pearson, inspecting field officer of militia, commanding at that post, called upon us to

---

who the King has appointed, and they want no other (Colonel Claus)." The letter
noted that this was the opinion of the Mohawks, Oneidas, and Tuscaroras, but
that the Cayugas, Senecas, and Onondagas refused to "answer" when asked if
they shared this view (Gordon Drummond to Prevost, 19 April 1814, LAC, RG8,
257:234–5). Nevertheless, JN afterwards attended a council at Grand River where
representatives of at least five of the Six Nations overturned the earlier message.
They confirmed their support for him through offering strings of wampum after he
told them about his discussions with Prevost in Quebec, including promises made
by the governor-in-chief, and informed them of British success against Napoleon in
Europe. Unfortunately, the record does not indicate what Sir George offered, but the
Haudenosaunee received the news "with pleasure" (Gordon Drummond to Noah
Freer, 28 June 1814, enclosing Extracts from a Council, n.d. [1814], ibid., 257:290–4,
quote on 293). In a postwar document, JN said that the number of followers he
had in terms of Six Nations warriors who chose to follow him was greatest among
the Cayugas, Onondagas, and Delawares (JN to J.F. Addison, 13 February 1817,
ibid., 261:26). Prevost continued to support JN, even though "strong jealousies and
unnecessary objections have been excited against Captain Norton"; and he asked
local commanders to try to reconcile William Claus and William Caldwell to JN, but
also wanted JN to stop encouraging warriors to leave the Indian Department officers
assigned to them (Noah Freer to Robert Loring, 9 July 1814, LAC, RG10, 3:1463–4).

12 Part of the American army under Major-General Jacob Brown crossed the Niagara
  River from Buffalo on 3 July and moved against Fort Erie. The fort's commandant,
  Major Thomas Buck of the 8th Foot, later was court-martialled and reprimanded
  for dereliction of duty because he only had offered token resistance to the invaders
  before surrendering his 150 men to 2,500 enemy soldiers, even though the time
  between the first shots being fired by his pickets near the shoreline and his
  capitulation totalled 14 hours.

join him, which we did instantly, and proceeded together with the flank company of the 100th [Regiment] up the river as far as Black Creek. Here he said that he had been informed that one division of the enemy was proceeding by a back road from Point Abino to the mouth of Chippawa, and that another was to cross in our rear at the lower end of the Grand Island. Therefore, to prevent the evil that might have occurred from such a manoeuvre – had it really been put into execution by the enemy – we returned to our former position.[13]

On the 4th of July, at about two o'clock in the afternoon, a dragoon came express from General Riall to inform us that the enemy was advancing and had reached Black Creek. We hastened to join him at Chippawa, but although we had used every possible dispatch, we did not arrive until after he had marched out to meet the enemy. We followed, and heard firing in front. We hastened our pace and we met the troops returning. Supposing the Americans to be in [the] rear, I hastened forward with those near me, but our rear was influenced by the retrograde movement and did not follow us. We remained in the flank till the troops had passed, and then retired. The enemy did not make his appearance in front of our position. He encamped at Street's farm (called the Grove) about two miles from Chippawa. As soon as we had repassed the bridge, it was destroyed. The houses on the side next the enemy were also burnt, lest he might approach under cover of them. From these proceedings, I concluded that the general had resolved to defend his position at Chippawa until he had received further reinforcements, [thus deciding] not to risk anything by acting offensively.

---

13 Major Thomas Pearson of the 23rd Foot was a brevet lieutenant-colonel and inspecting field officer of militia. Black Creek empties into the Niagara River opposite the central portions of Grand Island, 10 miles north of Fort Erie; Point Abino is west of the fort on Lake Erie (and both are within the boundaries of today's municipality of Fort Erie). A landing at the latter might have provided the Americans with an opportunity to move inland and then march around the British on the Niagara Peninsula to threaten their rear or right flank. A crossing from New York at Grand Island might have divided their opponents operating farther south from the main body to the north. Neither operation, however, occurred. At that point, the British elsewhere along the Niagara Peninsula did not know that Fort Erie had fallen, and assumed that part of the American army was occupied investing the post, thus thinking that there were fewer men moving against them along the Canadian shore of the river than there actually were. At the time, the Americans had 5,000 soldiers and 600 warriors along the Niagara River, compared to 3,000 British supported by 900 native combatants.

We encamped, or rather slept, on the ground upon the right flank of his position.[14]

In the morning, early, I called upon him [i.e., General Riall]. He expressed a desire that I should cause the enemy's position to be reconnoitred. I immediately dispatched a small party with directions to observe exactly the position of the enemy, without giving any alarm by firing at the advanced posts, and to return and give information of the same. Others, however, were sent the same way, and instead of a reconnoitring party, it became a band of skirmishers who began with firing at the sentries, whom the enemy having succoured, compelled them to retire.[15] We found that the enemy was encamped in Street's field, and that his flank next the woods was exposed to an attack from irregulars under their cover. We heard also from an inhabitant that came from twelve miles up the road that only one division of the enemy's army was now before us and that the other division, which had not yet joined, was the most numerous.

General Riall now proposed that I should lead my party over Chippawa, saying that the flank companies should support them. We got over with some difficulty, but not in sufficient force to attack the enemy, and none of the troops had yet followed us. The general and Lieutenant-Colonel Pearson came over and passed to reconnoitre the

---

14 On 4 July, one of the American brigades advanced north with the objective of seizing the bridge across the Chippawa (now Welland) River, but British forces slowed its movements by harassing it and destroying bridges across the other waterways on the Niagara Peninsula as they – outnumbered badly – slowly retired north. They then took up a position behind their defences on the north side of the Chippawa to await reinforcements, after destroying its bridge and the buildings on its south side that the invaders otherwise might have used for cover. The river, 80 yards across and protected by artillery (which had opened fire), represented a formidable barrier dividing the Canadian shore of the Niagara Peninsula in half. The Americans, realizing that they had lost the opportunity to secure the bridge and capture or demolish the defences located around it, withdrew two miles to the south side of Street's (now Ussher's) Creek, where other elements of their army joined them for the night of 4–5 July. The men assembled in the camp included 350 warriors from New York, mainly from Six Nations communities. The Grove was a farm belonging to Samuel Street, a prominent settler and militia officer.

15 On the morning of 5 July, the American army, located mainly on cleared land south of Street's Creek, faced the waterway. The invaders' right flank rested near the Niagara River, and their left near a forest. The people who fired on them from the bush consisted of warriors from the Six Nations and the west, along with some militiamen, which led the Americans to contract their left flank.

enemy. I joined them. In returning, the general told me that at two o'clock we would proceed to attack the enemy. It was then twelve o'clock.[16] I proposed, as the surest mode of attack as soon as the bridge could be repaired and the troops had passed over, that my party of about 250 men, followed by one hundred men of the Western Department, the same number of militia, and supported by the flank companies, should pass through the woods in such a manner as to arrive imperceptibly upon the [left] flank of the enemy, and from the covert of the wood open a heavy fire upon it.[17] His attention thus engaged, the main body of our troops might advance and attack him in front. A quarter of an hour after the general had returned, I received a note from him which mentioned that the engineer could not complete the bridge until four o'clock. As soon as it was done, the troops were drawn up, and passing over, advanced hastily. The militia were taken along the road. Advancing through a field till we reached the wood, we then took a direct course to the field which contained the hostile camp.[18]

---

16 The intelligence the British received on the size of the opposing force was wrong, because they assumed that Fort Erie still was under siege and because a large part of the American army arrived at Street's Creek after JN, Phineas Riall, and Thomas Pearson had completed their reconnaissance. Jacob Brown ultimately assembled over 4,000 men in his camp, of whom 2,100 would participate in the subsequent battle of Chippawa (in today's Niagara Falls, Ontario). Riall had 1,800 regulars, militia, and warriors. The British commander's plan was to march against Brown, defeat him, and then relieve Fort Erie.

17 The Western Department comprised the warriors from southwestern and northern Upper Canada and the Old Northwest, along with the Indian Department officials who served with them, but did not include warriors from these regions who had been assigned to JN.

18 The British planned to send a large body of light troops, militia, and warriors to join the skirmishers in the forest near the American left flank to draw the invaders' attention away from their front. With the Americans thus engaged against the British, Phineas Riall planned to advance against them with his main body of soldiers. (The terrain and vegetation – even in the "open" areas – would allow Riall to cross the Chippawa River and progress some distance unseen.) The men assigned to attack the American left moved through the forest that lay inland of the river in three parties. One group of natives and militia moved ahead close to the forest edge, the rest of the Euro-American troops followed them, and JN's party moved farther west into the woods on the right of the rest of the force. At the time, Gordon Drummond thought there were 200 warriors with JN and another 100 elsewhere (Drummond to Sir George Prevost, 10 July 1814, LAC, RG8, 684:60).

We had entered the wood a small distance when, through the foliage, we discerned the glistening of arms. Imagining it to be the scouts of the enemy, we pursued, but they outran us or eluded our pursuit from the intricate nature of the forest, impenetrable to the sight for any distance.[19] Having then waited for the rear to come up, we proceeded in as good order as it was possible, advancing by separate files. We had gone perhaps something more than half way to the point of our destination when a firing commenced on our left. We hastened forward and soon came in contact with the enemy. Ascending a gentle rise, we received their fire. They were concealed behind trees and fallen timber. We shouted and closed with them without firing till we reached them. They had not reloaded their pieces. They ran, many of them falling before us. We received several volleys from other parties of the same division, but we constantly advanced, driving one part into the field behind the regulars, the other dispersing through the woods. We now saw the columns of the enemy advancing through the field with colours flying. We fired among their condensed ranks, and they returned it with grape and musketry. We heard our bugle sound a retreat, and the troops, overwhelmed with an immense superiority of numbers, were obliged to retire. Our number was greatly diminished by the nature of the contest, some having scattered in pursuit of the enemy we had dispersed at the first onset, and others, having fallen in [the] rear as we advanced, never rejoined us after we had engaged. We therefore could only follow the example of our brother warriors. Many were killed by that division of the enemy with which we had encountered, and we brought in several prisoners. Among the latter were a major and [a] captain, several of the volunteers, and a few Indians. From these we learned that Lieutenant-Colonel Bull, commanding the volunteers, was among the killed, and that he had led out in that wing eight hundred volunteers from the militia and five hundred men of the tribes of Indians being within the American boundary.

When we approached Chippawa, we found that the troops had recrossed and that the bridge was demolished, excepting a log or two which yet remained. We called for a canoe to take over the wounded. The cannon was firing at the advancing column of the enemy and at some dragoons who approached in front of their right flank. We crossed

---

19 The Americans had pickets in the forest to monitor movements in that vicinity.

upon the log remaining at the bridge, and our return was welcomed by our friends who had passed before us.[20]

In this battle the nature of the ground was so varied, in woods and fields half-cleared of timber, that no one engaged could see more than what was doing in his presence, and could only have an imperfect idea of the transactions at a little distance. What I have already said relates only to that part which particularly fell within my view. This, which follows, is what I could collect from information and circumstances.

The loss of our friends gave us all a gloomy appearance. In every division, they seemed to think that they alone had more particularly fallen

---

20 The American commander, Jacob Brown, initially was not aware of the threat in his front from Phineas Riall, so he sent 850 regulars, militia, and warriors into the woods south of the point occupied by the opposing native and white force near his left flank at about 3 p.m. Their objectives were to move north, dislodge the men who were giving him so much trouble, and secure the wooded area south of the Chippawa River. (To distinguish themselves from their opponents, his men wore white cloths on their heads.) In the ensuing fighting, the Six Nations from New York took the lead in advancing against their enemies, who fell back but with many individuals being captured on both sides. Their movement only came to a halt when the warriors from New York came under heavy fire from Canadian militia and other warriors who had deployed alongside them. The attacking force withdrew for a time, but then re-engaged in an exchange of musketry until British light infantry joined the action, at which point those on the American side retreated while being pursued by their opponents, with some fighting occurring at close quarters. The people with JN came late to this engagement because they had moved farther inland from the river and deeper into the forest than the other combatants. After the British and their allies in the woods forced their enemy to withdraw, they engaged the infantry and artillery towards the American left flank, who stood exposed in the open field and could not withstand the fire directed against them. A portion of Brown's infantry therefore charged towards them to push back their opponents, who had to withdraw because they were outnumbered and too thinly deployed to withstand an assault by tightly organized infantry. Due to the volume of fire on his left flank, General Brown assumed that he likely would come under attack in his front. Therefore, he deployed other elements of his army to be ready to engage the rest of Phineas Riall's troops when they appeared before him on the more open land closer to the Niagara River. Brown's artillery and infantry brought Riall's advance to a halt. A close-range exchange of fire then followed until the British, defeated, withdrew back across the Chippawa River at the end of the three-hour battle. Lieutenant-Colonel Robert Bull of (James) Fenton's Pennsylvania Volunteer Regiment, mentioned by JN, was killed and scalped by a warrior after being taken prisoner. Although a comparatively senior officer in the operations in the forest, he did not exercise overall command as suggested by the text; rather, the primary leaders were Brigadier-General Peter B. Porter and Seneca chief Red Jacket.

a sacrifice to the misfortune of the day. When we parted at Chippawa, the troops who advanced on the road did not allow sufficient time for the flankers to gain the proper position. The Indians and militia who advanced on the road between us and the main river fell into an ambuscade prepared for them by the enemy (who, from the skirmishing in the morning, had expected them in that direction), and so completely were they ensnared that they were thrown into confusion and routed with great loss, and apparently were only saved by the simultaneous attack of the flank companies upon those who immediately pursued them and of our party upon the right wing of the ambuscade, which was prosecuted with such vigour as to rescue many that were just overtaken by the exulting enemy.

The main body, consisting of a division of the Royals [or 1st Regiment] on the right and another of the 100th on the left (amounting to about seven hundred men), advanced through a rough field in front of the enemy, who had ranged his front line under cover of a ravine. From this, he opened a fire very destructive to our troops, who were retarded from making a regular and impetuous charge by the nature of the ground, and their fire prevented from doing much execution from the precaution taken by the enemy. Thus combating against a great odds of number, as well as every disadvantage of position, they lost many gallant officers and brave soldiers. To save the survivors, a retreat was sounded. Few officers in this division escaped without a wound. The Marquess of Tweeddale, who commanded the 100th, and Lieutenant-Colonel Gordon of the Royals were both wounded, the former severely so as to deprive the army of his service. From appearances, as well as the acknowledgment of the enemy, we have reason to suppose that our artillery, under the direction of Captain Mackonochie, made great havoc in his ranks, and we know that his loss was by no means inconsiderable, notwithstanding his great force. This consisted of about five thousand regulars, eight hundred militia, and five hundred Indians. We had not more than fifteen hundred men of all descriptions. The battalion companies of the King's, which had recently arrived at Chippawa, and which had been much reduced by service and sickness, were not brought into action on this occasion, but the light company, which met the enemy's irregulars with great gallantry, lost some men.[21]

---

21 After the 5 July battle of Chippawa, the two armies returned to their camps, with the Americans located on the south side of Street's Creek and the British on the north side

The enemy gained no further advantage from this engagement than that which might arise from the loss we had sustained in the action, which, in a degree proportional to our inferiority of number, must have rendered us still less capable of opposing to his future progress a formidable resistance. We remained, however, in our former position for two days. In that time, our wounded were sent to Fort George and our baggage was also conveyed to the rear. The prophet of the Shawnees [Tenskwatawa] with many of these people and others from the west arrived in this time [from elsewhere on the Niagara Peninsula], and the hopes of being speedily reinforced by the whole body of warriors rejoiced us not a little. In this, however, we were greatly disappointed. On the evening of the 7th of July, the prophet and his people observed (or thought they had observed) the artillery throw some ammunition and an old iron 9-pounder into the water. This they immediately considered as preparatory to a flight. Immediately after dark, the shattered remains of the 100th moved to the rear to take [up a] position at Lundy's Lane, and, some laden carriages going at the same time, a Delaware came and informed me that the Indians, imagining a retreat to have commenced, were all preparing to march off [to the shores of Lake Ontario], and that he was sent by his tribe to inquire of me if the general with all the troops was really going to retire.[22] I hastened to the [native] camp, but I found that many were already gone and more ready to go. I required them to remain firm until I could go to the general to receive his instructions. To this, many agreed. I went to him at Chippawa and

---

of the Chippawa River. The British regulars and militia had lost 500 killed, wounded, or missing, while the Americans had suffered 325 casualties. The warriors from New York had as many as 16 killed and wounded and 10 missing; indigenous casualties on the British side are uncertain but were heavy. The Americans claimed that the Grand River and western natives had as many as 87 killed, five taken prisoner, and an unknown number wounded, although the Americans usually exaggerated losses among their enemies. George Hay, Marquess of Tweeddale, of the 100th Foot recovered from his wounds and saw action again in 1814. Major John Gordon was a brevet lieutenant-colonel in the 1st Foot (the Royal Scots, or JN's "Royals"). After Chippawa, he recovered, saw action at Lundy's Lane, but died of wounds at Fort Erie. James Mackonochie was a Second Captain in the Royal Artillery.

22 Lundy's Lane (in modern Niagara Falls, Ontario) was three miles north of Chippawa; thus a move there represented a withdrawal, which degraded the already poor morale among the warriors and threatened to reduce Phineas Riall's force severely should the natives leave the British lines.

he assured me that he had no intention of retreating. I returned to the camp and found the greatest confusion prevailing. Some of the troops had broken open a store belong to Mr Street and had divided the spirits with the Indians, in consequence of which many who remained were intoxicated to such a degree as to be entirely devoid of reflection. In the morning, there were not twenty remaining of the people from the west and Five Nations. The general desired that they should be recalled, and I dispatched Mr John Brant for that purpose, and afterwards followed him myself. He had overtaken the main body but had not been successful, and I could not pass St Davids [to follow the retiring warriors], lest I should be absent when the enemy might make an attack upon our position at Chippawa. All I found there returned with me, and I believe we might then have counted about fifty men.

In the afternoon it was perceived that the enemy had gained a position on our right flank on the opposite side of the [Chippawa] River from which his cannon would completely range the whole of our entrenchment; and from this movement it appeared very probable that he contemplated passing the river higher up, and thus passing our flank take us in [the] rear. The general, with much propriety, considering our force too feeble to risk another encounter with the enemy before we had been reinforced, ordered a retreat, and that evening we moved down to Fort George in good order.[23] The next morning he advised me to return to Burlington to endeavour to reassemble our Indians, which I immediately did. On joining Colonel Scott at Burlington, I found that he had concentrated the whole of his regiment, the 103rd, at that place and that he was in readiness to

---

23 A withdrawal to Fort George made sense because Phineas Riall did not have enough men to offer effective opposition to the Americans, who renewed their advance on 7–8 July, engaged in some skirmishing, and built a bridge across the Chippawa River inland of the British positions. Furthermore, the invaders were capable of threatening the British rear by crossing the Niagara River to the north. On 8 July, Riall's forces retired to Fort George, Fort Niagara, and a new post at the mouth of the Niagara River on the Canadian side, Fort Mississauga. On the 10th, Jacob Brown's army marched north and encamped on Queenston Heights. He expected the United States Navy's Lake Ontario squadron to appear off the British works and coordinate operations with him to drive his enemy out of the region. During the days that followed, American soldiers and their native allies looted and burned Canadian property, including 40 homes in St Davids.

move forward to attack the enemy in [the] rear should he attempt to invest General Riall at Fort George. More than a thousand militia also embodied and moved forward at the same time. We followed with five or six hundred Indians and came up with him at the Forty Mile Creek.[24]

---

24 This move of the natives probably occurred on 13 July. The officer mentioned was Lieutenant-Colonel Hercules Scott of the 103rd Foot, whose regulars and militia represented a threat to the Americans should Jacob Brown move north from Queenston towards the British fortifications at Niagara. The indigenous camp at Forty Mile Creek comprised people from the Grand River, southwestern and northern Upper Canada, and the Old Northwest. Many of those from the Grand, however, were unwilling to participate in operations against the Americans at that time.

8

Discredit, Battles at Lundy's Lane and Fort Erie, Murders, and the Defence of Grand River, 1814

John Norton's description of the battle of Chippawa included this sentence: "When we parted at Chippawa, the troops who advanced on the road did not allow sufficient time for the flankers to gain the proper position." In contrast, another combatant, William Hamilton Merritt, wrote, "The Indians under Captain Norton [i.e., the flankers] were to commence the attack on our right, in the wood … [but] took too long a circuit and got nearly in the rear of the American camp; consequently [they] did not get into action until it was over."[1] While that was an exaggeration in terms of timing, Lieutenant-General Gordon Drummond, in a more nuanced assessment, thought Teyoninhokarawen contributed to the British defeat because he took his warriors "too far into the woods to offer the assistance required of them."[2] Thus, Norton's journal obliquely acknowledged awareness of the blame attributed to his actions for the American victory, which undoubtedly was the subject of common discussion throughout the defenders' lines at the time and a source of distress for him. With the historical documentation available to us, it is difficult to judge how serious Teyoninhokarawen's timing was in contributing to the outcome of the battle, but it led Drummond and his second-in-command, Phineas Riall, to lose much of their confidence in him as a military leader. Then, at a council soon afterwards, which we will explore below, his reputation decayed further when the majority of Six Nations men and other warriors agreed to withdraw from the conflict at the request of American-resident Haudenosaunee representatives. Colonial officials blamed

---

1 William Hamilton Merritt, Journal, n.d., published in Sutherland, *Desire of Serving*, 40.
2 Gordon Drummond to Sir George Prevost, 10 July 1814, LAC, RG8, 684:60.

*Norton for that substantial blow to their military power, and even won-
dered if he had subverted Anglo-Iroquois relations on purpose. The decision
to abandon the campaign followed the catastrophe in which warriors had
killed their relatives while fighting on opposing sides at Chippawa. Norton
disagreed with the decision and tried to preserve the alliance with the King,
although it seems that he arrived at the meeting too late to have much influence on its outcome (even if he had been capable of doing so, which seems
doubtful). Consequently, the confidence that many army officers had shown
him dissolved, although he still maintained friendships with some and continued to be regarded as useful by individuals who had become wary of him.
Yet officials such as William Caldwell of the Indian Department worked
to discredit John Norton over both the council and the disruptions he had
caused through his distribution of presents to warriors and their families,
which had upset the department's management of native affairs. A number
of senior officers concluded that Norton's special status and the freedom from
departmental constraint that Sir George Prevost had given him had been a
mistake. Teyoninhokarawen also found himself ignored by most of the people
of the Grand because he decided to keep on fighting, in opposition to the
majority opinion – at least until near the end of 1814, when various parties
of warriors mustered to oppose one American force on the Niagara River and
another that moved against their settlements from the west. With the decline
of his reputation among a portion of the British military leadership and his
decision to keep fighting despite the general Haudenosaunee agreement not
to do so, his roles in the war after Chippawa were modest both militarily and
diplomatically. Doubts about his loyalty to the Anglo–First Nations alliance
and his hostility to the Americans, however, were misplaced, because he kept
on serving bravely at the head of the smaller number of men who followed
him against the Americans through the hard fighting of Lundy's Lane and
Fort Erie that dominated the struggle on the Niagara Peninsula during the
war's final months.*

Some of our men, who had left Burlington after us, arrived at this
place [Forty Mile Creek] and informed me that two Indians from the
American army had arrived there with an old chief of the Cayugas
(whom they had taken prisoner at Chippawa), that they had proposed
a meeting of the chiefs of the different tribes, and that the Onondagas and Shawnees, who had proceeded a few miles on the road after
us, returned to hear what they had to say. Colonel Scott expressing

a desire that I should return to expedite the march of the rear, and informing me that he would wait for further reinforcements, I rode back to Burlington and reached that place at sunset. As the council which had been assembled in consequence of the arrival of the Senecas [from the American lines] had dispersed, I proceeded to see the two men, one of whom I recognized, as it had only been four years since he had emigrated from the Grand River to the village of that nation on the American side of the line. They were seated together with the old man whom they had conducted home. I found that they had come to propose an exchange of prisoners, and that they had expected to have found one of their chiefs prisoner who had probably been killed in the action. They said that they had had a conference with our people in the presence of the officer commanding the garrison, [and] that they had entreated them to remain neutral because they hoped that, should they comply with this entreaty, the Americans would also permit them to remain peaceably at their homes. They said that at first they had held the language of peace towards them, advising them to remain neutral, alleging that they (the Americans) were sufficiently numerous themselves for every emergency of war and that they would never ask any Indian tribe for their assistance. "But," they added, "now they have changed their tone, and say, 'as the Indians with the British assist them, you must also help us, or we will consider you as our enemies and their secret friends.' We are," continued they, "in their power: we cannot withdraw our families from among them but we are certainly much averse to help them in war, for in so doing, we are brought to fight against relatives and friends."

I told them that their situation and that of the tribes who fought on the side of the King was very different. That it was to him that they looked as a protector and a father; that, therefore, it was very natural for them to exert themselves in support of his authority. But the Americans were totally dissimilar, being the common enemy of all the aboriginal race; that, therefore, none could have any object in fighting under their banner; that they made use of them as a hunter used a dog, pushing them always forward in the greatest danger without allowing them any share of glory. "If you are unable to resist their power, you can, however, elude compulsion by leaving your villages and retiring to the woods to hunt. Any expedient is better than to allow those who have got the most of your lands now to have your lives at their disposal. If by this means they can effect your utter destruction, they will be highly gratified. There will then be only women and children remaining to claim the little land which yet remains your property."[3]

These men appeared in haste to return home. I advised them to remain a few days, apprehending that the enemy might draw some information from them respecting our movements. But they urged that their people only awaited their return to leave the American army entirely, and said it was to avoid all suspicion that they had remained at the place where I had found them, and from which they could certainly make no observations on the fortifications of Burlington.[4] In the morning I told the officer at that post that if he would take the men in charge without treating them as common prisoners, I would persuade them to remain a few days there; but he replied that he had no other means of holding them unless in the common guardhouse. I thought it inconsistent with justice to make prisoners of the men after they had been admitted to hold a parley. And as my only motive for wishing them to be detained in a friendly manner was to prevent the enemy from obtaining intelligence of our move forward (that we might assail him [as] suddenly and unexpectedly as the thunderbolt), I was not so urgent to effect their detention when I perceived the many obstacles which retarded the accomplishment of my desire, and [was] buried in a multitude of uncertainties [over] our prospects and enterprises. Colonel Caldwell of the Indian

---

3 JN's conversation with the delegates from New York (whose identities, along with that of their prisoner, are unknown) occurred on 13 July. While his account of the exchange seems accurate, some people on the reservations in the state had wanted to fight for various reasons independent of white demands, as we saw earlier, such as to protect their interests in Grand Island or to express the warrior spirit that was important to men's identity. An additional point they made was that the American army and navy soon would overwhelm the British numerically, and thus further fighting would be pointless, which, according to one witness, "alarmed our Indians very much" (George Ironside to Duncan Cameron, 15 July 1814, LAC, RG10, 29:17114). JN's comment about the Americans "pushing" the warriors "forward in the greatest danger" conformed to the nature of combat he had witnessed, when their soldiers had not provided close support, in contrast to the greater degree of assistance that the British gave natives who fought alongside them. In the aftermath of this council, only small numbers of men continued in the field with the American and British armies in the Niagara theatre, even though many indigenous people remained in camp with the British. Later in the year, however, 100 Grand River warriors returned to the Niagara Peninsula, strengthening the small number present there for a time.

4 The meeting occurred in the camps on the low ground around Burlington Bay rather than at the fortifications on Burlington Heights.

Department, after expatiating of the propriety of apprehending these men, asserted that it was my office to cause them to be seized. I replied that I was no peace officer, and only seized men in arms against me, [and] that as they had been admitted in a friendly manner, I could not think it honourable now to make them prisoners as I had not heard of their having in any manner transgressed the rules observed on such occasions. But at the same time, if it was deemed necessary to detain their persons, let it be done by others, not by me. My business was to engage the enemy as soon as an opportunity occurred, and I must leave that of accusing and defending to those who had more leisure.[5]

---

5 "My business ..." captures JN's anger with the controversy surrounding this council. An Indian Department official recorded that William Caldwell, in the presence of a number of officers, had urged JN to detain the men at least until the results of the next major battle should become known. Caldwell offered either to take the blame for violating normal protocols or have the "Western Indians" seize the men, but he could not intervene further because of Sir George Prevost's orders forbidding interference with JN's primacy in Haudenosaunee-British relations. Thus, the delegates left for the American lines on 14 July (George Ironside to Duncan Cameron, 15 July 1814, LAC, RG10, 29:17114–5; see also Thomas Couche to Caldwell, 27 January 1815 [misdated 1814], ibid., 28:16667–8). JN's belief that he needed to show respect to men who came to parlay conformed to the period's military customs. In reflecting on the council, Major-General Phineas Riall stated: "I have much reason to be dissatisfied with the conduct of Captain Norton ... which may possibly be attended with very serious consequences, and which I am sorry to say places him ... in a very suspicious point of view. Two American Indians arrived at Burlington, bringing with them an old Cayuga chief who had been taken in action at Chippawa. Captain Norton was not only acquainted with the circumstances but permitted them to attend a council of the Six Nations in order to deliver a message from those in the interest of America. It is true, I believe, that the officer who was left in command at Burlington was informed of the circumstance, but he was ignorant of the customs of those people and uncertain how he should act and did not apprehend them. Whatever these fellows have said has caused much dissatisfaction among the Indians, and the western people have reason to suspect the Six Nations of treachery. Colonel Caldwell had told Norton that he should not only have prevented the American Indians from intercourse with his, but that he should have apprehended them immediately, which he would not do; and when I asked him why he had not done so, he replied that he had neither guard nor place to put them in, and that was the business of the officer commanding the posts. There is something extraordinary, I do think, in Mr Norton's conduct altogether in this business" (Riall to Gordon Drummond, 17 July 1814, LAC, RG8, 684:135–6). Riall was mistaken about JN's failure to prevent the council, because even according to William Claus he arrived as it ended, but Claus said that army officers lost faith in JN. He added that John Brant and other natives also had argued that the Senecas from the American side should have been prevented from leaving (William Claus to

I proceeded immediately with those who were ready to follow. On the road, I received a letter from General Riall informing me that, having placed Fort Niagara and Fort George in a posture of defence, he had withdrawn the remainder of his force, and was on the way to concentrate with us. At the Twenty Mile Creek, we rejoined the troops, [including] Indians and militia which had marched from Burlington on the west, and I learned that General Riall with the troops which he had led from Fort George were stationed a few miles in advance. From this place, we advanced to take position at the Twelve Mile Creek, but the troops were scattered between that place and the Twenty Mile, a distance of about six miles. The Glengarry Light Infantry under Lieutenant-Colonel Battersby held the same position with us, and many detachments of militia extended under the mountain as far as St Davids. They had some skirmishes with the advanced parties of the enemy and took a few prisoners, but he also made reprisals and took several of the militia.[6]

Unknown, 26 July 1814, LAC, RG10, 29:17127–30). For his part, General Drummond planned to investigate JN's conduct once he arrived on the Niagara Peninsula, and, if his suspicions that JN's fidelity was suspect should be "well-founded," he would send him to Quebec. Presumably the general thought it would be wise to remove him from the front lines and thereby prevent further injury, as, on another occasion, an influential Indian Department officer who behaved badly also was sent east to get him away from Niagara (Drummond to Sir George Prevost, 20 July 1814, LAC, RG8, 684:159; for removing another officer [Thomas McKee], see Drummond to Prevost, 31 March 1814, ibid., 682:286–7). That Gordon Drummond did not do so suggests that he regained some confidence in JN's integrity. Nevertheless, he continued to believe, along with others in authority, that JN's management of aboriginal affairs and his freedom to act outside of normal command structures damaged Anglo-First Nations affairs, and that something had to be done to remedy the situation (Drummond to Prevost, 15 December 1814, ibid., 257:378–80). Other people retained their negative opinions of JN following the defeat at Chippawa and the subsequent council. For instance, William Claus recorded that Major Thomas Pearson "is gone down violent against Norton, and is determined to tell Sir George that Norton is a scoundrel, a coward, and a traitor. He could not speak with temper when he mentioned his name to me" (Claus to Unknown, 3 October 1814, LAC, RG10, 3:1509). We do not know if there was something in particular that JN did to cause Pearson to speak so harshly about him.

6 Phineas Riall had troops in Forts Niagara, Mississauga, and George at the mouth of the Niagara River. Then, on 13 July, he moved other men elsewhere (mainly along the Lake Ontario shore of the Niagara Peninsula) so they could operate as a mobile force to take advantage of, or respond to, developing circumstances as well as scout American positions and harass their enemy. The opposing commander, Jacob Brown, remained on Queenston Heights but sent substantial numbers of men north to within

We had hitherto remained inactive because we waited direct orders from the general, many powerful reasons rendering this precaution necessary and convenient. I had therefore thought it advisable, particularly as I was indisposed, to remain inactive until I should be ordered to advance, as I might by such indulgence both improve my health and avoid blame.[7] Having heard, however, of the movements in the advance, I desired an order from our general to go forward, and I proceeded with a small party of Chippewas, Shawnees, Delawares, Wyandots, and Mohawks, leaving the main body deliberating at the Twelve Mile Creek.[8]

Having approached within a mile of St Davids, we met a deserter from the Americans. He was a Swiss belonging to the artillery. He reported that the enemy, having gone from Queenston, intended to encamp that night at the Cataract, that the force consisted of about five thousand men, and that he understood them to be on their retreat.[9] I sent a chief, well mounted, to inform the general and to call upon all the Indians to follow us. We then took the most direct path to come upon the enemy's route. However, when we had reached it we learned from

---

a mile of Fort George to probe British defences, contest control of the area between the two armies, and attempt to overawe the civilian population while he awaited the American Lake Ontario squadron and other reinforcements. The British pushed back and maintained contact with the Americans to monitor their movements and thereby prevent surprise. In the end, the squadron failed to appear, because its commander was ill and would not trust his ships and schooners to a subordinate. He also thought that the United States Navy had a higher calling than that of merely supporting the army. Deprived of the squadron's aid and facing other problems, such as sickness within his ranks, General Brown withdrew south to Chippawa on 24 July to gather supplies and reorganize his forces. He hoped to renew the campaign through bypassing the British forts at the mouth of the Niagara River in favour of an assault on Burlington Heights, but subsequent events did not allow him to do so. The Glengarry officer mentioned was Francis Battersby, formerly of the 8th Foot.

7 JN's comment seems to express his distress at the criticism of him over the recent council with natives from New York.

8 Note how JN's war party comprised warriors from different nations, which was not atypical. His "deliberating" seems to indicate that other people continued to discuss how they would behave in reflecting on the recent council, although some would continue in the field for a time; but note how the number of men who followed him was "small."

9 The information about the American withdrawal south from Queenston on 24 July from the Swiss deserter seems to have been the first news of this movement that the British heard.

the inhabitants that they had passed in very good order two or three hours before. We then proceeded by a back road towards Lundy's Lane, which was the road by which we expected our friends to arrive at the Cataract from the position in which we had left them. A young man, a volunteer of the militia living in that neighbourhood, undertook to be our guide. We passed by his father's house whom, although a peaceable inhabitant and an old man, the enemy had taken away prisoner.[10] We took a little repose in a barn and then proceeded, calculating to arrive there a little before the dawn.

On entering the road, we met a dragoon who informed us that Lieutenant-Colonels Drummond and Jones-Parry were following him.[11] They soon came up with us, as they were mounted and we were on foot. We continued on together. At the dawn, I passed on with my party to reconnoitre the position of the enemy. Lieutenant-Colonel Drummond, seeing my party small, sent about twenty militiamen under their captain to reinforce us. These men appeared very eager. When I wanted to restrain their speed, in order to approach more cautiously with the circumspection necessary to acquire an advantage from observing first without being observed, it was like endeavouring to hold in a fiery horse without a curb. At last, we descried the enemy's picket taking deliberate aim from an ambush. I called upon the whole that accompanied me to prepare, but the militia were yet more difficult to manage. They ran without regarding the reiterations of "Stop!" Only the young volunteer remained with the Indians. The Americans, on seeing them run, fired and advanced upon us, but a few rounds made them turn about again.[12]

Having now discovered the enemy's position – the sole object of our errand – we returned to the advance at the Cataract. There, I again met my gallant friend, Lieutenant-Colonel Drummond, who invited me to take up my quarters with him. After taking some breakfast, I lay down to repose a few hours. In the afternoon, hearing that my friends the

---

10 The identities of these individuals are unclear.

11 These officers were Lieutenant-Colonel William Drummond of the 104th Foot and Lieutenant-Colonel Love Parry Jones-Parry of the 103rd (and inspecting field officer of militia).

12 The skirmishing between JN's men and the American pickets on the morning of 25 July occurred near Deborah Wilson's tavern immediately south of Niagara Falls. It was not part of the battle of Lundy's Lane that occurred later that day, but one of a number of encounters that took place on both sides of the river at the time.

Indians had arrived at Lundy's Lane, we walked down there to see them. We met General Riall on the way. Going forward we found that only the Glengarry Light Infantry, Incorporated Militia, and some irregular militia had arrived with the Indians. There were, however, some fine pieces of artillery already planted on the eminence. This position was a collection of cultivated farms, clear of wood to some extent, of a mile in breadth and at least two miles in length, and this only separated from other fields by intervals of woods. A report came that a numerous body of the enemy were passing through a byroad on our right, and a party of Indians was required to be placed on the lookout in that quarter.[13]

Being assured from the nature of the ground that the main body of the enemy must advance in front should he come to attack us, and knowing that with our small number it was impossible to be formidable in every possible point of assault, I hoped for the greatest concentration in that part where it appeared to be the most probable that the enemy would make his attack. Therefore, after advising that a small party only should be dispatched to the right, I was making arrangements to have placed the main body of the Indian warriors in a piece of wood on the left hand when a report that the enemy was advancing caused me to follow my friend to our quarters. On arriving there, we discovered his vanguard, which had halted within two hundred paces, apparently waiting to be joined by the main body, which followed at a little distance, preparatory to making an attack upon us. Returning to Lundy's Lane – the enemy in sight advancing briskly – we found that an order for retreat had taken away most of our division, and the Indians and militia had followed the example. At the moment we were informed of this event, the rising of the dust from the road [to the rear] gave tokens of their return to the

---

13 This paragraph largely describes deployments in advance of the battle that occurred later that day along Lundy's Lane, a road that ran inland from the Niagara River and that bisected the Portage Road from Queenston. The British position was on high ground overlooking terrain that varied among fields, orchards, forest, and a cemetery. The landscape also was marked by fences and a number of buildings, with a small concentration of structures occupying the area around the intersection of the two roadways. The Battalion of Incorporated Militia of Upper Canada that JN mentioned had been formed earlier in the conflict for full-time service and possessed a high degree of proficiency. It had replaced the militia flank companies of the early war period noted before. JN's "irregular militia" probably referred to individuals and small parties of men who opposed the Americans but did so outside of the normal command structures.

field, and we soon had the satisfaction to learn that General Drummond and Lieutenant-Colonel Harvey, meeting the troops on the retreat, had ordered them to the right about to resume their position.[14]

The enemy entered the field in front in a condensed column, and our troops regained their position at the same time.[15] A part of the troops, with the artillery, faced the hostile division in front while the Glengarry proceeded by a lane [on the British right] to attack it in flank. We followed the example, as did some scattered parties of militia, but most of the Indians that yet remained with the army occupied an eminence on the left. They may have held in check the sharpshooters of the enemy (if it really was his intention to have pushed them forward in that direction), but their aid was much wanted in the attack we made upon the flank of the enemy's column. However, those who were there exerted themselves in thinning the hostile ranks by a well-directed fire. This was returned in volleys, which had less effect upon us as we were scattered according to the practice of irregular warfare, taking every advantage of which the open nature of the ground would admit. The enemy remained firm in the position which he had at first assumed, exposed to a galling fire in front and flank. Dread seemed to forbid his advance and shame to restrain his flight.[16]

---

14 Gordon Drummond arrived on the Niagara Peninsula from York on 25 July, the day of the battle of Lundy's Lane, and assumed command from Phineas Riall. Around 7 p.m., the British reoccupied the ground that Riall previously had held. (Riall had withdrawn from the site because he assumed he would be outnumbered badly, planning to reassemble at Queenston where other troops could reinforce him to face his enemy.) Given the positive way JN described General Drummond, it is difficult to know how aware he was of the general's dissatisfaction with him over his behaviour at Chippawa and the council near Burlington.

15 The American column that entered the field was the first of three brigades that formed the bulk of Jacob Brown's army that would fight that night. It was common to move troops in long columns for the sake of speed, such as along roads, before deploying into line to fire on their opponents. The events described here by JN occurred early in the evening, about 15 minutes after the British had reassumed their position at Lundy's Lane. The American brigade commander, Brigadier-General Winfield Scott, had not expected to meet strong opposition; therefore, he committed his troops without having conducted an adequate assessment of the British force.

16 Native forces and light troops often formed on the vulnerable flanks of a line of infantry and artillery, where they could harass their enemy and protect their own side from opposing movements to turn its flanks. At this point, in the first phase of the battle, only Winfield Scott's brigade of Americans was in the field to oppose them, and it was at least 400 yards away from the main British line. Thus its musketry could not inflict substantial injury, while the guns of its artillery were

In the twilight, we perceived the shattered remains of that column retiring. A calm ensued. Desirous to concentrate as many Indians as I could find, so as to be able to act collectively should our services be wanted, either to pursue or to defend, I took advantage of the pause to go in search of them. Having reached the road, I found the main body of our troops had just arrived from between the Twelve and Twenty Mile creeks, and yet stood in the road inclining to the left. I saw the 89th [Regiment] had just arrived from Niagara.[17] Turning to the spot occupied by the artillery near a log meeting house, one asked my opinion as to the fight being over for the night. At the same instant, another enquired what body of men it might be that were approaching from the Niagara Road on the left. Going towards them, I observed the moon glimmer faintly on the plates of their caps, the form of which denounced them to be our enemies.[18] Before I could speak, they fired. A few of our troops behind me, preparing to return the compliment, I hastened to regain the line. At this time, the horses attached to the guns, being startled, ran with the limbers through the ranks of our troops, overturning all in their way. This seemed to frustrate the intended resistance and to throw the little detachment near the guns into such confusion that the enemy gained a temporary possession.

I now descried General Drummond and Lieutenant-Colonel Harvey ride along the line of troops extending to the left, and, as I supposed

---

hampered because they sat on lower ground than their targets. In contrast, the Royal Artillery operated effectively against Scott's line. The British and the natives with JN fired on the American left flank at a range of 200 yards, which was farther than desirable in relation to the capabilities of their weapons, and thus their impact presumably was more modest than JN suggested.

17 As JN notes, British troops continued to reach Lundy's Lane from the northern parts of the Niagara Peninsula during the battle. The 103rd Foot, for instance, had marched 20 miles that day and had rushed forward as quickly as possible for the last few miles. American forces also arrived from their camp at Chippawa as the fighting unfolded.

18 Normally, it was not difficult to distinguish British from American regular infantry in daylight, but in the dark the colours of their coats were indistinct, a problem made worse by the fact that the tailoring, accoutrements, and other features of their uniforms were similar. The shape of the metal insignia on the caps of the two armies, however, were distinct should someone get close enough to see them. While JN described the battle well in terms of the parts he witnessed, and recorded broader impressions he learned from others, his overall narrative is incomplete, as is typical of participants in large-scale combat, whose perceptions are limited to the area over which they fought and whose understanding of the timing of events often is confused.

in consequence of the orders given, they wheeled so as to take in flank that body of the enemy which had advanced to the guns, and a sharp fire, which they opened upon them, held them in check. The troops which had just arrived on Lundy's Lane were ranged in an echelon. Another pause ensued, and for a few minutes, the night reassumed its natural tranquility. During this interlude, an American officer, having strayed from his division, was taken prisoner. On being brought before General Drummond, he requested to be sent to the rear with all haste, saying, "You are completely surrounded. In a few minutes you will be assailed from every side and I am averse to be exposed to the fire of my own friends as that is a danger out of my calculation." The ranks were closed and the soldiers ordered to kneel. The American officer had not been conducted many paces when the enemy recommenced a more heavy fire than any that had preceded. It would be difficult to name the time it continued; it ceased about half past ten o'clock. In this assault, General Drummond was badly wounded in the neck but he remained on the field.[19]

We now perceived that the enemy had retired, leaving the field covered with the dead and dying. They had also left our guns with some that had belonged to themselves. Having withstood so many repeated attacks, we remained for some time doubtful whether the contest had yet ended, and accordingly prepared to resist any further assault, and then reposed our wearied limbs on the cold ground until the dawn.

---

19 In the battle's second phase, American forces overran the British battery at about 9:30 p.m., and attempts to recapture it failed. Gordon Drummond withdrew north a short distance to reorganize his men for a counterattack. (He could not afford to lose his artillery if he were to fight again across open ground.) That decision led to the third and final phase that began around 10:45 p.m. The two sides fired heavy volleys at each other at close range, but Drummond again withdrew as he could not drive his enemy south. He counterattacked twice more, but without success, and then retired from the field. (JN mentioned some of the army's manoeuvres in this section. One was wheeling, which allowed a line of infantry to change its position to fire in a different direction. In echelon, the companies of a battalion took a different position from each other rather than standing in a straight multi-company line, with one company on a flank holding a position, the company beside it taking post a short distance farther in front, the next company standing even farther in front of the previous company, and so on. In this formation, the companies stood in a staggered line but had a clear field of fire in front of them. Armies at the time trained men to march in close and complex formations so that they could direct their musketry with maximum effect and minimum delay over rough terrain in rapidly changing battlefield conditions.)

Although [it was] the 25th of July, the night was chillingly cold. Then, advancing through the bloodstained field, we passed on till we had discovered the enemy in his former position. In doing this, we picked up many of the Americans who had straggled from the main body in the retreat. On the road lay several of the dead that had fallen out of the wagons as they were carrying them off.[20]

The enemy again advanced towards us. We awaited him at the field of battle but he disappointed us. He burnt a sawmill a mile and a half in advance of our position and retired.[21] The loss of the enemy, if we may judge from that which he had left on the field, was very great; but at the same time our loss was far from being inconsiderable. General Riall was severely wounded, and in conducting him aside to be dressed, he had fallen into the power of the enemy and was taken prisoner. Indeed, they had invested us in such a manner that many had wandered into their ranks and were taken prisoner, so that our number might have been diminished at least one-third, and those who remained effective were worn out with fatigue and destitute of ammunition.[22]

---

20 JN's text implies that the British held the field at the end of the five-hour battle of Lundy's Lane on 25 July, but it was the Americans who remained on the ground for a brief period as their opponents moved a short distance away for the rest of the night. Technically, Jacob Brown had won a tactical victory (although the Americans soon retired southwards). At the more important strategic level, Gordon Drummond had halted the American advance and shifted the initiative to his side as the invaders withdrew, first to Chippawa, and then to Fort Erie. Lacking ropes and having lost many horses, the Americans only removed one of the British guns but left two of their own behind, which their opponents acquired along with reclaiming their own pieces when Drummond reoccupied the battlefield once daylight returned (and when JN scouted ahead of the British position, apparently at dawn).

21 Around 7 a.m. on 26 July, 1,600 Americans marched north from Chippawa, as their senior officers thought they could win another encounter, although most of the exhausted soldiers were hostile to the prospect of renewing the contest. In the end, their officers decided against seeking battle once they came close to a similar number of British troops arrayed against them. In withdrawing, the Americans torched the village of Bridgewater Mills between Chippawa and Niagara Falls. They then burned buildings in and around Chippawa, broke camp, and marched south to Fort Erie later that day.

22 Both opposing generals, Gordon Drummond and Jacob Brown, had been wounded at Lundy's Lane, but Drummond was able to maintain his leadership role while Brown had to turn over immediate command to his subordinates until the beginning of September. As JN noted, Phineas Riall had been wounded, then captured. The British lost 875 killed, wounded, captured, and missing of their 3,500 combatants,

At about three o'clock in the afternoon, we retired from the field of battle to Queenston, a village at about seven miles distant. Here we took that rest which we so much required. Meeting with Captain Mackonochie, I passed the evening with him as pleasantly as a sleepy man possibly could do. The next day, in the afternoon, we were again required to follow the enemy. We set out, and that evening we stopped between the Cataract and Chippawa. At sunrise we began to cross the [Chippawa] River upon such rafts as we could hastily form, for the enemy had entirely destroyed the bridge.[23] A party of the 19th Dragoons passed over at the same time. They advanced on a back road by Black Creek, which led into the rear of Fort Erie, while we pursued the main road along the river's bank.[24]

In about a mile higher up we discovered five of the enemy riding towards us with a white flag. On coming up to them, we discovered them to be two officers and three dragoons. The officers said that they carried letters for General Drummond from their general. Thinking that the whole army followed us, I did not like them to pass on because I apprehended that they might make a discovery of our force and our movement. I therefore detained them till the [British] dragoons had rejoined us. One of the [American] officers, speaking of the late engagement, exclaimed that he hoped never to be again engaged in a night encounter similar to the last. "They had only themselves to blame," it was retorted from our side, "for coming to attack us at

---

in comparison to American losses of 860 of their 2,800 men engaged in the battle. Most of the British wounded, however, received minor injuries from small-calibre buckshot, which their enemies had loaded into each musket cartridge along with a proper ball, whereas the American wounded generally had suffered more debilitating injuries.

23 JN was part of an effort to send forth patrols and scouts. The largest part of the army, however, rested at Queenston and the forts at the mouth of the Niagara to recover from the battle and to guard its rear, because the American squadron belatedly had appeared at the western end of Lake Ontario. While the navy arrived too late to help Jacob Brown in his original plan to force the British out of the region, it kept its opponents concentrated at the north end of the Niagara Peninsula, providing the Americans in the south with time to strengthen defences at Fort Erie. The balance of power on the lake subsequently shifted to the Royal Navy in October as its shipbuilding efforts in Kingston outpaced those of the United States Navy.

24 JN's manuscript says "Black Rock" rather than "Black Creek," but obviously that was an error.

so late an hour. Had they approached more early, it might have been sooner concluded."

"We expected to have met with no resistance," he replied.

"From the experience of the past you had certainly no right to indulge in such expectation," it was returned.

"The firmness," he continued, "that was there displayed on the part of the British army certainly entitled every officer present to be *knighted*."

"What is much more certain," it was answered, "is that they were all *benighted*."

Through the medium of questions, apparently indifferent, they endeavoured to discover the position held by the general and the main body of the army. On that head, however, they were left in uncertainty. The dragoons returning to the road, we dismissed them.[25]

We retired a few miles to a place where there was a probability of procuring some provisions for the men, and there awaited further reinforcements. The next morning we advanced to a point opposite to Strawberry Island where a detachment of the Glengarry Light Infantry joined us shortly after (the main body of that corps, with some of the 19th Light Dragoons, taking up their quarters a mile or two in the rear of us). Towards the end of the night, a party of three or four of the dragoons of the enemy deserted to us. We remained here two days, apparently awaiting more reinforcements, having observed the [American] boat repassing at the ferry [between Black Rock and Frenchman's Creek] more than usual. In the afternoon, we received directions to advance. Our warriors led the van and were supported by the Glengarry Light Infantry. The party of the enemy stationed at the ferry retired before us, leaving a few men killed upon the ground. They fired upon us without doing us any injury. They left at the ferry some stores and provisions. At dark, we fell back upon the Glengarry, with which corps we remained all night.

About the dawn, we heard firing in our rear. I was informed by an officer that a detachment of our troops had passed over to the opposite side [of the Niagara River] and that this firing might proceed from their encounter with the troops of the enemy posted there. With a party of our warriors, we hastened to the waterside that we might pass over to

---

25 This meeting occurred on 28 July. It seems likely that JN was one of the speakers. It was common, when representatives of opposing armies met, to attempt to gain intelligence through what might seem like trivial conversation.

the assistance of our friends. We then saw them returning. We were now required to advance and feel the way to the position of the enemy at Fort Erie. We advanced and drove in the picket of the enemy with some loss. On our side, we had a worthy Wyandot warrior killed and a Muskogee wounded. We observed that an abatis had been formed by the enemy at the sortie from the wood into the open space which surrounded the fort and the fortified encampment of the enemy, under cover of which they had stationed several strong pickets. After having returned to the encampment, we learned that the detachment which had crossed the river (under Lieutenant-Colonel Tucker) had failed, from the enemy having destroyed the bridge at Scajaquada Creek before it could be passed or taken possession of, and the confusion which followed in consequence caused them to return. It was rather unfortunate that they did not know the stream to be fordable at less than a mile above the bridge, where its depth is only increased by the influx of the Niagara to a very small distance (the water flowing from the interior formed an ordinary brook, which the droughts of summer had rendered yet more inconsiderable).[26]

---

26 Gordon Drummond sent 600 men under Major John Tucker of the 41st Foot (a brevet colonel) to destroy the depots at Black Rock and Buffalo on the American shore opposite Fort Erie. Drummond's objective, if Tucker enjoyed success, was to force the soldiers in Fort Erie to come out and fight, surrender, or abandon their Upper Canadian foothold. The Americans, however, dismantled the bridge over Scajaquada (or Conjocta) Creek north of Black Rock and offered stiff resistance on 3 August, with 300 men secured in their defences on its south bank. The action resulted in 33 British and 10 American losses. (JN's manuscript says "St Lawrence" rather than "Niagara" River, which was an archaic practice.) While not a significant encounter in itself, it forced General Drummond to engage in difficult operations against Fort Erie through the following weeks. The American-held position, with 18 artillery pieces, consisted of the comparatively small Fort Erie and a large fortified camp on its south side, which extended to a strong point known as Snake Hill. Construction of the abatis (small logs used by themselves or in conjunction with earthworks, and enhanced with thorny vines and other obstacles) was part of the American effort to improve their defences. Artillery at Black Rock and on three schooners offered additional support to the garrison in Fort Erie (although British sailors captured two of the vessels in a surprise attack during the night of 12–13 August). The Muskogees, or Creeks, lived mainly in Georgia and the Mississippi Territory at the time; and this man may have been one of a modest number of southeastern people who had travelled far from their homes to join the Western Tribal Confederacy. Alternatively, he may have been associated with the Grand River for a long time, because a document from the 1780s listed Creeks among its residents (Census, 1784, published in Johnston, *Six Nations*, 52).

Although suffering much from the effects of a severe wound, General Drummond was indefatigable. The reinforcements of de Watteville's Regiment from Kingston had now arrived.[27] In the afternoon, the position of the enemy was reconnoitred. The next morning preparations were made for erecting a battery within six or seven hundred paces of the fort and entrenched camp of the enemy. (The latter appeared not to be yet completed.)[28] The position chosen for this work was joined by a ravine which extended to the right, inclining towards the outposts of the enemy and following the course of a morbid run that issued from an adjacent swamp in heavy rains, strong enough to form a trench, which now only contained a little stagnated water. It was required that we should take post on the right of the advance, which covered the working party. Here we found ourselves at the extremity of the ravine and within sight of a considerable party of the enemy. They fired at some of our men, which we returned with more effect, but we made no attempt to close because they were covered by the abatis and under the protection of the fort. The next day we returned to our former position but we did not find any of the enemy opposed to us in that quarter as we had the day preceding. In consequence of nothing occurring to attract their attention, the men, I perceived, began to scatter. To prevent the bad effects of inactivity, and to endeavour to obtain correct information of the outposts of the enemy extending to the lake, I detached a party of young men in that direction under the guidance of a noted war chief.[29]

---

27 The de Watteville Regiment consisted of soldiers of Swiss and other European origins.

28 With 3,500 men at that time, Gordon Drummond wanted to force the Americans to withdraw from Fort Erie to the New York side of the Niagara River or compel them to march out and engage him in open battle. He could not lay a proper siege because he lacked enough artillery, men, ammunition, equipment, and supplies to do so. Moreover, he could not isolate his enemies behind their walls and starve them out because they could receive provisions and reinforcements from Buffalo and Black Rock across the border. Nevertheless, after driving in the American pickets on 3 August, he built fieldworks and batteries, bombarded the fort over subsequent weeks, and engaged in other activities that mimicked a siege.

29 During Gordon Drummond's operations against Fort Erie described below, there were numerous skirmishes, often involving hundreds of men, as well as two larger-scale confrontations, with one consisting of a British assault on the fort itself and the other being an American attack in strength on their opponents' batteries. The "noted war chief" may have been Matoss, a Sauk from the upper Mississippi River. The fighting JN described likely referred to an incident on 6 August.

While the enemy in front made no appearance of hostility throughout the day, in the afternoon we heard a firing commence on our left
near the waterside. Desirous to assist our friends, I proposed moving
in that direction, and while my men hastened on under cover of the
ravine, I crossed it to acquaint Lieutenant-Colonel Drummond, who
commanded the detachment next to us. Before I had reached him,
I perceived through the foliage of the woods a number of men in
light coloured frocks coming towards me. At first sight, I supposed
them to be our men from the camp moving on to our assistance,
and only discovered my mistake when the foremost of them pointed
their rifles to me, calling out "Stop!" I paid no regard to them. They
fired. I found the few soldiers that were stationed hereabouts much
confused at being assailed from an unexpected quarter, but I soon
saw my gallant friend, Lieutenant-Colonel Drummond, encouraging
them to rally. Many of our warriors came running to our assistance,
and we compelled them [i.e., the Americans] to retire with some
loss. On our side we had a few killed and wounded. We remained in
front until near sunset. The enemy made repeated sorties and was
as often repulsed without our being able to ascertain their loss. They
advanced so small a distance in front of their abatis that they generally carried off the greater part of their killed and wounded. Our loss
was not considerable in number in these trifling encounters. In one
of them was killed Lieutenant McGregor of the Royals, much regretted by all who knew him, but the enemy acknowledged the loss of
several officers.[30]

Our battery began to play upon the enemy, both with round shot and
shells. He returned our fire and erected a battery on the opposite shore
[in New York] at the distance of a mile, which flanked our works. He
also fired round shot into our encampment from the other side of the
river but the fire of his artillery did very little execution. We thought
that ours did him much more injury, which is very probable as his force
was concentrated in [a] smaller space.

On the evening of the 14th of August, we advanced in company with
a party of the Glengarry to enable an engineer to reconnoitre a position
for another battery (that already erected being at too great a distance

---

30 The skirmish mentioned at the beginning of the paragraph occurred on 10 August
  between 160 Americans and an unknown number of men on the British side. The
  soldiers in frocks were riflemen rather than regular musket-equipped infantry. The
  officer mentioned was Lieutenant Gregor McGregor of the 1st Foot.

to make sufficient impression).[31] Returning to our encampment, we heard that an attack was to be made upon the enemy before the dawn of day; that the King's and de Wattevilles (about twelve hundred men) had marched to reach the lake by a circuitous road, and were to assault Snake Hill (a small fortification newly erected about half a mile from Fort Erie); [and] that the 103rd Regiment under Colonel Scott and the flank companies of the Royals, 41st, and 104th regiments under Lieutenant-Colonel Drummond were to advance from our batteries and attack Fort Erie and the entrenchments facing us. At our encampment I told my brother warriors that although we had received no directions to join in the attack, I could not consent to lie inactive whilst our friends the redcoats were going to undertake an arduous contest; that if any were inclined to follow, they should prepare to be in readiness to move forward at an equal distance between midnight and the dawn. All agreed to accompany me. Subsequently I learned that the Indian Department attached to the Indians from the vicinity of Detroit had received orders to follow a militia officer who had undertaken to guide them by a circuitous route called Buck's Road, which would bring them out on the open ground somewhere between the two main points of attack. Finding that I was left at liberty with my party, and apprehending that the route mentioned might *éloigne* those who followed it too far from the scene of action to allow them to give timely assistance to the troops engaged, I preferred joining the left division of the army destined to storm Fort Erie and the adjacent entrenchments.[32]

As we began to move forward, we heard the firing commence at Snake Hill. Hastening forward through the darkness of the night and closeness of the woods, we separated from a numerous division

---

31 Although destructive, neither side's artillery was as effective as the opposing commanders had hoped it would be. The British battery generally was too far away from Fort Erie to destroy the defences, and so the gunners directed much of their fire at the soldiers of the garrison. To improve their effectiveness, the British relocated their artillery closer to the American positions, completing the work late in August.

32 Snake Hill stood 800 yards south of Fort Erie at the end of the fortified American camp. The Americans levelled part of the hill and erected a battery on the site to secure their defences in that part of their works. British pickets held Buck's Road, to the west of the American position. Along with the native forces assembled by the Indian Department, they received orders to make a feint against the centre of the long west wall of the camp with the objective of distracting the Americans from the main objectives of a night assault, with Snake Hill to be assaulted second and the original Fort Erie third.

of our men, which constrained us to check our speed at a point of rendezvous previously appointed until they had joined us. We were within half a mile of Fort Erie when we heard the cracking of musketry and the roar of cannon announce the attack upon it.[33] We then ran forward as fast as the woods and darkness would permit, stumbling over logs and fallen trees. We passed the reserve, drawn up in a ravine, running against the fire to the glacis. As we arrived there, the explosion blew the broken fragments of buildings and works in all directions. It appeared to create a general confusion. We met the troops retiring from the fort, which they had gallantly entered. We saw none advancing, our own number nothing when compared to the host of foes which opposed us. After hesitating a little while, we retired with others to the ravine, on the summit of which we waited until the whole of our troops had retired. The enemy did not come out of his works, but continued firing round shot, grape, shells, and musketry. We left them there and followed our friends, enraged at their misfortune.

Our loss was very considerable in this affair both in officers and men. Colonel Scott, Lieutenant-Colonel Drummond, Captains Irwin and Torrens, Lieutenants Noël and Charleton, and some others were killed, and many more were wounded and taken prisoners. The unfortunate issue of this attempt appears to have originated from the entire failure of the division of the right, which had been sent to attack Snake Hill, which exposed that of the left (after it had beaten down all opposition and had gallantly entered the works) to the assault of the whole American army without cooperation or support. Thus checked by the resistance of a force very superior in number, it was entirely broken and overwhelmed by the explosion. On the right [at Snake Hill], the want of success was attributed to the flints having been taken out of the muskets of the de Wattevilles by order of their commanding officer to prevent them from firing [and warning the Americans], which it effectually did. But at the same time, by

---

33 Although the men of the picket and the warriors outside of JN's circle were supposed to have started the action by distracting the Americans from the main targets at Snake Hill and the original fort, they were delayed. The attack on Snake Hill thus occurred first rather than second, and the fighting at the main fort occurred subsequently. JN was mistaken in thinking the firing came from the fort, as it came from points to the south of the fort.

daunting the men, it might have had no less effect in checking their advance against the fire of the enemy.[34]

We expected seriously to have been attacked in our turn after this reverse, knowing that the force of the enemy was superior in number to our army even before it had been reduced by so severe a loss (which may be seen in the dispatch on the occasion).[35] In the afternoon [of 15 August], the rejunction of the division of the right [from the Snake Hill attack] placed us in a condition of resisting any attack of the enemy.[36] No attempt, however, was made on his part until the 20th when, in the morning, the alarm began by a few scattered shots on our left, apparently from the sentries of our picket. We advanced, directed by the report of the firing, in such a manner as to take the enemy in flank should he advance from that quarter, but it happened otherwise. We met a considerable detachment of riflemen and others, which had taken a circuit to pass the flank of the picket while the smaller party amused the left of our line in front. On discovering the enemy, we ran forward with all possible celerity. We gave them a well-directed fire; they attempted to advance but seemed checked by the well-aimed bullets, which brought some to the ground. At this time, their batteries were firing round shot, grape, and spherical shot upon us without much effect, and we discovered a party

---

34 The night assault on Fort Erie during the early hours of 15 August was a disaster. Not only did the Americans repulse the attackers, but they inflicted heavy casualties on the British. Many of the losses occurred among soldiers who managed to enter the fort but fell victim to a huge explosion when a gunpowder magazine located in a lower portion of the post blew up under them, likely accidentally. Of the 3,100 men engaged in the three-hour assault (of Gordon Drummond's total force of 4,850 at that moment), 905 were killed, wounded, taken prisoner, or reported missing, compared to 79 losses in the American garrison of 2,825. The flints had been removed from most of the muskets of the troops engaged in the attack around Snake Hill in order to prevent an early or accidental firing from warning the Americans of their movements. The defenders' pickets, however, spotted them and opened fire, thus raising the alarm. In the aftermath of the defeat, much of the blame fell on the troops assigned to enter the camp around Snake Hill, particularly in the de Watteville Regiment. The fallen officers in this account were friends of JN's, and those not mentioned earlier were Captain James Irwin and Lieutenant Thomas Charleton of the 103rd Foot, Captain S.B. Torrens of the 1st, and Lieutenant Horace Noël of the 8th.
35 As noted before, newspapers printed official reports of battles on a regular basis, while books, magazines, and pamphlets published during and immediately after the war reproduced them as well.
36 Following the failed attack on Fort Erie, the British artillery recommenced firing on the post at daylight on 15 August while the Americans returned fire and laboured to restore their defences after the damage created during the assault.

moving obliquely so as to envelop us. To baffle this attempt we divided. Leaving a part of our warriors to amuse those of the enemy in front, we hastened to meet the other division. On the first encounter the enemy seemed to hesitate, and in a short time began to retrograde, which move we hastened by closing upon them, both our divisions answering each other with vigorous shouts. We at last drove the enemy into their fort. They left a few lying on the ground but the greater part they carried off. We then retired without any further loss than a few men wounded and one of the Glengarry killed. We learned from deserters that the enemy lost sixty-eight men in killed and wounded. The fire from their cannon was yet continued after we had retired.[37]

About this time, a division of the 82nd [Regiment] joined the army; and notwithstanding the voyage [across the Atlantic] and long march from Quebec, they made a fine, gallant appearance.[38]

Constant exertions throughout the campaign had now reduced me to a low state, which together with a hurt in the breast, had put me out of condition to lead on with vigour.[39] I therefore retired for a few days for the recovery of my health. In a week or ten days, I returned to the encampment much recovered. I found that they had had another skirmish in my absence, in which the enemy had been beaten back as usual, although with some loss on our side. A detachment of the dragoons (19th) and of the Glengarry had taken and cut to pieces a picket of the enemy, the latter had insinuated themselves between them and the enemy's army, and when the dragoons advanced, they chased them into the water. We met some of the prisoners then taken on our way up to the camp.[40] Here we found that things were nearly in the same state

---

37 On 20 August, the Americans sortied against the British lines, and suffered 40–50 dead and an unknown number wounded and captured. British and native losses were negligible. As in most instances at Fort Erie, the majority of warriors came from non-Haudenosaunee nations. Gordon Drummond noted: "a feeble effort was made by the enemy to support his pickets when our Indians behaved with uncommon spirit and drove back the whole of his riflemen, supported by some hundred of his regular troops, without its being necessary for our troops to advance to their support" (Drummond to Sir George Prevost, 21 August 1814, LAC, RG8, 685:123).
38 A portion of the 82nd Foot arrived in the British camp on 24 August. It had sailed from France after campaigning in the Peninsular War for several years.
39 We do not know why JN had a "hurt in the breast" but it sounds like an injury rather than the sickness that had "reduced" him.
40 JN's text might refer to a skirmish that occurred on 6 September, with 21 American and two British losses.

in which we had left them, only a few additional batteries had been built, the army reinforced by the arrival of the 6th [Regiment] and the remaining division of the 82nd, and the encampment of the Indians had been removed to a greater distance from the batteries.[41]

We had now entered upon the month of September, which was this season ushered in by heavy and incessant rains. Nothing extraordinary took place more than the usual firing of shot and shells until the 17th of September when, in the afternoon and in the midst of a very heavy rain, four or five thousand of the enemy assailed our entrenchments unexpectedly and with such impetuosity as to carry them in despite the resistance made by the picket. In our encampment, the first notice we had of the attack was from the firing of musketry. We hastened forward on the extremity of the left flank and joined the Royals advancing in the same direction under the gallant Colonel Gordon. Near the battery we became mixed with the 6th and Glengarry. The lieutenant-colonel was severely wounded at the first onset from the fire of the riflemen. We advanced briskly upon them and drove them out of the works with great loss, but we found that they had completely damaged some of our guns. The 82nd, advancing briskly on the left to the support of the detachment of the King's – which yet bravely held out against the enemy – they recovered the entrenchment in gallant style. About three hundred Americans fell into our hands as prisoners and many lay dead on the ground. Among these were several militiamen, and we discovered that they had received a reinforcement of three thousand of the Genesee militia preparatory to making the attack upon us, in which it appears that they lost about seven hundred men.[42] In an [American]

---

41 The 6th Foot arrived at the British lines outside Fort Erie on 2 September. The army as a whole, not just the natives, relocated their camp at a safer distance from American fire, although it had the disadvantage of increasing the time it would take to support their batteries if they were to come under attack.

42 The Americans wanted the assault to cripple a new British battery located 700 yards from Fort Erie. Before they sortied from their defences, they had received a substantial number of militia reinforcements. By early September, for instance, they had upwards of 7,000 men at Fort Erie and in and around Buffalo. On 17 September, 1,875 men (including a small number of Senecas and Tuscaroras) advanced from Fort Erie, damaged the British artillery, and carried away or destroyed some ammunition before their opponents regained control. Gordon Drummond had 5,000 men around the fort at the time, but not all participated in the fighting because of the distance between his main camp and the batteries. Across two hours of close-quarters combat, the Americans suffered 510 men killed, wounded, and missing while the defenders had 580 losses (the majority of whom were taken prisoner).

officer's pocket, who had fallen, was found the account of the naval victory which they had gained over our fleet upon Lake Champlain.[43]

The heavy rains, which had fallen incessantly for two weeks past, now rendered it impossible to retain our inundated position longer without hazarding the destruction of the army by sickness. The trenches were filled with water, and the chilling blasts of autumn began to be felt. The troops on duty were exposed without shelter to the storm as well as to the shot of the enemy, and those reposing in the encampments were only out of reach of the fire from the hostile batteries. Our heavy cannon were removed from the batteries with some difficulty owing to the deplorable state to which the rains had reduced the roads. On or about the 20th of September we retired from our former position. The light brigade drew up in line on an extensive field near to Frenchman's Creek with intentions of giving battle to the enemy should he venture a sortie from his entrenchments. The main body of the army took up their quarters below Chippawa. A division under General de Watteville was stationed at Black Creek. The Glengarry Light Infantry, a small detachment of the 19th Dragoons, with a few of our men, were stationed between Black and Frenchman's creeks to cover people employed to get away grain in the neighbourhood.[44]

---

43 JN's comment about Lake Champlain refers to the American victory over the British squadron on 11 September. At the time, the British also had land forces engaged in operations against Plattsburg. Sir George Prevost, who commanded in person, however, decided to retire to Lower Canada after the naval defeat because the American squadron could support the defence of the town and threaten his communications lines, thus nullifying the impact of a victory on land, which also might be won only with heavy casualties, which he did not believe were acceptable. His reticence generated enormous criticism from his officers and government officials.

44 Before the 17 September attack on his lines, Gordon Drummond had decided to withdraw from his positions in front of Fort Erie after concluding that he probably could not take the post with the resources available to him. He also worried about the health and well-being of his ill-housed troops who suffered in unusually wet and cold weather for the time of year. On 21 September, most of the British moved north of the Chippawa River to various positions on the Niagara Peninsula, including Burlington Heights. The light brigade mentioned by JN consisted of 500 men of the Glengarry Light Infantry and the Incorporated Militia. Their movements were part of a plan to conceal the withdrawal from Fort Erie. Major-General Louis de Watteville was Drummond's second-in-command from early September 1814. Some skirmishing occurred as the Americans sent troops from Fort Erie to probe the British lines.

Having remained here about a week, I received directions to go with my little party to Fort Niagara in consequence of the enemy having been discovered in that quarter. We crossed the river, and scouring the woods for a few miles round, perceived only the traces of a very inconsiderable party, which had probably been employed in removing some grain and cattle from the farms approximate to the British garrison the preceding week.[45]

October had now arrived. The troops appeared to have taken up their winter quarters. The greater part of our men had also returned to their homes. The general also acceded to those who yet remained with me leaving the lines in order to rejoin their families and reassume the chase, the season for which had then arrived, and the falling leaf of autumn gave indications that the time for military operations of any extent in this country had ended for that year. He at the same time recommended that they would now endeavour to support themselves, as the means possessed by the commissariat were hardly sufficient to supply the troops.

I had hardly reached the Grand River when I heard that the American General Izard, with an army of six thousand men, was at Lewistown opposite to Queenston.[46] I received an express to hasten to the lines with as many men as could be collected. They were now too much scattered to find many at so short a notice. I therefore set out at the head of a party not exceeding a hundred.[47] We heard that our

---

45 The Americans thought of trying to take Fort Niagara, believing that its garrison was small, but did not do so. JN went as far as Four Mile Creek on the American side of the border on 29 September, did not see evidence of recent activity, and heard that the closest opposing party, a small one, was at Eighteen Mile Creek, and thus did not pose a threat. (JN to John Harvey, 30 September 1814, LAC, RG10, 3:1504–5). In the same letter, he noted that he only had "so small a party" with him, and he wrote that he was "particularly anxious to return to" Burlington Beach, "having heard yesterday that Mrs Norton is very unwell." He did visit her (JN to Colley Foster, 11 October 1814, ibid., 3:1529), and she recovered from her ailment.

46 The British discovered Major-General George Izard's force on 6 October, although they had heard about its movements earlier. Izard succeeded Jacob Brown on the Niagara Peninsula, with Brown taking a subordinate role under him. Izard sailed from Sackett's Harbour with 2,500 men, landed at the Genesee River (at modern Rochester), and then marched west to augment Brown's force. Meanwhile, another 1,000 men moved east from Detroit to enlarge the army further. With these developments, the initiative shifted to the Americans.

47 JN arrived back on the Niagara front on or about 23 October.

army had concentrated at Chippawa and the vicinity of the Cataract, and we took the direct road to join them. Within a few miles of their position, we learned that an encounter had taken place between the light brigade and the advance of the left division of the enemy's army, which had taken a circuitous route with the intention of crossing the Chippawa above the position held by our army. We arrived at head-quarters at the Cataract. We were informed that the enemy had retired towards Fort Erie subsequent to the failure of their attempt to force the position of our army. General Izard had shown himself with his army in front of Chippawa, while General Brown, passing by a road up Black Creek, reached Lyon's Creek on his way to the upper bridge on Chippawa. General Drummond detached Colonel Myers with the Glengarry and the flank companies of the other regiments to oppose any advance from that direction. These, meeting with a division of the enemy, fought with such spirit as led him to suppose their number much greater than it really was, and to think it advisable to retire without hazarding further, blaming General Izard for not having made a simultaneous attack upon Chippawa.[48]

We proceeded up the [Niagara] River to Black Creek and there took up our quarters together with the advanced picket of the Glengarry under Captain Fitzgibbon. Here we could perceive from the traces of the encampment that the American army was very numerous. Near this place, we met the general and his staff. They had been beyond French-man's Creek to reconnoitre the position of the enemy. He told me where he had seen the hostile army encamped (near to the ferry), and required us to watch their movements and to cut off their communication with the country. Having passed into the rear of the enemy, we found that it was not common for them to venture at any distance from the camp, that General Brown's army had recrossed the river to the side of the United States, that few people remained in Snake Hill, and that all

---

48 With some troops garrisoning his forts at the mouth of the Niagara River, Gordon Drummond took up a strong position along the Chippawa River and deployed men in advance in anticipation of an American thrust northwards from Fort Erie with the 6,300 soldiers they had on Canadian soil. There were several encounters in October but no decisive confrontation. The incident JN mentioned regarding Christopher Myers occurred on 19 October at Cook's Mills (in today's Welland), when 750 British encountered 900 Americans for less than an hour at a cost of 35 casualties on the British side, 70 on the American. It was the war's last noteworthy clash on the Niagara Peninsula.

appearances seemed to indicate that the Canadian frontier would in a few days be entirely evacuated by the enemy.[49]

A report that the enemy had landed near the mouth of the Grand River having reached the general, he directed us to return home. On the road, we discovered the report to have been incorrect.[50] At the beach [at Burlington], where I stopped, I heard that a wounded Indian was at Stoney Creek who reported that some of his companions had been killed.[51] I rode to the place to make enquiry in company with Mr A. Jones.[52] We found the wounded young man to be the son of the chief of the Delawares from Cattaraugus. He said that, accompanied by three young men of the same language, they had proceeded that far on their way to join the army, when, meeting with some of their friends returning from the lines who told them that the campaign was concluded, they had changed their destination and ascended the mountain [i.e., the Niagara Escarpment] with an intention to hunt a few days, having heard that some deer might be found in that direction. In about a mile and a half they came to two roads and made a fire in the woods, within 150 paces of a house, in order to pass the night there.

The sun was down. The young men had killed a few squirrels, which they boiled for their supper. After dark, a man came to them from the house and asked if there were only four of them. They answered in the affirmative. Before they had lain down to repose, he returned, and to their surprise, repeated the same question. Soon after his departure,

---

49 Gordon Drummond seemed dissatisfied with JN, writing that he "only arrived on this frontier three days ago, *after* the enemy had retreated" (Drummond to Sir George Prevost, 26 October 1814, LAC, RG8, 686:108). On 5 November, the American army evacuated Fort Erie, blew it up, and retired to Buffalo. British forces reoccupied the ruins shortly afterwards. Thus, the 1814 American invasion of the Niagara Peninsula came to a failed end. JN's "Captain Fitzgibbon" was Lieutenant James Fitzgibbon of the 49th Foot, mentioned earlier, who received a captaincy in the Glengarry Light Infantry in October 1813.

50 It seems that some Haudenosaunee people spread the rumour of an American landing at Grand River for malicious, but now unknown, purposes. Gordon Drummond asked JN to identify those responsible for the stories (Drummond to Sir George Prevost, 30 October 1814, ibid., 686:117).

51 Leaving Niagara on or about 26 October, JN intended to travel to the Grand via Burlington (ibid.).

52 Augustus Jones was a prominent surveyor and land speculator. He was the husband of Sarah, daughter of Henry Tekarihogen, and previously had had a relationship with a Mississauga woman, Tuhbenahneequay, mother of the Mississauga leader and Methodist minister of a subsequent generation, Peter Jones (Kahkewaquonaby).

they lay down to sleep. He then awoke from the noise of the fire or sensation of the wound he had received. He found two of his comrades lying dead, and a bayonet thrust into his body, beside the ball wounds. Struggling with his opponents and assisted by the comrade who was yet unhurt, they disengaged themselves and ran. The assassins fired again. He saw his comrade fall, and from weakness, he also fell; and finding he was pursued, he lay still. They passed without observing him, and finding their search ineffectual in the dark, they returned to the camp where he perceived a great blaze. I asked him if he thought it was the enemy and how many the party might have consisted of. He replied that he felt assured they were the country people of the neighbourhood and that there might have been about ten of them. Indeed, for my own part I could not for a moment have supposed it to be the enemy: Fort Erie was not only distant, but it was also very improbable that any scout of the enemy would loiter in remote parts of the woods at so great a risk, and only to glut their vengeance on a few individuals. (Mr A. Jones suspected the deed to have been perpetrated by some party of the enemy.) It was now too late to go to the place where the murder had been committed. Some of the Delawares then arriving on the same account, we agreed to ascend the mountain together the next morning and take the greater part of them home with us.

In the morning I heard that a Mr Green (the man of the house near which the murder had been committed), with his two brothers, had taken alarm when they heard that we were going to make search for the bodies of the deceased, and had left their house in the night. They went through a bad road eight miles to Burlington, there expressing strong apprehensions of the resentment of the Indians from the report of a murder having been committed in their neighbourhood. They asked the protection of Lieutenant-Colonel Jones-Parry, who sent or referred them to me, where I heard they came a little before daybreak after going seven miles through a very bad road, but the landlord [of a tavern?] sent them away by telling them that it was my intention to go to their place the next morning. After breakfast, we ascended the mountain (as it is called) or ridge. We came to the spot where the unfortunate young men had lighted their fire and made their camp. We found the bodies had been removed, the blood covered with leaves, and the traces of the encampment obliterated as much as possible. The house in sight was about 150 paces distant. The Indians, in general, expressed much resentment at the proprietor [Samuel Green], suspecting him to be an accomplice from the ignorance he pretended of the transaction. He complained to me that some of them had pillaged his house. What could be discovered I caused them to restore, observing to them that if he were innocent it was highly unjust to do him any injury, and if he were guilty it was much too slight a punishment, that in time we would discover, and then atonement should be made.

Turning to him, I observed, "Mr Green, I must expect that you can give us some account of this transaction which has occurred just at your door. The number of men that appear to have been concerned must, with the firing, have made some noise. Did you hear nothing nor perceive them while engaged in carrying away the bodies?" He answered, "I came home after dark from raising the frame of a mill in which the whole neighbourhood had been engaged. My wife told me that Indians were encamped at the corner of the field and I saw the blaze of the fire. Being tired, I soon went to bed. In the morning my wife told me that she had tried to awake me on hearing something like an alarm, but without effect, and the noise ceasing, she let me sleep on."

I resolved [to consider several points] in my mind: his apathy and indolence for a whole day in making no enquiry into the cause of the alarm of which his wife had acquainted him (although the camp was only 150 paces from his door), the great care that had been taken to conceal all traces that might develop [sic] the perpetration of the bloody deed, and the great apprehension he had shown in running to Burlington for protection as soon as he heard that we were on the move to make [a] search for the bodies. The result of my reflections was nothing in his favour. I thought it advisable, however, to make further researches before showing suspicion. I therefore sent him and his brother, in company with some Indians, in quest of a person that had been represented to me as a suspicious character, although the distance of his abode rendered it quite improbable that he could have been concerned in the recent event. The remaining party made every search for the bodies by following closely every track that was discernible going from the spot where the deed had been perpetrated. The next morning one body was discovered about half a mile from the camp. It had been thrown into a hole in a swamp, covered by water and mud about two feet deep; and soon after the other two were found at about two miles' distant in a different direction, laid among trees of fallen timber, and covered with leaves. Each body had several wounds of ball, buckshot, bayonet, and axe. The manner in which the poor lads had been mangled gave striking proofs of the barbarity of the insidious perpetrators of the murderous deed. At this time, the Greens returned with the person of whom they had gone in quest, who from every circumstance appeared clear of all suspicion, and was consequently dismissed. Their apprehensions were visibly increased at the discovery of the mangled bodies. They were put into custody and subsequently sent to York to await their trial. As soon as General Sir Gordon Drummond received information of this atrocious affair, he offered, by proclamation, a reward of one hundred pounds to whoever would give information on the guilty.[53]

While thus occupied I had received vague information of the advance of a body of one thousand Americans under Colonel McArthur from Detroit to the Grand River. I hastened forward with all the men I could collect, and within a few miles of the Grand River overtook a division of the 103rd under Lieutenant-Colonel Smelt proceeding to the same point. The next morning we went on to the ferry, and there learned that two days before the enemy had pushed forward a small division to that point, which had been gallantly opposed by a small party of Mohawks

---

53 JN's involvement in the story occurred at the end of October. The murdered people were young Delawares, of whom at least one had moved from New York to the Grand River, but their names have been lost to history. The brutality of the crime on the Niagara Escarpment near Stoney Creek underscored the tensions that existed between some elements of the native and settler populations in Upper Canada, often related to robberies committed across the cultural divide by both sides. Two interesting features of the incident are the fact that the British officer did not shelter the suspects, but sent them to JN and his native investigators (which was one of two groups who tried to find the perpetrators), while the indigenous people did not avenge the killings through traditional practices, but sent the prisoners to trial in the colonial courts. The suspects, however, either escaped shortly after the incident or were released because of a lack of evidence. Another description of these events JN wrote follows the *JMJN* text closely but includes a note about an unsuccessful investigation after the war. In that document, he declared: "Besides the justice of the case that all people living within the bounds of His Majesty's dominions should be protected in their lives and properties by the laws of the British Empire, it is evident that to allow to escape with impunity men with so base and unprovoked an assassination must have a very bad effect upon the minds of the Indians" (JN to J.F. Addison, 6 June 1817, LAC, RG8, 261:248). The murders continued to absorb JN's attention for several years. For instance, he conducted more research in 1818. Based on the evidence of white and native witnesses, JN thought the perpetrators included Samuel and John Green, and two people he identified as Bonham and Yager or Yeager (JN to Samuel Smith, 26 January 1818, LAC, RG10, 782:119–21; see also John Beverley Robinson to George Hillier, 17 November 1818, ibid., 782:147–8; JN to Sir Peregrine Maitland, 24 August 1819, ibid., 782:187–9).

and Cayugas, who fired across the river (not more than fifty yards wide at that place) with great spirit.[54]

We found, however, that no means of passing the river was left, neither boat nor canoe. I had, therefore, to send up the river for some large canoes capable of transporting about twenty men at a time. They arrived that evening, and the next morning we got over about one hundred of our men. Major Eustace of the 19th Dragoons, and Major Chambers, with a detachment of that corps, also passed over, and we proceeded on the track of the enemy. About twelve miles along the road we received information that they had not delayed at Long Point, as we had expected, but had hurried homewards again after having burnt a few mills and done some damage to the country. As they were all well mounted and had two days the start of us, we could have no hopes of overtaking them unless by persevering in pursuit for 150 miles, and my men were not in a condition to make speed for such a distance at this season of the year, being for the greater part without shoes or moccasins, and even without a necessary supply of ammunition. Thus situated, I could have no confidence unless the greatest alacrity should prevail on their [our?] side. We therefore returned to the Grand River. Here we found that the troops and militia assembled for the purpose had all returned to their quarters and their homes.[55]

---

54 Brigadier-General Duncan McArthur left Detroit on 22 October at the head of 720 men (including 70 warriors from Ohio and Michigan) to destroy crops, livestock, and property along the north shore of Lake Erie. He planned to assault the Six Nations of the Grand River, and, should circumstances allow, either move against Burlington or rendezvous with the American army at Fort Erie. While the raid was destructive against the civilian population in southwestern Upper Canada to the west of the Grand, McArthur decided not to attempt to cross that waterway. Nevertheless, his troops skirmished with warriors near the Mohawk village on 5–6 November and both sides suffered casualties, with one report saying the Americans lost 10 killed and one captured while the defending force had six Haudenosaunee men killed or wounded (John Brant to William Claus, 16 November 1814, ibid., 29:17367–8). McArthur thought that the river was too formidable to cross under fire against the forces arrayed against him, and learned that the American had decided to withdraw from Fort Erie, which rendered a crossing more or less pointless. Following his withdrawal, McArthur travelled 12 miles west and fought a successful action on 6 November against 400 militiamen and a small number of warriors at Malcolm's Mills (today's Oakland). Casualties were about 30 on the Canadian side and perhaps a third of that number on the American, but as many as 125 Canadians became prisoners, who the Americans paroled.

55 As well as JN's men, the British sent 375 regulars and militia from Niagara to the Grand River to reinforce local warrior and militia forces, but they did not arrive

We had now entered upon November and from the nature of the climate, the evacuation by the enemy of the position near Fort Erie (of which we had just received information), and the general results of all his attempts against us, we had reason to expect that we might pass the winter in tranquility unless a favourable opportunity should instigate us to make reprisals. The last predatory incursion of Colonel McArthur and the mounted Kentuckians might have been intended to distract our attention and divide our force while attacked by Generals Brown and Izard. The only object, however, effectually accomplished by this dashing enterprise was the destruction of four mills by one thousand men who had ridden from Kentucky, a distance of five hundred miles, and had been employed about two months at the rate of a dollar per day to each man. We were able to rebuild the mills in less time and at much less expense.

Some time antecedent to these occurrences, we received information that the enemy had made an attempt upon Michilimackinac, and had been completely foiled. The part at which they landed was occupied by a party of Indians with Mr R. Dickson. They opposed the Americans gallantly and obliged them to re-embark with loss. The son of Mr Dickson was wounded. Subsequently two of the enemy's armed vessels were taken by a detachment of the Newfoundland Regiment.[56]

FINIS

John Norton ended his narrative abruptly in late 1814, expecting to take to the field the following spring but, of course, that did not happen. Yet in 1815 and 1816, when writing his narrative, he did not produce a conclusion to his

---

until after the fighting had ended. McArthur retired to Detroit by mid-November after skirmishing, seizing prisoners, and destroying more property along the way. The loss of foodstuffs and the burning of mills exacerbated the problems faced by the British in feeding their forces, their allies, their dependents, and the civilian population over the following months. The officers mentioned in JN's account who have not been noted earlier are Major William Smelt, a brevet lieutenant-colonel who succeeded Hercules Scott to command of the 103rd Foot, and Captain John Eustace of the 19th Light Dragoons.

56 On 4 August, an American attack designed to retake Mackinac at the northern end of Lake Michigan from the British and their native allies failed. After most of the United States Navy squadron sailed back to Lake Erie, British soldiers and seamen,

story. American and British diplomats in the European city of Ghent finished peace negotiations on Christmas Eve 1814. Their governments subsequently ratified the treaty, which ended the war officially in mid-February 1815. The news reached Upper Canada later that month, followed by a national day of thanksgiving in April to commemorate the return of peace and the successful defence of British North America against the efforts of the United States to conquer the colonies.[57]

Great Britain – with the indispensable help of its First Nations allies – had achieved its primary war aims of not relinquishing any territory to the

---

accompanied by allied warriors, used rowboats to surprise one of the armed schooners left behind on Lake Huron to blockade Mackinac, and captured her on 3 September, which they then used to seize the second schooner on 6 September. Thus, the war in the upper lakes ended with the British controlling the region, which they supplied via fur trade routes leading from Montreal and York because Lake Erie remained in American hands. The wounded person mentioned was William Dickson, son of Robert Dickson and his wife Totowin (Helen), a prominent Dakota Sioux woman.

57 The official end of the war occurred on 16 February 1815, when the American government ratified the Treaty of Ghent. The British had done so on 27 December 1814, but the period's slow communications delayed Washington's decision. The United States had gone to war to change the international status quo in its favour. As noted earlier, Great Britain had made some concessions to the republic in an attempt to avoid a military confrontation before it learned of the American declaration of war, but it made none as a consequence of hostilities. Rather, it preserved everything it had possessed before the outbreak, and retained the rights it had exercised beforehand to control the high seas and use its navy against a future enemy as effectively as possible (as it would, for instance, in 1914 when it blockaded Germany in opposition to American protests). Essentially, the maritime irritants between the two powers evaporated due to Britain's victory over France and the consequent return of peace in Europe, not American belligerency. The government in London, however, did not press for concessions from the United States that it thought might be possible to obtain opportunistically (such as retaining parts of modern Maine, occupied by British forces), because of their desire to restore peace as quickly as possible. The only major shift included in the Treaty of Ghent was an agreement by President James Madison's government to join the United Kingdom in its efforts to suppress the Atlantic slave trade. Americans, however, ignored their nation's failure to achieve its goals. Instead, they celebrated victories at battles such as at Baltimore and New Orleans (while overlooking the very large number of successful raids into the United States during the British counterattacks of 1813 and 1814), and declared success in what they called "a second war of independence." Essentially, they twisted interpretations of what they had wanted the war to achieve to serve nationalistic and political agendas, which subsequent generations of patriotic historians in the United States have affirmed despite the evidence to the contrary.

United States, or of making any maritime or other concessions because of American belligerency. Yet the outcomes of the conflict were more complex and less satisfactory for the indigenous peoples of the Great Lakes, whether they had allied with one of the white powers or had remained neutral. The basis of the Treaty of Ghent was a return to the pre-war status quo. In conformity to that principle, Article IX addressed native affairs for those First Nations that had not signed peace treaties already (as had occurred in much of the Old Northwest). It required the white powers to end hostilities with aboriginal peoples and restore the rights, privileges, and possessions they had enjoyed in 1811. This provision was more meaningful south of the Anglo-American boundary, of course, because of the hostilities the republic had undertaken against the indigenous population within its borders, whereas natives in Canada had not taken up arms against the Crown on a community basis (and where individuals had done so, it occurred beyond the treaty's concern). The First Nations in the Old Northwest that had opposed the Americans had hoped to create an independent homeland for themselves, or at least establish a defined region where they could live free of the dominant society's abuse and exploitation. Article IX gave them less than they wanted. It only slowed settler expansion for a few years, because the republic's administration, while willing to return affairs to their 1811 state as part of the agreement to re-establish peace, had no intention of allowing the pre-war situation to persist into the future once it wanted to acquire indigenous lands or otherwise force its will upon native peoples. The government in London had tried to negotiate the creation of a distinct territory for its aboriginal allies, despite strident opposition from American diplomats. At one point in 1814, Prime Minister Lord Liverpool (Robert Jenkinson) had thought of continuing the fight into 1815 to achieve that goal. He decided, however, that such a course would not be in the best interests of either Great Britain or its Canadian colonies. The military situation in Europe in 1814 was uncertain enough that the troops recently sent to North America had to return across the Atlantic, while continuing the American war into a fourth year risked defeat and the loss of all or much of what had been defended successfully by 1814. Furthermore, the one area of strength the republic had shown in the conflict was in the Old Northwest, where it had recaptured territory lost in 1812 and had forced the majority of people in the Western Tribal Confederacy into peace agreements while the larger Anglo-American struggle continued.

Native people who had aligned with the United States in hopes that their support would purchase the republic's protection, such as many of the Haudenosaunee in New York, also experienced profound disappointment, being treated by the Americans no differently from those who had fought against

them and being forced to cede land and otherwise accommodate white society
on a devastating scale. For First Nations north of the Anglo-American border
who had opposed the invaders between 1812 and 1814, the war ended agree-
ably in the successful defence of the British provinces, although they too, like
all communities affected by the conflict, grieved their personal losses. Yet
there was widespread unhappiness that a separate homeland had not been
established on the American side of the western Great Lakes border for their
brethren who lived within the United States (and which likely would have
attracted some natives from British territory had it been created). In addition,
indigenous people in Canada after 1815 faced increased intrusions into their
lives from colonial bureaucracies, along with settler exploitation and pressure
to alienate land as immigrants from the British Isles flooded into the colony.
The extent of maltreatment was more modest than south of the international
boundary for several reasons, including the smaller populations of natives
and newcomers, different environmental and economic circumstances, and
stronger cross-cultural ties due to the alliance relationship between Great
Britain and the First Nations. Nevertheless, abuse did occur. For instance,
white authorities coerced the people of the Grand River to leave much of
the tract in the 1840s and start their lives anew on a smaller portion of the
original Haldimand Grant, in order to accommodate newcomers' desires for
land. As we shall explore below, John Norton did not live long enough to
see that injustice imposed on the people whose interests he had defended so
vigorously. Yet he likely had premonitions of the future in the late 1810s and
early 1820s, as he returned to his quest to secure Haudenosaunee title and
autonomy along the Grand River as soon as peace had been established and
he had fulfilled his promises to recruit Iroquois support to defend the province
against the American invaders.[58]

---

58 For fuller discussions, see Benn, *Iroquois in the War of 1812*, 174–93 (including material
on peace negotiations between opposing aboriginal groups); Benn, "Aboriginal
Peoples and Their Multiple Wars of 1812," 145–8.

Epilogue

John Norton in Upper Canada and Great Britain

At the beginning of 1815, people across Upper Canada assumed that the war might continue for some time. Thus, before news of the mid-February peace reached the province late that month, the administrative struggle between John Norton and his rivals in the colony persisted. Its characteristics were much the same as they had been before, marked by the Indian Department's attempts to restrict access to supplies for the people in his care, within its broader efforts to degrade his influence with the help of its indigenous supporters and Teyoninhokarawen's opponents (who were not necessarily the same people).[1] With the end of Anglo-American hostilities, Norton's

---

1 In January 1815 alone, the historical record preserves three such attempts to subvert JN. In one instance William Claus accused him of making "importunities" that had led one officer to order native stores to be delivered to him, which subverted the Indian Department's distribution of goods on a fair basis during a period of shortages (Claus to Edward MacMahon, 6 January 1815, LAC, RG10, 30:17538; see also Duncan Cameron to JN, 9 January 1815, ibid., 30:17544–5; JN to Cameron, 9 January 1815, ibid., 30:17547–9). To be fair, JN often did not follow the correct procedures for managing his responsibilities (e.g., Cameron to JN, 18 January 1815, ibid., 30:17600). A second centred on attempts to undermine JN's leadership by shifting the Munceytown Chippewas from his care to another officer (JN to Claus, 12 January 1815, ibid., 30:17561–2). A third instance that month related to the Indian Department's efforts to garner the support of its friends in the Grand River community (such as George Martin) to attack JN (Council Minutes, 20 January 1815, ibid., 30:17604–10). In that document, people expressed the hope that Claus would return as their "father" in place of JN because of the sufferings they had endured as "the government appears to pay little attention to Captain Norton," despite his

political enemies no longer had to worry about his undeniable value in defending the province, and therefore could aspire to bring their campaign to push him to the margins of Crown-Haudenosaunee relations to a close. The lieutenant-governor of Upper Canada, Francis Gore (who returned to the colony in 1815) wrote a revealing letter to the secretary of state for war and the colonies, Earl Bathurst (Henry Bathurst), which captured some of the animosity felt towards Teyoninhokarawen. Gore claimed that the army's patronage had elevated the Mohawk chief to "a species of influence incompatible with the subordination of the tribes to the views of His Majesty's Government, which it is so important to preserve."[2] That statement exposed the fundamental conflict between the colony's governors and John Norton. As we saw in the Introduction, Teyoninhokarawen, along with Joseph Brant and others, strove to preserve Six Nations freedom from unwanted external intrusions as much as the conditions and geographical realities of the time would allow, and thought the colonial government had an obligation to protect aboriginal people within British Norton America. In contrast, Francis Gore, William Claus, and their circle sought to impose their will over Iroquois affairs. Their desires arose partly from fear of indigenous military strength, as represented by Joseph Brant's threats to use force against the Crown to protect native interests in the 1790s. Brant's capacity to represent a serious danger had stemmed partly from his ability to attract support both from within the Six Nations of the Grand and from other native communities. Norton was suspect in his opponents' minds not only because of his association with Brant and because of all the things he had done before the war in opposition to the Indian Department, but also because, like his mentor, he had demonstrated that he could attract enough warriors to undermine Upper Canadian security should he decide to act against the provincial government. As with Joseph Brant, it is hard to imagine that he actually would have engaged in an armed rising against the established order, but these officials naturally considered such a possibility. As we saw earlier,

---

having been appointed by Sir George Prevost as their primary connection to their British allies (ibid., 30:17605). For other instances of these sorts of problems and JN's responses, see ibid., 30:passim.

2 Francis Gore to Lord Bathurst, 27 December 1815, LAC, CO42, 356:161.

Norton's reputation also had suffered from perceptions that he had failed to deploy warriors effectively at Chippawa in 1814, perhaps costing the British their victory. In addition, he had been condemned, unfairly, for undermining relations with the First Nations at the council following the battle, where many of the warriors decided to withdraw from the Niagara campaign. Other actions he took in opposition to the Indian Department's desires further enraged its officers, such as his use of the Crown's resources to distribute presents in order to enhance his position at the expense of William Claus and other departmental officials.

A greater incentive behind Gore's desires for "subordination," however, lay in desires to acquire native land and control indigenous communities for the benefit of settler society. Often the officials behind these efforts wanted to profit personally, rather than serve the broader interests of the Crown, the province, or Anglo–First Nations relations. Subordination would be more difficult to accomplish if aboriginal people opposed such desires through the efforts of talented individuals like Norton, who could muster resources within both their own and other native communities, as well as harness alternative sources of white authority (as Teyoninhokarawen did from the army and from sympathetic Britons across the ocean). The fact that John Norton had fought valiantly through 1812, 1813, and 1814 meant nothing to a number of people in the colonial elite, blinded by their hubristic desires and ambitions. In considering the divisions along the Grand River in their military and political behaviour, it is clear that the Six Nations Tract included many individuals who were more amenable to the Indian Department than at least a portion of those associated with Norton were. That fact allowed the department to malign Teyoninhokarawen and the people around him as dangerous militants, despite their contributions in repelling the American invasions of the colony. One outcome was that veterans who had allied with the Crown outside of John Norton's circle received more benefits than those within it, contrary to decisions made during the war to compensate people equitably for their losses and suffering. For instance, in 1817, Teyoninhokarawen complained that one of his Mohawk opponents and Claus's supporter, George Martin, distributed presents "in a manner as if they were intended to support party and foment division rather than to relieve the indigent or to reward the faithful warriors." The number mistreated was substantial: among the Mohawks alone, 150 people – more than a third of the tribe's population along the Grand River

– suffered from such favouritism.[3] In Haudenosaunee tradition, leaders relied, in some measure, on their ability to provide largesse from their white allies in garnering a following. Martin's actions, which aligned with the desires of the department and the anti-Norton groupings on the Grand, weakened Teyoninhokarawen's prominence, even though they caused distress among worthy and innocent individuals. This sort of conduct of course had been an ongoing scandal, as represented by events in 1814 and 1815 when the department had not provided enough rations to meet the needs of people in Norton's care, and then blamed him for the shortage as they attempted to degrade his standing.[4]

Gore's letter also denigrated Teyoninhokarawen by stating that he was "not an Indian, but a native of Scotland, a discharged soldier from the 65th Regiment ... who acquired the language and manner of the Indians whilst clerk to a trader in the Miamis so perfectly as to enable him to impose himself upon the public here and in Europe as a native Indian."[5] Thus, Gore not only condemned Norton as a fraud, in term of his ethnicity, who opposed government objectives, but made the offence worse because of the impertinence of a person of humble origins (a "soldier" and a "clerk") "imposing" himself on the public. Of course, Gore intended his assertion about Teyoninhokarawen's Scottish birth to hide the fact that Norton's father was a Cherokee, and that he held legitimate places in the Haudenosaunee world both as an adoptee and as a leader. Moreover, Gore noted that "this impostor" had achieved independence from the control of the Indian Department because of the support he had received, not only from the army but also from the former governor-in-chief of British North America, Sir George Prevost.[6] Anyone politically attuned when he penned those words knew that Prevost's reputation had collapsed, despite his successful defence of Canada, because many people thought he had bungled the Plattsburgh campaign in 1814. (Sir George took the dire initiative of seeking his own court martial to preserve his reputation, but died before it convened.) The fact that Norton enjoyed preferment from such a person stood as a condemnation in the eyes of Gore, anyone the lieutenant-governor could influence, and Prevost's detractors.

---

3 JN to J.F. Addison, 13 February 1817, LAC, RG8, 261:25–33 (quote on 33).
4 JN to Colley Foster, 23 February 1815, ibid., 258:29–32.
5 Francis Gore to Lord Bathurst, 27 December 1815, LAC, CO42, 356:161.
6 Ibid.

When Sir George Prevost returned to England, Lieutenant-General Gordon Drummond became the senior civil and military official in British North America for a time (and received a knighthood early in 1815). Acting on the recommendation of the Indian Department as it reduced its operations with the return of peace, Drummond offered Norton retirement with a substantial pension of two hundred pounds Halifax Currency per annum, along with two food rations per diem. He also made provisions for Teyoninhokarawen's wife, Catherine, to receive half that amount should she outlive him, but limited payment *"during pleasure."*[7] The general was not motivated by generosity but by frustration and fear. He thought that Norton had undermined the department's management of aboriginal affairs, but that "any measure which would be calculated to irritate or disappoint Captain Norton cannot but be considered as impolitic. For the character of this man is so strongly marked by great ability, design, and intrigue that, if tempted to change sides, he might prove a most dangerous enemy by stirring up dissentions among the tribes and rendering them hostile to His Majesty's government."[8] Thus, Claus and Drummond removed Teyoninhokarawen from active employment in the department, but did so with care. Losing access to the department's resources would inhibit his ability to support his followers, while Drummond intended the conditional nature of Norton's pension to restrain him from acting against the colonial bureaucracy. We can see how tense and frustrating the relationships were between Claus and other officials, on the one hand, and Teyoninhokarawen on the other, in a letter Norton sent just before Drummond made the offer. He wrote, "The complaints of the deputy superintendent-general ... and the rest of this worthy combination have been so great, so frequent, and so groundless that I only can advise them to bring forward their charges in a public manner if they are consistent with the good of the service." However, "if they are personal and only directed against myself, I am always ready, and tired of explanations with people who will not understand me."[9] Such a document from an ordinary

---

7 Colley Foster to JN, 18 April 1815, LAC, RG10, 12:10553–4. See also Sir John Johnson to Sir Gordon Drummond, 5 February 1815, ibid., 4:1643–6. Foster underlined "during pleasure," to make it clear that the authorities could cancel the pension at any time.

8 Sir Gordon Drummond to Sir George Prevost, 11 March 1815, LAC, RG8, 258:41–4, quote on 42–3.

9 JN to Duncan Cameron, 25 February 1815, ibid., 258:28.

official in the department easily could have led to dismissal without any compensation; but of course, Teyoninhokarawen was not an ordinary official. More significantly, he was a diplomatic and alliance chief from the comparatively powerful Six Nations of the Grand River, who also enjoyed a substantial degree of influence beyond his community across Upper Canada and among prominent individuals in the United Kingdom. Thus, a pension and retirement made more sense to protect the colony from a potential rising or other troubles with the native population. This was especially important because right after the war many people believed the Treaty of Ghent was more of a temporary truce than a permanent settlement between Great Britain and the United States (with, for instance, both powers building new defences and improving communications lines in anticipation of further hostilities).

Teyoninhokarawen responded to the offer to retire with some tartness, writing that it was "with pleasure" that he embraced "liberation from the disputes and intricacies of the Indian Department." Yet he seemed to think that it represented Drummond's "high consideration" of his service during the war. In accepting it, Norton nevertheless used his reply to ask the colonial authorities to promulgate regulations that would recognize and reward warriors who had fought with distinction with fairness in order prevent the Indian Department from discriminating against people it did not like.[10] His sharp words represented a riposte to some of the content of the letter offering retirement from Sir Gordon's secretary, Colley Foster. He asserted that Norton was partially responsible for "many misunderstandings and improper disputes" with William Claus, although Foster acknowledged that John Norton had "most fully at heart the good of His Majesty's government" and recognized the value of his contributions to the defence of British North America.[11] (Despite Drummond's desire to get rid of Teyoninhokarawen, he acknowledged Norton's skills as a war chief, writing that "this man is of the coolest and most undaunted courage, and has led the Indians with the greatest gallantry and much effect on many occasions, particularly at Queenston under the late Major-General Sir Isaac Brock.")[12]

---

10 JN to Colley Foster, 18 May 1815, ibid., 258:75–6.
11 Colley Foster to JN, 18 April 1815, LAC, RG10, 12:10553. The date of his retirement was 25 May (Foster to William Claus, 24 April 1815, ibid., 12:10556).
12 Sir Gordon Drummond to Lord Bathurst, 25 July 1815, published in Brymner, *Report on Canadian Archives*, xi.

While Norton retired from the Indian Department in 1815, he still was a Mohawk chief and capable of acting on behalf of those among the Six Nations who were willing to let him do so. From that position, he intended to pursue the land issues along the Grand River that had occupied much of his time before the war, now that peace had returned. He planned to visit the superintendent-general of the department, Sir John Johnson, in Montreal as the first step in resolving the controversies over the meaning and extent of the Haldimand Grant (as we explored in the Introduction). He probably did not expect Johnson to acquiesce to his demands, but likely believed he needed to make the effort. Therefore, he had decided to sail to Britain, where, among other plans, he would seek redress from the imperial authorities.[13] Hearing about his intentions, the Indian Department brought a group of congenial chiefs to a council in June 1815 in a manner reminiscent of the pre-war meeting that had denounced his earlier journey to England to address Six Nations land issues. Naturally, it occurred in Teyoninhokarawen's absence, and in York – an odd place for the Six Nations, but one where colonial officials could manage affairs more easily than if they were to meet closer to the Grand. One of Norton's Mohawk opponents, Henry Tekarihogen, spoke disparagingly about his political rival. In reference to Sir George Prevost's decision to give him an unusual degree of authority during the war, he said: "It is now two years since Norton went to Quebec [in 1814], as he said, with a deputation from the Six Nations; but we know nothing of the matter, and he returned with a very extraordinary appointment, unknown to us Indians, of which we complained to Major-General Riall whilst at the Beach [i.e., Burlington]. We are told that he is now out of the service. We will never consent that he shall again have a right to interfere in our affairs. We know nothing of him. He has no Indian blood in him. He is a bad man, and we cannot help fearing that he will injure us."[14] While it is true that Norton's appointment was "extraordinary," the rest of Tekarihogen's points were false, but reflected the lies the colonial administration used to deny Norton's indigenous ancestry and legitimacy within the Six Nations, while aligning him with the now-discredited governor-in-chief. For instance, the Haudenosaunee in fact knew what had transpired between Norton and Prevost, as Teyoninhokarawen had held a council to tell everyone

---

13 JN to Colley Foster, 25 May 1815, LAC, RG8, 695:80.
14 Henry Tekarihogen, Speech, 2 June 1815, LAC, RG10, 30:18022.

about his meeting when he returned from Quebec in 1814.[15] We can see the department's scheming as well in the next part of the speech. Tekarihogen continued, "Our present object is to request that our Great Father the King may be made acquainted with the character and conduct of this man, who we understand is going to England very soon, and we must express our hope that he will never again be employed in our affairs." He also complained that the tract's residents were divided into two parties over Norton, which unintentionally affirmed Teyoninhokarawen's support within the community; and of course most Six Nations people wanted control over their lands, and knew that Norton had worked hard to achieve that goal.[16] In the end, the records of this council would have no impact in London.

Teyoninhokarawen, now aged forty-five, took his son John, his wife Catherine, and a party of other individuals from the Grand River to Montreal to call upon Sir John Johnson, who simply would not deal with him or the other people in the delegation.[17] Norton and his family, but without the others, then sailed to the United Kingdom, arriving in August 1815. Along with trying to resolve the First Nations issues, he wanted to spend time with his Scottish family, his acquaintances from his 1804–5 visit, and men from the late war who already had returned to Britain. After several grim years of turmoil and danger, he undoubtedly expected to enjoy a holiday, and he decided to enrol his wife and son in a school in Scotland. Naturally, he wanted to finish his manuscript for publication, which he had been enlarging with the story of his adventures from the War of 1812. He also sought further military service "on the plains of Flanders," apparently having left Canada before news crossed the Atlantic proclaiming the end of the great Napoleonic struggles at Waterloo in June that year and the consequent reduction in the size of the armed forces.[18] Thus, his

---

15 Gordon Drummond to Noah Freer, 28 June 1814, enclosing Extracts from a Council, n.d. (1814), LAC, RG8, 257:290–4.

16 Henry Tekarihogen, Speech, 2 June 1815, LAC, RG10, 30:18023.

17 Sir John Johnson to Colley Foster, 21 August 1815, ibid., 487:4600; Johnson, Memorandum, 15 August 1815, LAC, MG19–F35, Series 2, Lot 738.

18 JN to Colley Foster, 18 May 1815, LAC, RG8, 258:75 (quote); Klinck, "Biographical Introduction," in *JMJN*, lxxxi–lxxxviii describes the Norton family's time and acquaintances in Britain in more detail than presented here. Klinck, however, erred about the date of the Nortons' arrival (second Duke of Northumberland to JN, 3 September 1815, BL, Northumberland MSS, 69A:333). See also, Morgan, *Travellers through Empire*, 45–50.

second attempt to become a commissioned officer in the British army failed, like the first during his previous visit across the ocean. He was successful, however, in petitioning for recognition of his contributions to the defence of Canada in relation to the number of warriors he had led in the field, as the authorities in London awarded him the rank of a non-serving major in the army.[19] (This gave one American newspaper the opportunity to denounce him and the King's ministers, proclaiming that "Norton, the Indian chief, celebrated for his murders on our frontier during the late war, has the brevet commission of major from the British government.")[20] In May, Lord Bathurst had Norton promoted to the local rank of lieutenant-colonel of the Six Nations and their aboriginal allies. With the return of peace, the position existed primarily as an honour and in anticipation of future hostilities with the United States, while his status among the Haudenosaunee was, in fact, something for the Six Nations rather than Bathurst to determine.[21] The affirmations presumably gratified Teyoninhokarawen, because he still found himself defending his loyalty in the face of accusations from Canada, although the government at the imperial centre dismissed the allegations.[22] (For instance, Lieutenant-Governor Francis Gore, with less subtlety of thought than Sir Gordon Drummond, made a futile attempt to revoke Norton's pension.)[23]

Norton received other forms of encouragement. For instance, in Dunfermline, not far from his birthplace, the town council bestowed the freedom of the burgh on him.[24] He dined with the famous

---

19 JN to Henry Goulburn, 29 January 1816, published in Cruikshank, "Campaigns," 43–6 (petition). The *London Gazette*, 2 March 1816, reported, "John Norton, Esq. alias Teyoninhokarawen, Captain and Leader of the Indians of the Five Nations, to have the local and temporary rank of major in Canada" from 15 February 1816.

20 *Niles' Weekly Register*, 11 May 1816.

21 Lord Bathurst to the Officer Administering the Government of Canada, 10 May 1816, quoted in Good, "Crown-Directed Colonization," 253. The annual *Army List* through the rest of JN's life, however, designated him as a major, but with the notation that he was "Captain and Leader of the Indians of the Five Nations." As a major, nevertheless, it was reasonable for him to be breveted as a lieutenant-colonel, and some documents from 1816 and later refer to him as "colonel" (e.g., *Louisville Public Advertiser*, 31 January 1824).

22 JN to J.F. Addison, 16 June 1818, LAC, RG8, 262:88–91.

23 Francis Gore to Lord Bathurst, 27 December 1815, LAC, CO42, 356:159–63.

24 Klinck, "Biographical Introduction," in *JMJN*, lxxxi–lxxxiii.

novelist Walter Scott, who became something of a friend and patron.[25] He received invitations from others in England and Scotland to visit their homes, including the well-known Whigs, the Earl and Countess of Levin (Alexander Leslie-Melville and Jane Melville).[26] In London, the Prince Regent received him.[27] Through the efforts of His Royal Highness and Henry Goulburn, the under-secretary of state for war and the colonies, Norton had high-quality rifles designed and manufactured for distribution to chiefs and warriors in Canada, including a double-barrelled model.[28] Naturally, Teyoninhokarawen visited and corresponded with people from his earlier travels to Great Britain. One of them, the Duke of Northumberland, dispatched other firearms, including a wall piece (a sort of very large musket with considerable range), along with other presents to Quebec so Norton could get them upon his return to Canada. Later, the third duke (also named Hugh Percy) helped Teyoninhokarawen by sending farm machinery to Canada and by paying a large portion of his debts, including school fees for his son, who remained in Scotland until 1819.[29] Other people also provided money and gifts to help meet John Norton's needs, which he undoubtedly appreciated because he habitually found it difficult to meet his financial obligations.[30]

Teyoninhokarawen had five major concerns relative to indigenous affairs that he wanted to deal with while in Britain. One was his ongoing quest to ensure that the Six Nations acquired control over the Grand River Tract. The others centred on economic viability, independence, broader land concerns, and defence. These four interconnected issues arose from his expansive vision for the First Nations across the Great

---

25 Communication from Paul Barnaby to Timothy Willig, 23 July 2012; Sir Walter Scott to George Canning, 28 June 1816, transcribed by Jane Millgate, both courtesy of Dr Willig; Klinck, "Biographical Introduction," in *JMJN*, xc; Adam Wilson to JN, n.d. (c.1820), AO, F440.

26 Lord Levin to JN, 20 April 1818, AO, F440.

27 Morgan, *Emigrant's Note Book*, 190.

28 Henry Tatham to JN, 23 March 1816, AO, F440; Alexander Davison to JN, 17 June 1816, ibid.; JN to Sir Henry Torrens, 31 December 1815, published in American and British Claims Arbitration Tribunal, *Cayuga Indians*, 3:1146; Band, "Tatham's Indian Guns," 3–7.

29 J.O. Johnstone to JN, 28 August 1818, AO, F440; Johnstone to JN, 4 August 1819, ibid.; Klinck, "Biographical Introduction," in *JMJN*, lxxxiii–lxxxv.

30 E.g., Robert Barclay to JN, 7 April 1817, AO, F440; William Lyon Mackenzie to JN, 15 February 1823, ibid.

Lakes region, but reverberated within the Haudenosaunee communities that were the principal focus of his chiefly endeavours. Recognizing the changing environmental conditions as newcomer settlement grew, Teyoninhokarawen promoted the modernization of aboriginal farming, as he had before the war. This included granting some families specific lands within a tract rather than requiring that all land be owned collectively, because he thought such a change would foster prosperity and recognize valiant military service. As he always had argued, he believed that agrarian reform would use less land than traditional subsistence patterns required, and thus would respond to the period's changing geographical realities. Furthermore, as he had assumed before the war, he thought that increasing the number of natives who employed Euro-American farming technologies and practices would help generate the wealth needed to comfort and sustain people, while giving them the financial security they needed to withstand unwanted external pressures. Beyond confirming Haudenosaunee rights to Six Nations holdings along the Grand, he wanted the government in London to create a thirty-by-fifty-mile tract in the Lake Huron and Georgian Bay region, close to the Iroquois living north of Lake Erie. He thought Algonquians occupying land elsewhere in Upper Canada and natives wishing to leave American persecution behind could join the existing population there. Large as it was, this tract would not be big by traditional standards in terms of supporting indigenous subsistence activities, but it would be more than sufficient if people followed his farm-centred economic model. By connecting the Haudenosaunee to other indigenous communities with an enlarged and concentrated population, he believed that British chances of repelling an American invasion of Canada in a future conflict would be greater. Yet he also realized that aboriginal peoples needed to maintain strength in order to protect their interests within the colonial environment, so his dream likewise addressed that concern. Fundamentally, as before, he saw the Americans as posing the graver threat to the First Nations, which demanded an alliance with Great Britain. Nevertheless, in seeking an honourable relationship with the King's government he did not want to compromise aboriginal sovereignty more than necessary. Therefore, as part of his plan, he argued that the connection between the Crown and the First Nations should be managed through the army on the British side, rather than through provincial authorities. Not only would such an arrangement make the best use of the forces available to defeat the Americans, but it also would serve as a stronger affirmation of native autonomy between the allies than one based on a bond with a colonial government.[31] In 1816, after studying the issues associated with Canadian defence during the recent war, and after listening carefully to Teyoninhokarawen's views on the subject, the British government transferred control of the Indian Department in Upper Canada from the civil authorities to the commander-in-chief of British North America (where it remained until 1830, when the lieutenant-governor again assumed responsibility for its operations). That immediate postwar decision basically met Norton's concern and infuriated Canadian officials, but it did so in a bureaucratic manner that preserved the department's expertise and capacity to serve the interests of the empire, and probably represented something less than Teyoninhokarawen had wished, as the reorganization resulted in few changes in the department's personnel.[32]

The government in London expressed support for the creation of a new tract near Georgian Bay.[33] Later, some Potawatomis and other people moved from the United States to the area. Nevertheless, Norton's grand dream of a large and concentrated native territory would remain unfulfilled. Looking into the future from the 1810s, Norton presumably could not have imagined how rapidly the Euro-American population of the Great Lakes would multiply, creating a massive demographic imbalance between it and the First Nations, with a corresponding hunger on the part of newcomers for land. Likewise, he probably could not foresee

---

31 JN to John Harvey, 30 September 1816, LAC, RG8, 260:21–3; JN to J.F. Addison, 10 August 1818, ibid., 262:129–31; JN to Henry Goulburn, 1 December 1815 (three letters of the same date), published in American and British Claims Arbitration Tribunal, *Cayuga Indians*, 3:964–8; JN to Goulburn, 6 December 1816, ibid., 3:968–9; Klinck, "Biographical Introduction," in *JMJN*, lxxxi–lxxxv; Good, "Crown-Directed Colonization," 252–61. To a large degree, JN's views on the military arose from his wartime experiences and the words he had heard from other natives during and after the conflict. In 1817, for instance, he wrote that the disreputable behaviour of the Indian Department and Upper Canadian officials contrasted with that of the army: "I am assured that the Indians themselves are warmly attached to the military, and have never attributed to them any part of the sufferings which they have endured since the war" (JN to J.F. Addison, 8 May 1817, LAC, RG8, 261:205).

32 An example of JN's influence in convincing London to transfer the Indian Department from the civil to the military authorities is Lord Bathurst to Sir John Sherbrooke, 5 July 1817, LAC, RG7, Lower Canada, Despatches from the Colonial Secretary to Governors, G9, 188. An example of a negative Upper Canadian reaction is Francis Gore to Lord Bathurst, 2 September 1816, LAC, CO42, 357:308–13.

33 Henry Goulburn to JN, 2 January 1816, published in American and British Claims Arbitration Tribunal, *Cayuga Indians*, 3:970–2.

the great period of modernization in transportation, communication, bureaucratic efficiency, and other realms that soon would occur. All of these, directly or indirectly, would facilitate the ever-greater oppression of native societies by American citizens, British subjects, and their leaders, beyond the already painful levels that existed in 1815 and 1816, while modernization itself provided proportionally fewer benefits to indigenous people than it did to Euro-Americans.

While in the United Kingdom, John Norton asked the British government for permission to lead a war party into the United States should the Americans violate the aboriginal provision of the Treaty of Ghent by entering hostilities against distant tribes within the republic, such as the Sioux or Cherokees. Predictably, London made it plain that such an enterprise would not be acceptable, because it wanted to maintain peace with its former enemy.[34] While there was some extravagance in Teyoninhokarawen's request, he was not completely alone in thinking about these issues. British officials on the Canadian side of the Great Lakes region, for instance, reacted negatively to American aggression against the tribes of the upper Mississippi River immediately after the war, demanding action for what they saw as a violation of the spirit, if not necessarily the letter, of the treaty. They too would be frustrated by the imperial government's unwillingness to endanger Canadian security on behalf of the First Nations who lived within the republic's borders.

John Norton worked with Henry Goulburn to resolve the Grand River land issues, which resulted in success from Teyoninhokarawen's perspective. Goulburn told him that "I am directed to assure you that there is no difficulty on the part of His Majesty's government to admit that the grant of the Grand River, which was after the peace of 1783 made to the Five Nations and their posterity, is a grant as full and as binding upon the government as any other made in Canada to individual settlers." (That statement even seemed to include the disputed northern reaches of the Grand.) He also wrote that the Six Nations had

---

34 JN to Henry Goulburn, 1 December 1815, ibid., 3:965; Goulburn to JN, 2 January 1816, ibid., 3:972; JN to Goulburn, 6 January 1816, ibid., 3:974. JN also failed to have London take up the matter of annuities owed to the Cayugas for the sale of land in New York, which the state unilaterally stopped paying to members of the tribe who had moved to Canada. The British government in JN's time did not believe it had the authority to intervene, but ultimately negotiated a settlement with the United States in the 1920s, with payments occurring in the 1930s.

the authority to apportion land within the tract as they saw fit, while the Crown possessed no such right unless the chiefs asked it to intervene. He stated further – as Norton probably had hoped would happen when he agreed to support the British in 1812 – that the Six Nations contributions to Canadian defence had been appreciated (despite some challenges during the war), which, in addition to pre-war arguments, inspired London to consider Teyoninhokarawen's requests "with every disposition to meet your wishes." Beyond these, Goulburn noted that the government would direct colonial authorities to provide fair compensation for indigenous individuals who had suffered in the war, among both the Haudenosaunee and the other aboriginal people in Canada.[35] In response, Teyoninhokarawen expressed his thanks for the government's decisions, writing that "the friendly disposition testified ... towards the chiefs and warriors of the Five Nations, who have aided in the defence of the province, is completely satisfactory." Vindicated, he nevertheless had enough doubt that he asked that the Prince Regent make a "special confirmation" to secure the imperial government's decision from potential opposition by colonial officials or future changes in British policy.[36] As we saw in the Introduction, he had asked for the same from the King when visiting England in 1804 and 1805.

After a generally agreeable and pleasant visit to Great Britain, John and Catherine crossed the ocean again during the summer of 1816, arriving in Quebec in September. There, Teyoninhokarawen presented London's dispatches in support of the Six Nations claims to the new commander and governor-in-chief, Sir John Sherbrooke, who responded favourably and sent orders to Lieutenant-Governor Francis Gore in Upper Canada to comply with their directions. Upon reaching the Grand River in November, Norton shared the good news of his success at a council of the Six Nations. Although he expected Gore to resist, he presumably thought the colonial bureaucracy ultimately would have to obey the decisions of its masters on the other side of the Atlantic.[37] Tragically, he found that his accomplishments would come to naught. The Indian

---

35 Henry Goulburn to JN, 2 January 1816, ibid., 3:970–2. See also Extract from Goulburn to JN, 2 January 1816, Enclosed in John Brant and Robert Kerr to Robert Wilmot, 4 March 1822, LAC, CO42, 369:247.
36 JN to Henry Goulburn, 6 January 1816, published in American and British Claims Arbitration Tribunal, *Cayuga Indians*, 3:973–4 (quote on 973).
37 JN to Lord Teignmouth, 13 February 1817, BFBSA, F3/Shore.

Department's agents and other colonial officials, as they had in the past, demonstrated a vigorous resilience to anyone opposing their agenda by ignoring their superiors across the ocean, partly through exploiting the distance between Britain and Canada to avoid close monitoring of their conduct. They also took advantage of their control over the distribution of information, used their enviable political skills, and worked with their allies within native and colonial societies. In the end, they got their way, even though London had attempted to mitigate their abuses by transferring them to the authority of the military commander-in-chief. Not all employees of the department were corrupt, and we see better attitudes and actions elsewhere and at other times, but the story as it related to the Six Nations in Norton's day was a grim one indeed. At one point, Teyoninhokarawen lamented that "the declaration made by Mr Goulburn on the part of His Majesty's government in confirmation of Sir Frederick Haldimand's grant ... does not appear to be much respected by the Upper Canada government." He asserted that provincial authorities denied Haudenosaunee ownership of the upper part of the Grand River, and threatened their property farther south. He blamed this behaviour on "a speculating junto ... who hope by purchase, the connivance of the executive here, and a corrupt party among the Mohawks ... to cut and slice the Grand River in such a manner as to render it unworthy to hold." He went on to complain about how "disgusting" it was that while colonial officials were "granting lands to everyone" in the settler community to reward wartime services, these same people seemed to be "constantly plotting how to get ours from us."[38] Those endeavours of course represented a stunning betrayal of Teyoninhokarawen's hopes that Six Nations efforts to defend Canada would secure them in their holdings. In combating this treachery, Teyoninhokarawen's prominent acquaintances in Britain, such as William Wilberforce and Robert Barclay, offered to represent Haudenosaunee interests to the imperial government if he would provide authorization to do so from the chiefs along the tract.[39] In the early 1820s, Norton also helped organize another mission to seek justice in

---

38 JN to Sir Roger Sheaffe, 23 February 1822, BL, Northumberland MSS, 68:181. See also JN to the third Duke of Northumberland, ibid., 68:191–2; JN to Henry Goulburn, 15 March 1822, LAC, CO42, 369:276–7. (JN referred to Haldimand as "Sir" in recognition of the knighthood he received in 1785 after leaving Canada.)

39 Robert Barclay to JN, 7 April 1817, AO, F440.

England by John Brant (Ahyouweaghs) and his cousin Robert John-
son Kerr, authorized by the Six Nations "sachems and principal war
chiefs."[40] They retraced Norton's journeys to London, took copies of
Goulburn's correspondence with them, obtained help from the third
Duke of Northumberland, and had the government in London reaf-
firm its desire to place the Grand River lands in the hands of the Six
Nations in fee simple. In return, however, imperial officials required the
Six Nations to give up claims to the disputed northern portions of the
Haldimand Tract, which now had been opened for white settlement.
When Brant and Kerr tried to complete the process back in Canada,
the Indian Department thwarted them by saying, as if London's decision regarding the undisputed portions of the grant was conditional,
that a change to the land regime would require cancelling the distribution of presents and subjecting the people of the tract to all the laws of
Upper Canada. These twin assaults on the alliance relationship with
the Crown and the independence of the Haudenosaunee – which the
government of King George IV did not seem to have contemplated in
its decision – were enough for a majority of chiefs to reject the change to
fee simple ownership. Furthermore, the department's agents said that
acceptance of the change would require unanimous consent within the
community, which they knew was impossible within the political environment of the Grand River. Thus, once again, colonial officials prevented the Six Nations from achieving objectives which authorities in
London were willing to grant to them. Land controversies persisted
through the decades. One consequence, as noted earlier, was that the
Six Nations were forced onto a smaller tract on the Grand in the 1840s.
Along with charges of the colony's mismanagement of its obligations
to the Haudenosaunee, the issues that Joseph Brant, John Norton, John
Brant, William Kerr, and others had tried to resolve in the Georgian era
have plagued Crown-Haudenosaunee relations continuously through
time and, to a large degree, remain unresolved today.[41]

---

40 Robert Kerr and John Brant to Lord Bathurst, 6 September 1821, with Enclosures, 17
    February 1821 and n.d. (1821), published in American and British Claims Arbitration
    Tribunal, *Cayuga Indians*, 3:1046–51 (quote on 1046).
41 Isabel Kelsay, "Tekarihogen ... John Brant," *Dictionary of Canadian Biography*; C.M.
    Johnston, "Six Nations of the Grand River Valley, 1784–1847," in Smith and Rogers,
    Aboriginal Ontario, 178–9; Six Nations Council, *Six Miles Deep*; Six Nations Council,
    Six Nations of the Grand River; Klinck, "Biographical Introduction," in *JMJN*,

Teyoninhokarawen undoubtedly burned internally over the questions arising from the land controversy. In addition, the treatment of veterans and problems arising from other matters largely unconnected to territorial issues frustrated him as he tried to arrange pensions, presents, and other aid for warriors who had served with him in the war, or for the families of those who had died while defending the province. He did these things not only for the residents of the Grand River, but also for natives elsewhere in southwestern Upper Canada, especially for individuals who had been associated with him during the conflict, because the Indian Department treated these people with particular callousness. In contrast, the governor-in-chief attempted to have William Claus and other officials behave honourably in meeting the Crown's commitments and without prejudicing the rights of those associated with Norton.[42] About the same time, Lord Bathurst wanted Teyoninhokarawen to report on Anglo-Haudenosaunee affairs, because he wished to maintain good relations with the Six Nations but remained uneasy about the management of indigenous affairs in Canada.[43] Beyond that affirmation of Norton's expertise and local knowledge, British officials called upon him for other services. For instance, he received a request to investigate whether four American soldiers who had been taken prisoner at the River Raisin in 1813 and then adopted by native people wanted to return home, and to help them if they wished to do so.[44]

---

lxxxviii–lxxxix; Good, "Crown-Directed Colonization," 274–85; Elbourne, "Broken Alliances." For John Brant's views and frustrations, see Brant to the third Duke of Northumberland, 6 June 1823, BL, Northumberland MSS, 68:185–7; for the demand for unanimity, see JN to Northumberland, 30 September 1823, ibid., 68:192–3. For a summary of the Kerr/Brant journey, see Paxton, *Brant*, 80–1.

42 E.g., J.F. Addison to JN, 30 November 1816, LAC, RG8, 1241:36–7; Addison to JN, 23 December 1816, ibid., 1241:40–1; Addison to JN, 25 January 1817, ibid., 1241:51–2; JN to Addison, 11? February 1817, ibid., 261:25–33; JN to William Claus, 20 February 1817, ibid., 261:47–48; Addison to JN, 22 March 1817, ibid., 1241:70–1; JN to Addison, 9 May 1817, ibid., 261:204–12; Addison to JN, 10 June 1817, ibid., 1241:87; JN to Addison, 16 August 1817, ibid., 261:280–2; JN to Addison, 16 June 1818, ibid., 262:88–92; JN to George Bowles, 20 February 1819, ibid., 262:288–91. Issues related to pensions began during the war itself (e.g., JN to Edward MacMahon, 26 October 1814, LAC, RG10, 3:1546–8).

43 J.F. Addison to JN, 15 April 1817, LAC, RG8, 1241:77–8.

44 J.F. Addison to JN, 22 February 1817, ibid., 1241:59–60. See also Sir John Sherbrooke to Lord Bathurst, 25 May 1817, ibid., 1240:112–13. For examples related to other matters, see Addison to JN, 29 March 1817, ibid., 1241:72–3; Addison to JN, 26 April

While worrying about issues of land tenure, autonomy, and moderniization, Norton attended to the needs of his family and to the broader community in other ways. He worked his farm, Hillhouse, on high ground overlooking the Grand River below today's Caledonia (apparently taking up residence there after the war). He also continued serving the Church, including baptizing people along the Grand in the absence of Anglican clergymen.[45] The missionary to the Six Nations and rector of Niagara, the Reverend Robert Addison, hoped that Teyoninhokarawen would translate all of the Gospels into Mohawk, noting that "Mr Norton, the great chief ... is the only person capable of such work, and if he undertakes it he will execute it well."[46]

Final Years

In a violent confrontation on 23 July 1823, John Norton wounded an Onondaga, Joseph Crawford (Kahishorowanen), while suffering a grazing wound to his head. Also known as Big Arrow, Crawford died two days later. He was twenty-eight, married to the daughter of an Oneida chief, and had two children. Norton was fifty-two. Observers then and since have called the event a duel, but period descriptions indicate that it occurred in the heat of an argument over the honour of Teyoninhokarawen's wife, Catherine, without the gentlemanly characteristics we normally associate with the idea of a duel. Norton had fostered Crawford since childhood, and he was the warrior we met earlier who an American officer shot unfairly in 1813. He lived with the Nortons, and may have had an affair with Catherine. According to Teyoninhokarawen, when he confronted Joseph Crawford the younger man dared him to a fight. Norton told him to choose his weapon; Kahishorowanen loaded a pistol, and Norton did the same. Teyoninhokarawen's adversary approached within a few feet, fired, lunged at him, and grabbed at Norton's gun. It fired, and the ball shot down through Crawford's thigh. Afterwards, Teyoninhokarawen recorded, "When I saw the poor young man stretched on the

1817, ibid., 1241:83; Addison to JN, 30 August 1817, ibid., 1241:99; Addison to JN, 27 December 1817, ibid., 1241:105–6.

45 Klinck, "Biographical Introduction," in *JMJN*, lxxxiii–lxxxviii; Habermehl and Combe, *Robert Addison*, 82; JN to the second Duke of Northumberland, 25 June 1816, BL, Northumberland MSS, 68:98.

46 Robert Addison Report and Journal, 6 September 1817, quoted in Young, "Addison," 184.

ground, and the recollections of past times crowded into my mind, pity succeeded to every other feeling."[1] He then wrote to the attorney-general of Upper Canada offering himself for trial at Niagara.[2]

Surviving documents tend to be mixed about Catherine's conduct but sympathetic towards her husband; yet it is nearly impossible to understand the intricacies of a marriage after the passing of two centuries.[3] Teyoninhokarawen feared that Crawford's relations would seek to avenge the death by killing him, although Norton's son thought that he could follow Mohawk customs by "covering" the grave through a condolence ceremony and by distributing gifts.[4] Justice came through the white court system at Niagara, however, with John Norton being found guilty of manslaughter and fined twenty-five pounds, which was a relatively light punishment. Even so, one newspaper claimed Teyoninhokarawen endured more than was necessary, noting that his "conduct in the affair (a duel with another chief) was truly honourable, and he would no doubt have been acquitted altogether if he had not, from feelings of delicacy, withheld his best defence" (presumably by revealing details about his wife and Joseph Crawford that he preferred to keep to himself).[5] Catherine Norton sought a reconciliation with her husband, hoping that God would forgive her sins and asking him not to forsake

---

1 JN to John Harvey, n.d. (August–September 1823), AO, F440.

2 Robert Thomson to JN, 8 August 1823, ibid.; William Claus to Archibald Johnson, 6 August 1823, LAC, RG10, 15:12240. See AO, F440 for additional documents. For more on the duel and trial, see Klinck, "Biographical Introduction," in *JMJN*, xcii–xciv.

3 E.g., Robert Thomson to Unknown, n.d. (1823, after the duel), AO, F440. In contrast to most commentators, however, JN's long-standing enemy in the Mohawk world, George Martin, suggested that the confrontation that led to Joseph Crawford's death was JN's fault (Martin to William Claus, 29 July 1823, LAC, MG19–F1, 12:185–6).

4 John Norton Jr to JN, n.d. (1823, after the duel), AO, F440.

5 *Gleaner* (Niagara), 20 September 1823. For JN's account of the trial, see JN to John Harvey, October? 1823, AO, F440. See also *Canadian Times*, 7 October 1823, which covered the trial in some detail, with the story reprinted in Washington by the *Daily National Intelligencer*, 21 October 1823, which demonstrated some ongoing awareness and interest in JN in the United States. In a brief note in an earlier edition, the *Intelligencer* commented sarcastically: "A duel was lately fought ... between Colonel Norton, the famous chief, and another chief of his neighbourhood, in which the former was slightly, and the latter mortally wounded. The savages are progressing in the arts of *civilization*" (2 September 1823).

her.[6] Nevertheless, he decided to leave his wife, but made provision for her financial needs. She then moved to the Delaware Moravian mission on the Thames River.[7]

Her husband left the province soon after his trial, travelling far south to the Cherokees, accompanied by his first cousin's son, John Charles Wolateagh, who had come to Canada in 1810 after Norton's earlier journey to his father's people. (Teyoninhokarawen had been planning such a journey for several years, but the duel served as an incentive to go.) A third man went with them, which one record suggests was Norton's son, but we do not know if that is correct. John Norton rented his farm, and hoped to support himself through hunting until he could pay his debts. He did not plan to stay in the south, and even thought of visiting England in 1824.[8]

John Norton's party travelled quickly, passing through St Louis on the Mississippi River on the way south in November 1823 (and raising suspicions about Teyoninhokarawen's motivations due to native-newcomer tensions at that moment).[9] At some point in 1824, the group

---

6 Catherine Norton to JN, 3 August 1823, AO, F440.

7 Lukenbach and Haman, "Extract from the Diary of the Indian Congregation at Fairfield," 146–7.

8 JN to J.F. Addison, 10 August 1818, LAC, RG8, 262:129–31; John Harvey to JN, 13 April 1822, AO, F440; JN to Unknown, October? 1823, ibid.; JN to the third Duke of Northumberland, 30 September 1823, BL, Northumberland MSS, 68:192–3; Robert Addison Report and Journal, 1 January 1824, quoted in Young, "Addison," 189; Klinck, "Biographical Introduction," in *JMJN*, xcii–xciv. The document that suggests JN's son went with him is San Fernando de Bexar, Memorandum, 30 October 1824, United States Senate, *Affairs of the Mexican Kickapoo Indians* 3:1902. Yet data from 1861 suggests that the third person may not have been his son John, who had a son born in 1825 in Canada and who may have had trouble returning home in time to have fathered a child who came into the world that year (LAC, RG31, Canada West Personal Census, Kent County, 1861, 5317). The relationship in which JN's son John had been born produced an elusive second child. It is possible that this individual may have been the third person, but the absence of any mention of such an individual in the historical record suggests that he or she had died some years earlier or otherwise no longer had contact with JN.

9 *Louisville Public Advertiser*, 31 January 1824. (Although published in Louisville, the report came from St Louis.) In a larger article titled "Indian Outrages," the *Advertiser* noted: "About eight weeks since, Colonel Norton, the celebrated British Indian partisan, who is well known on the Niagara frontier, passed through this place for the Arkansas under the pretence of visiting his Indian relations in that quarter. He was dressed in military costume and accompanied by two Indians." If the claim

reached the Presbyterian Dwight Mission to the Cherokees in the Arkansas Territory (near today's Russellville). Many of the Cherokees whom he had visited in 1809–10 had moved there from the east by this time, including his cousin Tahneh (Naomi), to whom he returned her son after his long absence. Wolateagh, sadly, only lived for about a year. According to a late 1830s source, he died in an accident when thrown from a horse while intoxicated, but contemporary records from the 1820s said he passed away due to "pulmonary consumption" (or tuberculosis).[10]

As well as getting away from the troubles in Canada, Norton wanted to "renew the old friendship between the northern Indians and the Cherokees."[11] He also dreamt of journeying across the southerly regions of what then was Mexican territory to the Pacific Ocean, partly along the Santa Fe Trail, thinking he might find a place in the west that could serve as a secure and congenial homeland where native peoples could live beyond the corruptions and controls of white society.[12] In fact, in October 1824 he was in San Antonio, where he served as a speaker for a large group of Shawnees who asked Mexican authorities for permission to emigrate from the United States to the Colorado River because of their land losses in the American republic.[13] People in Canada at the time did not seem to know that he had travelled to Mexican territory, because they continued to send mail to him in the area around the Dwight Mission.[14] If mail did reach him, he may have heard about three milestones: the birth of his grandson in 1825, the death of William Claus in 1826, and his wife's passing in 1827.[15]

---

about the "costume" was correct, it might have been a chief's coat of the kind white allies gave native people.

10 Washburn, *Reminiscences*, 153–4 (alcohol); "Journal at Dwight," 1825, 246–7; "Journal at Dwight," 1828, 311 (consumption).

11 Communication from Charles Rees noted in the Cherokee Mission Diary at Oochgeelogy, Georgia, 18 August 1828, published in Crews and Starbuck, *Records of the Moravians*, 8:n.p. (forthcoming).

12 Klinck, Biographical Introduction,' in *JMJN*, xcv–xcvi.

13 JN, Petition, 25 October 1824 and Related Documents, published in United States Senate, *Affairs of the Mexican Kickapoo Indians* 3:1901–2.

14 *Arkansas Weekly Gazette*, 12 October 1824, 11 October 1825.

15 LAC, RG31, Canada West Personal Census, Kent County, 1861, 5317; Robert S. Allen, "Claus, William," *Dictionary of Canadian Biography*; Lukenbach and Haman, "Extract from the Diary of the Indian Congregation at Fairfield," 146–7.

He intended to return to Upper Canada. We know this from a letter dated November 1825, sent from Laredo on the Rio Grande River to a friend in the province.[16] Sadly, he did not come home: John Norton died sometime in 1827.[17] He was fifty-six. The record of his death is vague, suggesting that there was nothing exceptional about his demise, and thus we might wonder if some sort of illness carried him off.[18]

Fifty-one years later, an elderly veteran of the War of 1812, John Smoke Johnson, who had not seen Teyoninhokarawen since 1823, misremembered him as a "Scotchman" (along with being confused about other facts related to Teyoninhokarawen, as we would expect with the passage of time and the constraints of age). Johnson's mistakes symbolized much of the John Norton legacy at that point in history. Teyoninhokarawen's unique and important document, part of which we have explored in this book, lay dormant in England. Most of the people who had known him had passed away. The memories of his life within, and contributions to, native society largely had been forgotten. Newspaper and other publications that mentioned him in his day no longer were read. Official records related to his life had been filed away and would not begin to be examined by modern scholars for two more decades, when Douglas Brymner, an archivist in Ottawa, attempted to understand Norton's story, adding to the limited efforts of earlier researchers. (One such person, for instance, was William L. Stone, who knew of him through researching his biography of Joseph Brant published in the 1830s.) From the above exploration of just one of the major components of Teyoninhokarawen's journal – the section on the War of 1812 – examined along with other documentation and scholarly efforts, we can appreciate how significant Norton was in First Nations history and

---

16 *Colonial Advocate*, 9 March 1826.

17 Communication from Charles Rees noted in the Cherokee Mission Diary at Oochgeelogy, Georgia, 18 August 1828, published in Crews and Starbuck, *Records of the Moravians*, 8:n.p. (forthcoming), recorded JN's death the previous year. Until recently, people have assumed JN died in October 1831, based on information from a putative nephew, Samuel Stevens (T. Gladwin Hurd to Fox Maule, 4 September 1851, LAC, RG8, 271:107), but the mission record seems definitive in comparison. Stevens wanted to collect several years' worth of JN's pension, since JN or his agent had not claimed payments after 24 February 1826 (J.B. Glegg, Memorandum, latter 1820s?, ibid., 271:109).

18 Searches by several historians for information on JN's passing have failed to produce more data.

in that history's wider connections to the past, a good portion of which still has consequences for people today. As stressed in the Introduction to this book, much remains to explore, evaluate, and say about this fascinating individual. The eighty-five-year-old John Smoke Johnson, while forgetting a few things, recalled – probably accurately, given other people's observations in the historical record – that John Norton was "a good-natured man" with "a very good character," who "was a great warrior and very brave."[19]

---

19 Albert Johnson to Lyman C. Draper, quoting John Smoke Johnson, 11 February 1878, State Historical Society of Wisconsin, Draper Manuscripts, Series F, Brant Papers, 14:23–4. Johnson's view that JN was a Scot, however, could reflect his opinion that identity came through one's mother's line, as was traditional in Haudenosaunee society. See also Brymner, *Report on Canadian Archives*, 1897.

Appendix A: The Six Nations Population on the Grand River, 1811 and 1814

This list of the Six Nations population along the Grand River Tract on the eve of the War of 1812 simplifies a more complex and somewhat confusing period document.[1] Aside from members of the Haudeno-saunee community (comprising the Six Nations and closely aligned people like the Delawares), there were individuals possessing other indigenous ancestries (such as Cherokees) who lived within the Iroquois community, as did some Euro-Americans and Afro-Americans, but the original record integrated them into the Haudenosaunee list for the most part. (A portion of the people lived in the nationally designated villages indicated on the Grand River map presented elsewhere in this book; others had homes outside of these settlements across the tract.) Thus, this list presents the population by cultural affiliations deter-mined by the census takers, largely based on residency; but we should remember that the Six Nations of the Grand formed a more diverse society than it indicates. This was due to the adoption of outsiders, the in-migration of people of a range of indigenous and non-aboriginal backgrounds, marriages across national boundaries, the birth of chil-dren from mixed unions, and personal preferences in choosing cultural alignments. Beyond the Iroquois communities of the Grand, there also were white, black, and Mississauga people who lived there separately from the Haudenosaunee, and who did not appear in the original docu-ment. The ratio of warriors to population in the early 1800s was 1:4.8,

---

1 Number of the Different Nations of Indians Living at the Grand River, Taken in June 1810 and 1811, n.d. (1811?), LAC, MG19–F1, 10:29.

which indicates that the Six Nations of the Grand River had a combatant strength of 400 men.[2]

Mohawks	436	
Oneidas and Tuscaroras	348[3]	
Onondagas	225	
Cayugas	412	
Senecas	39	
Akwesasnes	19	(from the Seven Nations of Canada)
Delawares	303	
Montours	31	(diverse Six Nations and other people)
Nanticokes	10	
Tutelos	105	
TOTAL	1,928	

A comparable list from the summer of 1814 counted 1,702 Six Nations people, exclusive of 32 Mississaugas who were not part of the Haudenosaunee community included in a tally of 1,734. The difference of 226 Iroquois individuals (1,928 vs 1,702) represented about 12 per cent of the 1811 population, assuming that these statistics were reasonably correct numerically, as they seem to be.[4] This substantial difference – predating additional losses to come later in the war – reflects deaths in, or consequent to, battle; other war-related mortality brought on through exposure, starvation, and increased vulnerability to illness; and the decision of some people to move away, either permanently or temporarily. Beyond this reduction in the size of the population, many people suffered physical wounds or injuries, some of which permanently affected their lives; and, of course, the war created both short- and long-lasting psychological and emotional trauma, the extent of which lies beyond history's ability to measure at two hundred years' distance. As we saw earlier, the majority of people abandoned the Grand River Tract late in 1813 when it seemed threatened by American forces. When they returned in 1814, they found

---

2 Benn, *Iroquois in the War of 1812*, 195–6; JN to J.F. Addison, 16 August 1817, LAC, RG8, 261:281.

3 It is difficult to separate the Oneidas and Tuscaroras because one group of 158 people on the 1811 list, designated as Aughhquagas (or Oquagas), probably included both tribes along with the separate entries on the same document for 143 Tuscaroras and 47 Oneidas.

4 A Return of the Indians on the Grand River, August 1814, LAC, MG19–F1, 10:229.

that disloyal settlers who had aligned with the invaders had robbed and vandalized their homes. Colonial authorities provided compensation for war losses to property, as well as food and supplies, along with pensions to wounded men and the families of the dead, but of course such payments, however welcomed and supportive, never could assuage the personal losses suffered by the Haudenosaunee fully.[5] From the above census records, the destruction of their property, the narrative left to us by John Norton, and the other surviving records of the conflict, we can assume the Six Nations of the Grand suffered on a scale comparable to the worst-afflicted indigenous and newcomer communities across the Great Lakes region.

---

5 Benn, *Iroquois in the War of 1812*, 122, 179–80, 184.

Appendix B: John Norton's Spelling of Native Names Where It Differed from Current Practice

This list presents Teyoninhokarawen's spelling of indigenous names in the part of his journal presented above where his use differed from today's common orthography, used in this book. Other sections of his journal and his broader correspondence record a range of additional spellings (including deviations from those below).

TODAY'S COMMON USE	NORTON'S SPELLING
Cattaraugus	Cataragaras
Cayuga	Cayugwa
Cuyahoga	Caighhague
Chippewa (Anishinabe or Ojibwa)	Chippawa
Claus, Joseph	Claws, Joseph
Conestoga (Susquehannock)	Conestogue
Kahnawake	Caghnawague
Kanesatake	Kaneghsatague
Kekionga	Kikaiskigh
Kickapoo	Kikapoo
Mackinac/Michilimackinac	Michillimackinac
Mississauga	Missisaga and Messisaga
Muskogee (Creek)	Muscogui
Munsee (Delaware)	Munsey
Myeerah	Mea Ire
Nottawagee (Iroquois or Haudenosaunee)	Nottowegui
Odawa	Ottawa
Oneida	Oniada
Onondaga	Onondague, but he also used Onondaga

Potawatomi	Poutewattomi
Sauk	Sakie
Scajaquada Creek	Skeuntyoghkwati Creek
Seneca	Ondowaga, but he also used Seneca
Shawnee	Shawanon
Sounehhooway (Thomas Splitlog)	Tharoutorea, and likely Karonteoreas
Tecumseh	Tecumthi and Tecumthe
Tekarihogen, Henry	Tekarihhogea and Tekarihogea
Tippecanoe	Tippicanoes
Wapakoneta	Wiappaghkwanetta

Acknowledgments

Like almost all historians I am indebted to many people, whose generosity helped me produce this book. Naturally, my greatest obligation is to John Norton himself for recording his story in expectation of sharing it with the public, although his ambition was not realized until long after his passing. I am most grateful to the twelfth Duke of Northumberland (Ralph Percy), who kindly agreed to let me publish this selection from Norton's original manuscript that resides in His Grace's collection. I am thankful for the Champlain Society's support for my edition of Norton's journal to stand beside its own fine volumes. Particular gratitude goes to four fellow historians. The first is Timothy Willig, who was most generous in sharing his research on Teyoninhokarawen as well as discussing the historiographical challenges we faced as I prepared this study, and as Dr Willig worked on the first full biography of this fascinating person (which my effort is not meant to be). There is no question that my book would have been a weaker contribution to scholarship without this help, and I hope my research will benefit his forthcoming study of John Norton. The second is Dianne Graves, who undertook valuable research for me in England. In addition, Donald Graves and Stuart Sutherland have shared their research and thoughts on the War of 1812 with me over many years with generosity and acuity.

Richard D. Merritt warrants my gratitude for regularly sharing his research, answering questions, and taking the time to provide comments and advice on a draft of my manuscript to strengthen it as it made its way towards publication. Jennafer Da Silva receives my appreciation for research she did as an undergraduate assistant at Ryerson University. I would like to express my appreciation to the following people for their kindnesses in sharing research and thoughts – often in detail and over a number of years: Dorothy and Marjorie Bain, Fred Bassett, Clark Bernat, Sara Byers, Mairi Cowan, Cynthia Cumfer, Heriberto Dixon, Brian Dunnigan, William Engelbrecht, David Faux, Alan Finlayson, Jim Folts, Michael Galbon, Peter Gibbons, Reg Good, Tanya Grodzinski, Tom Hatley, Laurence Hauptman, Robert Henderson, Richard Hill, Dennis Hillis, Keith Jamieson, Jon Jouppien, Laurie Leclair, Susan Lewthwaite, John MacLeod, Tom McCullough, Gerry Neilands, Trudy Nicks, Alison Norman, Christine Patrick, Andrew Potter, Theresa Regnier, Linda Sabathy-Judd, Roger Sharpe, Raymond Skye, Donald Smith, Peter Smith, Marianne Stopp, John Triggs, Anne Unyi, Ouinai Walosi, Gavin Watt Sr, Paula Whitlow, Roy Winders, and the late William Sturtevant.

In addition, I acknowledge my gratitude to the staff at the University of Toronto and Ryerson University libraries, and to the people at similar institutions who cooperated with them in providing interlibrary loan services, along with the individuals in various archives, museums, and similar institutions who were so helpful answering questions during this research project.

As always, I thank Ann Joan Procyk for her excellent editorial advice and for listening patiently while I worked through my thoughts in conversation over dinner. I also would like to recognize the many people through the years from within and beyond the indigenous world who contributed to my formation as a historian through their conversation and the texts they wrote, especially the participants at the Conference on Iroquois Research, who have stimulated my thoughts almost every year since I first attended its annual meetings in 1990. This book reflects their innumerable contributions to my development. Two scholars who require special mention are individuals I never met – James J. Talman and Carl F. Klinck – who brought the *Journal of Major John Norton* to the public's attention in 1970 after a century and a half of obscurity, and consequently made my work easier and richer.

I began writing this book before moving from the museum world into full-time academia, and so I did not have access to the funding normally available for such projects and thus, like many historians, paid my own research expenses. Once I came to Ryerson University in 2008, however, I benefited from several grants (such as a Faculty of Arts Special Projects Grant that allowed Michael Morrish to draw the maps of the lower Great Lakes and the Grand River Tract that grace this book; I also express my gratitude to Michael for his work). Importantly, this book has been published with the help of a grant from the Federation for the Humanities and Social Sciences, through the Awards to Scholarly Publications Program, using funds provided by the Social Sciences and Humanities Research Council of Canada.

Finally, I wish to acknowledge my appreciation to the people who worked on creating an attractive and accessible publication at the University of Toronto Press. Len Husband was a most enthusiastic acquisitions editor, while a range of other individuals worked on bringing this book out, including Frances Mundy, Marilyn McCormack, Breanna Muir, and people who quietly did their jobs in the background. As well, I would like to extend my appreciation to Jonathan Adjemian of The Editing Company for his fine work in copy editing the text, and to Teresa Wingfield for her excellent design work. I also would like to thank the anonymous reviewers of the manuscript for their helpful insights, and the various decision-makers at UTP who supported this project.

Image Credits

1 *John Norton, Teyoninhokarawen, the Mohawk Chief*, Mary Ann Knight, 1805. Courtesy of Library and Archives Canada, 1984–119–1. Quote: Charles William Janson, *The Stranger in America* (London: James Cundee, 1807), 287n.

2 *The Three Cherokees, Came over from the Head of the River Savanna to London, 1762* (detail), attributed to George Bickham the Younger, c.1762. © Trustees of the British Museum, 1982, U.3745.

3 *Fort Niagara from the Canadian Shore*, Anonymous, c.1780. Courtesy of the Old Fort Niagara Association, OF1989.102.

4 Untitled (Mohawk schoolroom), James Peachey, 1786, published in Daniel Claus (attributed author), *A Primer for the Mohawk Children: Waerighwaghsawe Iksaongoenwa* (London: C. Buckton, 1786). Courtesy of the John Carter Brown Library, Brown University, 06809–1.

5 *Indian of the Nation of the Shawanoes* (1796), Jean-Baptiste Pierre Tardieu after Victor Collot, 1805, published in Collot, *A Journey in North America* (Paris: Arthus Bertrand, 1826). Courtesy of the John Carter Brown Library, Brown University, 06078–6.

6 *A View of Fort George, Navy Hall, and New Niagara, Taken from the United States' Fort of Old Niagara*, Edward Walsh, "Sketches from Nature …," 1804. Courtesy of the William L. Clements Library, University of Michigan, FF 1803 Wa, Accession P-201.

7 *Thayendanegea (Joseph Brant)*, William Berczy, c.1807. Courtesy of the National Gallery of Canada, 5777.

8 *Mohawk Village on the Grand River or Ouse*, Elizabeth Simcoe, c.1795. © The British Library Board, c13588–09.

9 *Bust of a Mohawk Indian on the Grand River* (detail), Sempronius Stretton, 1804. Courtesy of Library and Archives Canada, 1990–336–1.13V.

10 *Costume of Domiciliated Indians of North America*, Joseph Stadler after George Heriot, published in Heriot, *Travels through the Canadas* (London: Richard Phillips, 1807). Courtesy of the Toronto Public Library, JRR 2046.

11 Untitled (native woman), attributed to George Heriot, but likely James Peachey, late 1700s. Courtesy of the Musée du Nouveau Monde.

12 John Norton (and Joseph Brant?), trans., *Nene Karighwiyoston Tsinihorighhoten ne Saint John: The Gospel according to Saint John* (London: Phillips and Fardon for the British and Foreign Bible Society, 1804). Courtesy of the Toronto Public Library.

13 Pipe Tomahawk, 54 × 24 × 4 cm, c.1804–5. © Trustees of the British Museum, Am1981,17.1.

14 *Colonel William Claus*, Andrew Plimer, c.1792. Courtesy of Library and Archives Canada, 1989–407–5.

15 *Sir George Prevost*, Robert Field, c.1810. Courtesy of Library and Archives Canada, 1948–125–1.

16 *Map of Detroit River and Adjacent Country, from an Original Drawing by a British Engineer* (1812; details), Henry Schenk Tanner, 1813. Courtesy of Library and Archives Canada, 80101/189.

17 *The Battle of Queenston, October 13th, 1812*, Thomas Sutherland after James Dennis, 1816. Courtesy of the McCord Museum, M924.

18 *View of Amherstburg*, Margaret Reynolds, 1813. Courtesy of Parks Canada Agency – Fort Malden National Historic Site, FF77.44.1.

19 *Deputation of Indians from the Chippewa Tribes to the President of Upper Canada, Sir Frederic Ph. Robinson, KCB, Major-General, etc. in 1815*, Rudolf Steiger, 1815, Courtesy of the National Gallery of Canada, 30237.

20 *Plan of York* (1818), George Phillpotts, 1823. Courtesy of Library and Archives Canada, H2/440/Toronto/1818 (1823).

21 *Fort Meigs* (1813), Anonymous after Joseph Larwell, c.1846, published in Henry Howe, *Historical Collections of Ohio* (Cincinnati: Author, 1850). Courtesy of the Toronto Public Library.

22 *The Niagara Frontier*, published in Francis Hall, *Travels through the United States and Canada in 1816 and 1817* (London: Longman, Hurst, Rees, Orme, and Brown, 1818). Courtesy of the Toronto Public Library.

23 *Capture of Fort George* (1813), William Strickland, published in the *Port Folio*, 1817. Courtesy of the Samuel E. Weir Collection, RiverBrink Art Museum, 009.41.

24 *No. IV, Upper Canada, Plan of Niagara River* (detail), A. Gray, 1810. Courtesy of Library and Archives Canada, e010700978.

25 *Colonel Johnson's Mounted Men Charging a Party of British Artillerists and Indians at the Battle Fought near Moraviantown* (1813), Ralph Rawdon

after Anonymous, 1814–17. Courtesy of Library and Archives Canada, C-007763.

26 *The House of Captn Brandt, a Celebrated Indian Chief, at the Head of the Lake (Ontario)*, Edward Walsh, "Sketches from Nature …," 1804. Courtesy of the William L. Clements Library, University of Michigan, FF 1803 Wa, Accession P-201.

27 *Quebec from Cape Diamond* (detail), Frederick Christian Lewis after George Heriot, published in Heriot, *Travels through the Canadas* (London: Richard Phillips, 1807). Courtesy of Library and Archives Canada, 1989–479–8:B.

28 *Deputation of Indians from the Mississippi Tribes to the Governor-General of British North America, Sir George Prevost*, Rudolf Steiger, 1814. Courtesy of Library and Archives Canada, 1989–264.

29 *Ground Sketch of Niagara Falls and the Rapids and Vicinity*, Samuel and Josiah Neele after Robert Gourlay, 1822, published in Gourlay, *Statistical Account of Upper Canada* (London: Simpkin and Marshall, 1822). Courtesy of the Toronto Public Library.

30 *View of the Falls of Niagara from the Bank near Burch's Mills*, Frederick Christian Lewis after George Heriot, published in Heriot, *Travels through the Canadas* (London: Richard Phillips, 1807). Courtesy of the Toronto Public Library, JRR 1325.

31 *Battle of Niagara from a Sketch by Major Riddle* (1814), William Strickland, published in the *Port Folio*, 1815. Courtesy of the Samuel E. Weir Collection, RiverBrink Art Museum, 009.21.

32 *Siege and Defence of Fort Erie* (1814; detail), John Vallance after D.B. Douglas, published in John Lewis Thomson, *Historical Sketches of the Late War between the United States and Great Britain* (Philadelphia: Thomas DeSilver, 1816). Courtesy of the John Carter Brown Library, 03897–10.

33 *Battalion Infantry*, Charles Hamilton Smith, 1815. Courtesy of the Anne S.K. Brown Military Collection, Brown University Library, 2-SIZE UC485.G7 S65x 1815.

34 *London, Taken Near the New Custom House*, Robert Havell after Thomas Sautelle Roberts, 1816. © Trustees of the British Museum, 1880,1113.1633.

Bibliography

"A." "Sketch of the Life of Lieutenant-Colonel Towson." *The Portico* 3, no. 1 (1817): 211–23.

Abler, Thomas S. *Cornplanter: Chief Warrior of the Allegany Senecas.* Syracuse: Syracuse University Press, 2007.

Allen, Robert S. *His Majesty's Indian Allies: British Indian Policy and the Defence of Canada, 1774–1815.* Toronto: Dundurn, 1992.

Alnwick Castle, Duke of Northumberland Collection. John Norton. "Journal of a Voyage, of a Thousand Miles, down the Ohio; from the Grand River, Upper Canada; – Visit to the Country of the Cherokees: – through the States of Kentucky and Tenessee [*sic*]: and an Account of the Five Nations, Etc. from an Early Period, to the Conclusion of the Late War between Great Britain and America."

American and British Claims Arbitration Tribunal. *Cayuga Indians.* 4 vols. Washington, DC: Government Printing Office, 1913.

Anderson, Chad Leslie. "The Storied Landscape of Iroquoia: History and Memory on the New York Frontier, 1750–1840." PhD diss., University of California, Davis, 2012.

Anger, Donald G. *"Scruples of Conscience": The War of 1812 in the Sugarloaf Settlement.* Port Colborne: Port Colborne Historical and Marine Museum, 2008.

Antal, Sandy. *A Wampum Denied: Procter's War of 1812.* Ottawa: Carleton University Press, 1997.

Aquila, Richard. *The Iroquois Restoration: Iroquois Diplomacy on the Colonial Frontier, 1701–1754.* Detroit: Wayne State University Press, 1983.

Archives of Ontario (AO). F440. John Norton Fonds.

– F1015, MU1063. Alexander Fraser Fonds.

– MS234. Peter Russell Copy Book, Indian Correspondence.

Armstrong, Frederick H. *Handbook of Upper Canadian Chronology*, rev. ed. Toronto: Dundurn, 1985.

Atkinson, James R. *Splendid Land, Splendid People: The Chickasaw Indians to Removal*. Tuscaloosa: University of Alabama Press, 2004.

Band, Robert W. "Tatham's Indian Guns: A Gift for Mohawk Warriors." *Arms Collecting* 37, no. 1 (1999): 3–7.

Barbuto, Richard V. *Niagara 1814: America Invades Canada*. Lawrence: University of Kansas Press, 2000.

Benn, Carl. "The Military Context of the Founding of Toronto." *Ontario History* 81, no. 4 (1989): 303–22.

– "Iroquois Warfare, 1812–14." In *War along the Niagara: Essays on the War of 1812 and Its Legacy*, edited by Arthur Bowler, 60–76. Youngstown: Old Fort Niagara Association, 1991.

– *Historic Fort York, 1793–1993*. Toronto: Natural Heritage, 1993.

– "The Iroquois Nadir of 1796." In *Niagara 1796: The Fortress Possessed*, edited by Brian L. Dunnigan, 50–8. Youngstown: Old Fort Niagara Association, 1996.

– *The Iroquois in the War of 1812*. Toronto: University of Toronto Press, 1998.

– "Native Military Forces in the Great Lakes Theatre, 1812–15." In *The Incredible War of 1812: A Military History*, by J. Mackay Hitsman, 1965; rev. by Donald E. Graves, 302–3. Toronto: Robin Brass, 1999.

– *The War of 1812*. Oxford: Osprey, 2002.

– "Brant, Joseph." In *Oxford Dictionary of National Biography*, edited by Colin Matthews et al., 7:377–9. Oxford: Oxford University Press, 2004.

– "Norton, John." In *Oxford Dictionary of National Biography*, edited by Colin Matthews et al., 41:177–9. Oxford: Oxford University Press, 2004.

– "Iroquois Confederacy." In *Encyclopedia of the New American Nation*, edited by Paul Finkelman, 2:240–4. Detroit: Charles Scribner's Sons, 2006.

– *Fort York: A Short History and Guide*. Toronto: City of Toronto Culture, 2007.

– *Mohawks on the Nile: Natives among the Canadian Voyageurs in Egypt, 1884–1885*. Toronto: Dundurn, 2009.

– "Iroquois External Affairs, 1807–15: The Limitations of the New Order." In *The Sixty Years' War for the Great Lakes, 1754–1814*, edited by David Skaggs and Larry L. Nelson, 291–302. 2001. East Lansing: Michigan State University Press, 2010.

– "Missed Opportunities and the Problem of Mohawk Chief John Norton's Cherokee Ancestry." *Ethnohistory* 59, no. 2 (2012): 261–91.

– *Native Memoirs from the War of 1812: Black Hawk and William Apess*. Baltimore: Johns Hopkins University Press, 2014.

– "Aboriginal Peoples and Their Multiple Wars of 1812." In *Routledge Handbook of the War of 1812*, edited by Donald R. Hickey and Connie D. Clark, 132–51. New York: Routledge, 2016.

– "The John Norton Portraits." *Iroquoia*, 4 (2018): 7–39.

Bodleian Library, University of Oxford. Wilberforce Papers: Slavery Religion, and Politics, Part 1, MSS Wilberforce, C.4, Fol. 109.

Born, Lester K., comp. *British Manuscripts Project*. Washington, DC: Library of Congress, 1955.

Boyce, Douglas W., ed. "A Glimpse of Iroquois Cultural History through the Eyes of Joseph Brant and John Norton." *Proceedings of the American Philosophical Society* 117, no. 4 (1973): 286–94.

Bradley, James W. *Evolution of the Onondaga Iroquois: Accommodating Change, 1500–1650*. Syracuse: Syracuse University Press, 1987.

British and Foreign Bible Society Archives (BFBSA). Cambridge University Library: British and Foreign Bible Society Library. 1/5/2. Correspondence Books, vol. 2.

– F3/Shore. Lord Teignmouth's Letters.

British Library (BL). MSS of the Duke of Northumberland, Letters and Papers (Northumberland MSS).

Brown, George Williams, et al., eds. *Dictionary of Canadian Biography*. 15+ vols. Toronto: University of Toronto Press, 1966–.

Browne, George. *The History of the British and Foreign Bible Society from Its Institution in 1804, to the Close of Its Jubilee in 1854*. 2 vols. London: British and Foreign Bible Society, 1859.

Brymner, Douglas. *Report on Canadian Archives, 1896*. Ottawa: Queen's Printer, 1897.

"C__L," D. Letter to the Editor. *Monthly Magazine; or British Register* 20, no. 2 (1805): 101–2.

Calloway, Colin G. *Crown and Calumet: British-Indian Relations, 1783–1815*. Norman: University of Oklahoma Press, 1987.

Campbell, William J. *Speculators in Empire: Iroquoia and the 1768 Treaty of Fort Stanwix*. Norman: University of Oklahoma Press, 2012.

Carnochan, Janet. "Early Records of St Mark's and St Andrew's Churches, Niagara." Ontario Historical Society *Papers and Records* 3 (1901): 7–73.

"Censor." Letter to the Editor. *Monthly Magazine; or British Register* 35, no. 5 (1813): 403–4.

Chartrand, René. *Forts of the War of 1812*. Illustrated by Donato Spedaliere. Oxford: Osprey, 2012.

Claus, Daniel (attributed author). *A Primer for the Mohawk Children: Waerighaghsawe Iksaongoenwa*. London: C. Buckton, 1786.

Committee of Chiefs Appointed by the Six Nations Council of Grand River. "The Tradition of the Origin of the Five Nations' League." 1900. *New York State Museum Bulletin* 184 (1916): 61–109.

Crews, C. Daniel, and Richard W. Starbuck, eds. *Records of the Moravians among the Cherokees*. 4+ vols. Tahlequah, OK: Cherokee National Press, 2010–.

Crooks, James. "Recollections of the War of 1812." c.1853. Niagara Historical Society *Publications* 28 (c.1916): 28–41.

Cruikshank, Ernest A. *The Fight in the Beechwoods* [Beaver Dams]. 2nd ed. Welland: Lundy's Lane Historical Society, 1895.

– "The Battle of Fort George." Niagara Historical Society *Publications* 1 (1896): 4–30.

– "The Blockade of Fort George." Niagara Historical Society *Publications* 3 (1898): 1–79.

– *Drummond's Winter Campaign*. 2nd ed. Lundy's Lane: Lundy's Lane Historical Society, 1900.

– "A Study of Disaffection in Upper Canada in 1812–15." *Proceedings and Transactions of the Royal Society of Canada* 6, sec. 2 (1912): 11–65.

– ed. "Reminiscences of Colonel Claus." *Canadiana* 1, no. 12 (1889): 177–87, and 2, nos. 1–3, 8–9, 10–12 (1890): 7–11, 24–8, 55–9, 127–30, 203–6.

– ed. "Campaigns of 1812–14: Contemporary Narratives by Captain W.H. Merritt, Colonel William Claus, Lieut.-Colonel Matthew Elliott, and Captain John Norton." Niagara Historical Society *Publications* 9 (1902): 3–46.

– ed. *Documentary History of the Campaign upon the Niagara Frontier*. 9 vols. Welland and Lundy's Lane: Lundy's Lane Historical Society, 1902–8. (NB: titles and volume numbering are inconsistent between printings and even within particular editions.)

– ed. *Documents Relating to the Invasion of Canada and the Surrender of Detroit, 1812*. Ottawa: Government Printing Bureau, 1912.

– ed. "Some Letters of Robert Nichol." Ontario Historical Society *Papers and Records* 20 (1923): 41–71.

– ed. *The Correspondence of Lieut. Governor John Graves Simcoe*. 5 vols. Toronto: Ontario Historical Society, 1923–31.

– ed. "Petitions for Grants of Land in Upper Canada, Second Series, 1796–99." Ontario Historical Society *Papers and Records* 26 (1930): 97–379.

Cruikshank, Ernest A., and A.F. Hunter, eds. *The Correspondence of the Honourable Peter Russell*. 3 vols. Toronto: Ontario Historical Society, 1932–6.

Curnoe, Greg. *Deeds/Nations*. Edited by Frank Davey and Neal Ferris. London: London Chapter, Ontario Archaeological Society, 1996.

Currie, William Wallace. *Memoir of the Life, Writings, and Correspondence of James Currie*. 2 vols. London: Longman, Rees, Orme, Brown, and Green, 1831.

Densmore, Christopher. *Red Jacket: Iroquois Diplomat and Orator*. Syracuse: Syracuse University Press, 1999.

DeVries, Laura. *Conflict in Caledonia: Aboriginal Land Rights and the Rule of Law.* Vancouver: UBC Press, 2011.

Dowd, Gregory Evans. *A Spirited Resistance: The North American Indian Struggle for Unity, 1745–1815.* Baltimore: Johns Hopkins University Press, 1992.

Dunnigan, Brian L. *Frontier Metropolis: Picturing Early Detroit, 1701–1838.* Detroit: Wayne State University Press, 2001.

Edgar, Matilda, ed. *Ten Years in Upper Canada in Peace and War, 1805–1815, Being the Ridout Letters.* Toronto: William Briggs, 1890.

Edinburgh Annual Register for 1816 9 (1820).

Elbourne, Elizabeth. "Broken Alliance: Debating Six Nations' Land Claims in 1822." *Cultural and Social History Journal* 9, no. 4 (2012): 497–525.

Elliott, James E. *Strange Fatality: The Battle of Stoney Creek, 1813.* Montreal: Robin Brass, 2009.

Engelbrecht, William. *Iroquoia: The Development of a Native World.* Syracuse: Syracuse University Press, 2003.

Feltoe, Richard. *Redcoated Ploughboys: The Volunteer Battalion of Incorporated Militia of Upper Canada, 1813–1815.* Toronto: Dundurn, 2012.

Fenton, William N. Review of *The Journal of Major John Norton. American Historical Review* 79, no. 4 (1974): 1258–60.

– "Cherokee and Iroquois Connections Revisited." *Journal of Cherokee Studies* 3 (1978): 242–6.

– *The Great Law and the Longhouse: A Political History of the Iroquois Confederacy.* Norman: University of Oklahoma Press, 1998.

– ed. "Answers to Governor Cass's Questions by Jacob Jemison, a Seneca (ca. 1821–1825)." *Ethnohistory* 16, no. 2 (1969): 113–39.

Finlayson, Allan James. "Major John Richardson: A Study of an Artist, His Historical Models, and His Milieu." MA thesis, Carleton University, 1977.

Fitzgibbon, Mary Agnes. *A Veteran of 1812: The Life of James Fitzgibbon.* Toronto: William Briggs, 1894.

Fogelson, Raymond D. "Major John Norton as Ethno-Ethnologist." *Journal of Cherokee Studies* 3 (1978): 250–5.

Fort Malden National Historic Site. Caldwell Family Papers.

Fredriksen, John C., comp. *Free Trade and Sailors' Rights: A Bibliography of the War of 1812.* Westport: Greenwood, 1985.

– comp. *War of 1812 Eyewitness Accounts: An Annotated Bibliography.* Westport: Greenwood, 1997.

French, Christopher. "Journal of an Expedition to South Carolina." 1761. *Journal of Cherokee Studies* 2, no. 3 (1977): 275–96.

Fulford, Tim. *Romantic Indians: Native Americans, British Literature, and Transatlantic Culture, 1756–1830.* Oxford: Oxford University Press, 2006.

Ganter, Granville, ed. *The Collected Speeches of Sagoyewatha, or Red Jacket.* Syracuse: Syracuse University Press, 2006.

Gates, Lillian F. "Roads, Rivals, and Rebellion: The Unknown Story of Asa Danforth, Jr." *Ontario History* 76, no. 3 (1984): 233–54.

Gilpen, Alex R. *The War of 1812 in the Old Northwest.* East Lansing: Michigan State University Press, 1958.

Glenney, Daniel J. "An Ethnohistory of the Grand River Iroquois in the War of 1812." MA thesis, University of Guelph, 1973.

Glover, Jeffrey. "Going to War on the Back of a Turtle: Creation Stories and the Laws of War in John Norton's *Journal*." *Early American Literature* 51, no. 3 (2016): 599–622.

Good, Reg. "Crown-Directed Colonization of Six Nations and Métis Land Reserves in Canada." PhD diss., University of Saskatchewan, 1994.

Gourlay, Robert. *Statistical Account of Upper Canada.* 2 vols. London: Simpkins and Marshall, 1822.

Graves, Donald E. *Red Coats and Grey Jackets: The Battle of Chippawa, 5 July 1814.* Toronto: Dundurn, 1994.

– *Where Right and Glory Lead! The Battle of Lundy's Lane.* 1993. Toronto: Robin Brass, 1997.

– *Field of Glory: The Battle of Crysler's Farm, 1813.* Toronto: Robin Brass, 1999.

– *And All Their Glory Past: Fort Erie, Plattsburgh, and the Final Battles in the North, 1814.* Montreal: Robin Brass, 2013.

– ed. *Merry Hearts Make Light Days: The War of 1812 Journal of Lieutenant John Le Couteur, 104th Foot.* Ottawa: Carleton University Press, 1993.

Gray, William. *Soldiers of the King: The Upper Canadian Militia, 1812–1815.* Erin, ON: Boston Mills, 1995.

Graymont, Barbara. *The Iroquois in the American Revolution.* Syracuse: Syracuse University Press, 1972.

Great Britain. Adjutant-General. *Regulations and Orders for the Army.* London: W. Clowes, 1811.

– *Parliamentary Papers. Third Report of the Royal Commission on Historical Manuscripts.* London: HMSO, 1872.

– War Office. *A List of the Officers of the Army and Royal Marines.* London: C. Roworth, annual editions, 1810s–20s.

Grodzinski, John (Tanya). *Defender of Canada: Sir George Prevost and the War of 1812.* Norman: University of Oklahoma Press, 2013.

Habermehl, Fred C., and Donald L. Combe. *Robert Addison: Scholar, Missionary, Minister.* Niagara-on-the-Lake: St Mark's Anglican Church Archives Committee, 2012.

Hagopian, John S. "Joseph Brant vs Peter Russell: A Re-examination of the Six Nations' Land Transactions in the Grand River Valley." *Histoire Sociale/Social History* 30, no. 60 (1997): 300–33.

Hall, Francis. *Travels in the United States and Canada in 1816 and 1817*. London: Longman, Hurst, Rees, Orme, and Brown, 1818.

Harper, Russell. "An Early History of Haldimand County." 1950. Typescript by Ian Thompson. http://www.media.wix.com/ugd/b8858b_2be1e3b921b 2b50d38369a16c5535cf7.pdf.

Hauptman, Laurence M. *Conspiracy of Interests: Iroquois Dispossession and the Rise of New York State*. Syracuse: Syracuse University Press, 1999.

Heath, William. *William Wells and the Struggle for the Old Northwest*. Norman: University of Oklahoma Press, 2015.

Heriot, George. *Travels through the Canadas*. 2 vols. London: Richard Phillips, 1807.

Herrick, James W. *Iroquois Medical Botany*. Edited by Dean R. Snow. Syracuse: Syracuse University Press, 1995.

Hickey, Donald R. "The War of 1812: Still a Forgotten Conflict?" *Journal of Military History* 65, no. 3 (2001): 741–69.

– *Don't Give Up the Ship! Myths of the War of 1812*. Toronto: Dundurn, 2006.

– *The War of 1812: A Forgotten Conflict*, rev. ed. Urbana: University of Illinois Press, 2012.

Hill Sr, Richard W., ed. *War Clubs and Wampum Belts: Hodinöhsö:ni Experiences of the War of 1812*. Brantford: Woodland Cultural Centre, 2012.

Hill, Susan. *The Clay We Are Made of: Haudenosaunee Land Tenure on the Grand River*. Winnipeg: University of Manitoba Press, 2017.

Hinderaker, Eric. *The Two Hendricks: Unraveling a Mohawk Mystery*. Cambridge: Harvard University Press, 2010.

Hitsman, J. Mackay. *Safeguarding Canada, 1763–1871*. Toronto: University of Toronto Press, 1968.

– *The Incredible War of 1812: A Military History*. 1968; rev. by Donald E. Graves. Toronto: Robin Brass, 1999.

Horne, Thomas Hartwell. *An Introduction to the Critical Study and Knowledge of the Holy Scriptures*. 5th ed. 2 vols. London and Edinburgh: T. Cadell and W. Blackwood, 1825.

Horsman, Reginald. *Matthew Elliott, British Indian Agent*. Detroit: Wayne State University Press, 1964.

– *Expansion and American Indian Policy, 1783–1812*. 1967. Norman: University of Oklahoma Press, 1992.

Howe, Henry. *Historical Collections of Ohio*. Cincinnati: Author, 1850.

Huneault, Kristina. "Miniature Objects of Cultural Covenant: Portraits and First Nations Sitters in British North America." *Canadian Art Review (RACAR)* 30, no.1/2 (2005): 87–100.

"H.W." "Original Account of a Meeting or Talk of Indians." *Supplement to Vol. III of the Monthly Repository of Theology and General Literature* (1809): 709–15.

Ingersoll, Thomas N. *To Intermix with Our White Brothers: Indian Mixed Bloods in the United States from Earliest Times to the Indian Removals.* Albuquerque: University of New Mexico Press, 2005.

Irving, L. Homphray, comp. *Officers of the British Forces in Canada during the War of 1812–15.* Welland: Canadian Military Institute, 1908.

Jamieson, Keith, and Michelle A. Hamilton. *Dr Oronhyatekha: Security, Justice, and Equality.* Toronto: Dundurn, 2016.

Janson, Charles William. *The Stranger in America, 1793–1806.* London: James Cundee, 1807.

Jemison, G. Peter, and Anna M. Schein, eds. *Treaty of Canandaigua, 1794: 200 Years of Treaty Relations between the Iroquois Confederacy and the United States.* Santa Fe: Clear Light, 2000.

Jennings, Francis. *The Ambiguous Iroquois Empire: The Covenant Chain Confederation of Indian Tribes with the English Colonies from Its Beginnings to the Lancaster Treaty of 1744.* New York: W.W. Norton, 1984.

– *Empire of Fortune: Crowns, Colonies and Tribes in the Seven Years War in America.* New York: W.W. Norton, 1988.

Jennings, Francis, William N. Fenton, Mary A. Druke, and David R. Miller, eds. *The History and Culture of Iroquois Diplomacy.* Syracuse: Syracuse University Press, 1985.

Johnston, Charles Murray. "William Claus and John Norton: A Struggle for Power in Old Ontario." *Ontario History* 57, no. 2 (1965): 101–8.

– ed. *The Valley of the Six Nations: A Collection of Documents on the Indian Lands of the Grand River.* Toronto: Champlain Society, 1964.

Jordan, Kurt. *The Seneca Restoration, 1715–1754: An Iroquois Local Political Economy.* Gainesville: University of Florida Press, 2008.

Jortner, Adam. *The Gods of Prophetstown: The Battle of Tippecanoe and the Holy War for the American Frontier.* New York: Oxford University Press, 2012.

"Journal at Dwight." *Missionary Herald, Containing the Proceedings of the American Board of Commissioners for Foreign Missions* 21, no. 8 (1825): 244–8; and 24, no. 10 (1828): 311–13.

Kelsay, Isabel Thompson. *Joseph Brant, 1743–1807: Man of Two Worlds.* Syracuse: Syracuse University Press, 1984.

Kerber, Jordan A., ed. *Archaeology of the Iroquois.* Syracuse: Syracuse University Press, 2007.

King, Duane. "Who Really Discovered the Cherokee-Iroquois Linguistic Connection?" *Journal of Cherokee Studies* 2, no. 4 (1977): 400–4.

Klinck, Carl F. "New Light on John Norton." *Transactions of the Royal Society of Canada* 4, series 4, sec. 2 (1966): 167–77.

– *Giving Canada a Literary History: A Memoir of Carl F. Klinck.* Edited by Sandra Djwa. Ottawa: Carleton University Press for the University of Western Ontario, 1991.

Lépine, Luc. *Les officiers de milice du Bas Canada, 1812–1815.* Montreal: Société généalogique canadienne-français, 1996.

Library and Archives Canada (LAC). Colonial Office 42. Colonial Office Fonds.

– Manuscript Group 19–F1. Daniel Claus and Family Fonds.

– Manuscript Group 19–F35. Superintendent of Indian Affairs in the Northern District of North America Fonds.

– Manuscript Group 21–Add.MSS–8075. Joseph-Geneviève de Puisaye Fonds.

– Record Group 7. Governor-General's Papers.

– Record Group 8, C Series. British Military and Naval Records.

– Record Group 10. Indian Affairs Records.

– Record Group 31. Upper Canada/Canada West Census Returns (Statistics Canada Fonds).

– Ridout, Thomas. *Plan Shewing the Lands Granted to the Six Nation Indians, Situated on Each Side of the Grand River, or Ouse, Commencing on Lake Erie, Containing about 674,910 Acres*, 1821.

[Loskiel, George]. *The History of the Moravian Mission among the Indians of North America.* London: T. Allman, 1838.

Lukenbach, Abraham, and Adam Haman. "Extract from the Diary of the Indian Congregation at Fairfield in Upper Canada, for 1827." *Periodical Accounts Relating to the Missions of the Church of the United Brethren Established among the Heathen* 11, no. 124 (1829):145–8.

Malcomson, Robert. *Lords of the Lake: The Naval War on Lake Ontario, 1812–1814.* Toronto: Robin Brass, 1998.

– *Warships of the Great Lakes, 1754–1834.* Annapolis: Naval Institute Press, 2001.

– *A Very Brilliant Affair: The Battle of Queenston Heights, 1812.* Toronto: Robin Brass, 2003.

– *Historical Dictionary of the War of 1812.* Lanham: Scarecrow Press, 2006.

– *Capital in Flames: The American Attack on York, 1813.* Montreal: Robin Brass, 2008.

Martindale, Barbara. *Caledonia along the Grand River.* Toronto: Natural Heritage, 1995.

McClinton, Rowena, ed. *The Moravian Springplace Mission to the Cherokees.* 2 vols. Lincoln: University of Nebraska Press, 2007.

Melhorn Jr, Donald F. "'A Splendid Man': Richardson, Fort Meigs and the Story of Metoss." *Northwest Ohio Quarterly* 69, no. 3 (1998): 133–60.

Memorial of the Inhabitants of Buffalo. Washington, DC: Jonathan Elliot, 1817.

Merritt, Richard D. *On Common Ground: The Ongoing Story of the Commons in Niagara-on-the-Lake*. Toronto: Dundurn, 2012.

Mills, John Jackson. *A View of the Political Situation of the Province of Upper Canada in North America*. London: W. Earle, 1809.

Monture, Rick. *We Share Our Matters: Two Centuries of Writing and Resistance at Six Nations of the Grand River*. Winnipeg: University of Manitoba Press, 2014.

Morgan, Cecilia. *Travellers through Empire: Indigenous Voyages from Early Canada*. Montreal and Kingston: McGill-Queen's University Press, 2017.

Morgan, John C. *The Emigrant's Note Book and Guide; with Recollections of Upper and Lower Canada during the Late War*. London: Author, 1824.

Murray, J.E. "John Norton." Ontario Historical Society *Papers and Records* 37 (1945): 9–16.

National Archives, United Kingdom (NAUK). MPG1/62. Nesfield, N.A. *Map of the Niagara District in Upper Canada*, 1815.

– WO12/7378. War Office Papers. 65th Foot, First Battalion, 1783–97; Commissary-General of Musters Office and Successors; General Muster Books and Pay Lists.

Nelson, Larry L. *A Man of Distinction among Them: Alexander McKee and British-Indian Affairs along the Ohio Country Frontier, 1754–1799*. Kent, OH: Kent State University Press, 1999.

– "Dudley's Defeat and the Relief of Fort Meigs during the War of 1812." *The Register of the Kentucky Historical Society* 104, no. 1 (2006): 5–42.

New York Public Library. MSSColl 927, Thomas Addis Emmet Collection.

New York State Library (NYSL). BD13350–1, "Headley" (Charles Winn-Allanson Winn, second Baron Allanson and Winn; sometimes Allanson-Winn). "Account of the Descriptions Given by Mr Norton Concerning His Country, Customs, and Manners, 12 March 1805."

– SC10440. Phelps and Gorham Papers, 1772–1895.

Newberry Library (NL). MS654. John Norton Letter Book. (Also known as the Ayer Manuscript.)

– MS3204. Edward E. Ayer Manuscript Collection.

Newspapers: *American and Commercial Daily Advertiser* (Baltimore); *American Beacon and Commercial Diary* (Norfolk); *Arkansas Weekly Gazette* (Little Rock); *Bath Chronicle and Weekly Gazette* (UK); *Buffalo Gazette*; *Canadian Times* (Montreal); *Chronicle, or Harrisburg Visitor*; *Colonial Advocate* (York); *Daily National Intelligencer* (Washington); *Gleaner* (Niagara); *Gleaner* (Wilkes-Barre); *Lancaster Journal* (Pennsylvania); *London Gazette*; *London Morning*

Post; *Louisville Advertiser*; *Massachusetts Spy* (Worcester); *Missouri Gazette and Public Advertiser* (St Louis); *New York Evening Post*; *New York Statesman*; *Niles' Weekly Register* (Baltimore); *Olio* (New York); *Quebec Gazette*; *Reporter* (Brattleboro); *Upper Canada Gazette* (York); *Vermont Mirror* (Middlebury); *War* (New York); *Washington City Weekly Gazette*; *Weekly Aurora* (Philadelphia); *Western Courier* (Louisville).

Norton, John. *Ne Raowenna Teyoninhokarawen Shakonadonire ne Rondaddegenshon ne Rondadhawakshon Rodinonghtsyoni Tsiniyoderighwagennoni ne Raorighwadogenghte ne ne Sanctus John: Address to the Six Nations Recommending the Gospel of Saint John*. London: Phillips and Fardon, 1805.

– *The Journal of Major John Norton, 1816*. Edited by Carl F. Klinck and James J. Talman. 1816/1970. Toronto: Champlain Society, 1970.

– *The Journal of Major John Norton, 1816*. Edited by Carl F. Klinck and James J. Talman. 1816/1970. With a new introduction by Carl Benn. Toronto: Champlain Society, 2011. (This is the edition used in this book, cited as *JMJN*.)

– [and Joseph Brant?], trans. *Nene Karighwiyoston Tsinihorighhoten ne Saint John: The Gospel According to Saint John*. London: Phillips and Fardon for the British and Foreign Bible Society, 1804.

Ostler, Jeffrey. "'To Extirpate the Indians': An Indigenous Consciousness of Genocide in the Ohio Valley and Lower Great Lakes, 1750s–1810." *William and Mary Quarterly* 72, no. 4 (2015): 587–622.

Ostola, Lawrence. "The Seven Nations of Canada and the American Revolution." MA thesis, Université de Montréal, 1989.

Owen, John. *The History of the Origin and the First Ten Years of the British and Foreign Bible Society*. 2 vols. 1816. New York: James Eastborn, 1817.

Parker, Arthur C. "The Senecas in the War of 1812." *New York History* 15 (1915): 78–90.

Parmenter, Jon. *The Edge of the Woods: Iroquoia, 1534–1701*. East Lansing: Michigan State University Press, 2010.

Paxton, James W. *Joseph Brant and His World*. Toronto: James Lorimer, 2008.

Pilkington, Walter, ed. *The Journals of Samuel Kirkland*. Clinton, NY: Hamilton College, 1980.

Public Speeches Delivered at the Village of Buffalo, on the 6th and 8th Days of July 1812, by Hon. Erastus Granger, Indian Agent, and Red Jacket, One of the Principal Chiefs and Speakers of the Seneca Nation, Respecting the Part the Six Nations Would Take in the Present War against Great Britain. Buffalo: S.H. and H.A. Salisbury, 1812.

Quaife, Milo M., ed. *The John Askin Papers*. 2 vols. Detroit: Detroit Library Commission, 1928–31.

Rammage, Stuart A. *The Militia Stood Alone: Malcolm's Mills, 6 November 1814*. Summerland, BC: Author, 2000.

Review of *The History of the British and Foreign Bible Society*. *Quarterly Review* 36, no. 71 (1827): 1–28.

Rice, Brian. *The Rotinonshonni: A Traditional Iroquoian History through the Eyes of Teharonhia:Wako and Sawiskera*. Syracuse: Syracuse University Press, 2013.

Richardson, John. *Richardson's War of 1812*. 1842. Edited by Alexander Clark Casselman. Toronto: Historical Publishing, 1902.

Richter, Daniel K. *The Ordeal of the Longhouse: The Peoples of the Iroquois League in the Era of European Colonization*. Chapel Hill: University of North Carolina Press, 1992.

Sabathy-Judd, Linda, trans. and ed. *Moravians in Upper Canada: The Diary of the Indian Mission of Fairfield on the Thames, 1792–1813*. Toronto: Champlain Society, 1999.

Samuel Gedge Limited. *Catalogue 23*. Norwich: Samuel Gedge, 2016.

Scadding, Henry. *Leaves They Have Touched: Being a Review of Some Historical Autographs*. Toronto: no pub., 1874.

Scotland's People. Church of Scotland, Parish Church of Crail, Old Parish Registers, 1655–1857. https://www.scotlandspeople.gov.uk/.

Shannon, Timothy J. "Dressing for Success on the Mohawk Frontier: Hendrick, William Johnson, and the Indian Fashion." *William and Mary Quarterly* 53, no. 1 (1996): 13–42.

– *Iroquois Diplomacy on the Early American Frontier*. New York: Penguin/Viking, 2008.

Sheaffe, Roger Hale. "Documents Relating to the War of 1812: The Letter Book of Gen. Sir Roger Hale Sheaffe." *Publications of the Buffalo Historical Society* 17 (1913): 271–381.

Shore Jr, John. *Memoir of the Life and Correspondence of John Lord Teignmouth*. London: Hatchard and Son, 1843.

– *Reminiscences of Many Years*. 2 vols. Edinburgh: David Douglas, 1878.

Short, Adam, and Arthur G. Doughty, eds. *Documents Relating to the Constitutional History of Canada, 1759–1791*. Ottawa: S.E. Dawson (King's Printer), 1907.

Six Nations Council. *Six Miles Deep: Land Rights of the Six Nations of the Grand River*. Ohsweken: the Council, n.d. (c.2014).

– *Six Nations of the Grand River: Land Rights, Financial Justice, Resolutions*. Ohsweken: the Council, n.d. (c.2015).

Skaggs, David Curtis. *William Henry Harrison and the Conquest of the Ohio Country*. Baltimore: Johns Hopkins University Press, 2014.

Smith, Donald B., and Edward S. Rogers, eds. *Aboriginal Ontario: Historical Perspectives on the First Nations*. Toronto: Government of Ontario and Dundurn, 1994.

Smith, Michael. *A Geographical View of the Province of Upper Canada; and Promiscuous Remarks on the Government*. 3rd ed. Philadelphia: Author, 1813.

Snow, Dean R. *The Iroquois*. Cambridge, MA: Blackwell, 1994.

Snyder, Charles M., ed. *Red and White on the New York Frontier: A Struggle for Survival*. Harrison, NY: Harbor Hill, 1978.

Spragge, George W., ed. *The John Strachan Letter Book*. Toronto: Ontario Historical Society, 1946.

Staats, Sheila. *Warriors: A Resource Guide*. Brantford: Woodland Cultural Centre, 1986.

Stagg, J.C.A. *Mr Madison's War: Politics, Diplomacy, and Warfare in the Early American Republic*. Princeton: Princeton University Press, 1983.

– *The War of 1812: Conflict for a Continent*. New York: Cambridge University Press, 2012.

Stanley, George F.G. "The Significance of Six Nations Participation in the War of 1812." *Ontario History* 55, no. 4 (1963): 215–31.

State Historical Society of Wisconsin. Draper Manuscripts.

Stone, William L. *Life of Joseph Brant – Thayendanegea*. 2 vols. New York: Alexander V. Blake, 1838.

– *The Life and Times of Sa-go-ye-wat-ha, or, Red-Jacket*. New York: Wiley and Putnam, 1841.

Stopp, Marianne P. "John Norton – Teyoninhokarawen." Manuscript Submission Report 2010–29. National Historic Sites and Monuments Board of Canada, 2010.

Sugden, John. *Tecumseh: A Life*. New York: Henry Holt, 1997.

Sutherland, Stuart. *His Majesty's Gentlemen: A Directory of British Regular Army Officers of the War of 1812*. Toronto: Iser, 2000.

– ed. *"A Desire of Serving and Defending My Country": The War of 1812 Journals of William Hamilton Merritt*. Toronto: Iser, 2001.

Sword, Wiley. *President Washington's Indian War: The Struggle for the Old Northwest, 1790–1795*. Norman: University of Oklahoma Press, 1985.

Tanner, Helen Hornbeck. "The Glaize in 1792: A Composite Indian Community." *Ethnohistory* 25, no. 1 (1978): 15–39.

– ed. *Atlas of Great Lakes Indian History*. Norman: University of Oklahoma Press, 1987.

Taylor, Alan. "A Northern Revolution of 1800? Upper Canada and Thomas Jefferson." In *The Revolution of 1800: Democracy, Race, and the New Republic*, edited by James Horn, Jan Ellen Lewis, and Peter S. Onuf, 383–409. Charlottesville: University of Virginia Press, 2002.

– *The Divided Ground: Indians, Settlers, and the Northern Borderland of the American Revolution*. New York: Alfred A. Knopf, 2006.

– *The Civil War of 1812: American Citizens, British Subjects, Irish Rebels, and Indian Allies.* New York: Alfred A. Knopf, 2010.

"Teyoninhokarawen the Indian Chief." *Christian Observer* 9, no. 8 (1810): 524–5.

Thomson, John Lewis. *Historical Sketches of the Late War between the United States and Great Britain.* Philadelphia: Thomas DeSilver, 1816.

Tiro, Karim M. *The People of the Standing Stone: The Oneida Nation from the Revolution through the Era of Removal.* Amherst and Boston: University of Massachusetts Press, 2011.

Toronto Public Library (TPL). Sir David William Smith Papers.

– William Dummer Powell Papers.

Trigger, Bruce G., ed. *Handbook of North American Indians* 15 (Northeast). Washington, DC: Smithsonian Institution 1978.

Tupper, Ferdinand Brock. *The Life and Correspondence of Major-General Sir Isaac Brock, KB.* Guernsey: H. Bedstone, 1845.

United States Senate. *Affairs of the Mexican Kickapoo Indians.* 3 vols. Washington, DC: Government Printing Office, 1908.

Wallace, Anthony F.C. *The Death and Rebirth of the Seneca.* 1969. New York: Vintage, 1972.

Wallot, Jean-Pierre. *Intrigues françaises et américaines au Canada, 1800–1802.* Montreal: Éditions Leméac, 1965.

Walsh, M.B. "General Hull's Campaign along the Detroit: Shots Not Fired on 16 August 1812?" *War of 1812 Magazine* 18 (2012). http://www.napoleon -series.org/military/Warof1812/2012/Issue18/Shots1MAINSECTION.pdf

Washburn, Cephas. *Reminiscences of Indians.* 1838. New York: Johnson Reprint, 1971.

Watt, Gavin K. *Rebellion in the Mohawk Valley.* Toronto: Dundurn, 2002.

Western University. AFC407. John Norton (Teyoninhokarawen) Collection.

– B1900–1943. Carl F. Klinck Papers.

Whitaker, Nathaniel. *A Brief Narrative of the Indian Charity School in Lebanon in Connecticut, New England.* 2nd ed. London: J. and W. Oliver, 1767.

White, Patrick C.T., ed. *Lord Selkirk's Diary, 1803–1804.* Toronto: Champlain Society, 1958.

White, Richard. *The Middle Ground: Indians, Empires, and Republics in the Great Lakes Region, 1650–1815.* Cambridge: Cambridge University Press, 1991.

Whitehorn, Joseph. *While Washington Burned: The Battle for Fort Erie, 1814.* Baltimore: Nautical and Aviation Publishing, 1992.

William Reese Company. "A Collection of Profiles by Thomas Pole, MD." 2017. https://www.williamreesecompany.com/pages/books/ WRCAM52382/thomas-pole/a-collection-of-profiles-by-thomas-pole-m-d -manuscript-title

Willig, Timothy D. *Restoring the Chain of Friendship: British Policy and the Indians of the Great Lakes, 1783–1815.* Lincoln: University of Nebraska Press, 2008.

Wood, William, ed. *Select British Documents of the Canadian War of 1812.* 3 vols. Toronto: Champlain Society, 1920–8.

Young, A.H., ed. *The Parish Register of Kingston, Upper Canada, 1785–1811.* Kingston: British Whig Publishing, 1921.

– "The Rev. Robert Addison: Extracts from the Reports and (Manuscript) Journals of the Society for the Propagation of the Gospel in Foreign Parts." Ontario Historical Society *Papers and Records* 19 (1922): 171–91.

Zaslow, Morris, ed. *The Defended Border: Upper Canada and the War of 1812.* Toronto: MacMillan, 1964.

Index

Page numbers may refer to material in the text and/or the footnotes. See Appendix B for John Norton's spelling of indigenous names where it differed from today's common practices.

A.W. (Adam or Andrew Wilson), 6–9
Addison, Robert, 62, 203, 292
Akwesasne, or St Regis, 14, 182, 190, 192–3, 300
Albany, 13, 35, 44, 46, 52
Allan, William, 161
Allcock, Henry, 49
Alnwick Castle, 6
American Council of Learned Societies, 6
American Revolution, 17–21, 78, 91, 96, 107, 142; outcomes and fears, 21–4, 38–40, 45, 48–9, 53, 57–8, 79, 83–4, 87, 91–2, 96, 165, 184; veterans, 31, 36, 50–1, 88, 101, 130, 137, 172
Amherstburg: in 1812, 98, 101, 104, 107–8, 110, 112–13; in 1813, 145–6, 148–50, 152–4, 156, 164, 209–13, *pls. 16, 18*
Ancaster, 82, 214, 228, *pl. 22*
Anderson, Christian, 24, 26–7, 124

Anglo-Cherokee War, 25, 71, 94, *pl. 2*
Anishinabeg, terminology, 11. *See also* Chippewas
Anne, Queen, 36
Arosa, or George Silverheels (Seneca), 94–6
Askin, John, and family, 30
Assiginack, Jean-Baptiste, or Blackbird (Odawa), 197–8, 202

Ball's farm, 203, 207
Baltimore, 272
Barclay, Robert, 289
Barclay, Robert Heriot, 210–11
Barham, Baron, 64
Bath, 60
Bathurst, Earl, 218, 276, 283, 291
Battersby, Francis, 245–6
Beaver Dams, 101, 189–93, 195, *pl. 22*
Berwick, 26
Big Arrow, or Joseph Crawford/ Kahishorowanen (Onondaga), 197–8, 292–3

Big Captain Johnny, or Moluntha (Shawnee), 154

Big Rock, or Brownstown, 100, 108–10, *pl. 16*

Bisshopp, Cecil, 173–4, 200–1

Black Creek, 231, 253, 263, 265

Black Hawk, or Makataimeshekiakiak (Sauk), 143–4

black people, 3, 15, 36, *pls. 19, 28*; terminology, 12

Black Rock: in 1812, 91, 120–3, 137; in 1813, 200–1, 220–1; in 1814, 253–6, *pl. 22*

Black Swamp Road, described, 201–2, *pl. 22*

Blackbird, or Jean-Baptiste Assiginack (Odawa), 197, 202

Bladensburg, 179

blind warrior (Mohawk?), 85

Boerstler, Charles, 191–2

Bonham, 269

Bostwick, John, 216

Brant, John, or Ahyonweaghs (Mohawk), 129, 195, 238, 244, 290–1

Brant, Joseph, or Thayendanegea (Mohawk): adopted and promoted JN, 24–5, 33–7, 52, 70; American Revolution, 21, 31, 33, 36, 38, 107; Anglican, 45, 62; author and translator, 5, 62; Aaron Burr plot, 44–6; chiefly status, 36, 38–9, 55–7, 64–6, 70; death, 69–70; Five/ Six Nations, 49; Grand River lands and issues, 22, 39–49, 54–9, 64–7, 276; homes, *pls. 8, 26*; Indian Department rank, 36, 70; Duke of Northumberland's friend, 5, 50–2, *pl. 13*; on JN's

mission to Britain, 49–53, 55–6, 65, 67; portrait, *pl. 7*; post-revolutionary affairs in the US, 42–5; Sandusky interests, 45; tensions with JN, 62, 66–7, 69; united Buffalo Creek/Grand River council, 48, 56–7, 59, 65; mentioned, 4, 75, 76, 82, 84, 101, 132, 142, 290, 296

– relatives (Mohawks): Catherine, or Ohtowakeshson/ Adonwentishon, 132, 166, *pl. 26*; Christina, or Aoghyatonghsera, 33; Elizabeth Johnson, 132; Isaac, or Karaguantier, 33; Molly, or Margaret/Gonwatsijayenni, 132, 171. *See also* John Brant

Bridgewater and Burch's Mills, 252, *pls. 22, 29–30*

brigade major, defined, 124

Bright Horn, or Waskweela/ Wathethewela (Shawnee), 154

British and Foreign Bible Society, 6, 26, 53, 62, 121, *pl. 12*

Brock, James, 169

Brock, Sir Isaac: assumed command and prepared defences, 75, 80–1, 98–9; death, funeral, and monument, 125, 134, 136–7; Detroit campaign, 97, 101–14, *pl. 16*; Haudenosaunee relations, 75–6, 80–5, 93–4, 98–9, 101–3, 108, 113, 118–19, 132; knighted, 139; Niagara campaign, 118–35; mentioned 141, 169, 280

Brown, Jacob, 230, 233, 235, 239, 245–6, 252–3, 264–5, 271

Brownstown, or Big Rock, 100, 108–10, *pl. 16*

Brush, Henry, 114

Brymner, Douglas, 296
Buck, Thomas, 230
Buffalo: in 1813, 139, 175, 183, 220–1; in 1814, 226, 228, 230, 255–6, 262, 266, *pl. 22*
Buffalo Creek, 35, 48, 56–7, 65, 221, 228
Bull, Robert, 234–5
Bullock, Richard, 133
Burlington region, or Head of the Lake: in 1813, 159, 165–6, 175–9, 181–2, 184, 190, 201, 208, 212, 214–16; in 1814, 224–8, 238, 241–6, 249, 263–4, 266–8, 270, 281; *pls. 22, 26*
Burr, Aaron, and filibusters, 43–6
Butler, Thomas, and family, 171–2, 197

Caldwell, William, 228–30, 241, 243–4
Camden, Marquess, 52, 59
Canard River, 108, *pl. 16*
Carrying River, or Rivière du Portage, 149
Castlereagh, Viscount, 68
Cataract. *See* Niagara Falls
Cattaraugus, 266
Cayuga Creek, 119
Cayugas: before 1812, 19, 22, 27–9; in 1812, 86, 102, 130, 132, 136, 140; in 1813, 176, 199, 202; in 1814, 230, 241, 244, 270; in postwar period, 287; Gayogohono, 11; Ourehouare, 140; son of Karhagohha or Hawk, 102; mentioned, 3, 11, 13, 15. *See also* Haudenosaunee
Chambers, Peter, 99, 102–4, 270
Champlain Society, 7–10

Chandler, John, 179
Charleton, Thomas, 259–60
Châteauguay, 183, 216
Chauncey, Isaac, 161
Cherokees: before 1812, 3–6, 24–9, 31, 63, 70–1, 81, 94, 109, *pl. 2*; from 1812, 37, 287, 294–6; at Grand River, 37, 299; as Iroquoians, 37; Kennitea, 25; Kuwoki and Little Keowee, 71; JN's aunt, 25–6; John Norton (father of JN), 3, 24–9, 278; Tahneh, 176, 295; warfare, 164; John Charles Wolateagh , 176, 294–5. *See also* John Norton
Chewett, William, 161
Chickasaws, Jimmy Underwood, 32
chiefs' medals, *pls. 9, 28*
Chippawa and Chippawa River, 119, 122, 124; in 1812, 125, 127, 130, 132, 138, 140; in 1813, 173–4, 190; in 1814, 160, 226, 229–41, 244–6, 249–50, 252–3, 263, 265, 277, *pls. 22, 29*
Chippewas, or Ojibwa/Anishinabeg: before 1812, 22, 45, 77; in 1812, 104–7, 113, 118; in 1813, 143, 147–8, 160, 163, 176, 190, 192, 196–9, 204–6, 213; in 1814, 224, 229, 246, 275; in 1815, *pl. 19*; Munceytown, 275; JN's terminology, 11; Splitnose, 163–4
Chisholm, James, 135
Chisholm family, 127
Chrystie, John, 134, 180
clans, 14–15, 37, 51
Clark, Andrew, 153
Clark, Thomas, 189–90
Claus, Joseph (Mohawk), 169–70

Claus, William, or deputy
    superintendent-general, 44, 169;
    death, 295; portrait, *pl. 14*;
  – relations with JN,
    Haudenosaunee, and other
    natives: before 1812, 24–5, 32,
    44, 51–70, 83; in 1812, 76, 82–3,
    102, 140, 157; in 1813, 157, 182,
    187, 190, 195, 199–200, 203–8; in
    1814, 228–30, 244–5; in postwar
    period, 275–7, 279–80, 291
Clench, Ralph, 132
Clerk, Alexander, 179–80
Cleveland, or Cuyahoga, 164
Coffin, John, and family, 27–8, 124
Conestogas, or Susquehannocks, 90
Cook's Mills, 265
Cooke, Edward, 52, 59
council meetings: 1770s Onondaga,
    48; 1790s Buffalo Creek and
    Albany, 35; 1790s Ohio country,
    30–2; 1799 Grand River, 24–5,
    36; 1801 Buffalo Creek, 48; 1803
    Grand River, 48, 51, 57; 1805
    Niagara and Buffalo Creek, 56–7,
    59, 65; 1806 Grand River, 41, 66–7;
    1807 Grand River, 67–9; 1808
    Grand River, 69–70; 1811 Ancaster
    and Grand River, 82; 1812 Fort
    George 136; 1812 Grand River,
    82–92, 99–103; 1812 Queenston,
    94–6; 1813 Amherstburg, 212–13;
    1813 Burlington region, 184–5,
    215; 1813 Detroit region, 145–6,
    149; 1813 Fort Meigs region,
    209; 1814 Burlington, 240–6, 277;
    1814 Grand River, 230, 281–2;
    1814 Quebec, 226–7, 281, *pl. 28*;
    1815 York, 281–2; 1816 Grand
    River, 288

council practices: 48, 85–9, 92, 96, 136,
    149. *See also* wampum
Craig, Sir James, 68
Crail, 24
Crawford, Joseph, or Big Arrow /
    Kahishorowanen (Onondaga),
    197–8, 292–3
Creeks, or Muskogees, 37, 255
Crysler's Farm, 183, 216
Cuyahoga, or Cleveland, 164

Danforth, Asa, 45
Dearborn, Henry, 118, 161, 175, 177,
    180, 191
deCew, John, and his property, 172,
    174, 189, 191. *See also* Beaver
    Dams
Delaware Town and Township, 104,
    146
Delawares, or Lenni Lenapes /
    Munsees: before 1812, 15, 90;
    in 1812, 104–7, 110, 118, 129; in
    1813, 147–8, 176, 199, 205–6, 213;
    in 1814, 224, 227, 230, 237, 246,
    266–9; in postwar period, 275;
    Catherine Norton, 29, 60, 183,
    203, 226–7, 264, 279, 282, 288,
    292–5; Christiana, 148; Delaware
    Town, 146; Jacob, 148; Joseph
    Jacobs, 148; Moraviantown /
    Fairfield, 105, 148, 214;
    Munceytown, 275; murders, 90,
    266–9; New Fairfield, 105, 294
Dennis, James, 134–5
deputy superintendent-general. *See*
    William Claus
deserters: American, 112–13, 123,
    133, 136, 139, 156, 166, 208, 246,
    254, 261; British/Canadian, 98,
    108, 132, 189, 203; First Nations,

126; Norton men, 26–8, 44; JN's father-in-law, 203

Detroit: before 1812, 22, 30, 34; in 1812, 83, 91, 97–9, 103, 105, 107–18, 123, 139, *pl. 16*; in 1813, 142–6, 149–51, 153, 156, 158, 162, 212–13; in 1814, 264, 269–71

Detroit-Raisin River Road, described, 108

Detroit River region, detailed period map, *pl. 16*

Deyonihnhogawen (Seneca), 38

Dickson, Robert, 142–3, 145–6, 150, 209, 271

Dickson, William (Sioux), 272

diplomacy:
   – Anglo-American: before 1812, 20–3, 34, 79, 83, 86–7; 1812 and after, 16, 118, 136–7, 216, 223, 272–4, 287
   – between First Nations: before 1812, 14–15, 17–18, 30–2, 35, 40, 78–80; in 1812, 86–92, 94–6, 99, 106–8; in 1813, 216; in 1814, 240–1. *See also* Western Tribes
   – First Nations-Great Britain: before 1812, 17–23, 30, 42–3, 47–8, 51–63, 68–9, 75–9, 81–2; in 1812, 102, 116–18, 132; in 1813, 142–5, 165–6, 175–6, 192–3, 208, 215–16; in 1814, 223–4, 243; in postwar period, 273, 287–8, 290
   – First Nations-United States: before 1812, 20–3, 30, 35, 42–3, 45, 77–8, 88, 92, 95; in 1812, 100–2, 116–17; 1813 and after, 16, 175–6, 184, 206, 208, 214, 216, 273–4, 287
   – treaties: 1768 Stanwix, xi, 18, 20; 1783 Paris, 20–3, 79, 83–4; 1794 Jay's, 23, 83; 1795 Greenville, 23, 79, 146; 1814 Ghent, 272–4, 280, 287; unspecified First Nations-American, 184, 273

disease and sickness: before 1812, 15, 20; in 1812, 112, 123, 139–40; in 1813, 182–3, 202–3, 207–9; in 1814, 225, 236, 246, 261, 263–4; in postwar period, 296, 300

division (military term), as used by JN, 157; Right, Centre, Left, 208

Dockstader, John, 45

Dorchester, Baron, 52, 57–8

Dowwisdowwis. *See* John Norton, names

Drummond, Sir Gordon: in 1813, 217–18; in 1814, 227–8, 240, 245, 249–53, 255–6, 260–3, 265–6; in 1815, 279–80, 283

Drummond, William, 247, 257–9

Dudley, William, 163

Dundas Street, described, 104

Dunfermline, 283

Durand, James, 135

Dwight Mission, 295

Echo, or Raweanarase/Young Clear Sky (Onondaga), 82, 84

editorial decisions: *JMJN*, period documents, statistics, and terminology, 9–12

Eighteen Mile Creek, 264

Eldridge, Joseph, 197

Elliott, Alexander (Shawnee), 153–4

Elliott, Matthew, 153–4, 209, 212–13, 228–9

Elliott, William, 114

European wars: 1792–1815, 43, 49–50, 64, 86, 122, 222, 230, 261, 272–3, 282; 1914–18, 272

Eustace, John, 270–1
Evans, Thomas, 124

Fallen Timbers, 23, 32–3, 107
father, diplomatic meaning, 92
fencibles, described, 132
filibusters and private expansionists,
    43–6, 87
First Nations:
  – diversities and outsider
    adoptions, 3, 14–15, 24–5, 35–7,
    43, 46, 109, 139–40, 144, 192, 255,
    278, 291, 299, *pls. 19, 28*
  – dress, 60, 106, 123, 148, 227, 235,
    270, 294, *pls. 1–2, 4–5, 7, 9–11,
    18–19, 28*
  – motivations for belligerency or
    neutrality: before 1812, 19–20,
    22–3, 43, 69; in 1812: 4, 75–97,
    99–102, 106–10, 115–17; in 1813,
    143–4, 146, 155, 159, 165, 175–6,
    182–7, 192–3, 205–6, 208, 211–15;
    in 1814, 223, 240–3, 273
  – warfare, characteristics of:
    command, 130; dances, songs,
    and associated practices, 61, 63,
    101, 129; horses in battle, 147–8;
    veteran status, *pl. 9*; withdrawal
    from campaigns, 164, 192–3;
    withdrawal from combat, 126.
    See also scalps and scalping;
    weapons and ammunition
Fitzgibbon, James, 189–93, 265, 266
Five Mile Meadows, 166–7, 218
Fort Dearborn, 115
Fort Erie: in 1812, 91, 118, 122–4, 137–
    9, 140; in 1813, 156, 165–7, 173–4,
    181; in 1814, 132, 226, 230–3, 237,
    252–63, 265–7, 270–1, *pls. 22, 32*;
    mentioned, 160, 204, 241

Fort George: before 1812, 34–5, 59,
    pl. 6; in 1812, 93, 118, 124–7, 130,
    136–8; in 1813, 121, 155, 158–9,
    162, 165–77, 179–83, 186–9, 191,
    193–209, 212, 217, *pls. 22–4*; in
    1814, 229, 237–9, 245–6, 253, 265;
    mentioned, 4, 225
Fort Mackinac, or Michilimackinac,
    97, 104, 107–8, 115, 199, 222–3,
    271–2
Fort Madison, 141
Fort Malden. *See* Amherstburg
Fort Meigs, 145, 149, 157, 162–4, 183,
    209, *pl. 21*
Fort Miamis, 22–3, 33
Fort Mississauga, 167, 238, 245–6,
    253, 265
Fort Niagara: before 1812, 20, 27,
    56, 165, *pls. 3, 6*; in 1812, 124–5,
    136–8; in 1813, 162–3, 166–9,
    181–2, 216–21, 226, *pls. 22–4*;
    in 1814, 238, 245, 253, 264–5,
    pl. 22
Fort Recovery, 31–2
Fort Schlosser, 119–20
Fort Stanwix, treaty and line, xi, 18,
    20
Fort Stephenson, 209
Fort Wayne, 141, 152
Fort York, 159–60
Forty Mile Creek, 173–7, 180–1,
    186–90, 193, 215, 239, 241, *pl. 22*
Four Mile Creek (NY), 264
Four Mile Creek (UC), 173, 190,
    194–5, 198, 201–3, *pl. 22*
Foxes, or Mesquakies, 15
Francis, Thomas and William, 216,
    219–20
Frenchman's Creek, 122, 139, 254,
    263, 265, *pl. 22*

Frenchtown, or Raisin River, 108–9, 113–14, 135, 145–52, 154–5, 291
Frey, Barent, 137–8
Frontenac, Comte de, 140
Fry, Philip, 45

Ganeodiyo, or Handsome Lake (Seneca), 63, 78
Genesee River, 264
George III, King (specifically, not figuratively): honoured Joseph Brant, 70; in indigenous discourse, 54, 84–5, 87, 89–90, 92, 95–6, 102–3, 186, 229, 242, 282; request to confirm Grand River lands, 53–4. *See also* Royal Proclamation
George IV, King, formerly Prince Regent, 218, 223, 284, 288, 290
Georgian Bay region, 45–6, 224, 285–6
Gnadenhutten, 90
Gordon, James, 236–7, 262
Gore, Francis, 65–8, 80–1, 276–8, 283, 286, 288
gospels, Mohawk translations, 7, 62–3, 121, *pl. 12*
Goulburn, Henry, 284, 287–90
Grand Island, 98, 117–20, 122, 221, 231, 243, *pl. 22*
Grand River Tract:
– before 1812/after 1814: Brock's Monument contribution, 136; creation, 21–2, 39–40, 53; descriptions and conditions, 39–40, 66–70, 255, 274, 285, *pl. 8*; Euro-American residents, 49; external pressures and land issues before 1815, 35, 39–62, 64–70, 81–5, 101; external pressures and land issues from

1815, 274–8, 281–92; immigration to/away, 21–2, 41–2, 45, 54–5, 57, 206–7, 242, 266; investments, interest payments, and annuities, 55, 66–7, 82–3, 287; political groups, 39, 51, 53–7, 59, 70, 76, 79–80, 83, 88, 93, 275–6, 282, 289. *See also* Joseph Brant; council meetings; Great Britain, government; Haudenosaunee; John Norton; presents, payments, and pensions; supplies; *individuals*; *nations*
– 1812–14: at the outbreak, 93–102; 1812 Detroit campaign, 102–14; 1812 Niagara campaign, 115–40; 1813 campaign, 155, 165–221; 1813 crises, 165–6, 175–87, 214–15; 1814, Niagara campaign, 227–66; 1814 defence of Grand River, 266, 269–71; conditions at Grand River and refugee camps, 140, 155, 157, 159, 175, 225, *pl. 26*; proximity to Niagara fighting, *pl. 22*; political groups, 76, 79, 83, 101, 116–18, 182, 186, 215, 229–30; property destroyed, 216; warriors burned Tuscarora, 221. *See also* council meetings; diplomacy; First Nations; Haudenosaunee; John Norton; presents, payments, and pensions; *individuals*; *nations*
Granger, Erastus, or American agent, 88–9, 95
Grant, Alexander, 64
Great Britain, government (also London/imperial centre/King George/Crown): honoured JN, 32, 34, 223, 283–4; influenced by

JN, 286, 288; sovereignty and indigenous land ownership, 13, 18, 286; strategic considerations, 22–3, 87, 118, 141, 222, 272–3, 287; views on Grand River, 41, 53, 57–9, 68–9, 272–3, 287–8, 290. *See also* American Revolution; diplomacy; Indian Department; Royal Proclamation; treaties; Upper Canada, government; War of 1812

Great Peace, 13

Green family: John, Samuel, and Samuel's wife, 267–9

Haldimand, Sir Frederick: death, 57; grant, 39–40, 42, 49–50, 52–8, 64–5, 67, 75, 82–3, 85, 274, 281, 289–90, *pl. 34*; knighthood, 289

Hamilton, Christopher, 219

Hamilton Cove, 125

Handsome Lake, or Ganeodiyo (Seneca), 63, 78

Harrison, William Henry, 146, 148–9, 150–1, 154, 156, 158, 162–3, 184, 211–14

Harvey, John, 177–9, 218, 249, 250

Hatt, Samuel, 135

Haudenosaunee, or Iroquois: confederacy, 13–14; history, economy, and society before 1812, 13–23, 31–71, 101; leadership, decision making, and personal freedoms, 13–15, 33, 36–9, 48, 56–7, 70, 76, 85, 91, 95, 101, 117–18, 126, 130, 141–2; New York/Pennsylvania residents in combat, 1812–14, 181–2, 201, 204–8, 212, 221, 226, 234–7, 240–1, 262; terminology, 49.

See also Cayugas; Grand River Tract; Kayengwiroghtongh's brother; Mingos; Mohawks; Oneidas; Onondagas; Sandusky Senecas; Senecas; Seven Nations; Tekeantawea; Tuscaroras; *communities*; *individuals*
– gender: male identity, 19, 37, 90, 116, 129, 163, 243, 280, 297; marriage and status, 29, 38, 48; women and governance, 14, 33, 37–9, 56, 91, 95

Hawk, or Karhagohha, son of (Cayuga), 102

Head of the Lake. *See* Burlington region

Headley, Baron, 37

Hendrick, or Tejoninhokarawa (Mahican?/Mohawk), and Hendrick Peters, or Theyanoguin (Mohawk), 36

Hillhouse, 292

Historical Manuscripts Commission, 6

historiographical issues: Aaron Burr plot, 44–6; conflation of JN's sons, 30; editorial decisions, 9–12; JN's desertion from the army, 27–8; 44; JN's Cherokee and Mohawk identities, 3, 24–7, 34–5, 176, 278, 296; JN's female partners, 29; mistake in affirming JN held hereditary office, 37–8; mistake in assuming British government purposely could not find the Haldimand Grant, 53; mistake about JN's arrival in England, 282; *Mohawk Memoir* objectives, 8–9; nature of Grand River holdings, 40;

recommended texts on Grand
River, 40; recommended
texts on Haudenosaunee, 13;
recommended texts on JN, 3, 5;
recommended texts on War of
1812, 80
Holcroft, William, 128
hostages, 185
Hoyatategh and his son (Mingos/
Senecas), 146
Hull, William, 98, 100–4, 106–15, 137,
139, 152
Hunter, Peter, 48–9, 52, 55, 64
Hurons, or Wendat, 14, 17

Indian Department:
– administration and personnel,
19, 34–6, 47–8, 70, 73, 76, 101,
107, 112, 132, 142–4, 195, 228–9,
279, 285–6, 289
– Haudenosaunee affairs and
opposition to JN: before 1811, 8,
24, 34, 43–5, 47–51, 54–7, 66–70,
81, 132; in 1811–12, 76, 83–4, 91,
97–8, 101–2, 140; in 1813, 142–3,
145, 155, 175, 182–3, 188, 192,
195, 199, 202–4, 206, 209, 218;
in 1814, 223–9, 241–4, *pl. 27*; in
postwar period, 275–82, 286,
288–91, *pl. 34*
– JN's employment in, 34–6, 76,
107, 112, 142–4, 195, 208, 224–5,
229, 245, 279–81
– relations beyond the
Haudenosaunee, 84, 87, 98,
142, 144–6, 148, 151–4, 164,
195–6, 203–4, 206, 209, 213, 217,
223–4, 229, 233, 258. *See also*
John Brant; Joseph Brant;
William Caldwell; Andrew

Clark; William Claus; Robert
Dickson; Alexander Elliott;
Matthew Elliott; Sir John
Johnson; Sir William Johnson;
Robert Kerr; William Johnson
Kerr; Charles de Langlade;
Louis Langlade; George Martin;
Thomas McKee; John Norton; Sir
George Prevost; Upper Canada,
government
infantry, described: battalions,
132; brigades, 124, 263; flank
companies, 94, 248; Incorporated
Militia, 248; light division, 201;
line, grenadier, and light infantry
94, 109, 132, 214, 249, 251, *pl. 33*;
volunteers, 94. *See also* weapons
and ammunition
Iroquoia, 13–18, 20–2, 48
Iroquois. *See* Haudenosaunee
Irwin, James, 259–60
Izard, George, 264–5, 271

Jacobs, Joseph or Josephus
(Delaware), 148; parents
Christiana and Jacob/
Gendaskund, 148
Jefferson, Thomas, 46
Jishkaaga, or Little Billy (Seneca),
86–9
Johnson, John Smoke, or
Sakayengwaraton (Mohawk),
140, 176, 296–7
Johnson, Sir John, 44, 281–2
Johnson, Sir William, 19, 39, 44, 132,
171
Jones, Augustus, 266–7
Jones, Peter, or Kahkewaquonaby
(Mississauga), 266
Jones-Parry, Love Parry, 247, 267

Kahishorowanen, or Joseph
    Crawford/Big Arrow
    (Onondaga), 197, 292–3
Kahnawake, 14, 35, 182, 190–3, 205,
    220
Kanesatake, 14, 182, 190–3
Karhagohha, or the Hawk, son of
    (Cayuga), 102
Kayengwiroghtongh's brother
    (unspecified Haudenosaunee),
    206–7
Kekionga, 152
Kennitea (Cherokee), 25
Kerr family (Mohawk/Mohawk
    connections): Robert Johnson, or
    Theyandanegea, 171, 290; Robert
    Joseph, 171; Walter, 131–2, 171;
    William Johnson, 129, 132, 173,
    188, 290
Kickapoos, 152
King, Charles, 138–9
King, William, 138–9
King's Head Inn, or Government
    House, 166
Kingston: in 1813, 157–9, 162, 165,
    175, 182, 186, 208, 211–12, 215,
    225; in 1814, 226, 229, 253, 256
Kirkland, Samuel, 62
Kitson, James, 147
Klinck, Carl F., 3, 7, 9, 30, 37–8, 282
Kuwoki and Little/New Keowee, 71

La Belle Fontaine, 111
Lake Champlain, 263, 278
Lake Road, Niagara, described, 172
Langlade Jr, Charles de (Odawa),
    196–7
Laredo, 296
Law family: Elizabeth, John, George,
    and George Jr, 195

Lenapes. *See* Delawares
Leonard, Nathaniel, 220
Levin, Earl and Countess of, 284
Lewiston, 119, 122–3, 128, 135, 220–1,
    pl. 22
Liddell, Andrew, 167–8, 171
Little Billy, or Jishkaaga (Seneca),
    86–9
Liverpool, 52
Liverpool, Earl of, 273
Lloyd, Thomas, 170–1
local rank, described, 99
Logan, John (Shawnee), 109
Logan, Johnny, or Captain Johnny/
    Spemicalawba (Shawnee), 109,
    154
London (city, not government), 5–6,
    36, 50–64, 282–91, *pls. 2, 34*
Long Point: in 1812, 91, 99, 103–4; in
    1813, 154, 210, 216, 219–20; in
    1814, 270
Loskiel, George, 63
Lundy's Lane, 237, 241, 247–52,
    pls. 29–32; mentioned, 4, 171
Lyon's Creek, 265

Macdonell, John, 135–6
Mackonochie, James, 236–7, 250, 253
Macomb, William, 111
Madison, James, 87, 93, 118, 222–3,
    272
Maguaga, 110, 145
Mahican, putative: Henrick/
    Tejoninhokarawa, 36
Makataimeshekiakiak, or Black
    Hawk (Sauk), 143–4
Malcolm's Mills, 270
Martin, George, or Shononhsese
    (Mohawk), 82–3, 102–4, 113, 275,
    277–8, 293

Martin, John, 219
Masons, 226
Matoss (Sauk), 256
Maumee River. *See* Miami River
McArthur, Duncan, 114, 269–71
McDouall, Robert, 151–2
McFarland, John, 218
McGregor, Gregor, 257
McGregor, John, 107
McGregor's Creek, 105, 212
McIntyre, Angus, 132, 163
McKee, Thomas, 245
McLean, Donald, 161
McLean, William, 171
McNeale, Neal, 160
Merritt family: Thomas, 169; William
    Hamilton, 127, 196, 240
Mesquakies, or Foxes, 15, 77
Miami, or Maumee, River, 30, 149–54,
    162–3, 209, *pl. 21*
Miamis, 22, 110; Kekionga, 152
Michigan, martial law, 149
Michilimackinac, or Mackinac: 97,
    104, 107–8, 115, 199, 222–3, 271–2
militia. *See* infantry; JN, opinions of;
    regiments and other formations
Mingos: before 1812, 14–15, 20,
    22, 29, 31; 1812–13, 77, 146–7;
    Hoyatategh and his son, 146
Mississauga Point and lighthouse,
    167–8, *pls. 23–4*
Mississaugas: in 1813, 160, 190, 192,
    199; at Grand River, 299–300;
    land losses, 40, 42, 53; Peter
    Jones, 266; threatened Crown, 43;
    Tuhbenahneequay, 266
Mississippi region, 77, 79–81, 104,
    142, 209, 222, 255–6, 287, *pl. 28*;
    JN in, 294; mentioned, 23
Mohawk chapel, *pl. 8*

Mohawks: before 1812, 13, 15, 19,
    22, 28–9, 35, 40–1, 49, 51, 300;
    in 1812, 83, 85, 88, 101, 117, 130,
    140; in 1813, 172, 176, 184, 192–3,
    199; in 1814, 230, 246, 269–70,
    300; in postwar period, 277–8,
    289, 293; JN's adoption, 3, 24–5,
    36–7; language distinctions, 126;
    member of the Haudenosaunee
    confederacy, 15, *pl. 9*; village,
    83, 101, 270, *pl. 8*. *See also*
    Akwesasne; blind warrior;
    John Brant; Joseph Brant;
    Joseph Claus; Grand River;
    Haudenosaunee; Hendrick; John
    Smoke Johnson; Kahnawake;
    Kanesatake; Kerr family; George
    Martin; John Norton; Sarah,
    daughter of Henry Tekarihogen;
    Tyendinaga; Henry Tekarihogen
Moira, Earl of, 50–2, 59
Moluntha, or Big Captain Johnny
    (Shawnee), 154
Montreal, 20, 44, 141, 183, 212, 214,
    272, 281–2; mentioned, 14, 27, 28,
    154, 216
Moraviantown, or Fairfield, 105,
    148, 184, 211–15, 224–5, *pl. 25*;
    mentioned, 104, 109, 153, 222,
    227
Mountain Road, Niagara, described,
    191
Muir, Adam, 109, 152
Munceytown, 275
Munsees. *See* Delawares
murders and attempted murders: by
    Euro-Americans, 90, 197–8, 216,
    266–9; by First Nations, 134, 150–1,
    163–4, 192, 235; JN accused of,
    121, 283; by unknown, 220–1

Murray, John, 215–16, 218–19
Muskingum River, 90–1
Muskogees, or Creeks, 37, 255
Myeerah (Wyandot), 109, 111, 150
Myers, Christopher, 170, 265

Nanticokes, 3, 300
Naomi, or Tahneh (Cherokee), 176, 295
naval affairs: Atlantic Ocean: 64,
    86, 222–3, 272–3; Great Lakes,
    downriver of Niagara Falls,
    141, 157–62, 166–9, 186–8, 203,
    227, 238, 246, 253, pls. 3, 20, 23;
    Great Lakes, upriver of Niagara
    Falls, 98, 102, 122–3, 183, 210–11,
    213, 222–3, 255, 271–2; Lake
    Champlain, 263
naval vessels: Caledonia, 122–3,
    Detroit, 122–3; General Hunter,
    110; Madison, 160, 169; Mercury,
    64; Oneida, 160; Prince Regent,
    158; Queen Charlotte, 110; Sir Isaac
    Brock, 157–9, 161; Superior, 227;
    Wolfe, 162, 186
Navy Hall, 138, pls. 6, 24
Nawash (Odawa), 228
Nepean, Sir Evan, 51, 58, 61–2
New Fairfield, 105, 294
New France, 13–14, 140
New Orleans, 272
New York City, 51–2
New York election, 157
Niagara, or Newark, town: before
    1812, 34–5, 43, 56, pl. 6; in 1812,
    93, 118, 120, 122–4, 126, 132, 137;
    in 1813, 145–6, 155–9, 165–74,
    179, 180–3, 193–208, 217–18, 220,
    pls. 23–4; in 1814, 238–9, 250, 266;
    in postwar period, 292–3. See also
    Fort George

Niagara Escarpment, described, 172,
    174–5, pl. 22
Niagara Falls, or Cataract/Falls: in
    1812, 119, 121–2, 137; in 1813,
    220; in 1814, 229, 246–7, 252–3,
    265, pls. 22, 29–30
Niagara portage, described, 119, 248
Niagara region, detailed period
    maps, pls. 22, 24, 29, 32
Nöel, Horace, 259–60
Normee, or Splitnose (Chippewa),
    164
Northumberland, Duke of:
– (second): assisted
    Haudenosaunee, 51–3, 67–8,
    pl. 13; commissioned portraits
    of JN and Catherine, 60; death,
    6; gifts from, 284; indigenous
    modernization, 55, 286–7; JN's
    journal dedication, 5; view of
    JN, 55
– (third), 284, 290
Norton, Catherine, or
    Karighwaycagh/Kitty
    (Delaware): death, 295; duel,
    292–4; marriage, 29, 183, 203;
    pension, 279; portraits, 60,
    travels, 226–7, 282, 288; unwell,
    264
Norton, John, or Teyoninhokarawen
    (Cherokee/Mohawk):
– abstract of life, roles, and
    views, 3–4, pls. 1–34. See also
    historiographical issues
– appearance, manner, and dress,
    60–2, 227, 294–5, pl. 1
– chronology: childhood, 24–7;
    military service, 27–8; entered
    native world, 27; taught at
    Tyendinaga, 28–9, 35; visited

Grand River, 29; Ohio trader, warrior, and translator, 29–34, 52; moved to Canada, joined/left Indian Department, adopted by Mohawks and became a leader, 24–5, 34–9, 43–9; in Britain, 49–64; at Grand/succeeded Joseph Brant, 64–71; Cherokee journey, 28, 70–1; late pre-/ early war period, 75–96, 98; 1812 Detroit campaign, 98–114; 1812 Niagara campaign, 115–40; 1813 Detroit theatre and return to Grand/Niagara regions, 142–64; 1813 battles of Fort George and Stoney Creek, 162–82; 1813 blockade of Fort George, 193–208; 1813 capture of Fort Niagara and late year activities, 216–21; 1814 visit to Quebec, 222–7; 1814 Niagara campaign, 227–66; 1814 murder investigation, 266–9; 1814 defence of the Grand, 266, 269–71; 1815 in Canada, 275–82; 1815–16 in Britain, 60, 282–8; 1816–23 at Grand, 288–94; 1823–7 in US and Mexico, 294–6; death, 296. *See also* John Norton, abstract of life, roles, and views
– duel, 292–4
– family: children John, Tehonakaraa, and unknown, 29–30, 50, 209, 282, 284, 293–4; parents John Norton and Christian Anderson, 24–9, 35, 50, 124, 278, *pl. 2*; grandson, 295; putative nephew Samuel Stevens, 296; relatives, Cherokee, aside from father: aunt, 25–6; uncle Kennitea, 25; cousin

Tahneh, 176, 294–5; cousin John Charles Wolateagh, 176, 294–5; visits to, 26, 63, 81; relatives, Scottish, aside from mother: Andersons, 26; Susan Wilson, 6; visits to, 26, 60, 282–4; relatives, in-laws, 29–30, 35, 203; wives/partners: Catherine, or Karighwaycagh/Kitty, 29–30, 60, 183, 203, 226–7, 264, 279, 282, 292–5; unidentified Mohawk and Onondaga women, 27, 29–30, 35, 50, *pl. 11*
– income, work, land, and debts, 34–5, 52, 112, 143, 279, 284, 292, 294
– journal, history of, 4–8, 186, 282, *pl. 34*
– languages, 26–7, 33, 142, 226
– leadership, nature of: army commission, 49–50, 60, 282–3; Joseph Brant's patronage, 33–7, 66–7, 69; "Captain of the Confederate Indians," 141–2, 199; cross-cultural, 33, 36, 142, 223–9, 246, 276, 295, *pls. 18–19, 28*; diplomatic and political, 36–9, 65–7, 69–70, 118, 182–3, 199–200, 223–5, 240–5, 278, 280–1, *pl. 27*; in Indian Department, 34–6, 76, 107, 112, 142–5, 195, 199–200, 208, 223–5, 229, 240–5, 279–81, 283; personal skills, 33–4, 61, 76, 226; pine tree chief, 38; war chief, 4, 31, 38, 118, 130, 143, 150, 159, 165–6, 175–6, 224–5, 228, 240–1, 276, 283
– loyalties: British and Mohawk/ Haudenosaunee, 46–7, 49–50, 55, 85, 142–3, 166, 175–6, 229, 241,

276–8, 283, 285; connections to non-Haudenosaunee natives, 3, 29, 30, 33, 71, 143–4, 223–5
– Masonic connection, 226
– murders: accused by American press, 121, 283; investigated Delaware killings, 266–9
– names: Dowwisdowwis, 35, 57; Teyoninhokarawen, meaning and link to predecessor, 36–8; signature, 11
– portraits: by Mather Brown/ John Francis Rigaud, Mary Ann Knight, Thomas Phillips, Thomas Pole, Solomon Williams, 60, 309, *pl. 1*; exhibited at Royal Academy, 60
– postwar and earlier army commissions, 49–50, 60, 282–3
– press and other publications on, 6, 120, 151, 177, 179, 187, 205, 283, 293–5
– printing apprenticeship and printing press, 26
– reliability of, 7–8, 144, 182–3, 185–6
– religion: Anglican, 62; Anglican and Quaker support, 52–3, 60, 62; Christian warrior, 84, 103, 105, 151, 274; Dwight Mission, 295; evangelism and teaching, 28, 46, 62–4, 71, 292; marriages and partnerships, 29–30, 63, 203; Presbyterian baptism, 24, 62; respect for, and participation in, native faith, 4, 28, 61, 63, 85, 92, 102, 109, 126, 164; scriptural translation, 7, 26, 62–3, 121, 292, *pl. 12*
– terminology and spelling, 9–12, 49, 206, 302–3

– third-person voice, 31, 119, 126, 128–9, 168
– views of JN on: acquisition of Grand River, 40–2, 52–5, 75–6, 81–2, 85, 186, 274, 282, *pl. 34*; alcohol, 30, 67, 100, 103–4, 151, 220, 228, 238, *pl. 18*; Americans, 46–7, 50, 75, 85, 90, 100, 242–3; battle of Beaver Dams, 193; battle of Chippawa, 236, 240; British army, 75, 156, 185; Isaac Brock, 75, 81–5, 93, 136–7; William Claus and the Indian Department, 65–7, 69, 152, 199, 279, 285–6; criminal law, 269, 293; Crown-First Nations relations, 46–7, 53–5, 75–6, 85, 90, 199–200, 223–4, 242–3, 285–8; Delawares and Chippewas, 104; descent, 140; Matthew Elliott, 229; Euro-American prejudice, 113, 134, 150–1; James Fitzgibbon, 189; Handsome Lake, 63; Haudenosaunee conditions in US, 90–2, 242–3; honour, 53, 59, 85, 87, 90, 185, 218, 226, 243–4, 285, 292–3; George Martin, 103, 277; William Hamilton Merritt, 196; militia, 79; mistreatment of natives in Canada, 47–50, 52, 54, 266–9; native independence and modernization, 42, 47, 55, 60–1, 66–70, 75–6, 274, 285–7, *pl. 10*; native military customs, 63, 164, 192–3; new homes for natives, 36, 44–6, 50, 81, 144, 285–7, 295; pan-tribal relations, 18, 46; possessions, 30; Sir George Prevost, 208; Baron de

Rottenburg, 208; Royal Navy, 64; strategy and tactics, 54, 149, 156–8, 174–5, 184–5, 194–6, 199, 211, 249; Tecumseh and Tenskwatawa, 109, 214; treaties, 47; unwarranted violence, 163–4, 266–9; John Vincent, 156; "wandering Indians" vs Wyandots, 150–1. *See also*, George III, in indigenous discourse; John Norton, religion
– views on JN by: Lord Bathurst, 218; Canadian officials, 43–4; Viscount Castlereagh, 68; William Claus, 24–5, 32, 44, 55–6, 69–70, 76, 187, 199–200, 203, 207–8, 228–30, 244, 275; Gordon Drummond, 240, 245, 249, 261, 266, 279–80, 283; Francis Gore, 276–8; Grand River residents, 54, 65, 67, 70, 76, 79, 117, 175, 229–30, 240–1, 275–6, 281; Haudenosaunee from US, 89; Charles William Janson, 61, *pl. 1*; John Smoke Johnson, 296–7; George Martin, 83, 281–2, 293; William Hamilton Merritt, 240; Sir Edward Nepean, 61–2; second Duke of Northumberland, 55; Thomas Pearson, 245; Sir George Prevost, 142, 150, 223–5, *pl. 15*; Prince Regent, 218; Phineas Riall, 240, 244; Baron de Rottenburg, 199–200, 208; Thomas Scott, 226; Sir Roger Sheaffe, 136, 142, 150; Lord Teignmouth, 61; John Vincent, 156; "Z" and other unknowns, 33, 61, 121. *See also* JN, press and other publications on

– *Wacousta* and John Richardson, 61
– wounds and illness: in 1812, 136; in 1813, 182–3, 203, 207–9, 224; in 1814, 226, 261; in postwar period, 292–3; death, 296
Norton, John, father of JN (Cherokee), 24–8, 29, 71
Norton, John, son of JN (Mohawk), 29, 282, 284, 293–4
Nottawagees, 205–6
Nowlan, Maurice, 219–20
Nyles, Silas, 120

Odawas, or Ottawas: before 1812, 15, 22; in 1812, 107; in 1813, 147, 190, 196–7, 199, 213; in 1814, 228–9; Blackbird, 197, 202; Charles de Langlade Jr, 196–7; Nawash, 228
Ogilvie, James, 167, 178, 179
Ohio River, 5, 20, 23
Ohio War, 22–4, 29–34, 52, 77, *pls. 5–7*
Ojibwas. *See* Chippewas
Old Northwest: before 1812, 31, 34, 48, 76–9, 87; in 1812, 104, 115–16, 141–2; in 1813, 142–4, 146, 211, 224; in 1814, 233, 239, 273; original boundaries, 23
Ondowaga, 94. *See also* Senecas
One Mile Creek, 170, *pls. 22, 24*
Oneidas: before 1812, 19, 21, 49, 78, 91–2; 1812–14, 100, 136, 230; Joseph Crawford's family, 292; in Haudenosaunee confederacy, 3, 13, 15–16, 18; Oquagas, 300; gospel translation, 62. *See also* Haudenosaunee
Onondagas: before 1812, 13, 19; in 1812, 86, 95, 99, 130, 136; in 1813, 185, 187, 197, 199; in 1814,

230, 241; in postwar period,
292; council house and fire, 70,
82–3, 99, 230; Joseph Crawford,
197, 292–3; Echo, 82, 84; in
Haudenosaunee confederacy,
3, 15; JN's partner and in-laws,
29–30, 35; Tehonakaraa, 29–30.
See also Haudenosaunee
Oquagas, 300. *See also*
Haudenosaunee
oral tradition, 4–5, 186
Oriskany, 20
Oswegatchie, 14
Oswego, 227
Ottawa River, 13–14, 182, 190, 193
Ottawas. *See* Odawas
Ourehouare (Cayuga), 140
Owen, John, 6, 60, 62
Oxford, 103, 113

parole. *See* prisoners
Paxton Boys, 90
Pearson, Thomas, 230–3, 245
Pelly, Charles, 64
Pike, Zebulon, 161
Plattsburgh, 263, 278
Plenderleath, Charles, 178–9
Point Abino, 231, *pl. 22*
Pontiac War, 90
population: Euro-American, 78; First
Nations, 15, 37, 93, 299–301
Porter, Peter B., 235
Potawatomis, 22, 77, 110, 146–7, 150,
152–3, 286, Winamac, 154
Powell, John, 174
prejudice and racism, 96, 101, 113,
150–1, 200–1, 208, 221, 269
presents, payments, and pensions:
before 1812, 6, 32, 47, 69; in 1812,
93, 116, 140; in 1813, 148, 176,
186, 193, 199–200; in 1814, 186,

223–4, 227–8, 241; in postwar
period, 277, 290–1; gifts and
pension to JN and Catherine,
64, 218, 223, 227, 279–81, 283–4.
See also supplies
Presque Isle, 91
Prevost, Lady Catherine Ann, 227
Prevost, Sir George, or commander of
the forces: death, 278; favoured
JN over Indian Department,
141–3, 146, 150, 182, 199, 208,
218, 223–5, 227–30, 241, 244, 275,
278, 281–2, *pl. 27*; at Fort George,
207–8; JN met, 208, 218, 223–4,
226, 281–2; JN sought help from,
175, 224, 226–7; plans for, and
views, of JN, 8, 142–5, 146, 150–1,
156; Plattsburg campaign and
court martial, 278–9; portrait,
pl. 15; truce with Americans, 118
Prince Regent, later George IV, 218,
223, 284, 288, 290
prisoners: indigenous customs, 14,
63, 109, 139–40, 192, 291; paroles
and exchanges, 112–13, 136–7,
146, 180, 241–2; payment for,
94, 109, 193; treatment and
mistreatment, 96, 100, 109, 134,
150–1, 153, 163–4, 192–3, 216,
235, 243–4, 251
prize money, described, 112
Procter, Henry: in 1812: 104–5, 107,
110; in 1813, 143, 147–52, 156,
158, 162, 164, 208–10, 212–14, 226
Prophetstown, 90, 109, 145, 152
Puisaye, Comte de, 218

Quebec (city), 64, 223, 226–7, 245,
281–2, 288, *pl. 27*; mentioned, 27,
52, 137, 146, 222, 230, 261, 284
Quebec (old province), 39–40, 52

Queenston and Queenston Heights: in 1812, 94–6, 121–37, 139, 140–2, 160, 280, *pl. 17*; in 1813, 172–3, 182, 189, 191, 195, 217–18, 220; in 1814, 238–9, 245–6, 249, 253; mentioned, 4, 31, 118, 180, 181, 248, 264, *pl. 22*
Queenston, or York, Road, described, 172

Raisin River, or Frenchtown, 108–9, 113–14, 135, 146–52, 154–5, 291
Raisin River Massacre, 150–1
Raweanarase, or Young Clear Sky / Echo (Onondaga), 82, 84
Red Jacket, or Sagoyewatha (Seneca), 57, 86, 235
refugees: American Revolution, 20–2, 42, 58, 105; 1812–14, 121, 165, 175, 183–4, 213–15, 224–5, 227–8, *pl. 26*
regiments and other formations, American:
 – 1st Regiment of Artillery: Nathaniel Leonard, 220
 – 2nd Artillery: Winfield Scott, 134, 180, 249
 – 4th Regiment of Infantry, 112
 – 13th Infantry: John Chrystie, 134, 180; Joseph Eldridge, 197; William King, 138–9
 – 14th Infantry: Charles Boerstler, 191–2
 – 22nd Infantry, 169
 – Kentucky Militia, 147
 – New York Militia, 120, 262; Lewis Nyles, 120; Stephen Van Rensselaer, 123–4, 134–5, 137; William Wadsworth, 134
 – Ohio Militia: Henry Brush, 114; Duncan McArthur, 114

 – Pennsylvania Volunteer Regiment: Robert Bull, 234–5
regiments and other formations, British/colonial:
 – 1st Regiment of Foot Guards: Cecil Bisshopp, 173–4, 200–1
 – 1st Regiment of Foot, or Royal Scots/Royals, 26, 236, 258, 262; James Gordon, 236–7, 262; Gregor McGregor, 257; JN's father, 26, *pl. 2*; Archibald Stewart, 194, 198, 201; S.B. Torrens, 259–60
 – 6th Foot, 262
 – 6th Garrison Battalion: John Harvey, 177–9, 218, 249–50
 – 8th Foot, or King's, 124, 152, 157, 160–1, 167, 170, 173, 178–9, 194, 236, 258, 262; Francis Battersby, 245–6; Thomas Buck, 230; Thomas Evans, 124; Thomas Lloyd, 170–1; Robert McDouall, 151–2; Neal McNeale, 160; Horace Nöel, 259–60; James Ogilvie, 167, 178, 179; Robert Young, 194
 – 19th Light Dragoons, 203–4, 253–4, 261, 263, 270–1; John Eustace, 270–1
 – 23rd Foot: Thomas Pearson, 230–3, 245
 – 41st Foot, 99, 103, 109–10, 112, 125, 128, 134, 137–8, 147, 162–3, 173, 178, 194, 201, 213, 258; Richard Bullock, 133; Peter Chambers, 99, 102–4, 270; Angus McIntyre, 132, 163; Adam Muir, 109, 152; Henry Procter, 104–5, 107, 110, 143, 147–9, 150–2, 156, 158, 162, 164, 208–10, 212–14, 228; Paddy Russell, 164; William Saunders, 201; John Tucker, 255

– 49th Foot, 125, 134–5, 137–8, 167, 169, 171, 173, 177–9, 189, 191, 211; James Brock, 169; Alexander Clerk, 179–80; James Dennis, 134–5; James Fitzgibbon, 189, 190–3, 265–6; Charles Plenderleath, 178–9; John Williams, 134–5
– 65th Foot, 27–8; Norton family, 27–8, 33, 278, *pl. 3*
– 70th Foot: Thomas Scott, 226
– 82nd Foot, 261–2
– 89th Foot, 250
– 100th Foot, 215, 218–19, 231, 236–7; Christopher Hamilton, 219; John Martin, 219; John Murray, 215–16, 218–19; Maurice Nowlan, 219–20; Marquess of Tweeddale, 236–7
– 103rd Foot, 238, 250, 258; Thomas Charleton, 259–60; James Irwin, 259–60; Love Parry Jones–Parry, 247, 267; Hercules Scott, 238–9, 241, 258–9, 271; William Smelt, 269, 271
– 104th Foot, 194, 211, 258; William Drummond, 247, 257–9, 266, 279–80; John Le Couteur, 202
– Brant's Volunteers, 107
– Butler's Rangers, 138; Thomas Butler, 171–2; Barent Frey, 137–8
– de Watteville Regiment, 256, 258–60, 263
– "Detroit militia," 162
– Essex Militia: Matthew Elliott, 153–4, 209, 212–13, 228–9; William Elliott, 114
– Glengarry Light Infantry, 131, 160, 167–71, 178, 180, 245, 248–9, 254, 257, 261–3, 265; Francis Battersby, 245–6; Alexander Clerk, 179–80; James Fitzgibbon, 189, 190–3, 265–6; Robert and Walter Kerr, 131, 171; Andrew Liddell, 167–8, 171; Robert McDouall, 151–2; William McLean, 171; Christopher Myers, 170, 265; Alexander Roxburgh, 167, 171
– Incorporated Militia, 248, 263
– "irregular militia," 248
– Lincoln Militia: Thomas Clark, 189–90; James Durand, 135; Samuel Hatt, 135; George and George Law Jr, 195; John Powell, 174
– Niagara Light Dragoons and Provincial Dragoons, 127, 188–9, 196; William Hamilton Merritt, 127, 196, 240
– Norfolk, or Long Point, Militia, 99, 103, 154, 216; John Bostwick, 216
– Queen's Rangers: JN's father-in-law, 203
– Royal Newfoundland Regiment, 123, 137, 147, 167, 170–1, 173, 178, 271; William Winter, 167
– Royal Regiment of Artillery, 128, 138, 178, 250; William Holcroft, 128; Charles King, 138–9; James Kitson, 147; James Mackonochie, 236–7, 250, 253
– Upper Canada Militia: leaders appointed by JN, 107; problems of, 98; staff and inspecting field officers, 135–6, 174, 216, 230–1, 247
– York Militia: William Allen, 161; William Chewett, 161; James Chisholm, 135

religion:
– Christian: Anglican, 62, 83, 292, *pl. 8*; British and Foreign Bible Society, 6, 26, 53, 62–3, 121; Clapham Sect, 53; clergy and missionaries, 6, 19, 24, 28, 41, 62–3, 81, 105, 143, 148, 161, 176, 203, 266, 292; general, 17, 45, 115–16, 151, *pl. 9*; gospels, 7, 62–3, 121, *pl. 12*; Methodist, 266; Moravian, 63, 90, 105–6; Presbyterian, 24, 62, 295; Quaker, 62, 90; Roman Catholic, 14, 62; Society for the Propagation of the Gospel, 28. *See also* Norton, John, religion
– First Nations traditional: condolence and covering graves, 28, 63, 136, 149, 293; general, 76–7, 89, 92, 96, 115–16; Great Peace, 13; Handsome Lake, 63, 78; in governance, 13, 37–9; post-battle, 164; war dances, songs, and associated practices, 61, 63, 101, 129. *See also* scalps and scalping; Tenskwatawa
Riall, Phineas, 228–33, 235, 238–40, 244–5, 248–9, 252, 281
Richardson, John, 61
Richelieu River, 28
River Road, Niagara, described, 124
Rottenburg, Baron de, 156, 194, 199–201, 206, 208, 211, 217
Roundhead, or Stayeghtha (Wyandot), 109, 111, 122, 143, 148–9, 150
Rousseau, Jean–Baptiste, 86
Roxburgh, Alexander, 167, 171

Royal Navy. *See* naval affairs; naval vessels
Royal Proclamation, xi, 18–19, 40–1, 43, 58

Sackett's Harbour: in 1813, 156–7, 162, 165, 175, 186, 211; in 1814, 227, 264
Sagoyewatha, or Red Jacket (Seneca), 57, 86, 235
St Andrew's Church, Niagara, 172, *pl. 23*
St Clair region, 99, 106–7, 113, 143, 224
St Davids: in 1813, 172, 190–1, 194, 196, 198, 201, 206–7, 217; in 1814, 238, 245–6, *pl. 22*
St Lawrence River, 11, 13–14, 62, 64, 182, 190, 193, 208, 212, 216, 223
St Louis, 77, 294
St Mark's Church, Niagara, 194, *pls. 6, 24*
St Regis, or Akwesasne, 14, 182, 190, 192–3, 300
Sakayengwaraton, or John Smoke Johnson (Mohawk), 140, 176, 296–7
Sandusky, 209–10
Sandusky Senecas, 22, 29, 45
Sandwich: in 1812: 98, 105, 107–8, 110, 112; 1813–14, 148, 154, 214, *pl. 16*
Sanschagrin, Marie Louise (Shawnee), 154
Sarah, daughter of Henry Tekarihogen (Mohawk), 266
Sauks, 77, 152, 213; Black Hawk, 143–4; Matoss, 256
Saunders, William, 201
Scajaquada, or Conjocta/ Conjockoquaddy, Creek, 255, *pl. 22*

scalps and scalping, 63, 121, 139, 227
Scioto River, 29
Scott, Hercules, 238–9, 241, 258–9, 271
Scott, Thomas and Walter, 33, 226–7, 284
Scott, Winfield, 134, 180, 249
Secord, John, 169
Secord, Laura, 189
Selkirk, Earl of, 52, 63
Senecas: before 1812, 3, 13, 15, 19, 90; in 1812, 86–9, 94–5, 117, 122, 128; in 1813, 146, 185, 187, 201, 204, 221; in 1814, 230, 242, 244, 262; in Haudenosaunee confederacy, 3, 13; Arosa, 94–6; Deyonihnhogawen, 38; Handsome Lake, 63, 78; Hoyatategh and his son, 146; Little Billy, 86–9; Red Jacket, 57, 86, 235; Tehaosemsghte, 38; village, 99. See also Haudenosaunee; Sandusky Senecas
Seven Nations of Canada, 14–15, 20, 62, 192–3, 196, 300. See also Akwesasne; Haudenosaunee; Kahnawake; Kanesatake
Seven Years' War, 13, 18, 25, 89–90, 94
Shawnees: before 1812, 18, 22, 32, 90, pl. 5; 1812–14, 110, 152–4, 237, 241, 246; as Algonquians, 15; Captain Johnny and Big Captain Johnny, 154; Bright Horn, 154; Andrew Clark, 153; Alexander Elliot, 153–4; John Logan and Johnny Logan, 109, 154; JN and Mexican negotiations, 295; relations with Western Tribes, 76–7, 92, 153–4; Marie Louise Sanschagrin, 154; Wapakoneta 154. See also Prophetstown; Tecumseh; Tenskwatawa

Sheaffe, Sir Roger: in 1812, 124–5, 130–3, 136–9, 140–2; in 1813, 145, 155, 157–62
Sherbrooke, Sir John, or governor-in-chief, 288, 291
Shononhsese, or George Martin (Mohawk), 82–3, 102–3, 108, 113, 275, 277–8, 293
Silverheels, George, or Arosa, and his ancestor (Senecas), 94–6
Simcoe, John Graves, 34
Sioux, 287; William Dickson and Totowin (Helen), 272
Six (formerly Five) Nations Confederacy. See Haudenosaunee
Sixteen Mile Creek, 188, pl. 22
Smelt, William, 269, 271
Smyth, Alexander, 137, 139
Snake Hill, 255, 258–60, 265, pls. 22, 32
Society for the Propagation of the Gospel, 28
Sounehhooway, or Thomas Splitlog/ Tharoutorea (Wyandot), 109, 121, 147, 149
Spanish colonies, 87
Spemicalawba (Johnny Logan), 109, 154
Splitlog, Thomas, or Sounehhooway/ Tharoutorea (Wyandot), 109, 121, 147, 149
Splitnose, or Normee (Chippewa), 163–4
Stayeghtha, or Roundhead (Wyandot), 109, 111, 122, 143, 148–50
Stevens, Samuel, 296
Stewart, Archibald, 194, 198, 201
Stone, William L., 296
Stoney Creek, 160, 166, 177–82, 184–7, 215–16, 225, 266, pl. 22; mentioned, 4, 156, 269

Strachan, John, 161
Strawberry and Squaw islands, 122–3, 254, *pl. 22*
Street, Samuel, and his property, 231–3, 238
Street's Creek, 232, 233, 236
Stuart, John, 28
supplies, 1812–14: captured, 106, 112–13, 115–16, 128, 161, 164, 183, 188, 192–3, 201, 214, 217, 219–21, 227, 238, 262; challenges, for Americans, 109–10, 113, 156, 180, 209, 246; challenges, for British, 99, 105, 141, 153, 158, 161, 180, 182, 193, 203, 210, 214, 220, 222, 228, 252, 256, 264, 271; challenges, for First Nations, 116, 123, 140, 155, 157, 180, 184, 193, 203, 208, 210–11, 213, 222–5, 227–9, 264, 270, 275, 278, 301. *See also* presents, payments, and pensions
Susquehannocks, or Conestogas, 90

Tahneh, or Naomi (Cherokee), 176, 295
Talman, James J., 3, 7, 9, 53
Tecumseh (Shawnee): before 1812, 76–7; in 1812, 97, 109–11, 115; in 1813, 121, 143–5, 151–3, 162–4, 184, 209–11; killed and butchered, 184, 213–14, *pl. 25*; sister, 227
Tehaosemsghte (Seneca), 38
Tehonakaraa (Onondaga), 29–30
Teignmouth, Baron, 53, 61, 62
Tejoninhokarawa, or Hendrick (Mahican?/Mohawk), 36
Tekarihogen, Henry (Mohawk), 48, 50, 54, 101, 266, 281–2

Tekeantawea (unspecified Haudenosaunee), 207
Ten Mile Creek, 190, 194, 198, 217, *pl. 22*
Tenskwatawa, or the prophet (Shawnee), 76–8, 98, 109, 115, 144, 184, 218, 237
Teyoninhokarawen. *See* John Norton, names
Thames, or Tranche, River, 99, 105–7, 211–14, 224, 294
Thayendanegea. *See* Joseph Brant
Theyandanegea, or Robert Johnson Kerr, 290
Theyanoguin, or Hendrick Peters (Mohawk), 36
Thorpe, Robert, 65
Tippecanoe, 79, 90
Tonawanda, 183, 221
Torrens, S.B., 259–60
Totowin, or Helen (Sioux), 272
treaties. *See* diplomacy
truces: Prevost-Dearborn, 118; Sheaffe-Van Rensselaer, 136–7
Tucker, John, 255
Tuhbenahneequay (Mississauga), 266
Tuscarora, 221
Tuscaroras: before 1812, 19, 21, 49, 78, 92; 1812–14, 153–4, 221, 230, 262; in Haudenosaunee confederacy, 3, 13, 15–16, 49. *See also* Haudenosaunee
Tutelos, 3, 15, 49, 300
Tweeddale, Marquess of, 236–7
Twelve Mile Creek, 172, 188–9, 191–4, 245–6, 250, *pl. 22*
Twenty Mile Creek, 173, 245, 250, *pl. 22*
Two Mile Run or Creek, 167–9, 203, *pls. 22, 24*
Tyendinaga, 22, 28, 35, 62, *pl. 4*

Underwood, Jimmy (Chickasaw), 32
United Empire Loyalists, 19–20, 22, 42, 45, 137, 172
United States, government, or Madison administration/ Washington: declaration of war, 79–80, 92–3; expansion, 21, 77, 86–8, 91, 222–3, 272–4; strategic considerations, 91, 141, 175, 211–12, 222–3. *See also* American Revolution; diplomacy; treaties; War of 1812; George Washington
United States Navy. *See* naval affairs; naval vessels
University of Cambridge, 60
Upper Canada:
  – government: Haudenosaunee land and rights, 41–7, 55–61, 64–5, 68–70, 276–8, 288–90. *See also* William Claus; Great Britain, government; Indian Department; John Norton, views on
  – fear of invasion and sedition (excluding 1812–14), 42–6, 55, 59, 65, 68, 276–7
Upper Canadians, loyalty and disaffection: 43, 78–9, 83, 91, 103, 106–7, 121, 132, 159, 189–92, 216, 300–1

Van Rensselaer, Stephen, 123–4, 134–5, 137
Vincent, John, 155, 159, 167, 169–70, 172–80, 190, 192, 194, 211–12, 215, 217, 228
Vrooman's Point, 126

Wabash River, 31–2, 109, 152, *pl. 5*
Wacousta, 61
Wadsworth, William, 134

wampum, 24, 28, 63, 88, 95, 106, 108, 230, *pl. 2*
Wapakoneta, 153–4
War of 1812: causes and pre-war concerns, 75–80, 86; course of, summaries, 97–8, 115–18, 141–5, 157–8, 162, 165–6, 181–4, 211–17, 222–3, 272; declaration of war, 93; outcomes, 272–4; postwar fears, 275, 285, 287
Washington (place, not government), 179, 293
Washington, George, 20, 22
Waskweela, or Wathethewela/Bright Horn (Shawnee), 154
Watteville, Louis de, 263
weapons and ammunition, described: artillery, 128, 131, 138; bows, *pl. 5*; edged 107, 148, *pl. 13*; firearms and musketry discipline, 36, 109, 129, 177, 196–8, 249–50, 253; native use, 107; stands, 112; wall piece, 284; weapon design inspired by JN, 284
Wendat, or Hurons, 14, 17. *See also* Wyandots
Wenros, 17
Westbrook, Andrew, 104
Western Battery, 160
Western Posts, 22–3, 27, *pl. 3*
Western Tribes (alliance): before 1812, 76–80, 84, 86–7, 117; in 1812, 92, 97, 99, 101, 115–16, 143; in 1813, 121, 143–4, 183–4, 211, 213–15, 220; in 1814, 222, 255, *pl. 26*; in postwar period, 273. *See also* Tecumseh; Tenskwatawa
Whitaker, Captain, 45
Wilberforce, William, 53, 289
Willcocks, Joseph, 132

Williams, John, 134–5

Wilson, Adam or Andrew (A.W.), 6–9

Wilson, Deborah, and her tavern, 247,
  pl. 29

Wilson, Susan, 6

Winamac (Potawatomi), 154

Winchester, James, 135, 146–8, 150–1,
  154

Winder, William, 179

Windham, William, 68

Winter, William, 167

Wolateagh, John Charles (Cherokee),
  176, 294–5

Wyandots: before 1812, 22, 31; in
  1812, 100, 104, 108; in 1813, 147,
  149, 151, 154, 213; in 1814, 246,
  255; Brownstown or Big Rock,
  100, 108–10, *pl. 16*; Myeerah, 109,

111, 150; Roundhead, 109, 111,
  122, 143, 148–9, 150; Thomas
  Splitlog, 109, 121, 147, 149

Yager, or Yeager, 269

Yeo, Sir James, 186, 188, 227

York: before 1812, 43, 48–9; in 1812,
  81; in 1813, 145, 157–62, 175,
  229, *pl. 20*; in 1814, 269, 272; in
  1815, 281; mentioned, 31, 59,
  80, 82, 104, 124, 155, 182, 215,
  225, 249

Young, Robert, 194

Young Clear Sky, or Echo/
  Raweanarase (Onondaga), 82, 84

Youngstown, 219

"Z," identity of, 27